The Musical Woman

The Musical Woman
An International Perspective

1983

JUDITH LANG ZAIMONT,
EDITOR-IN-CHIEF

**CATHERINE OVERHAUSER
AND JANE GOTTLIEB,**
ASSOCIATE EDITORS

GREENWOOD PRESS
Westport, Connecticut • London, England

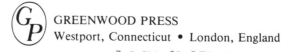

ISBN: 0-313-23587-2
ISSN: 0737-0032

First published in 1984

Greenwood Press
A division of Congressional Information Service, Inc.
88 Post Road West, Westport, Connecticut 06881

Printed in the United States of America

10 9 8 7 6 5 4 3 2 1

Contents

Illustrations and Tables

ILLUSTRATIONS

TABLES

Acknowledgments

The editors wish to express their appreciation for the support of Marilyn Brownstein and James Sabin of Greenwood Press. They, together with their staffs, provided technical assistance, constructive suggestions, and enthusiasm at every step of the way.

Introduction

Who is "the musical woman"?

To the average concertgoer she is probably an internationally acclaimed performer, such as Joan Sutherland, Janet Baker, Alicia de Larrocha or Jacqueline du Pré. To the more general music lover she is most likely, again, an internationally known theatrical singer (Barbra Streisand, Edith Piaf, Lena Horne) or singer-songwriter (Judy Collins, Carole King).

Limited identifications of this sort hardly do justice to the true scope of women's very real presence in every facet of the music world. All over the globe women are and have been active as

> composers and composer-arrangers: Thea Musgrave, Germaine Taille-ferre, Toshiko Akiyoshi
>
> conductors: Sarah Caldwell, Margaret Hillis
>
> critics and cultural reporters: Joan Peyser, Barbara Jepson
>
> historians and scholars: Edith Borroff, Miriam Stewart-Green
>
> directors of cultural or performing institutions: Beverly Sills (New York City Opera), Marta Istomin (Kennedy Center)
>
> record producers: Marnie Hall (Leonarda Productions, Inc.), Teresa Sterne (Nonesuch)
>
> music publishers: Bea Friedland (Da Capo Press), Clara Lyle Boone (Arsis Press)
>
> teachers: Nadia Boulanger, Rosina Lhevinne, and
>
> concert producers: Patricia Chiti (Donne in Musica, Rome), Katherine Hoover (annual Festival of Women's Music, New York).

The women mentioned above are just a few of the many already active in these fields—all of which are non-performance oriented.

Although a few of these women music professionals have attained high visibility, most have slipped past the notice of many musically aware people. They are practitioners in areas that are essentially "behind the scenes," areas traditionally understood to be reserved for men. When their presence *is* noted, these women are frequently classified under labels which, while accurately identifying their occupations, serve to perpetuate their separation from the main body of their colleagues: "woman composer," "woman conductor."*

Such appellations, akin to the phrase "male nurse," are unwieldy and perhaps distasteful. In the future, as women continue to be noted as outstanding practitioners of their craft, they will be viewed simply as music professionals, rendered unremarkable by virtue of their sex. Until that time, however, women's achievements in these areas must be brought to the attention of the public more forcibly. This is the objective of *The Musical Woman*.

What is *The Musical Woman*?

It is a continuing publication chronicling women's achievements around the world in all aspects of the art save solo performance: as composers, conductors, critics and commentators, scholars, and entrepreneurs. The emphasis will be on highlighting the achievements of outstanding women music professionals of the twentieth century, especially those of the present day. Subsequent volumes will appear at regular intervals.

Each volume will be organized in two parts: a gazette section, tabulating recent and current data concerning women's musical activities worldwide, and a section of essays.

The gazette will include lists by year of major events in numerous categories: composers' honors and awards, important performances, published music, recordings issued, and information on national and international conferences and festivals. The gazette for this volume has been prepared by Associate Editor Jane Gottlieb and includes material for the years 1980, 1981, and 1982 and a forecast for the first part of 1983.

The essay section contains articles by individual authors, many of whom are themselves dedicated and successful women music professionals. The articles are arranged within eight standing departments:

Music Festivals and Concert Series

The Music Business—Women at the Helm

Featured Musicians: Critical Appraisals

Genre Surveys

---

*The Musical Woman plans to continue to use these phrases, in the spirit of "factual reportage." However, readers are encouraged to submit one-word alternatives for possible adoption in future volumes.

National Surveys
Music Profession Overviews
Music Education
Music Scholarship: Special Topics

Included are critical appraisals of notable figures, living and dead; surveys of composers grouped by nationality and/or medium or style; overviews of the current state of affairs for particular groups of music professionals, such as critics or conductors; essays about individuals who have devoted their careers to promoting music composed by women; and more general essays relating to women in music education and to special topics of music scholarship and research.

Two of these departments are of special interest, Featured Musicians: Critical Appraisals and Music Scholarship. Much of the literature specifically dealing with women musicians that has already appeared is conspicuously lacking in informed, impartial critical assessments, particularly of today's composers. *The Musical Woman* plans to publish this material regularly. Similarly, already-published research is often not the "last word" on a particular topic. For this reason, *The Musical Woman* offers the very broadly conceived department Music Scholarship, which will continue to publish updated research on topics that may have been initially explored elsewhere.

All fifteen articles in the present volume are original publications; all but one were commissioned especially for *The Musical Woman*. Given the book's nature, the editors expect that the great majority of essays to appear in future volumes will also be commissioned originals, although the inclusion of reprints of previously published articles may be appropriate on occasion.

It is quite clear that no single volume can be comprehensive in its coverage of such a broad range of subjects; for instance, women's contributions to popular music and jazz will be more fully taken up in later volumes. Thus, the emphasis of each book will differ—to a greater or lesser degree—from that of preceding volumes.

This first volume serves as a model for the entire series. Its essays offer detailed views of the present state of affairs for women music critics and opera conductors in the United States; surveys of the achievements of women composers in Britain and, in the United States, of composers working in electronic media and jazz; features on the music of one experimental and two traditional composers; first-person narratives by four entrepreneurial "pioneers"; and a guide to the creation of a comprehensive curriculum for the study of women in music at the college level. Miriam Stewart-Green's important descriptive list of 414 specially selected art songs, which is featured in the Music Scholarship section, forms a valuable adjunct to her previous publications on vocal music by women.

Though these fifteen essays were written by fifteen independent authors, certain crosscurrents and patterns thread their way through whole groups of articles. For example, the four entrepreneurs—concert producers Chiti and Maves, publisher Boone, and record producer Hall—share with the reader many revealing facts about the individual economic circumstances influencing the course of their careers. The big contrast here is not between the "commercial" enterprises of recording and publishing and the more "artistic" vocation of concert producer, but between the present economic climates influencing all arts-related undertakings in America versus those abroad.

Another example of a hidden pattern has to do with the neoclassic presence that informs the music of two of the featured composers, Bacewicz and Talma. Though Bacewicz disavowed the stylistic label and Talma acknowledges it, both composers did study with Nadia Boulanger at formative points in their careers, and the term is justifiably used to describe particular facets of the music of each.

A third subterranean current, the question of the influence of the demands of home life on a woman's musical career, is tapped in the essays by Kosloff and Jepson on opera conductors and music critics, respectively. Musicians' working hours, like actors', are apt to be evening ones, and Kosloff talks of domestic responsibilities interfering with Eve Queler's early success, while Jepson quotes several critics' views—pro and con—on the advisability of pursuing a full family life and career at the same time.

Essays in future volumes of *The Musical Woman* will undoubtedly reveal many similar parallelisms.

We welcome correspondence from our readers. In particular, we would like to receive suggestions for essay topics to be treated in future volumes (or abstracts of completed articles) as well as information about musical happenings for inclusion in the gazette. All gazette entries should include as much specific data as possible: date, location, scope of the event, titles of compositions, names of performers, and any other pertinent details. Send all correspondence to: Judith Lang Zaimont, *The Musical Woman*, c/o Greenwood Press, 88 Post Road West, P.O. Box 5007, Westport, CT 06881. We look forward to your sharing in the continuation of a most stimulating and rewarding project.

Judith Lang Zaimont
Catherine Overhauser

The Musical Woman

Part I
GAZETTE

This issue of the Gazette is divided into five chapters: "Performances," "Festivals," "Prizes and Awards," "Publications," and "Discography." Information was taken from various sources: newsletters of composer organizations (for example, The American Music Center and the International League of Women Composers), publishers' announcements, concert programs, and press releases. Composers were solicited directly through a notice placed in the June-July 1982 issue of the ILWC *Newsletter*. We appreciate the response from composers here and abroad and acknowledge the generous time they spent in methodically listing performance dates and other activities.

For foreign events information was solicited specifically from Music Information Centers and women composers' organizations abroad. Responses were inconsistent, and foreign representation hopefully will increase in future volumes. In this volume all composers and events are listed in a single alphabetical sequence by year and with country abbreviations. At the end of "Performances" brief country summaries list active composers in particular countries, when this information was provided by the Music Information Center.

Performances are listed by seasons running from September through August (for example, September 1982 through August 1983). Emphasis was placed on listing premieres (indicated with an *). We have attempted to provide complete information for each listing: title, instrumentation, date of composition, performers, place, and exact date of performance, but this was not always possible. Listings were eliminated when too much information was lacking (for example, "new work of Jane Smith to be performed next season in Milwaukee").

Commissions or awards connected to a particular work are listed in the performance section and are indicated by a †. Notices of other prizes and commissions not connected with a specific performance (or when the information was not complete enough) are listed in "Prizes and Awards."

"Publications" lists new publications, compiled from composers' correspondence, publishers' brochures, newsletters, and the publications lists in *Notes: Quarterly Journal of the Music Library Association*. Educational pieces and music for children are listed alongside "serious" works.

The discography is a list of available recordings by women composers, compiled from the current *Schwann* catalog, various record company catalogs (CRI, Opus One, 1750 Arch Records), and distribution service catalogs. The separate jazz discography is a selected list, with emphasis placed on records containing original works by women jazz composers. Readers are referred to the New Music Distribution Service (500 Broadway, New York, NY 10012) and Ladyslipper, Inc. (P.O. Box 3124, Durham, NC 27705) to obtain recordings.

Future volumes of the Gazette will also include a section on newly published scholarship and criticism on women in music. Readers are referred to the comprehensive bibliography included with Carol Neuls-Bates's article in this volume. The following new and forthcoming publications are also noted:

Dahl, Linda. *Stormy Weather: The Untold Story of Women in Jazz.* Chelsea House, 1982.

Frasier, Jane. *Women Composers: A Discography.* Detroit Studies in Music Bibliography. Detroit, MI: Information Coordinators, projected spring 1983.

Placksin, Sally. *American Women in Jazz: 1900 to the Present; Their Words, Lives, and Music.* New York, NY: Seaview Books, 1982.

Finally, a note on comprehensiveness. It is virtually an impossible task to document fully the activities of women composers in the past three years. The lists in this first volume of the Gazette provide a sampling of the diversity and scope of activities worldwide. Again, we look forward to increased reader participation in future volumes and welcome all correspondence.

Performances

(* indicates premiere; † indicates commission or award related to a particular work. Country codes indicate country of origin or citizenship for composers other than U.S. composers.)

1982-1983 SEASON

*Anderson, Laurie. *United States*, parts I-IV (a two-evening performance). Brooklyn, NY: Brooklyn Academy of Music, 2/3-4, 5-6, 7-8, 9-10/83.

Blaustein, Susan. *Songs*, for mezzo-soprano and piano. Guild of Composers concert. New York, NY: 12/2/82.

*Bouchard, Linda. *Concert-Drama*, in eight tableaux for three singers and chamber ensemble. New York, NY: Manhattan School of Music, 12/82.

    Web-Trap. National Association of Composers U.S.A. concert. New York, NY: St. Stephen's Church, 4/24/83.

Chance, Nancy Laird. *Exultation and Lament*. Group for Contemporary Music. New York, NY: Manhattan School of Music, 5/3/83.

Coulthard, Jean (Canada). *Vancouver Lights—A Soliloquy*. Vancouver Bach Choir. Vancouver, BC: 2/83.

Diemer, Emma Lou. *Four Poems by Alice Meynell*. Bay Area Women's Philharmonic concert. San Francisco, CA: San Francisco Civic Center, 11/14/82.

    Summer of '82, for 'cello and piano. Geoffrey Rutkowski, 'cello, Wendell Nelson, piano. Performed in Goettingen, Bordeaux, and Padua, 10/82.

*†Even-Or, Mary (Israel). *Ad Infinitum*, for string orchestra (1982). Rubin Academy of Music Orchestra. Tel-Aviv: 12/82. Commissioned by the Rubin Academy of Music, with the help of Maestro Antal Dorati.

    Cardioyda, for brass quintet (1982). Bonn Brass Quintet. W. Germany: 11/82.

Fowler, Jennifer (U.K.). *Chant with Garlands*, for orchestra (1974). BBC Northern Symphony Orchestra, John Hopkins, conductor. Manchester: 1/83.

    †Invocation to the Veiled Mysteries, for flute, clarinet, bassoon, violin, 'cello, and

piano (1982). Seymour Group. Sydney: 10/82. Commissioned by the Seymour Group and the Australia Council.

Piece for an Opera House, for two pianos (1973). John Lavender, Penelope Thwaites, pianists. London: Wigmore Hall, 12/82.

Gideon, Miriam. *Spirit above the Dust*. Group for Contemporary Music. New York, NY: 92d Street YMHA, 4/19/83.

*Giteck, Janice. *A'Agita*, one-act opera. Seattle, WA: Cornish Institute, spring 1983.

Glanville-Hicks, Peggy. *Three Gymnopedies*. Bay Area Women's Philharmonic concert. San Francisco, CA: San Francisco Civic Center, 11/14/82.

Greene, Diana. *Sohoma*. Susan Belling, soprano, Brooklyn Philharmonia, Lukas Foss, conductor. New York, NY: Cooper Union, 3/4-5/83 (New York premiere).

*Ivey, Jean Eichelberger. *Pantomime*, for clarinet and xylophone. Hodie ensemble. Baltimore, MD: 3/27/83.

Solstice, for soprano with instruments. Washington Contemporary Music Forum. Washington, DC: 12/13/82, 1/17/83.

Jazwinski, Barbara. *Deep Green Lies the Grass along the River*. New York New Music Ensemble. New York, NY: Carnegie Recital Hall, 1/13/83 (New York premiere).

*La Barbara, Joan. *Vlissingen Harbor*. Monday Evening Concerts ensemble, Steven Mosko, conductor. Los Angeles, CA: Los Angeles County Museum of Art, 12/6/82.

*†Lauber, Anne (Canada). *Valse concertante*, for piano and orchestra (1981-82). Quebec Symphonic Orchestra, P. Hetu, conductor. Quebec: 12/7/82. Commissioned by the Canadian Arts Council.

LeBaron, Anne. *Rite of the Black Sun*. New Music Consort. New York, NY: Symphony Space, 1/25/83.

*†Louie, Alexina (Canada). *Afterimages*, for two pianos (1981). Ralph Markham, Anne Broadway, pianists. Paris: Radio-France Broadcast, 2/83. Written under a grant from the Canadian Council.

*†*Refuge*, for accordion, vibraphone, and harp (1981). New Music Concerts. Ontario: 10/8/82. Commissioned by the CBC.

*†*Sanctuary*, for chamber ensemble (1982). New Music Concerts. Ontario: 10/8/82. Written under a grant from the Ontario Arts Council.

*†*Songs of Paradise*, for orchestra. Thunder Bay Orchestra, Dwight Bennett, conductor. Ontario: 2/83. Written under a grant from the Canadian Council.

Maconchy, Elizabeth (U.K.). *Proud Thames Overture*. Bay Area Women's Philharmonic, Antonia Brico, conductor. Berkeley, CA: University of California at Berkeley, 2/19/83.

Mageau, Mary (Australia). *Concerto Grosso*, for flute, 'cello, harpsichord, timpani, percussion, and string orchestra. Brisbane Baroque Trio, Queensland Theatre Orchestra, Georg Tintner, conductor. Brisbane: 11/27/82.

Mamlok, Ursula. *Sextet*. National Association of Composers U.S.A. concert. New York, NY: St. Stephen's Church, 11/14/82.

Marez-Oyens, Tera de (Netherlands). *Mixed Feelings*, for percussion and tape (1973); *Photophonie*, electronic work for four tracks and eight light sources. Amsterdam: 10/82.

Musgrave, Thea (U.K.). *Horn Concerto*. Barry Tuckwell, horn, St. Louis Symphony

Orchestra, Leonard Slatkin, conductor. St. Louis, MO: Powell Symphony Hall, 1/15-16/83.

Pentland, Barbara (Canada). *Disasters of the Sun*, for mezzo and chamber ensemble (1976). Vancouver New Music Society. Vancouver: 10/24/82.

Perry, Julia. *Short Piece*, for orchestra. Bay Area Women's Philharmonic, Antonia Brico, conductor. Berkeley, CA: University of California at Berkeley, 2/19/83.

Procaccini, Teresa (Italy). *Un Cavallino Adventuroso*, op. 33. Bay Area Women's Philharmonic concert. San Francisco, CA: San Francisco Civic Center, 11/14/82.

Ran, Shulamit. *Excursions*. Music Today, Gerard Schwarz, conductor. New York, NY: Merkin Concert Hall, 1/12/83 (New York premiere).

For an Actor, monologue for clarinet. Jean Kopperud, clarinet. New York, NY: Merkin Concert Hall, 11/2/82.

*Reich, Amy. *The One Turning*. Jane Struss, mezzo, Pro Arte Chamber Orchestra, Myron Romanul, conductor. Cambridge, MA: Sanders Theatre, 2/26/82.

*Ricard, Gisele (Canada). *Une Autre Création du Monde*, by Gisele Ricard and Bernard Bonnier, for electronic instruments, character/actor, and character/setting. Quebec City: Institut Canadien, 11/5/82.

*Rudow, Vivian Adelberg. *Force III*. Baltimore Symphony Orchestra, Sergiu Comissiona, conductor. Baltimore, MD: 12/2-3/82.

Semegen, Daria. *Arc*, music for dancers (1977). Electronic Music Plus Festival. Knoxville, TN: University of Tennessee, 10/22/82.

†Silver, Sheila. *Chariessa*, for soprano and piano. Jane Bryden, soprano, Frank Weinstock, piano. New York, NY: Carnegie Recital Hall, 2/17/83 (New York premiere). Winner of League-ISCM National Composers Competition.

*Silverman, Faye-Ellen. *No Strings*. Brooklyn Philharmonia, Lukas Foss, conductor. New York, NY: Cooper Union, 3/4-5/83.

*†*Winds and Sines*, for full orchestra. Indianapolis Symphony Orchestra, Raymond Harvey, conductor. Terre Haute, IN: Indiana State University Contemporary Music Festival, 9/30/82. One of three winners of the Indiana State University composition contest.

Singer, Jeanne. *Songs of Reverence*. National Association of Composers U.S.A. concert. New York, NY: St. Stephen's Church, 11/14/82.

Tower, Joan. *Amazon II*, reorchestrated for chamber orchestra. Houston Symphony Chamber Orchestra. Houston, TX: 3/12/83.

†*Sequoia*. New York Philharmonic, Zubin Mehta, conductor. New York, NY: Avery Fisher Hall, 9/23,28/82. This work was also chosen as the representative American composition in the New York Philharmonic's "United Nations Day Program," 10/24/82, televised over WNET-TV.

*Walker, Alice. *The Ponder Heart*, an opera based on the book by Eudora Welty. Jackson, MS: New Stage Theatre, 9/10/82.

Wallach, Joelle. *String Quartet*. National Association of Composers U.S.A. concert. New York, NY: St. Stephen's Church, 4/24/83.

Whisps, for solo piano (1973). Max Lifchitz, piano. New York, NY: Interlude Concert Loft, 10/10/82.

†Zallman, Arlene. *Three Songs from Quasimodo*. New York New Music Ensemble. New York, NY: Carnegie Recital Hall, 1/13/83. Winner of League-ISCM National Composers Competition.

Zwilich, Ellen Taaffe. *Passages*. Music Today, Gerard Schwarz, conductor. New York, NY: Merkin Concert Hall, 11/3/82 (New York premiere).

1981-1982 SEASON

*Anderson, Laurie. *It's Cold Outside*. American Composers Orchestra, Dennis Russell Davies, conductor. New York, NY: Alice Tully Hall, 11/30/81.

Archer, Violet (Canada). *Fanfare and Passacaglia*, for orchestra. Fox Valley Symphony Orchestra of Portland, OR. Appleton, WI: 11/21/81; Menasha, WI: 11/22/81.

*Barkin, Elaine. *De Amore*, mini-opera for four female and four male singer-speakers and ensemble. Oberlin College Workshop, Judith Layng, director. Oberlin, OH: Oberlin College, 2/14/82.

  Media Speak, for nine speakers, saxophone, and slides based on texts concerning nuclear reactors. Los Angeles, CA: University of California at Los Angeles, 4/17/82.

†Blaustein, Susan. *Due Madrigali di Torquato Tasso*, for mezzo and chamber ensemble. Contemporary Chamber Ensemble, Arthur Weisberg, conductor. New York, NY: Carnegie Recital Hall, 10/15/81. Winner of League-ISCM National Composers Competition.

  Fantasie, for piano solo. Alan Feinberg, piano. New York, NY: Symphony Space, 4/14/82.

  Ricercare. Group for Contemporary Music. New York, NY: Manhattan School of Music, 4/28/82.

*Bobrow, Sanchie. *Little Black Fish*, children's musical. New York, NY: Hartley House Theatre, 9/12/81.

Bouchard, Linda. *Before the Cityset*, for eight violas with oboe, horn, and percussion in the balcony (1981). Linda Bouchard, conductor. New York, NY: Manhattan School of Music, 5/6/82.

  †*Ma Lune maligne*, for flute, viola, harp, and percussion (1981). Los Angeles, CA: California State University, 2/5/82. First prize winner, NACUSA Composers Contest, 1981.

  Stormy Light, for string quartet (1981). New York, NY: New Music for Violas concert, 11/81.

  *†*Viennese Divertimento*, for oboe, viola, 'cello, piano, and percussion. New York, NY: 5/22/82. Commissioned by Maria Pelikan.

*Britain, Radie. *A Musical Portrait of Thomas Jefferson*, for string quartet. Rome, Italy: 3/27/82.

  Translunar Cycle, for 'cello and piano. Diego Villa, 'cello; Ching Lee, piano. Denton, TX: North Texas State University, 2/26/82.

Brockman, Jane. *Sonata*, for clarinet and piano (1981). David Harman, clarinet; Benita Rose, piano. New York, NY: Symphony Space, 11/24/81 (New York premiere).

*†Brouk, Joanna. *Lalinia Electral (The Lake, the Sky)*. Bay Area Women's Philharmonic, Laurie Steele, conductor. Berkeley, CA: First Congregational Church, 3/21/82. Orchestrated version commissioned by the Bay Area Women's Philharmnic.

*Bruner, Cheryl. *Brass Quintet*. Pittsburgh New Music Ensemble. Pittsburgh, PA: University of Pittsburgh, 3/24/82.

  Star Fear. Lynn Webber, soprano; Beverly Nero, piano. Pittsburgh, PA: University of Pittsburgh, 1/20/82.

*Brush, Ruth. *A Legend*; *If I Could Help Santa Claus*, for women's voices. Bartlesville, OK: First Christian Church, 12/12/81.

*Carlson, Roberta. *The Cookie Jar*, a children's opera. Children's Theatre Company. Minneapolis, MN: 3/1/82.

Chance, Nancy Laird. *Duos*, for violin and 'cello. Contemporary Music Forum. Washington, DC: Library of Congress, 5/17/82 (concert of music by women).

Clayton, Laura. *Simichai-ya*, for saxophone, tape, and Echoplex. New York, NY: Carnegie Recital Hall, 2/11/82.

†Clement, Sheree. *String Quartet*. Atlantic String Quartet. New York, NY: Carnegie Recital Hall, 3/25/82 (New York premiere). Winner of League-ISCM National Composers Competition.

*Coates, Gloria. *Between*, for two tapes and seven instruments. East Berlin Festival. East Berlin, Germany: 9/21/81.

Music on Open Strings. St. Paul Chamber Players, William McClaughlin, conductor. Minneapolis, MN: Walker Arts Center, 3/18/82.

Sinfonietta della Notte. Leif Segerstam, conductor. Lund, Sweden: 7/4/82.

Conrad, Laurie. *Etoiles / Morning*; *Elegy / Songs XI / Dawn*; *The Rose / Thaw*; *Songs of Will-Red Sun*. New York, NY: Lincoln Center Library, 1/15/82 (American Women Composers concert).

Coolidge, Lucy. *Etchings*. New York: Lincoln Center Library 1/15/82 (American Women Composers concert).

*Cory, Eleanor. *Surroundings: Keeping Things Whole; Praise for a Patch of Quiet; Air*. Beverly Morgan, mezzo; Christopher Oldfather, piano. New York, NY: Columbia University, 3/11/82.

*Dembo, Royce. *The Audience*, chamber opera. Golden Fleece Ltd. New York, NY: Soho Repertory Theatre, 5/7/82.

*Diemer, Emma Lou. *God Is Love*, for choir and tape (1982). Washington, DC: Church of the Reformation, 5/82.

*†*Le Rag*, for symphonic band (1981). Virginia Intercollegiate Band, Emma Lou Diemer, conductor. Norfolk, VA: Old Dominion University, 2/82. Won second prize in the Virginia College Band Directors National Association Symposium for New Band Music, 1982.

Seven Etudes, for piano (1965); *Encore*, for piano (1981). Betty Oberacker, piano. Los Angeles, CA: University of Southern California, 4/82 (Second International Congress on Women in Music).

Solotrio, for xylophone, vibraphone, and marimba. Marta Ptaszynska, percussion. Mexico City: New Music Forum, 4/82.

*Dinescu, Violeta (Rumania) *Arabesks*, for flute and percussion (1981). Bucharest: Radioteleviziunea Romana broadcast, 2/1/82.

Elogium, for trumpet and trombone (1981). Bucharest: Radioteleviziunea Romana broadcast, 10/20/81.

Immagini, for flute (1981). Bucharest: Nottarra Museum, 2/28/82.

Para Quittarra (1982). Bucharest: Nottarra Museum, 5/27/82.

The Play, for children's choir and percussion. Mannheim: 5/8/82.

Satya I, for violin (1982). Bucharest: Nottarra Museum, 4/25/82.

Satya IV, for clarinet (1982). Darmstadt: 7/23/82.

*Dlugoszewski, Lucia. *Cicada Terrible Freedom*, for chamber ensemble. New York, NY: Carnegie Recital Hall, 5/31/82.

Dungan, Olive. "Olive Dungan: this is your life." Program of her compositions presented by the Miami Music Teachers' Association. Miami, FL: University of Miami, 10/18/81.

*Ekizian, Michelle. *Hidden Crosses*, for voices and chamber ensemble (1981). New York, NY: Symphony Space, 11/24/81.

*Even-Or, Mary (Israel). *Esspresioni-musicali*, for children's choir. Haefroni Girls' Choir. Tel-Aviv: 2/82.

  Shika, songs of Japanese Haiku, for mixed choir (1979). Jerusalem Rubin Academy of Music Choir. Jerusalem: 6/82.

  Tone-colors, for piano solo (1981). Ady Even-Or, piano. Haifa: Haifa Auditorium, 12/81.

Fine, Vivian. *The Women in the Garden*, a chamber opera. Boston Musica Viva, Richard Pittman, conductor. Cambridge, MA: Sanders Theatre, 10/2/81.

Fontyn, Jacqueline (Belgium). *Symphony "Les 4 sites,"* for orchestra. Belgian National Orchestra, George Octors, conductor. Ottignies, Belgium: Cultural Centre, 11/19/81.

*Fowler, Jennifer (U.K.). *The Arrows of Saint Sebastian II*, for bass clarinet, 'cello, and tape (1981). Alan Brett and Harry Sparnaay. London: 9/81.

  Veni Sancte Spiritus—Veni Creator, for twelve solo singers (1971). B.R.T. Radio Choir of Brussels. Brussels, Belgium: 1981 ISCM World Music Days, 9/81.

*Gideon, Miriam. *Sonata*, for piano. Robert Black, piano. New York, NY: Merkin Concert Hall, 3/29/82.

*†Giteck, Janice. *Tree*, for chamber orchestra. San Francisco Symphony, Edo de Waart, conductor. San Francisco, CA: 12/19/81. Commissioned by Edo de Waart.

Grigsby, Beverly. *Augustine, the Saint*. California State University at Northridge Opera Workshop. Los Angeles, CA: University of Southern California, 4/3/82 (Second International Congress on Women in Music).

Grossman, Deena. *Three Colors*, for oboe (1981). Brenda Schuman-Post, oboe. San Francisco, CA: San Francisco State University, 6/12/82 (Bay Area Women's Philharmonic chamber concert).

*Harting, Julie. *Invocation*, for soprano, tenor, and chamber ensemble. Linda Bouchard, conductor. New York, NY: Manhattan School of Music, 3/24/82.

Hays, Doris. *Homing*. New York, NY: Cooper Union, 4/16/82 (New York premiere).

  Southern Voices, for orchestra. Chattanooga Symphony Orchestra. Chattanooga, TN: Tivoli Theatre, 5/6/82.

  Tunings, for soprano, violin, 'cello, and piano. Contemporary Music Forum. Washington, DC: Library of Congress, 5/17/82 (concert of music by women).

Hoover, Katherine. *Homage to Bartok*. Sylvan Wind Quintet. New York, NY: Carnegie Recital Hall, 3/5/82.

  Psalm 23, for chorus and orchestra. New York, NY: Cathedral of St. John the Divine, 10/24/81.

*Ivey, Jean Eichelberger. *Sea-Change*, for orchestra and tape. Baltimore Symphony Orchestra, Joseph Silverstein, conductor. Baltimore, MD: Lyric Theatre, 3/3-4/82.

  Two Songs, for high voice, flute, and piano. Constance Beavon, mezzo; Kim French, flute; Max Lifchitz, piano. New York, NY: Carnegie Recital Hall,

3/2/82; Charleston, SC: Piccolo Spoleto Festival, 5/31/82.

Jeppsson, Kerstin (Sweden). *Triadic Songs*, for soprano and piano (1968-69); *Women's Songs* (1973); *Three Russian Poems*, for soprano and clarinet (1973); *Four Miniatures*, for piano solo (1972); *Three Songs* from *Five Chorals in Folk Tune*, for soprano and organ (1980-81). Stockholm: 1982.

*Kesselman, Wendy. *A Tragic Household Tale*, opera. Lenox Arts Center Music Theatre Group. Lenox, MA: 7/82.

*†Kessler, Minuetta. *Quartet*, op. 109. Lowell, MA: Lowell University, 11/15/81. Commissioned by the Massachusetts Music Teachers' Association.

Kolb, Barbara. *Crosswinds*, for wind ensemble and percussion. Bay Area Women's Philharmonic, Laurie K. Steele, conductor. San Francisco, CA: San Francisco State University, 1/30/83.

    Rebuttal, for two clarinets. Laurel Hall, Marilyn Martella, clarinets. San Francisco, CA: San Francisco State University, 6/12/82 (Bay Area Women's Philharmonic chamber concert).

    Three Lullabies (1980). David Starobin, guitar. New York, NY: Third Street Music School Settlement, 2/9/82.

*La Barbara, Joan. *Silent Scroll*. Newband ensemble. New York, NY: Symphony Space, 4/25/82.

Larsen, Libby. *Weaver's Song and Jig*. Houston Symphony Chamber Orchestra, C. William Harwood, conductor. Houston, TX: St. Luke's Methodist Church, 10/24/81.

*LeBaron, Anne. *After a Dammit to Hell*. Jay Barksdale, bassoon. New York, NY: St. Stephen's Church, 3/11/82.

    Rite of the Black Sun. New Music Consort, Claire Heldrich, conductor. Jamaica, NY: Hillside Center Auditorium, 12/6/81.

    The Sea and the Honeycomb, for soprano, flute, clarinet, piano, and percussion. Syracuse Society for New Music. New York, NY: Carnegie Recital Hall, 1/19/82.

*†LeFanu, Nicola (U.K.). *The Old Woman of Beare*, for soprano and thirteen players (1981). Rosemary Hardy, soprano; Lontano Ensemble, Lionel Friend, conductor, 11/3/81. Commissioned by Macnaghten Concerts.

    †A Penny for a Song, for soprano and piano (1981). Penelope Price-Jones, soprano; Philip Martin, piano. Dublin: Trinity College, 1/8/82. Commissioned by the performers with funds from the Arts Council of Great Britain.

Levine, Amy Miller. *Contrasts*, for voices, percussion, and chamber orchestra. Elayne Jones, percussion; Bay Area Women's Philharmonic, Laurie K. Steele, conductor. San Francisco, CA: San Francisco State University, 1/30/82.

†Lutyens, Elisabeth (U.K.). *Wild Decembers*. Philharmonia Orchestra, Sir Charles Groves, conductor. London: 2/14/82. Commissioned for the fourth Milton Keynes February Festival.

*McIntosh, Diana (Canada). *Extensions*; *Luminaries*; *Sonograph*. New York, NY: Carnegie Recital Hall, 1/11/82.

*McMillan, Ann. *A Little Cosmic Dust*, for piano and tape. Max Lifchitz, piano. New York, NY: Interlude Concert Loft, 6/13/82.

McPartland, Marian. Various jazz selections. Marian McPartland Trio and the New York Pro Arte Chamber Orchestra. New York, NY: Merkin Concert Hall, 2/16/82.

*†Mageau, Mary (Australia). *The Line Always There*, for SSAA, flute, percussion, and piano four hands (1981). Choir of Mt. Gravatt College, Ian McKinley, conductor. Brisbane: Brisbane Grammar School, 10/28/81. Commissioned by the Australia Society for Music Education.

*Mamlok, Ursula. *Concerto for Oboe and Orchestra*, two-piano and percussion version. New York, NY: Manhattan School of Music, 3/11/82.

 *Panta Rhei, for violin, 'cello, and piano. Ben Hudson, violin; Chris Finkel, 'cello; Aleck Karis, piano. New York, NY: Manhattan School of Music, 1/25/82.

†Marez-Oyens, Tera de (Netherlands). *Charon's Gift*, for piano and tape (1982). Vivian Taylor, piano. Ann Arbor, MI: 3/14/82 (Women in Music Conference). Received special mention at the 12th International Electroacoustic Music Festival in Bourges, France.

 Episodes, for orchestra and variable ensembles (1976). Overijsels Philharmonic Orchestra, Tilo Lehmann, conductor. Hengelo, Holland: 5/27/82; Zwolle, Holland: 5/28/82.

 *Imploring Mother, for soprano, clarinet, basset horn, and piano (1982). Abbandono Ensemble. Zwolle, Holland: 6/14/82.

Martin, Judith. *Oceanside in the Well Tempered Being*, for electronic and acoustic ensemble and theatre. New York, NY: Experimental Intermedia Foundation, 4/6/82.

 **The Secret Circuit*, space opera. Brooklyn Philharmonia, Tania Leon, conductor. Brooklyn, NY: Brooklyn Academy of Music, 3/13/82.

 **Songs for a New World*. Sonora ensemble. Brooklyn, NY: 6/26/82.

Miranda, Sharon Moe. *American Fanfare*. Bay Area Women's Philharmonic, Laurie K. Steele, conductor. San Francisco, CA: San Francisco State University, 1/30/82.

*Monk, Meredith. *Specimen Days*, for twelve voices, two electric organs, and two pianos. The House Ensemble. New York, NY: Public Theatre, 12/2/81.

Musgrave, Thea (U.K.). *A Christmas Carol* (1979). Sadler Wells Company, Peter Mark, conductor. London: 12/16/81 (British premiere).

 **From One to Another*, for viola and fifteen strings (1982). St. Paul Chamber Orchestra, Thea Musgrave, conductor. St. Paul, MN: 3/18/82.

 The Last Twilight. Brooklyn Philharmonia. Brooklyn, NY: Brooklyn Academy of Music, 3/4/82 (New York premiere).

 *†*Peripeteia*, for orchestra (1981). Royal Philharmonic Orchestra, Thea Musgrave, conductor. London: Royal Festival Hall, 11/2/81. Commissioned by the Royal Philharmonic Orchestra with funds from the Arts Council.

*Mygatt, Louise. *Chorale-variations*. Rebecca La Breque, piano. New York, NY: Carnegie Recital Hall, 2/5/82.

Nordenstrom, Gladys. *Rondo*, for flute and piano (1948). Anne Diener Giles, flute; Zita Carno, piano. Los Angeles, CA: University of California at Los Angeles, 12/5/81.

Oliveros, Pauline. *Lullaby for Daisy Pauline*; *Breathe-in-Breathe-out*; *Horse Sings from Cloud*. New York, NY: Paula Cooper Gallery, 1/29/82.

†Parker, Alice. "Meet the Composer" concert. New York, NY: Bloomingdale House of Music, 4/18/82. Concert sponsored by a grant from Meet the Composer.

Procaccini, Teresa (Italy). *Clown Music*, op. 36. Judith Fischer, flute; Randy Israel, oboe; Laurel Hall, clarinet; Patty Paulson, bassoon; Janis J. Leiberman, horn. San Francisco, CA: San Francisco State University, 6/12/82 (Bay Area Women's Philharmonic chamber concert).

Radigue, Elaine (France). *Adnos III, Prelude to Milarepa*. New York, NY: Experimental Intermedia Foundation, 4/30/82.

*Raigorodsky, Natalia. *The Promise of Peace,* a scenic oratorio. Opera Theatre of Washington, Doris Mattingly, conductor. Washington, DC: American University, 10/18/81.

*Ran, Shulamit. *A Prayer*. Contemporary Chamber Players. Chicago, IL: University of Chicago, 1/22/82.

*Richter, Marga. *Duesseldorf Concerto*. Duesseldorf Ensemble, Wolfgang Trommer, conductor. Salzburg, Austria: 5/20/82.

The Music of Marga Richter: *Landscapes of the Mind II*, for violin and piano; *Soundings*, for harpsichord; *Sonata,* for piano; *Sonora* (1981); *String Quartet no. 2*. New York, NY: Merkin Concert Hall, 10/18/81.

*Rodgers, Lou. *Miyako*, chamber opera. Golden Fleece Ltd. New York, NY: Soho Repertory Theatre, 5/7/82.

Rubin, Anna. *Marguerite's Dance*, for flute, 'cello, and percussion. Contemporary Music Forum. Washington, DC: Library of Congress, 5/17/82 (concert of music by women).

*†St.-Marcoux, Micheline Coulombe (Canada). *Constellation I*, electronic. Bourges, France: Festival de Bourges, 6/9/82. Commissioned by the Groupe de Musique Experimentale de Bourges.

Horizon I, for flute solo. Marielena Arizpe, flute. Mexico City: Cuatro Foro Internacional de Música Nueva, 3/21/82.

Luminance, for orchestra. Vancouver Symphony Orchestra, Akiyama, conductor. Vancouver, BC: 3/82.

Trakadie, for percussion and tape; *Zones*, for tape with slides; *Arksalalartoq*, for tape and singer; *Miroirs*, for tape and harpsichord; *Episodiquement*, for three percussionists. Toronto: Fourth Annual Festival of Electronic Music, 2/26/82.

*Samter, Alice (West Germany). *Gemini*, for piano four hands. T. Yamashita, M. Takahashi, pianists. West Berlin: British Center, 10/2/81.

Klaviertrio. Valentina Teutsch, violin; Zdravka Güttler 'cello; Manfred Theilen, piano. West Berlin: 12/10/81.

*Schonthal, Ruth. *Sonata Concertante*, for 'cello and piano. Maxine Neuman, 'cello; Ioan Stein, piano. Hofheim, W. Germany: 10/2/81. Also performed at the American Women Composers concert, Lincoln Center Library, 1/15/82.

Semegen, Daria. *Jeux des quatres*. New York, NY: Lincoln Center Library, 1/15/82 (American Women Composers concert).

*†*Music for Contrabass Solo*. Lynn Milano, contrabass. Rochester, NY: Eastman School of Music, 11/8/81. Commissioned by the New York State Music Teachers Association.

Shatin, Judith. *Wind Songs*, for wind quintet (1980). Sylvan Wind Quintet. New York, NY: Carnegie Recital Hall, 3/5/82 (New York premiere).

*Shore, Clare. *Prelude and Variations* (1981). Rebecca La Breque, piano. New York, NY: Carnegie Recital Hall, 2/5/82.

Silsbee, Ann. *De Amore et morte*, for soprano, clarinet, violin, 'cello, and piano. Syracuse Society for New Music. New York, NY: Carnegie Recital Hall, 1/14/82 (New York premiere).

   Trialogue, for clarinet, violin, and piano. Contemporary Music Forum. Washington, DC: Library of Congress, 5/17/82 (concert of music by women).

*Silverman, Faye-Ellen. *Trysts*, for two trumpets. Don Tison, Langston Fitzgerald, trumpets. Baltimore, MD: 4/25/82.

   *Speaking Together. Dinos Constantinides, violin; Eugene Cline, piano. Baton Rouge, LA: Louisiana State University School of Music, 2/12/82.

Singer, Jeanne. *From Petrarch*; *Memoria*; *Suite in Harpsichord Style*. New York, NY: Lincoln Center Library, 1/15/82 (American Women Composers concert).

*Smith, Julia. *Prairie Kaleidoscope*, song cycle. Lynne Anders, soprano; Ruth McDonald, piano. Ann Arbor, MI: University of Michigan, 3/14/82 (Conference on Women in Music).

   *Suite, for wind octet. North Texas State University Wind Ensemble. Denton, TX: North Texas State University, 2/25/82.

*Solomon, Elide M. *Scenes from Childhood*. White Plains, NY: County Center, 10/14/81.

   *Stangetziana, for woodwind quartet. New York, NY: Lincoln Center Library, 6/16/82.

*Southam, Ann (Canada). *Glass Hours*, sixteen pieces for piano and tape (1981). Christina Petrowski, piano (Piece no. 5). Ottawa: 4/82.

   *†*Natural Resources or What to Do Till the Power Comes On* (sound game for found sound, 1981). Toronto: Comus Theatre, spring, 1982. Commissioned by the Canadian Electronic Ensemble under a grant from the Ontario Arts Council.

*Spektor, Mira J. *Lady of the Castle*, chamber opera. Theatre for the New City. New York, NY: 2/4/82.

   *Sunday Psalm. Lawrence Chelsi, baritone. New York, NY: Madison Presbyterian Church, 5/3/82.

Still, Ruth. *Triplex*, for three trumpets. Joyce Johnson Hamilton, Marilyn Meyers, Karen Baccaro, trumpets. San Francisco, CA: San Francisco State University, 6/12/82 (Bay Area Women's Philharmonic chamber concert).

*Sugai, Esther. *Calling*, for three didjeridu and tape. Seattle, WA: 3/6/82.

Swados, Elizabeth. *Alice at the Palace*, a musical fantasy based on books by Lewis Carroll. Meryl Streep, Alice. Broadcast on WNBC, 1/16/82.

   *The Haggadah: musicalization of the Passover story. New York, NY: Public Theatre, 4/1/82.

Talma, Louise. *Variations on Thirteen Ways of Looking at a Blackbird*, for tenor, oboe, and piano. Paul Sperry, tenor. New York, NY: Carnegie Recital Hall, 10/15/81.

Tashjian, B. Charmain. *Songs of the Sea*, for mezzo, viola, and piano. Carol Loverde, mezzo; Audrey Pedersen, viola; Darlene Cowles, piano. Chicago, IL: Cultural Center, 3/82.

*Tower, Joan. *Wings*, for solo clarinet. Laura Flax, clarinet. New York, NY: Merkin Concert Hall, 12/14/81.

Van de Vate, Nancy. *Adagio for Orchestra*. National Gallery Orchestra, Richard Bales, conductor. Washington, DC: 4/12/82.

   *Cantata, for women's voices. Veil of Isis, Joan Gallegos, conductor. Los Angeles,

CA: University of Southern California, 4/1/82 (Second International Congress on Women in Music).

Concertpiece, for 'cello and small orchestra. San Francisco Conservatory Orchestra, Joan Gallegos, conductor. San Francisco, CA: 1/28/82.

Short Piece, for brass quartet. Basel Brass Quartet. Basel, Switzerland: 3/13/82.

*†Vercoe, Elizabeth. *Fanfare*, for three trumpets and timpani. M.I.T. Brass Ensemble. Wellesley, MA: Wellesley College, 9/18/81. Commissioned for the inauguration of the president of Wellesley College.

Irreveries from Sappho. Melinda Spratlan, soprano; Allen Boude, piano. South Hadley, MA: Mt. Holyoke College, 11/4/81.

*Wang, An-Ming. *Little Yellow Bird*. Helen Kwok-Hui, soprano; Lin Kung-Chin, piano. Taipei, Taiwan: Shih Chien Hall, 7/17/82.

Petite valse; *Arabesque*; *Toccata*, three piano pieces. Platteville, WI: University of Wisconsin, 10/15/81.

Weigl, Vally. *Songs of Remembrance*, for mezzo, flute, and piano. New York, NY: Interlude Concerts, 5/23/82.

Three Discourses, for flute and 'cello. Gwendolyn Mansfield, flute; David Moore, 'cello. New York, NY: Donnell Library, 10/3/81.

*†Weir, Judith (U.K.). *Ballad*, for baritone solo and orchestra (1981). Stephen Varcoe, baritone; Scottish National Orchestra, Sir Alexander Gibson, conductor. Glasgow, Scotland: 9/17/81. Commissioned by the Scottish National Orchestra Society for Musica Nova 1981.

*†*Music for 247 Strings*, for violin and piano. Paul Barritt and William Howard. London: 10/5/81. Commissioned by the performers with funds from the Greater London Arts Association.

*Wylie, Ruth Shaw. *Music for Three Sisters*, for clarinet, flute, and piano. Contemporary Music Forum. Washington, DC: Library of Congress, 5/17/82 (concert of music by women).

*†Zaimont, Judith Lang. *From the Great Land*, women's songs (1982). Bayreuth, Germany: North Star Consort, 5/6/82 (followed by six performances in the U.S., 5/82). Commissioned through the Exxon Fund for the University of Alaska-Fairbanks's North Star Consort.

Two Songs, for soprano and harp. Seattle, WA: ASUC Annual Conference, 4/23/82.

Zallman, Arlene. *Three Preludes*, for piano. Charles Fisk, piano. New York, NY: Merkin Concert Hall, 1/23/82 (New York premiere).

*Zwilich, Ellen Taaffe. *Passages*, for soprano and chamber ensemble. Janice Felty, soprano; Boston Musica Viva, Richard Pittman, conductor. Boston, MA: 1/29/82.

*†*Three Movements*, for orchestra. American Composers Orchestra, Gunther Schuller, conductor. New York, NY: Alice Tully Hall, 5/5/82. Joint commission: National Endowment for the Arts/American Composers Concerts, Inc.

1980-1981 SEASON

Archer, Violet (Canada). *The Bell*. Ottawa Choral Society, Ottawa Symphony Orchestra. Ottawa: 3/2/81.

Capriccio, for 'cello and piano. Claude Kenneson, 'cello; Brian Harris, piano. London: Wigmore Hall, 6/20/81.

Prairie Profiles, for horn, baritone voice, and piano. David Hoyt, horn; Harold Wiens, baritone; Janet Scott-Hoyt, piano. Edmonton: 2/23/81.

Primeval. David Astor, tenor; Harold Brown, piano. Banff, Alberta: Banff Festival of the Arts, 8/10/81.

Psalm 145, for a cappella mixed choir. Richard Eaton Singers, Larry Cook, conductor. Edmonton: 7/16/81.

Sinfonietta, for orchestra. R.A.I. Orchestra of the Italian Radio. Rome: 3/17/81.

*Baker, May Winder. *Simfony for Frank*. Arch Ensemble for Experimental Music. San Francisco, CA: Performance Gallery, 5/3/81.

Barthelson, Joyce. *Lysistrata*, opera in one act. New York University Opera Studio, Thomas Martin, conductor. New York, NY: New York University, 3/81 (First National Congress on Women in Music).

*Beecroft, Norma (Canada). *Cantorum Vitae*, for 'cello, flute, percussion, two pianos and tape. days months and years to come ensemble. Vancouver: Vancouver East Cultural Centre, 3/1/81.

*Blaustein, Susan. *Commedia*. Speculum Musicae. New York, NY: Symphony Space, 12/16/80.

*Bobrow, Sanchie. *Three Frames of Mind*, for solo flute. Gina Bertucci, flute. New Brunswick, NJ: Rutgers University, 4/30/81.

Life Song, a stage piece for Passover. New Brunswick, NJ: Rutgers University, 4/9/81.

*Bolz, Harriett. *Sonic Essay and Fugue*, for organ. Adel Heinrich, organ. Waterville, ME: Colby College, 3/22/81.

Bouchard, Linda. *Glances*, for 'cello and dancer (1980). Marymount Dance Workshop Production. New York, NY: 4/5/81.

*Britain, Radie. *Alaskan Trail of '98*. West Texas State University Orchestra, Gary Garner, conductor. Canyon, TX: 5/3/81.

In the Beginning. New York Horn Quartet. New York, NY: 3/27/81.

Prelude to a Drama. Air Force Symphony Orchestra, George Howard, conductor. Los Angeles, CA: 6/14/81.

Prison (lament), for chamber orchestra. Alberto Bolet, conductor. Los Angeles, CA: 5/31/81.

Program of her compositions. Bernice DuLong, soprano; Joy Bottle, piano. Los Angeles, CA: MacDowell Club, 6/14/81.

*Bruner, Cheryl. *Circles*. Beverly Nero, piano. Pittsburgh, PA: University of Pittsburgh, 10/28/80.

Five Bagatelles, for string quartet. Pittsburgh New Music Ensemble. Pittsburgh, PA: 2/5/81.

*Chance, Nancy Laird. *Exultation and Lament*, for alto saxophone and timpani. Tallahassee, FL: Florida State University, 5/8/81.

*Clement, Sheree. *Prelude no. 5*, for piano. Allen Shawn, piano. New York, NY: Symphony Space, 2/10/81.

Coates, Gloria. *Music on Open Strings*. New Amsterdam Symphony Orchestra, Rachel Worby, conductor. New York, NY: New York University, 3/81 (First National Congress on Women in Music).

*Collins, Janyce. *As in a Twilight of Roses*. Brigitte Jones, harp. Redlands, CA: 12/12/80.

*Davidson, Tina. *Lazy Afternoon Music*, for two violins, flute, clarinet, and bassoon. Bennington, VT: Bennington College, 8/18/81.

*Dembo, Royce. *Duet Metamorphic*, for piano duet. David Henry, Barbara Brown, pianists. Platteville, WI: University of Wisconsin, 12/4/80.

   Songs, for soprano, horn, and piano. Charlotte Surkin, soprano; Christopher Costanzi, horn; John Klingberg, piano. New York, NY: 3/20/81.

   Sonority no. 1, for piano. Rosemary Platt, piano. Platteville, WI: University of Wisconsin, 12/4/80.

Diemer, Emma Lou. *Add One #1*, for electronic piano and tape (1981). Marilyn Shrude, piano. Bowling Green, OH: Bowling Green State University, 4/81.

   Add One #2, for synthesizer and tape (1981). Emma Lou Diemer, synthesizer. Santa Barbara, CA: University of California at Santa Barbara, 4/81 (Conference on Women in Music).

   Homage to Cowell, Cage, Crumb and Czerny, for two pianos (1981). Marjorie and Wendell Nelson, pianists. Westminster, MD: Western Maryland College, 4/81 (also performed at Shanghai Conservatory and Central Conservatory in Beijing, China, 5/81).

   *†*Three Hymn Anthems*, for choir, congregation, organ, brass, and percussion (1980). Duke University Chapel Choir. Durham, NC: Duke University, 10/80. Commissioned by Duke University.

*Dinescu, Violeta (Rumania). *Memories*, for string orchestra (1980). Craiova Philharmonic. Bucharest: 6/13/81.

*Even-Or, Mary (Israel). *Music to a Poem*, for voice, flute, and 'cello (1979). Mira Zakai, alto; Uri Shoham, flute; Marcel Bergman, 'cello. Jerusalem: 3/81.

*Fine, Vivian. *Gertrude and Virginia*. Rosalind Rees, soprano; Kimball Wheeler, mezzo; five-member ensemble, Vivian Fine, conductor. New York, NY: 6/8/81.

   *†*Oda a las Ranas*, for women's chorus, flute, oboe, 'cello, and percussion. Anna Crusis Choir, Catherine Roma, conductor. Philadelphia, PA: 6/13/81. Commissioned by the Anna Crusis Choir.

   *†*Trio,* for violin, 'cello, and piano. Mirecourt Trio. Oak Park, IL: Frank Lloyd Wright Unity Temple, 4/4/81. Commissioned by the Mirecourt Trio.

*Forman, Joanne. *Ikarus*, one-act opera. Southwest Chamber Opera. Albuquerque, NM: 1981.

*†Fowler, Jennifer (U.K.). *Music for Piano, Ascending and Descending* (1980). Michael Finnissey, piano. London: British Music Information Centre, 12/80. Commissioned by Michael Finnissey and the Vaughan Williams Trust.

   Piece for E.L., for solo piano (1981). Michael Finnissey, piano. London: 3/81.
   Voice of the Shades, for soprano, oboe (or clarinet), and violin (1976-1977). Hong Kong: Asian Composers Conference and Festival, 3/81.

*Gardner, Kay. *Ladies Voices*, opera. Southwest Chamber Opera. Albuquerque, NM: 1981.

*Gideon, Miriam. *Morning Star*, a song cycle in Hebrew on poems of childhood. Judith Raskin, soprano. New York, NY: 92nd Street YMHA, 1/18/81.

   *†*Spirit above the Dust*, song cycle on American poetry for voice and chamber ensemble. Yale Contemporary Ensemble, Arthur Weisberg, conductor. New Haven, CT: Yale University, 2/11/81. Commissioned by the Elizabeth Sprague Coolidge Foundation of the Library of Congress in honor of the fiftieth anniversary of the Music Library Association.

*†Gillick, Lyn. *Cages*, for guitar and tape. Wayne Reynolds, guitar. Memphis, TN:

Orpheum Theatre, 2/20/81. Commissioned by Ballet South, George Latimer, choreographer.

*Giteck, Janice. *Breathing Songs from a Turning Sky*. New Music Performance Group. Seattle, WA: 4/5/81.

*Grigsby, Beverly. *Dithyrambos*, for violin and 'cello. New Repertory Ensemble. New York, NY: Carnegie Recital Hall, 12/9/80.

*Hays, Doris. *Only*, for prepared piano and tape recorders. Loretta Goldberg, piano. New York, NY: New York University, 5/7/81.

*Hovda, Eleanor. *Journey Music*. Orchestra of Our Time, Joel Thome, conductor. New York, NY: Merkin Concert Hall, 1/20/81.

*Kessler, Minuetta. *Variations on a Jewish Lullaby*, for flute and harp. Donna Hiecken, flute; Ruth Saltzman, harp. Providence, RI: Beth El Temple, 1/23/81.

Kolb, Barbara. *Homage to Keith Jarrett and Gary Burton*. Atlanta Chamber Players. Atlanta, GA: 3/2/81.

*Larsen, Libby. *Scudding*. Ruth Dreier, 'cello. New York, NY: Third Street Music School Settlement, 2/9/81.

*Lauber, Anne (Canada). *Fantasy on a Known Theme*, for piano and youth orchestra (1980). Tristan Van Nguyen, piano; Joliette Youth Orchestra, Paul Boivin, conductor. Joliette, IL: 5/81.

*LeBaron, Anne. *Creamy Hands*, for harp, trombone, and klangpieldose. Cologne, W. Germany: 8/2/81.

   Rite of the Black Sun. New Music Consort. New York, NY: Carnegie Recital Hall, 12/11/80.

*†LeFanu, Nicola (U.K.). *Like a Wave of the Sea*, for mixed choir and ensemble of early instruments (1981). Nottingham University Choir and instrumentalists. Nottingham: 3/1/81. Commissioned by Nottingham University.

   Trio, for flute, 'cello, and percussion (1980). Lontano Ensemble. London: 6/15/81. Commissioned by the ensemble.

†Louie, Alexina (Canada). *Incantation*, for clarinet and prepared tape. Music Inter Alia. Ontario: 2/81. Written under a grant from the Canadian Council.

*Lutyens, Elisabeth (U.K.). *Diurnal* (eleventh quartet). Medici Quartet. London: 1981.

*Mageau, Mary (Australia). *Cantilena*, for flute and percussion (1980). Adelaide Brown, flute; Richard Hills, percussion. Brisbane: Queensland Conservatorium of Music, 8/2/81.

   Pacific Ports, for piano four hands (1979). Jeanette Castle, Danielle Nowland, pianists. Brisbane: North Brisbane College, 5/13/81.

   Statement and Variations. Michael Kimber, viola. Lawrence, KS: University of Kansas, 3/4/81.

*Marez-Oyens, Tera de (Netherlands). *Cellogism*, for 'cello and piano (1980). Gert Jan Van de Weerd, 'cello; Maria Hol, piano. Amsterdam: 11/23/80.

   Concerto, for horn and tape (1980). Johan Donker Kaat, horn. Utrecht: 11/17/80.

*Moore, Anita. *Quintet for Brass*. Grace Avenue Brass Ensemble. New York, NY: Manhattanville College, 3/21/81.

Ostrander, Linda. *O, Faces*, a children's musical by Linda Ostrander and Sara Beattie. Elma Lewis School of Fine Arts Children's Theatre. Roxbury, MA: 6/81.

*Owen, Blythe. *Processional on an Austrian Hymn*. William J. Ness, organ. Berrien Springs, MI: Andrews University, 8/9/81.

   *Trio, for clarinet, 'cello, and piano. Lennart Olson, clarinet; Roy Maki, 'cello; Blythe Owen, piano. Traverse City, MI: 10/14/80.

*Phillips, Bryony (New Zealand). *Cloudwhisperer*, song cycle for mezzo and piano. Gillian Kendrick, mezzo; Peter Watts, piano. Auckland, New Zealand: 8/16/81.

   *First Love, song cycle for soprano and piano (1979). Mary Pound, soprano; Ingrid Wahlberg, piano. Takapuna, New Zealand: 2/28/81.

*Pizer, Elizabeth. *Look Down Fair Moon*, for soprano and piano. Anna Carol Dudley, soprano; Lois Bradywynne, piano. San Francisco, CA: San Francisco State University, 1/30/81 (Bay Area Conference on Women in Music).

   *Sunken Flutes. Santa Barbara, CA: University of California at Santa Barbara, 4/11/81 (Santa Barbara Conference on Music by Women).

*Polin, Claire. *Felina, Felina*. Delaware Valley Composers concert. Philadelphia, PA: 3/15/81.

*Preobrajenska, Vera. *Preludium*, for organ solo. Eugene, OR: University of Oregon, 11/8/80.

   **Suite for Strings*. Santa Cruz Chamber Orchestra, Lewis Skeizov, conductor. Santa Cruz, CA: First Methodist Church, 12/22/80.

*Procaccini, Teresa (Italy). *Clown Music*, for wind quintet. Quintet of the Americas. New York, NY: New York University, 3/81 (First National Congress on Women in Music).

Ricard, Gisele (Canada). *Immersion*. Dominican Republic: Décimo Curso Latino-americano de Música Contemporanea, 1/81.

   **Passacaille 22/11-44*, multimedia work. AmaQ concert. Quebec City: Institut Canadien de Québec, 1981.

*Richter, Marga. *To Whom?* New Calliope Singers, Peter Schubert, conductor. New York, NY: 3/6/81.

*Rodgers, Lou. *Thursday's Child*, opera. Golden Fleece, Ltd. New York, NY: Theatre 22, 10/31/80.

Rogers, Patsy. *A Woman Alive: Conversation against Death*. Joyce McLean, soprano; ensemble, Aileen Passloff, director. New York, NY: New York University, 3/81 (First National Congress on Women in Music).

*St. John, Kathleen. *The Winds of Aeolus*. Quintet of the Americas. New York, NY: New York University, 3/81 (First National Congress on Women in Music).

*Samter, Alice (West Germany). *Gott schuf die Sonne*. Ferry Lendvay, cymbal; Janice Williams, soprano; Rosario Marciano, piano. Vienna, Austria: Palais Palffy, 9/9/80.

   Rivalités, Patricia Becler, flute; Bruce Berry, 'cello; Maria Palacios, clarinet; Leah Rummel, piano. Denton, TX: 4/7/81.

   *Trialog, for violin, contrabass, and piano. Marianne Boettcher, violin; Klaus Stoll, contrabass; Ursula Boettcher, piano. West Berlin: British Center, 5/13/81.

*Scherchen-Hsiao, Tona (France). *Between*, acoustical part of a future multimedia project for five musicians and electronic tape. New York, NY: The Kitchen, 1981.

Schonthal, Ruth. *Music for Horn and Chamber Orchestra* (1979). Robert Johnson, horn; New Amsterdam Symphony Orchestra, Rachel Worby, conductor. New

York, NY: New York University, 3/81 (First National Congress on Women in Music).

*Semegen, Daria. *Music for Clarinet Solo.* Jack Kreiselman, clarinet. New York, NY: Carnegie Recital Hall, 11/28/80.

*Shatin, Judith. *Follies and Fancies,* chamber opera. Ash Lawn, VA: 8/14/81.

*Shore, Clare. *July Remembrances,* for soprano and chamber orchestra. Daureen Podenski, soprano; Patricia Handy, conductor. New York, NY: Juilliard School, 2/20/81.

  **Woodwind Quintet.* New York, NY: Juilliard School, 2/20/81.

*Silverman, Faye-Ellen. *Oboe-sthenics.* James Ostryniec, oboe. Innsbruck, Austria: 10/29/80.

*Singer, Jeanne. *American Indian Song Suite,* arranged for mixed chorus. Coro de Camera de la Universidad Nacional, Elsa Gutierrez, conductor. Bogotá, Colombia: 9/29/80.

  **Go in Peace,* for men's chorus with tenor solo. Austin Miskell, tenor; Coro de Ibague, Nelly de Vuksic, conductor. Bogotá, Colombia: 12/18/80.

*Solomon, Elide M. *Hommage à Picasso* (1980). Elide M. Solomon, piano. New York, NY: Carnegie Recital Hall, 10/19/80.

*Solomon, Joyce. *Sing My People.* Brooklyn Philharmonia. Hempstead, NY: Hofstra University, 6/19/81.

*Thomas, Marilyn Taft. *Elegy.* Pittsburgh New Music Ensemble, David Stock, conductor. Pittsburgh, PA: University of Pittsburgh, 10/28/80.

*Tower, Joan. *Sequoia.* American Composers Orchestra, Dennis Russell Davies, conductor. New York, NY: Alice Tully Hall, 5/18/81.

*Van Appledorn, Mary Jeanne. *Lux: Legend of Santa Lucia.* Gary Garner, conductor. Cincinnati, OH: University of Cincinnati College Conservatory of Music, 8/6/81.

*Van de Vate, Nancy. *Nine Preludes for Piano.* Platteville, WI: University of Wisconsin, 12/4/80.

  **Sonata,* for piano. Sallie Warth Schoen, piano. Maryville, TN: Maryville College, 10/23/80.

  String Quartet no. 1. Ridge String Quartet. San Francisco, CA: 8/8/81.

  **Trio,* for bassoon, percussion, and piano. Paul Barrett, bassoon; Wiliam Niley, percussion; Nancy Van de Vate, piano. Honolulu, HI: Unitarian Church of Honolulu, 12/7/80.

  Variations, for chamber orchestra. Santa Cruz Chamber Orchestra, Lewis Keizer, conductor. Santa Cruz, CA: 5/9/81.

†Vercoe, Elizabeth. *Herstory I* (1975). Cheryl Cobb, soprano; Dean Anderson, percussion; Randall Hodgkinson, piano. Boston, MA: broadcast over WGBH as a prize winner in the WGBH-Boston Musica Viva Competition for New Music.

  *†*Persona,* for solo piano. Vivian Taylor, piano. New York, NY: New York University, 3/27/81 (First National Congress on Women in Music). Commissioned by Vivian Taylor for the Congress.

*Weigl, Vally. *Bird of Life,* for clarinet solo. Naomi Drucker, clarinet. New York, NY: Donnell Library, 10/11/80.

  **Only the Moon Remembers,* for mezzo, oboe, clarinet, and bassoon. Constance Beavon, mezzo; Charleston Woodwind Players. Charleston, SC: Piccolo Spoleto Festival, 5/31/81.

*Three Dialogues, for clarinet and violin. Richard Stoltzman, clarinet; Lucie Stoltzman, violin. Berkeley, CA: 4/19/81.

*†Weir, Judith (U.K.). *An mein Klavier*, for piano (1980). Michael Finnissey, piano. Bracknell, GB: 7/20/80. Commissioned by South Hill Park Festival of English Music, Bracknell.

*†*Cello Sonata* (1980). Oxford, GB: 2/6/81. Commissioned by Rohan de Saraon and Lise-Martine Jeanneret with funds from the Arts Council.

*†*Isti Mirant Stella*, for orchestra (1981). Scottish Chamber Orchestra, Jerzy Maksymiuk, conductor. Orkney, Scotland: 6/23/81. Commissioned by the St. Magnus Festival with assistance from the Scottish Arts Council.

*†*Pas de deux*, for violin and oboe (1980). Alan Wilkinson and Sarah Ionides. Warwick University: 11/30/80. Commissioned by the performers with funds from the Southern Arts Association.

*†*Thread!* for narrator and eight players (1981). Roger Savage, narrator; New Music Group of Scotland, Edward Harper, conductor. Stirling, Scotland: 3/2/81. Commissioned by the New Music Group of Scotland with assistance from the Scottish Arts Council.

Zaimont, Judith Lang. *A Calendar Set*—two excerpts. Used as a key theme of music score for the PBS documentary "The Artist Was a Woman," national TV broadcast, 5/81.

Capriccio. Elizabeth Hicks, flute. New York, NY: Lincoln Center Library, 10/3/80.

Three Ayres. Western Wind Ensemble. New York, NY: 6/81 (Festival IV of Women's Music).

*Ziffrin, Marilyn J. *Quintet*, for oboe and string quartet. Basil Reeve, oboe; Primavera String Quartet. Henniker, NH: New England College, 4/9/81.

Sono, for 'cello and piano. David and Janet Wells. New London, NH: Summer Music Associates, 8/19/81.

1979-1980 SEASON

*Archer, Violet (Canada). *Four Duets*, for violin and 'cello. Tom Rolston, violin; Shawna Rolston, 'cello. Banff, Alberta: Banff Festival of the Arts, 7/25/80.

*Berleant, Andrea. *Pieces*, for string quartet. Bennington, VT: Bennington Composers' Conference, 7/13/80.

†Bouchard, Linda. *Anticipation of Priscilla*, for mezzo, flute, violin, viola, 'cello, piano, and percussion. Bennington, VT: Bennington College, 4/80. Commissioned by the Dromas Ensemble.

*Chance, Nancy Laird. *Duos III*, for violin and 'cello. New Times Concerts. Baton Rouge, LA: 6/80.

*Coates, Gloria. *Music on Open Strings*. Bavarian Radio Orchestra, Elgar Howarth, conductor. Munich: 11/14/80.

Nonet. Rome: Braschi Palace, 3/23/80.

Six Movements, for string quartet. Ensemble Classique. Cologne: 4/7/80.

Valse triste. Warsaw: Warsaw Autumn Festival, 8/80.

*Diemer, Emma Lou. *Scherzo*, for electronic tape (1980). Knoxville, TN: University of Tennessee, 4/80.

Toccata, for piano (1979). Nozomi Takahashi, piano. Santa Barbara, CA: University of California at Santa Barbara, 4/80.

*Even-Or, Mary (Israel). *Music for Strings* (1979). Haifa Symphony Orchestra. Jerusalem: 11/79.

Reflections, for four recorders (1980). Mor-Li ensemble. Haifa: Museum of Modern Art, 3/80.

Ferreyra, Beatriz (France). *Echos* (1978). Tel Aviv: ISCM World Music Days, 2/7/80.

*Fine, Vivian. *Lieder*, for viola and piano. Jacob Glick, viola; Vivian Fine, piano. New York, NY: Lincoln Center Library, 5/2/80.

Music. Huntingdon Trio. New York, NY: Federal Hall, 6/29/80.

*Fowler, Jennifer (U.K.). *Tell Out My Soul*, for soprano, 'cello, and piano (1980). Piace Consort. London: Wigmore Hall, 6/80.

Frasier, Jane. *Joy, Peace and Singing*. John Anderson, flute; Women's Concert Choir, Carol Bisanz, conductor. Greeley, CO: University of Northern Colorado, spring, 1980.

*†Gardner, Kay. *Winter Night, Gibbous Moon*, saga for eleven flutes. Longy School of Music Flute Choir, Trix Kout, conductor. Boston, MA: 4/27/80. Commissioned by Trix Kout for the Longy School of Music Flute Choir.

*Gideon, Miriam. *Spiritual Airs*, for tenor and seven instruments. Constantine Cassolas, tenor; New Repertory Ensemble, Dinu Ghezzo, conductor. New York, NY: Carnegie Recital Hall, 2/6/80.

*Goldfader, Laura. *Natural Forces*, an operetta. Amy Snyder, conductor. Bennington, VT: 6/80.

*Hays, Doris. *Southern Voices*. New York, NY: Third Street Music School Settlement, 2/29/80.

Jeppsson, Kerstin (Sweden). *Impossible*, for alto and chamber ensemble (1977). Helsinki: Nordic Music Days, 1980.

String Quartet no. 1 (1974). Norrköping, Sweden: Swedish Music Spring Festival, 1980.

*Kolb, Barbara. *Three Lullabies*, for solo guitar. David Starobin, guitar. Paris: American Cultural Center, 3/27/80.

*Laufer, Beatrice. *In the Throes* . . . Shreveport Symphony Orchestra, John Shenaut, conductor. Shreveport, LA: 6/14/80.

*†LeFanu, Nicola (U.K.). *Farne*, for orchestra (1980). University of London Orchestra, Ian Reid, conductor. Bradford: 3/28/80. Commissioned by the University of London Orchestra.

*Louie, Alexina (Canada). *Pearls*. days months and years to come ensemble. Vancouver: Vancouver East Cultural Center, 6/15/80.

*†Mageau, Mary (Australia). *Sonata Concertante* (in stilo moderno). Adelaide Brown, flute; Gary Williams, 'cello; Mary Mageau, harpsichord. Brisbane: University of Queensland, 5/14/80. Written with a commission from the Australia Council.

*Mamlok, Ursula. *Grasshoppers*, sixteen humoresques for orchestra. Pittsburgh, PA: University of Pittsburgh, 11/25/80.

When Summer Sang, for flute, clarinet, violin, 'cello, and piano. Da Capo Chamber Players. New York, NY: Carnegie Recital Hall, 4/28/80.

*Marez-Oyens, Tera de (Netherlands). *Ballerina on a Cliff*, for piano (1980).

Gertrud Firnkees, piano. Munich: 5/5/80.

Mosaic, for oboe, clarinet, horn, bassoon, and piano (1979). Mozart Quintet. Hilversum, Holland: 5/30/80.

Three Hymns, for mezzo and piano (1979). Meta Bourgonjen, mezzo; Ro Van Hessen, piano. Brussels: 3/21/80.

*†Musgrave, Thea (U.K.). *The Last Twilight*, for large SATB chorus, brass, and percussion (1980). Santa Fe, NM: Paolo Soleri Theatre, 7/20/80. Commissioned by the New Mexico D. H. Lawrence Festival, and based on Lawrence's poem "Men in New Mexico."

Mary, Queen of Scots, opera (1977). Scottish Opera, Meredith Davies, conductor. London: 4/2/80 (London premiere).

*Oliveros, Pauline. *Fwynnghn*, a funky fairytale. Valencia, CA: California Institute of the Arts, 3/80.

Ostrander, Linda. *Sci-Fi*: a musical. Cambridge, MA: Lesley College, 5/80.

*Phillips, Bryony (New Zealand). *Dreams in the Grass*, for reciter, mezzo, and recorder (1979); *Widow's Lament*, for unaccompanied soprano (1978); *Tanka: Reality*, for unaccompanied soprano (1978); *Night Hours*, for mezzo and recorder (1979). Takapuna, New Zealand: 3/30/80.

*†*Great Sea*, for boys' choir, trumpet, and percussion (1980). Auckland Boys' Choir. Auckland, New Zealand: 1980. Commissioned by the Auckland Boys' Choir.

Kasumi, Haiku cycle for tenor and piano (1978). Richard Phillips, tenor; Douglas Mews, piano. Auckland, New Zealand: Kenneth Maidment Theatre, 10/3/80.

*†*The Picture of Christ*, for tenor and piano. Richard Phillips, tenor; Alan Pow, piano. Auckland, New Zealand: Auckland Town Hall, 8/21/80. Winner in the song category of the Auckland Composition Contest.

The Shadow of Your Presence, song cycle for soprano and piano (1980). Wendy Dixon, soprano; Moya Rea, piano. Auckland, New Zealand: Outreach Cultural Centre, 6/23/80.

*Pizer, Elizabeth. *Interfuguelude*, for string quartet (1977-1979). Members of the Honolulu Symphony. Honolulu, HI: University YWCA, 8/17/80.

*Polin, Claire. *Summer Settings*, for solo harp. J. Passer, harp.

Vigniatures, for violin and harp. G. Schaff, violin; J. Passer, harp. Philadelphia, PA: 1/26/80.

*Preobrajenska, Vera. *Hebraic Suite*. Santa Cruz Chamber Orchestra, Lewis Keizer, conductor. Aptos, CA: 3/7/80.

*†Reverdy, Michele (France). *Arcane*, for clarinet, violin, 'cello, piano, and percussion (1979). Laboratorio de Interpretation Musical (LIM). Madrid: Institut Français de Madrid, 3/20/80. Written for the LIM.

Through the Looking-Glass, for narrator, female voice, clarinet, viola, two trombones, and piano (1979). Intervalles Ensemble. Paris: Centre Culturel Suédois, 5/20/80. Written for the ensemble.

*Roger, Denise (France). *Musique pour flûte et harpe* (1979). Emmanuel Burlet, flute; Sylvie Beltrando, harp. Paris: 1980.

Psaume (pour un mort), for baritone and eleven instruments. Michel Verschaeve, baritone, l'Ensemble Instrumental de la Police Nationale, Michel Meriot, conductor. Paris: 1980.

Scintillements, for clarinet solo (1979). André Tillous, clarinet. Paris: 1980.

* †St.-Marcoux, Micheline Coulombe (Canada). *Mandala I*, for flute, piano, oboe, 'cello, and percussion. days months and years to come ensemble, Patrick Wedd, conductor. Vancouver: Vancouver East Cultural Center, 6/15/80. Commissioned by the ensemble.

* †Scherchen-Hsiao, Tona (France). *Tzing*, for brass quintet (1979). Paris: 1980. Commissioned by Radio-France.

*Schonthal, Ruth. *Music for Horn and Chamber Orchestra*. Brooks Tillotson, horn; Columbia University Orchestra, Howard Shanet, conductor. New York, NY: Columbia University, 3/28/80.

* †Shore, Clare. *Sonata*, for clarinet and bassoon. Deborah Pittman, clarinet; Cindy Gady, bassoon. Brooklyn, NY: Boro Hall, 3/10/80. Commissioned by Deborah Pittman.

String Quartet no. 1. New Milford, CT: Charles Ives Center for American Music, 8/21/80.

*Silverman, Faye-Ellen. *Three Guitars*. Peabody Guitar Ensemble. Baltimore, MD: 4/4/80.

Yet for Him. Bonnie Lase, flute; Eric Edberg, 'cello; Mary Steyer King, piano. Baltimore, MD: 4/29/80.

*Simons, Netty. *Songs for Wendy*. Jane Manning, soprano; Simon Rowland Jones, viola. Isle of Man, GB: 8/25/80.

*Singer, Jeanne. *Inteligencia*. Henry Roa, bass; Pable Arevalo, piano. Bogotá, Colombia: National Museum of Colonial Art, 3/27/80.

* †Snyder, Amy. *Feast of the Stones*, Mass for thirty trombones and percussion. Bay Bones Trombone Choir, Amy Snyder, conductor. San Francisco, CA: St. Mary's Cathedral, 2/10/80. Commissioned by the ensemble.

Tashjian, B. Charmain. *Antiphonies I* (1977). Bowling Green, OH: Bowling Green State University New Music Festival, 5/80.

*Van de Vate, Nancy. *Five Preludes*, for piano. Nancy Van de Vate, piano. Honolulu, HI: 5/7/80.

*Vercoe, Elizabeth. *Herstory II* (1979). Elisabeth Van Ingen, soprano; Pat Hollenbeck, percussion; Janice Weber, piano. Boston, MA: Boston University, 5/9/80.

*Weigl, Vally. *Songs Newly Seen in the Dusk*, for medium voice and 'cello. Constance Bevin, mezzo; David Moore, 'cello. Charleston, SC: Piccolo Spoleto Festival, 5/30/80.

Songs of Love and Leaving, for mezzo, baritone, clarinet, and piano. Shirley Love, David Holloway, Larry Sobol, and Richard Woitach. New York, NY: Carnegie Recital Hall, 10/4/79.

†Weir, Judith (U.K.). *King Haraid Sails to Byzantium*, for six players (1979). Fires of London, Peter Maxwell Davies, conductor. London: Queen Elizabeth Hall, 5/19/80 (London premiere). Commissioned for Fires of London by the St. Magus Festival Society with funds from the Scottish Arts Council.

*Zaimont, Judith Lang. *Calendar Collection* (1979). Judith Zaimont, piano. New York, NY: 2/21/80.

A Calendar Set, excerpts. Gary Steigerwalt, piano. New York, NY: WQXR radio broadcast "Piano Personalities" 6/12/80.

*Piano pieces: *In Good Spirits*; *Deceit*; *The Harpsichord*; *The Guitar*. New York, NY: Carnegie Recital Hall, 2/14/80.

**Psalm 23*, for voice and ensemble. Bronxville, NY: Sarah Lawrence College, 3/9/80.

SELECT COUNTRY SUMMARIES

(Lists of active women composers provided by Music Information Centers.)

CANADA

British Columbia: Jean Coulthard, Diane Morgan Morley, Barbara Pentland, Sylvia Rickard, Euphrosyne Keefer, Jean Ethridge, Joan Hansen, Kristi Allik, Sherilyn Fritz, Hildegarde Westerkamp, Linda Catlin Smith, Marian Newman (age 9).

Quebec: Micheline Coulombe St.-Marcoux, Gisèle Ricard, Anne Lauber, Marcelle Deschênes, Helen Hardy, Margaret Davies, Elma Miller, Sharon Smith, Gayle Young, Maggie Burston, Wendy Bartley, Kye Marshall, Freny Patell.

Ontario: Jean Anderson, Norma Beecroft, Alexina Louie, Ann Southam, Judy Specht.

FRANCE

The Centre de Documentation de la Musique Contemporaine lists the following women composers: Yvonne Aaron, Odette Allouard-Carny, Alice Bienvenu, Thérèse Brenet, Joanna Bruzdowicz, Monic Cecconi, Jeanine Charbonnier, Nicole Clement, Adrienne Clostre, Yvonne Desportes, Rolande Falcinelli, Beatriz Ferreyra, Graciane Finzi, Odette Gartenlaub, Ida Gotkowsky, Betsy Jolas, Suzanne Joly, Nicole Lachartre, Edith Lejet, Eliane Lejeune-Bonnier, Marcelle de Manziarly, Nicole Philiba, Renée Philippart, Alina Piechowska, Elaine Radigue, Michele Reverdy, Jeanine Richer, Denise Roger, Claire Schapira, Tona Scherchen-Hsiao, Danièle Sevrette.

HUNGARY

The Music Information Center of Hungary lists the following women composers: Erzsébet Szönyi, Katalin Székely.

NETHERLANDS

Women composers listed by Donemus, Amsterdam: Caecilia Andriessen, Saar Bessem, Fania Chapiro, Nancy Van Der Elst, Else Van Epen-De Groot, Tera de Marez-Oyens, Marjo Tal, Sylvia Welman, Margriet Hoenderos, Marga Mulder.

SCANDINAVIA

Denmark: Diana Pereira, Gudrun Lund, Vivian Dahl, Else Marie Pade, Brigitte Alsted.

Finland: Anneli Arho, Helvi Leiviska, Kaija Saariaho.

Norway: Ruth Bakke, Gudrun Nordraak Feyling, Synne Skouen, Maj Sonstevold, Anne-Marie Orbeck, Ase Hedstrom, Anna Jastrzebska.

Sweden: Kerstin Jeppsson, Carin Malmöf, Laura Netzel, Elfrida Andrée, Svea Welander, Madelaine Isaksson.

Festivals

1984 (PROJECTED)

Third International Congress on Women in Music. Jeannie G. Pool and Esperanza Pulido, coordinators. Mexico City, 1984.

1982-1983

Op. 2 Women in Music: a conference sponsored by the University of Michigan School of Music. Ann Arbor, MI: May 5-8, 1983.

Nordiska Kammarmusikdagar: Women in Music festival. Stockholm, August 22-26, 1982.

Second International Congress on Women in Music, sponsored by the University of Southern California's Program for the Study of Women and Men in Society. Jeanne G. Pool, artistic director. Los Angeles, CA: University of Southern California, April 1-4, 1982.

Women in Music: a conference sponsored by the University of Michigan School of Music. Ann Arbor, MI: March 11-14, 1982.

Women of Note: 1982 Festival of Women in Music, sponsored by the Canadian Music Centre in cooperation with the Canadian Broadcasting Corporation. Carolyn G. Lomax, chairwoman. Guelph, Ontario: University of Guelph, May 6-9, 1982.

1981

Bay Area Conference on Women in Music. San Francisco, CA: San Francisco State University, January 30-31, 1981.

Conference on Contemporary String Quartets by Women Composers, sponsored by the San Francisco Conservatory of Music. San Francisco, CA: August 7-8, 1981.

First National Congress on Women in Music, sponsored by the Department of Music and Music Education, New York University. Jeannie G. Pool, national coordinator. New York, NY: New York University, March 26-29, 1981.

Santa Barbara Conference on Music by Women. Emma Lou Diemer, coordinator. Santa Barbara, CA: University of California at Santa Barbara, April 11-12, 1981.

1979-1980 AND ANNUAL EVENTS

Conference/Workshop on Twentieth Century String Quartets by Women Composers, cosponsored by the International League of Women Composers and the First National Congress on Women in Music. Jeannie G. Pool, national coordinator. New York, NY: Trinity School, March 8, 1980.

Donne in Musica: rassegna di compositrici dalle Corti ai giorni d'oggi. Particia Chiti, artistic director. Rome: March 1980, annual.

Frau und Musik. Festival of Women's Music. Bonn and Cologne: November 20-23, 1980.

Michigan Womyn's Music Festival. Popular and folk music. Mt. Pleasant, MI: August, annual.

New York Women's Jazz Festival, sponsored by the Universal Jazz Coalition, Inc. New York, NY: June 1978, annual.

Piccolo Spoleto Festival: Minority Artists' Project of the College of Charleston. David Maves, director, Minority Artists' Project. Charleston, SC: June 1979, annual.

Women's Interart Center. Festivals of Women's Music, presented by the Women's Interart Center. Katherine Hoover, festival coordinator. New York, NY: February 1978, annual.

Women's Jazz Festival. Kansas City, MO: annual.

Prizes and Awards

Ellen Taaffe Zwilich received the 1983 Pulitizer Prize in Music for her composition *Three Movements for Orchestra*. She is the first woman composer to receive the award since its inception in 1943.

1982

General

1982 NEA Fellowship recipients: Nancy Chance, Doris Hays.

Amy Larsen, Balinda Takahashi, and Elizabeth Chur were three of the five winners of the Purchase New Music Ensemble's Little People's Composition Contest, for composers ages five to twelve. (The winning compositions will be published by Rydet Music Publishers.)

Individual Composers

Archer, Violet (Canada). Award of merit from the McGill University Alma Mater Fund, 9/82.

Brush, Ruth. Award from the National Federation of Music Clubs.

Chance, Nancy Laird. One of two winners of the ASCAP-Rudolf Nissim Composer Competition for orchestral works.

Davies, Margaret (Canada). Prizewinner in the 1982 Okanagan Music Festival Composers Competition.

Diemer, Emma Lou. ASCAP Standard Award for performances and publications annually since 1962.

Dinescu, Violeta (Rumania). Mannheim II Prize of the International Competition for Composers. Prize from the National Pioneers of Rumania.

Ekizian, Michelle. One of the seventeen winners of 1982 BMI awards to student composers.

Mageau, Mary (Australia). ASCAP Standard Awards 1981 and 1982.

Miller, Elma (Canada). Orchestral work *Genesis* was winner of third prize in the CAPAC Sir Ernest MacMillan Awards Competition.

Musgrave, Thea (U.K.). Recipient of Guggenheim Fellowship in Music.

Pizer, Elizabeth. First prize in the 1982 Biennial National League of American Pen Women Composition Contest. Three awards in the 1982 Delius Composition Contest.

Preobrajenska, Vera. *Slavic Tone Poem*, second prize from the National League of Artists and Pen Women.

Ran, Shulamit. Honored by the Chicago Junior Association of Commerce and Industry.

Silverman, Faye-Ellen. *Oboe-sthenics*, one of three works chosen to represent the U.S. at the International Rostrum of Composers/UNESCO meetings in Paris, 6/82.

Thomas, Karen P. Charles Ives Scholarship from the Charles Ives Society.

Vercoe, Elizabeth. *Herstory II*, awarded prize in the Competition of the League of American Pen Women. Award in the 1982 Internationaler Wettbewerb für Komponistinnen.

1981

General

1981 NEA Fellowship recipients: Wendy Biller, Margaret Garwood, Barbara Kolb, Priscilla McLean, Ursula Mamlok, Katherine Pogue, Kathleen St. John.

Euphrosyne Keefer and Sherilyn Fritz were winners in the Okanagan Music Festival for Composers Competition, 1981 (Canada).

Amy Larsen and Laura Murray were two of the three winners of the Purchase New Music Ensemble's Little People's Composition Contest.

Sheila Silver and Arlene Zallman were two of the six winners of the 1981 League-ISCM Composers Competition.

Susan Wilbrant's *Creatures* and Ann Gebuhr's *Synthesis* were runners-up in the Fifth Annual Pittsburgh Flute Club's Composition Contest.

Individual Composers

Archer, Violet (Canada). Honorary Life Academic Member of the Academia Tiberina in Rome. Performing Rights Organization of Canada Award for Outstanding Success in Concert Music, 1981.

Bouchard, Linda. *Ma lune maligne*, first prize winner in the National Association of Composers U.S.A. Composition Contest, 1981. Grant from the Canadian Council for the Arts, 1980-1981.

Brush, Ruth. Cowinner in the Ninth Annual Songs of Oklahoma Heritage Contest.

Gideon, Miriam. Honorary degree from the Jewish Theological Seminary, New York.

Karpman, Laura. One of twenty-five recipients of the ASCAP Foundation Grants to Young Composers.

LeBaron, Anne. *Rite of the Black Sun*, prizewinner in the 1981 Internationaler Wettbewerb für Komponistinnen.

McTee, Cindy. Honorable mention in the ASUC-SESAC Student Composition Contest.

Mamlok, Ursula. American Academy of Arts and Letters Prize.
Monk, Meredith. Recording of *Dolmen Music* (ECM1-1197), Preis der Deutschen Schallpattenkritik, 1981.
Schonthal, Ruth. Certificate of merit from the Yale School of Music Alumni Association for distinguished service in the field of music.
Semegen, Daria. Grant from the Alice M. Ditson Fund of Columbia University for a recording. Meet the Composer grants to appear at the Manhattan School of Music, Eastman School of Music, and the New York Cultural Center.
Van de Vate, Nancy *Quintet* for brass, special mention in the 1981 University of Kansas Brass Quintet Composition Contest.
Weigl, Vally. Commendation of Excellence from BMI for "long and outstanding contributions to the world of concert music."
Zwilich, Ellen Taaffe. Ernst von Dohnanyi Citation.

1979-1980

General

1980 NEA Fellowship recipients: Ruth Anderson, Susan Blaustein, Nancy Chance, Emma Lou Diemer, Joan La Barbara, Anne LeBaron, Mary McCarty, Barberi Paull, Elizabeth Phillips, Daria Semegen, Judith Shatin, Ellen Zwilich.
1979 NEA Fellowship recipients: Lucia Dlugoszewski, Joanne Forman, Janice Giteck, Doris Hays, Katherine Hoover, Barbara Kolb, Deanna LaValle, Annea Lockwood, Priscilla McLean, Thea Musgrave, Maggi Payne, Katherine Quittner, Marga Richter, Daria Semegen, Diane Thome, Joan Tower.
Susan Blaustein's *Fantasy* for piano solo and Sheree Clement's *String Quartet* were two of the six winners in the 1980 League-ISCM Composers Competition.
The Johann Wagenaar Foundation awarded a prize to Ro Van Hessen and Meta Bourgonjen for their project "Honneur aux Dames," a continuing project to promote and perform the music of women composers.

Individual Composers

Archer, Violet (Canada). Honored by the Alberta Registered Music Teacher's Association for her "outstanding contribution to Canadian music."
Clayton, Laura. One of six recipients of the 1980 Charles Ives Scholarships.
Dinescu, Violeta (Rumania). Prize from the Union of Composers of Rumania.
Lee, Hope Anne (Canada). One of two prizewinners in the first PRO Canada Young Composers Competition, 1979.
Reverdy, Michele (France). Lili Boulanger Prize, 1979.
Scherchen-Hsiao, Tona (France). Koussevitzky Prize, 1979.
Semegen, Daria. Meet the Composer grants to appear at SUNY at Stony Brook, Hamilton College, and Jersey City State College.
Singer, Jeanne. Choral work *Come Greet the Spring*, first prize winner in Composers' Guild National Competition. Two awards in the 1980 Biennial Competition of the National League of American Pen Women.

Tower, Joan. *Amazon II*, semifinalist in the Kennedy-Freidheim awards for new orchestral works.

Vercoe, Elizabeth. *Herstory II*, finalist in the 1980 Politis International Competition; the same work, award in the 1981 GEDOK International Competition. *Sonaria*, for 'cello alone, award in the 1980 F. G. Espinosa International Competition.

Wallach, Joelle. First prize in the 1980 Sigma Alpha Iota Inter-American Music Competition.

Zaimont, Judith Lang. *Songs of Innocence*, award in the Los Alamos International Wind/String Chamber Music Competition.

COMMISSIONS

(See also "Performances" for commissions relating to a specific performance.)

Anderson, Jean (Canada). *Introduction and Dance*, for tenor, saxophone, and piano (1982). Commissioned by the Ontario Arts Council for 1983 New Music Alliance Competition.

Bauld, Alison (Australia). Arts Council Bursary to write a masque based on *The Tempest* (1980).

BBC commission for a radio piece in the form of a scene from *Richard III* (1982).

Beecroft, Norma (Canada). *Hedda*, for orchestra and electronic tape (1981-1982). Commissioned by the National Ballet of Canada, to be premiered 2/83.

Diemer, Emma Lou. *Clap Your Hands*, for choir and organ (1982). Commissioned by the First United Methodist Church, Shreveport, LA.

Elegy for organ duet (1982). Commissioned by Marilyn Mason.

Dlugoszewski, Lucia. *Wilderness Elegant Tilt*, for strings, winds, and piano. Commissioned by the Chamber Music Society of Lincoln Center, to be premiered in 1983.

Fowler, Jennifer (U.K.). Work for amateur choir, commissioned by the Musicum Collegium and the Australian Council, 1982.

Lauber, Anne (Canada). *Conte symphonique*, commissioned by the Toronto Symphony Orchestra and the Orchestre Symphonique de Québec, to be premiered 10/83.

McIntosh, Diana (Canada). Commissioned by the Canadian Music Educators Association for a mixed-media work.

Mageau, Mary (Australia). Commissioned by St. Margaret's College to write an orchestral work, to be completed in 1983.

Marez-Oyens, Tera de (Netherlands). *The Odyssey of Mr. Goodevil*, an oratorio for two narrators, four soloists, two choirs and orchestra. Commissioned by the Dutch Ministry of Culture, 1981.

St.-Marcoux, Micheline Coulombe (Canada). Commissioned by the Canada Music Competition, Tremplin International, for the following: *Mandala II*, for piano solo; *Composition I*, for horn solo; *Jesod I*, for soprano and piano; *Jesod II*, for tenor and piano; *Horizon I*, for flute solo; *Horizon II*, for oboe solo; *Integration I*, for 'cello solo; *Integration II*, for violin solo (1980-1981).

Currently working on commissions from Le Quatour d'Ondes de Montréal and Les Marionettes de Montréal, to be completed 1983.

Silverman, Faye-Ellen. NEA Consortium Commission for a brass quintet. Commissioned jointly by the American Brass Quintet, Mt. Vernon Brass Quintet, Southern Brass Quintet, and Catskill Brass Quintet.

Tower, Joan. Commissioned by Collage, Boston-based chamber ensemble, for a chamber work to be premiered at Harvard University, 2/83.

New work for flute and guitar commissioned by Carol Wincenc and Sharon Isben, to be premiered in St. Paul, MN, 4/83.

New work for solo piano commissioned by Gilbert Kallsh.

Young, Gayle (Canada). Commissioned by William Buxton of the University of Toronto for a new work for computer and Amaranth (stringed instrument designed and built by the composer).

Zaimont, Judith Lang. *De Caeleste Infinitate*, for string quartet (1979). Commissioned by the Primavera Quartet.

Lamentations (1982). NEA Consortium Commission. Commissioned jointly by the Gregg Smith Singers, I Cantori, Dale Warland Singers, and the Philadelphia Singers, to be premiered in 1983.

The Magic World, ritual music for three (1979). Commissioned by Duncan Brockus of the Connecticut Opera.

Serenade: to Music, for SSATTB a cappella (1981). Commissioned by the Western Wind Ensemble.

Song cycle commissioned for the First International Arts Song Festival, University of Central Arkansas, to be premiered by Paul Sperry, 5/83.

Publications

COLLECTIONS AND SERIES

Broude Brothers Ltd. Nine centuries of music by women. Includes works by Francesca Caccini, Elisabeth Jacquet de la Guerre, Isabella Leonarda, Louise Reichardt, Barbara Strozzi, and Judith Lang Zaimont.

Da Capo Press Women Composers Series. Includes works by Amy Beach, Rebecca Clarke, Cecile Chaminade, Louise Farrenc, Fanny Mendelssohn Hensel, Louise Reichardt, Clara Schumann, and Ethel Smyth.

European American Music Women Composers Series. Includes works by Amy Beach, Cécile Chaminade, Rebecca Clarke, Louise Farrenc, Agathe Grøndahl, Josephine Lang, Fanny Mendelssohn Hensel, Mary Carr Moore, Louise Reichardt, Clara Schumann, and Ethel Smyth.

Galaxy Music Corp. Anthology of contemporary piano music by women composers. Ruth Schonthal and Judith Lang Zaimont, editors. Projected 1985.

INDIVIDUAL COMPOSERS (ANNOUNCEMENTS RECEIVED)

Archer, Violet. *Divertimento*, for oboe, clarinet, and bassoon. Dorn Publications, 1982.
Divertimento, for saxophone quartet. Dorn Publications, 1982.
Little Suite, for trumpet and piano. Leeds Music, 1980.
Proud Horses, SATB a cappella. Peer Southern, 1981.
Sonata, for bassoon and piano. Dorn Publications, 1982.
Sonata, for horn and piano. Berandol Music Ltd., 1980.
Sonatina, for clarinet and piano. Dorn Publications, 1982.
Sonatina, for oboe and piano. Dorn Publications, 1982.
Suite, for solo flute. Dorn Publications, 1982.
Twelve Miniatures, for violin and piano. Waterloo Music, Ltd., 1982.
Other new works of Violet Archer are available through the Canadian Music Center.
Barkin, Elaine. . . . *in its surrendering* . . . , for solo tuba (1981). Association for the Promotion of New Music.

. . . the supple suitor . . . , for mezzo and instrumental ensemble (1979). Association for the Promotion of New Music.

Blaustein, Susan. *Canzo*, for soprano and instrumental ensemble (1979). Association for the Promotion of New Music.

Fantasie, for piano (1980). Association for the Promotion of New Music.

Boyd, Anne. *The Little Mermaid*, opera for schools and young people. Faber, 1980.

Colley, Betty. *Styles,* for piano. Kjos West, 1982.

Cory, Eleanor. *Surroundings*, for mezzo and piano (1980). Association for the Promotion of New Music.

Desportes, Yvonne. *Branle-bas de combat*, pour percussion et piano. Billaudot, 1981.

Le Coeur battant, petite pièce pour percussion et piano. Billaudot, 1981.

Encueillant les laugriers, pour percussion et piano. Billaudot, 1981.

Un petit concert pour lutins, pour percussion et piano. Billaudot, 1981.

Premier concours, pour percussion et piano. Billaudot, 1981.

Diemer, Emma Lou. *Carols*, for organ (1949). Sacred Music Press, 1980.

Concerto, for flute (1963). Southern Music Co., 1982.

Concerto, for harpsichord and chamber orchestra (1958). Seesaw Music Corp., 1981.

The Four Seasons, for high voice and piano (1969). Seesaw Music Corp., 1982.

God Is Love, for choir and tape (1982). Arsis Press, 1982.

Psalm 121 (1956). Seesaw Music Corp., 1980.

Solotrio, for xylophone, vibraphone, and marimba (1980). Music for Percussion Inc., 1982.

Songs of Reminiscence (1956). Seesaw Music Corp., 1980.

Suite, for orchestra (1954). Seesaw Music Corp., 1981.

Symphony No. 2 (1959). Seesaw Music Corp., 1981.

Three Hymn Anthems (1980). Hinshaw Music, Inc., 1980.

Toccata, for piano (1979). Arsis Press, 1980.

Dondeyne, Désiré. *Neuf grands duos concertants*, pour clarinettes. Transatlantiques, 1979.

Dring, Madeleine (1923-1977). *Five Betzeman Songs,* for high voice and piano. Weinberger, 1980.

Three Dances, for piano solo. Cambria, 1981.

Valse française, for piano. Cambria, 1980.

Fowler, Jennifer. *The Arrows of Saint Sebastian II* (1981). Universal Edition

Music for Piano—Ascending and Descending (1980). Universal Edition

Piece for E. L., for piano solo (1981). Universal Edition

Revelation, for string quintet (1981). Universal Edition

Tell Out My Soul, for soprano, 'cello, and piano (1980). Universal Edition

Veni Sancte Spiritus—Veni Creator (1979). Universal Edition

Frasier, Jane. *Festivous Sonata*, for piano. Arsis Press, 1981.

Joy, Peace, and Singing, for SSA choir and flute. Studio PR, 1982.

Gallina, Jill. *Santa and the Snowmobile*, a musical play for the elementary grades. Shawnee Press, 1980.

Gideon, Miriam. *Fantasy on a Javanese Motive*, for 'cello and piano. Highgate, 1981.

Spirit above the Dust. C. F. Peters, 1981.

Gorton, Karen. *Folk Suite*, for woodwind quintet. Shawnee Press, 1981.

Gotkovsky, Ida. *Capriccio*, pour violon et piano. Billaudot, 1981.

Images de Norvège, pour clarinette et piano. Billaudot, 1981.

Variations pathétiques, pour alto saxophone et piano. Billaudot, 1980.

Hunnicutt, Judy. *Alleluia! Sing to Jesus*, unison and two-part anthems with hand-bells or keyboard. Ausburg, 1981.

Ivey, Jean Eichelberger. *Sea-Change*. Carl Fischer, Inc.

Vocal works: *Two songs*, for high voice, flute (or clarinet) and piano; *Crossing Brooklyn Ferry*, for baritone and piano; *Absent in the Spring*, for mezzo and string trio. Boosey & Hawkes (projected).

Jennings, Carolyn. *Cat and Mouse*, settings of four poems by John Ciardi for two and three part chorus. Schirmer, 1980.

John, Patricia. *Serenata*, for harp. Pantile Press, 1981.

Jolas, Betsy. *O Wall*, opéra de poupée pour quintette à vent. Heugel, 1980.

Quatre duos, pour alto et piano. Heugel, 1979.

Kavasch, Deborah H. *The Owl and the Pussycat*, for voices and narrator. Reimers, 1980.

Kolb, Barbara. *Songs before an Adieu*. Boosey & Hawkes, 1981.

Soundings, for orchestra. Boosey & Hawkes, 1981.

LaChartre, Nicole. *Pôttchô I, II*, pour flûte seule. Leduc, 1981.

Lauber, Anne. *Divertissement*, pour flûte et guitar. Doberman, 1981.

LeBaron, Anne. *Rite of the Black Sun*. Associated Music Publishers.

Loudová, Ivana. *Dramatic Concerto*, for solo percussion and wind orchestra. C. F. Peters, 1981.

Maconchy, Elizabeth. *Fantasia*, for clarinet and piano. Chester, 1981.

Mageau, Mary. *Duet Book*. vol. III (1980). Allans Music. Publication was commissioned by the Federation of Australian Music Teachers.

The Line Always There, for SSAA, flute, percussion, and piano four hands (1981). AMUSE, Ross Baker Music. Publication was commissioned by the Australian Society for Music Education.

Mamlok, Ursula. *Festive Sounds*, a concertino for wind quintet. C. F. Peters, 1981.

Merryman, Marjorie. *The River Sang*, for voice and orchestra (1981). Association for the Promotion of New Music.

Mygatt, Louise. *Through the Edge*, for soprano, clarinet, violin, percussion. and piano (1979). Association for the Promotion of New Music.

Nelson, Sheila M. *Pairs for 'Cellos*, easy duets for 'cello groups to play. Boosey & Hawkes, 1980.

Threes and Fours, for 'cellos. Boosey & Hawkes, 1980.

O'Hearn, Arletta. *Love Jazz*, for piano solo. Kjos West, 1981.

O'Leary, Jane. *Piece II*, for piano (1980). Association for the Promotion of New Music.

Ostrander, Linda. *Sonnet to Sleep*, choral. Plymouth Music Co.

Ran, Shulamit. *For an Actor*, monologue for clarinet. Theodore Presser, 1980.

Reigel, Esther and Rachelle Saltzman Waring. *The Little Camel Boy*, for narrator, children's choir, optional SATB choir. Shawnee Press, 1981.

Richer, Jeanine. *Piège 6*, pour guitar. Transatlantiques, 1979.

Roger, Denise, *Berceuse*, pour clarinette et piano. Billaudot, 1980.

St.-Marcoux, Micheline Coulombe. *Composition I*; *Horizon II*; *Integration II*. Editions Salabert.

Moments. Editions Québec-Musique.

Sciortino, Patrice. *Magisme*, pour flûte et piano. Billaudot, 1981.

Semegen, Daria. *Music for violin solo.* Galaxy Music Corp. The publisher received a 1982 Paul Revere Award for Excellence in Typography from the Music Publishers' Association, for the production of this score.

Tailleferre, Germaine. *Trio*, pour piano, violon, et violoncello. Lemone, 1980.

Tate, Phyllis. *Compassion*, an ode for soprano and alto soli, SATB chorus, and organ or orchestra. Oxford, 1981.

Tower, Joan. *Amazon.* Associated Music Publishers.

Townsend, Jill. *The Circus Comes to Town*, music for string orchestra. Chester, 1981.

Czech Song and Dance, for string orchestra. Chester, 1981.

Dance Suite, for string orchestra. Chester, 1981.

Van de Vate, Nancy. *Sonata*, for piano. Arsis Press.

Wallach, Joelle. *On the Beach at Night Alone*, for solo chant and mixed voices. C. F. Peters, 1981.

Weigl, Vally. *Carl Sandburg Cantata.* C. F. Peters.

Dear Earth. Arsis Press.

Lyrical Suite. C. F. Peters.

Zaimont, Judith Lang. *Calendar Collection*, twelve preludes for the developing pianist. Alfred Publishing Co., 1980.

A Calendar Set, for piano (1978). Leonarda Productions, 1980.

The Chase, for SSATB and piano (1972). Galaxy Music Corp., 1982.

Judy's Rag, for piano solo (1972). Leonarda Productions, 1981.

Nocturne, for piano (1978). Galaxy Music Corp., 1982.

Soliloquy from *Greyed Sonnets* (1975). Galaxy Music Corp., 1981.

Song Cycle. Galaxy Music Corp., projected 1983.

Three Choruses from *Sacred Service for the Sabbath Evening* (1976). Galaxy Music Corp., 1981.

Two Songs, for soprano and harp (1978). Lyra Publishing Co., 1982.

Zallman, Arlene. *Shakespeare Sonnet CXXVIII*, for baritone and piano (1980). Association for the Promotion of New Music.

Three Preludes, for piano (1979). Association for the Promotion of New Music.

Zwilich, Ellen Taaffe. *Chamber Symphony* (1979). Merion Music, 1981.

Passages, for soprano and chamber ensemble. Theodore Presser Co.

Discography

COLLECTIONS

Anthology of Electronic Music by Women Composers. Emma Lou Diemer, ed. Folkways Records (projected release).

Piano Music of Scandinavian Women Composers, released by Danish Society, Kvinder i Musik (projected release).

Piano Works by Women Composers. Rosario Marciano, pianist. Includes works of Elisabeth Jacquet de la Guerre, Maria Theresa von Paradis, Maria Szymanowska, Katharina Cibbini-Koželûh, Fanny Mendelssohn Hensel, Clara Schumann, Ingeborg von Bronsart, Agathe Backer-Grøndahl, Teresa Carreño, Cécile Chaminade, Germaine Tailleferre, Amy Beach, and Grażyna Bacewicz. Turnabout TV 34685.

Woman's Work. Includes compositions of Anna Amalia (Duchess of Saxe-Weimar), Anna Amalia (Princess of Prussia), Eldrida Andre, Lili Boulanger, Ingeborg von Bronsart, Francesca Caccini, Cécile Chaminade, Louise Farrenc, Louise Heritte-Viardot, Elisabeth Jacquet de la Guerre, Josephine Lang, Maria Malibran, Fanny Mendelssohn Hensel, Maria Theresa von Paradis, Irene Wieniawska Paul, Clara Schumann, Germaine Tailleferre, and Pauline Viardot-Garcia. Gemini Hall 1010.

INDIVIDUAL COMPOSERS

Aderholt, Sarah. *String Quartet* (1978). Leonarda LPI 111.

Anderson, Beth. *I Can't Stand It*; *Ocean Motion Mildew Mind*. Beth Anderson 45 (45 rpm).

    Torero Pieces (1973). 1750 Arch Records 1752.

Anderson, Laurie. *New York Social Life* (1977); *Time to Go* (for Diego, 1977). 1750 Arch Records 1765.

    O Superman. One Ten Records OT-005.

    You're the Guy I Want to Share My Money With. Giorno Poetry Systems GPS-020/21.

Anderson, Ruth. *Dump*; *S U M*. Opus One #70.

I Come Out of Your Sleep, electronic. Opus One #63.

Points (1973-1974). 1750 Arch Records 1765.

Anna Amalia (Duchess of Saxe-Weimar, 1739-1807). *Concerto for 12 Instruments and Cembalo Obbligato*; *Divertimento for Piano and Strings*. Turnabout 34754.

Archer, Violet. *Episodes*. Melbourne SMLP 4024.

Improvisations, for piano. Melbourne SMLP 4031.

Landscapes. CBC Canadian Collection SM 274.

Psalm 145, for mixed chorus a cappella. World Records WRC1-1601.

Sinfonietta. CBC Canadian Collection SM 226.

Sonata, for alto saxophone and piano; *Sonata*, for clarinet and piano; *Sonata*, for horn and piano. CBC RCI 412.

Three French Canadian Folksongs. Turnabout Canadian Collection CTC-32003.

Three Sketches, for orchestra. CBC Canadian Collection SM 119.

Trio no. 2. CBC RCI 241.

Seven-record set of her music. Canadian Broadcasting Corp. (projected release, 1983).

Bacewicz, Grażyna (1913-1969). *Piano Sonata no. 2*. Avant Records 1012.

Backer-Grøndahl, Agathe (1847-1907). Piano music. Genesis 1024.

Ballou, Esther Williamson (1915-1973). *Prelude and Allegro* (1955). CRI SD 115.

Sonata, for 2 pianos. CRI SD 472.

Barkin, Elaine. *String Quartet* (1969). CRI SD 338.

Two Emily Dickinson Choruses. CRI SD 482.

Bauer, Marion (1897-1955). *From the New Hampshire Woods*, op. 12, for piano; *Turbulence*, op. 17, no. 2 (1942). Northeastern 204.

Suite, for strings (1955); *Prelude and Fugue* (1948). CRI SRD 101.

Beach, Amy Marcy Cheney (1867-1944). *Cabildo*, chamber opera. Leonarda LPI 119 (projected release).

Concerto, for piano and orchestra, op. 45. Turnabout 34665.

Piano Music. Genesis 1054; Northeastern 204.

Piano Trio, op. 150 (In *Chamber works by Women Composers*). Vox SVBX-5112.

Quartet for Strings, op. 89 (1929). Leonarda LPI 111.

Quintet in F-sharp Minor, for piano and strings, op. 67. Turnabout 34556.

Sonata in A Minor, for violin and piano, op. 20. New World NW 268.

Theme and Variations, for flute and string quartet, op. 80. Leonarda LPI 105.

Three Browning Songs, op. 44. CRI SD 462.

Woodwind Quintet: Pastorale Musical Heritage Society 3578.

Benary, Barbara. *In Scrolls of Leaves*. Folkways 31312.

Bernard, Marie. *Petite suite québeçoise*, for soloists, choir, and orchestra. Alliance des Chorales du Québec. ACQ 1001/PDC 8001.

Beyer, Johanna (1888-1944). *Music of the Spheres* (1938). 1750 Arch Records 1765.

Bond, Victoria. *Peter Quince at the Clavier*; *Monologue*, for 'cello. Protone 150.

Bonds, Margaret. *Troubled Waters* (1967). Opus One #39.

Boulanger, Lili (1893-1918). *Clairières dans le ciel*, for soprano and piano. Spectrum 126; Leonarda LPI 118 (projected release).

Cortège, for piano; *D'un vieux jardin*. Avant Records 1012.

Faust et Hélène, cantata (1913); *Pour les funérailles d'un soldat* (1912). Varèse Sarabande 81095.

Nocturne (1918); *Cortège* (1919). Vox SVBX 5112.

Nocturne; *D'un matin de printemps*, for flute and piano. Leonarda LPI 104.

Brockman, Jane. *Tell-Tale Fantasy*, for piano (In *Music by Women Composers*, Rosemary Platt, pianist). Coronet 3105.

Brown, Gladys. *Black Tea*. Opus One #53.

Callaway, Ann. *Theme and Seven Variations*, for piano (In *Music by Women Composers*, Rosemary Platt, pianist). Coronet 3105.

Chaminade, Cécile (1857-1944). *Concertino*, for flute, op. 107. RCA ARL1-3777; Coronet S-1724.

Concertstück, for piano and orchestra, op. 40. Orion 78296; Turnabout 34754.

Piano music. Genesis 1024.

Piano Trio no. 1 in G Minor, op. 11. Vox SVBX-5112.

Sonata in C Minor, for piano, op. 21. Pelican 2017.

Chance, Nancy Laird. *Daysongs*, for flute and percussion (1974). Opus One #72.

Duos III, for violin and 'cello (1980). Opus One #85.

Ritual Sounds, for brass and percussion (1975). Opus One #69.

Clarke, Rebecca (1886-1979). Selected songs for tenor and piano. Leonarda LPI 120 (projected release).

Trio for violin, 'cello, and piano (1921). Leonarda LPI 103.

Cory, Eleanor. *Designs*, for piano trio. CRI SD 459.

Octagons (1976). Opus One #69.

Coulthard, Jean. *Aegean Sketches*. Melbourne SMLP 4031.

Cradle Song. Westminster WGS 8124.

Ecstasy (from *Spring Rhapsody*). Master Recordings MA-377.

Five Medieval Love Songs. CBC SM 180.

Five Part Songs. RCA CC/CCS 1020; RCI 226.

Four Etudes (nos. 1 & 4). Baroque BC 2837.

Lyric Sonatina. Melbourne SMLP 4032.

Sonata, for 'cello and piano. Columbia ML-5942; CBC SM 305.

Sonata, for piano. CBC RCI 289.

Song to the Sea. CBC Canadian Collection SM 215.

String Quartet no. 2. CBC Canadian Collection RCI 386.

Variations on B.A.C.H. CBC RCI 289.

Crawford-Seeger, Ruth (1901-1953). *Diaphonic Suite No. 1*, for solo oboe (1930). CRI SD 423.

Diaphonic Suite no. 2, for bassoon and 'cello (1931). Gasparo 108 CX.

Preludes, for piano, nos. 6-9 (1927-1928); *Piano Study in Mixed Accents*. Northeastern 204.

Preludes, for piano (complete); *Piano Study in Mixed Accents*. CRI SD 247.

String Quartet (1931). Gasparo GS 205; Nonesuch H-71280.

Suite, for wind quintet (1952). CRI SD 249.

Three Songs (1933). New World NW 285.

Two Movements, for chamber orchestra (1926). Delos 25405.

Daniels, Mabel (1878-1971). *Deep Forest* (1931) (In *Orchestral Music by Women Composers*). CRI SRD 145.

Three Observations (1943). Desto 7117.

Davis, Sharon. *Though Men Call Us Free*, for soprano, clarinet, and piano. WIM 13.

Dia, Beatrice de, Contessa (ca. 1160-1212/1214). *A chantar m'er de so qu'ieo non volria*. Telefunken 95673.

Diemer, Emma Lou. *The Compositions of Emma Lou Diemer: Laughing Song; Psalm 134; O Come, Let Us Sing unto the Lord; Fragments from the Mass; Hast Thou not Known; Three Poems by Alice Meynell; Madrigals Three; Wild Nights! Wild Nights!* Golden Crest ATH-5063.

    Declarations (1973); *Toccata and Fugue*, for organ (1979). Capriccio Records (projected release).

    Sonata, for flute and piano (1958). Golden Crest RE-7074.

    Toccata, for flute chorus (1968). Golden Crest S-4088.

    Toccata, for piano (1979) (In *Music by Women Composers*, Rosemary Platt, pianist). Coronet 3105.

    Youth Overture (1959). Inter-American Musical Editions OAS-007.

Dlugoszewski, Lucia. *Angels of the Utmost Heavens*. Folkways 33902.

    Fire Fragile Flight. Candide CE 31113.

    Space Is a Diamond. Nonesuch H-71275.

    Tender Theatre Flight Nageire. CRI SD 388.

Dvorkin, Judith. *Maurice* (1955). CRI SD 102.

Escot, Pozzi. *Fergus Are*, for organ. Delos 25448.

Farrenc, Louise (1804-1875). *Nonetto*, op. 38. Leonarda LPI 110.

    Trio in E Minor, op. 45, for flute, 'cello, and piano. Leonarda LPI 104.

Fine, Vivian. *Alcestis*, ballet music (1960) (In *Orchestral Music by Women Composers*). CRI SRD 145.

    Concertante, for piano and orchestra (1944). CRI SD 135.

    Paean. CRI SD 260.

    Quartet, for brass (1978); *Momenti*, for piano (1978); *Missa brevis*, for mezzo and four 'celli (1972). CRI SD 434.

    Sinfonia and Fugata, for piano. CRI SD 288.

Fontyn, Jacqueline. *Spirales*, for two pianos. ALPHA DBM-F-259.

Forman, Joanne. *In Time for Daffodils; Maggie, Milly and Molly and May; I Thank You God for Most This Amazing; La luna asoma; Noche*. Opus One #34.

    Three García Lorca Songs (1973). Opus One #44.

Gainsborg, Lolita Cabrera. *Lullaby*, for piano. Pelican 2017.

Gardner, Kay. *Emerging*. Urana WWE 83.

    Mooncircles. Urana WWE 80.

Gideon, Miriam. *The Adorable Mouse*. Serenus SRS 12050.

    Lyric Piece, for strings (1941). CRI 170.

    Nocturnes; Songs of Youth and Madness. CRI SD 401.

    Piano Suite no. 3. CRI SD 288.

    Questions on Nature; The Condemned playground, CRI SD 343.

    Rhymes from the Hill (1968); *Hound of Heaven* (1945). CRI SD 286.

    The Seasons of Time, songs on Tanka poems of ancient Japan. Serenus SRS 12078.

    Symphonia Brevis (1953). CRI 128.

Gilbert, Pia. *Transmutations*, for organ and percussion; *Interrupted Suite*. Protone 150.

Glanville-Hicks, Peggy. *Nausicaa*, selections (1961). CRI SD 175.

    Prelude for a Pensive Pupil, for piano. CRI SD 288.

    Three Gymnopedies. Varèse 81046.

Greenwald, Jan. *Duration 2*, electronic. CRI SD 443.

Grimani, Maria (18th century). *Sinfonie* (1713) (In *Women's Orchestral Works Performed by the New England Women's Symphony*). Galaxia.

Gyring, Elizabeth (1886-1970). *Piano Sonata no. 2*. CRI SD 252.

Hays, Doris. *Sunday Nights*, for piano (1977). Finnadar 720.

Hildegarde, Saint (Hildegarde von Bingen, 1098-1179). *Kyrie*, for women's choir. Leonarda LPI 115.

Hoover, Katherine. *Divertimento*, for flute and string trio (1975). Leonarda LPI 105.
   Princess Isabelle, for flute and piano. Leonarda LPI 104.
   Trio, for violin, 'cello, and piano (1978). Leonarda LPI 103.

Howe, Mary (1882-1964). *Castellana*, for two pianos and orchestra (1935). CRI 124.
   Spring Pastoral (1936) (In *Orchestral Music by Women Composers*). CRI SRD 145.
   Stars; *Sand*. CRI SRD 103; CRI 124.

Hoy, B. Hendricks. *Piano sonata no. 2*; *Eight Preludes*. Encore 1001.

Ivey, Jean Eichelberger. *Hera, Hung from the Sky*. CRI SD 325.
   Pinball, electronic. Folkways 33436.
   Terminus, for mezzo and tape; *Aldebaran*, for viola and tape; *Three Songs of Night*; *Cortège*. Folkways 33439.

Jolas, Betsy. *Quatour III*; nine etudes (1973). CRI SD 332.

Kessler, Minuetta. *Ballet Sonatina*; *Sonata Concertante* for violin and piano; *Clarinet Sonata*; *Fantasy*, for oboe. Afka SK-288.

Kolb, Barbara. *Crosswinds* (1974) (In *Women's Orchestral Works Performed by the New England Women's Symphony*). Galaxia.
   Figments, for flute; *Chansons bas*; *Three Place Settings*. Desto 7143.
   Looking for Claudio; *Spring River Flowers Moon Night*. CRI SD 361.
   Rebuttal, for two clarinets. Opus One #14.
   Solitaire; *Trobar Clus*. Turnabout 34487.
   Three Lullabies, for guitar (1980). Bridge 2001.

Kosse, Roberta. *Return of the Great Mother*, oratorio. Ars Pro Femina 77.

La Barbara, Joan. *Cathing* (1977); *Thunder* (1976). Chiaroscuro 196.
   Reluctant Gypsy. Wizard 2279.
   Tapesongs. Chiaroscuro CR 196.
   Voice Is the Original Instrument. Wizard 2266.

La Guerre, Elisabeth-Claude Jacquet de (1664-1729). *Samson*, cantata; *Le Sommeil d'Ulisse*, cantata. Leonarda LPI 109.
   Suite in D Minor, for keyboard. Avant Records 1012.

Lang, Josephine (1815-1880). Songs. Leonarda LPI 107.

Layman, Pamela. *Gravitation I*, for solo violin (1974). Grenadilla 1032.

LeFanu, Nicola. *The Same Day Dawns* (1964); *But Stars Remaining* (1970); *Deva* (1979). Chandos ABR 1017.

Leginska, Ethel (1886-1970). *Three Victorian Portraits*, for piano (1959). Orion 75188.

Leonarda, Isabella (1620-1704). *Messa prima*, op. 18. Leonarda LPI 115.

Lockwood, Annea. *Glass World*. Tangent TGS-104.
   Tiger Balm; electronic. Opus One #70.
   World Rhythms (1975). 1750 Arch Records 1765.

Lutyens, Elisabeth. *And Suddenly It's Evening*, for tenor and eleven instruments (1966). Decca/Argo ZRG 638.

Five Bagatelles (1962); *Five Intermezzi* (1943); *Piano e forte* (1958); *Plenum 1*, for piano (1972). Pavilion/Pearl SHE 537.

Plenum IV, for voice and organ duet (1974). Gamut/Vista VPS 1039.

Stevie Smith Songs (1948). Transatlantic/Unicorn UNS 268.

This Green Tide, for clarinet and piano; *This Green Tide*, for basset-horn and piano; *Valediction*, for clarinet and piano. Chantry CH T005.

MacGregor, Laurie. *Intrusion of the Hunter*, for percussion (1973-1974). CRI SD 444.

McLean, Priscilla. *Dance of the Dawn* (1974). CRI SD 335.

Interplanes, for two pianos. Advance FGR-19S.

Invisible Chariots. Folkways 6050; Folkways 33540.

Variations and Mozaics on a Theme of Stravinsky (1975). Louisville LS-762.

McMillan, Ann. *Gateway Summer Sound*. Folkways 33451.

Whale I. Folkways 33904.

Maconchy, Elizabeth. *Proud Thames*, overture (1954). Lyrita SRCS 57.

Serenata Concertante, for violin and orchestra (1962); *Symphony*, for double string orchestra (1953). Lyrita SRCS 116.

Mageau, Mary. *Contrasts*, for solo 'cello. Grevillea Records GRV 1070.

Sonate Concertante. Grevillea Records GRV 1080.

Variations on Scarborough. Grevillea Records 1081.

Mahler, Alma (1879-1964). Songs, for mezzo and piano. Leonarda LPI 118 (projected release).

Mamlok, Ursula. *A Cycle of German Songs*, for soprano and piano. Leonarda LPI 120 (projected release).

Haiku Settings, for soprano and harp. Grenadilla 1015.

Stray Birds (1963). CRI SD 301.

Variations, for solo flute. CRI SD 212; Opus One #72.

Manziarly, Marcelle de. *Dialogue*, pour violoncello et piano. Laurel-Protone Records L.P. 13.

Trilogue II, for violin, 'cello, and piano. Laurel Records LR 109.

Marez-Oyens, Tera de. *Safed*, electronic (1968). Composers' Voice CV 7903.

Martinez, Marianne (1744-1812). *Sonata* in A Major for piano. Pelican 2017.

Maurice, Paule (1910-1967). *Tableaux de Provence*, for saxophone and piano. Crystal S-105.

Mekeel, Joyce. *Planh*, for solo violin (1975); *Corridors of Dream*. Delos 25405.

Vigil, for orchestra (1977). Louisville 768.

Mendelssohn Hensel, Fanny (1805-1847). *Piano Trio* in D Minor, op. 11. Crystal 642; Vox SVBX-5112.

Sechs Lieder, op. 1, for tenor and piano. Leonarda LPI 112.

Songs. Leonarda LPI 107.

Monk, Meredith. *Dolmen Music*. ECM 1-1197.

Key, invisible theatre. Lovely Music Ltd. LML-1051.

Songs from the Hill and Tablet. Wergo SM-1022.

Musgrave, Thea. *Chamber Concerto* no. 2 (1966). Delos 25405.

A Christmas Carol, opera in two acts. Moss Music Group MMG 302.

Concerto, for clarinet and orchestra (1967). Argo ZRG 726.

Concerto, for horn and orchestra (1971); *Concerto,* for orchestra (1967). Decca Head 8.

Mary, Queen of Scots. Moss Music Group MMG 301.

Rorate Coeli (1973). Abbey LPB 708.

Newlin, Dika. *Piano Trio*, op. 2 (1948). CRI 170.

Nordenstrom, Gladys. *Zeit XXIV (Pandula)*, for soprano. Orion 79348.

Norman, Ruth. *Molto allegro* (1970); *Prelude IV* (1974). Opus One #35.

Nunlist, Juli. *Two Pieces*, for piano (1961). CRI SD 183.

Oliveros, Pauline. *Bye Bye Butterfly* (1965). 1750 Arch Records 1765.

Outline, for flute, percussion, and string bass (1963). Nonesuch H-71237.

Sound Patterns (1964). Odyssey 32160156.

Trio, for flute, piano, and page turner. Advance FGR-9S.

Pakhmutova, Alexandra. *Concerto* in E-flat, for trumpet and orchestra (1955). Monitor 2030.

Pentland, Barbara. *Duo*, for viola and piano. RCA CC/CCS-1017; CBC RCI 223.

Interplay. Melbourne SMLP 4034.

String Quartet no. 1. Columbia ML-5764; CBC RCI 141.

String Quartet no. 3. CBC Canadian Collection RCI 353.

Suite Borealis. Melbourne SMLP 4031.

Symphony for Ten Parts. RCA CC/CCS 1009; CBC RCI 215.

Toccata. CBC Canadian Collection SM 162.

Perry, Julia (1924-1979). *Homunculus C. F.*, for ten percussionists. CRI SD 252.

Short Piece, for orchestra (1952) (In *Orchestral Music by Women Composers*). CRI SRD 145.

Stabat mater (1951). CRI SD 133.

Pierce, Alexandra. *Job 22:28*. Zanja ZR-2.

Polin, Claire. *Cader Idris*, for brass quintet. Opus One #61.

Margo'a, for solo flute; *Synaulia II*. Orion 79330.

O Aderyn Pur, for flute, saxophone, and tape. Opus One #12.

Rainier, Priaulx. *String Quartet*. Leonarda LPI 117 (projected release).

Ran, Shulamit. *Private Game*, for clarinet and 'cello. CRI SD 441.

Reichardt, Louise (1779-1826). Songs, for tenor and piano. Leonarda LPI 112.

Richter, Marga. *Sonata*, for piano (1954). Grenadilla 1010.

Robert, Lucie. *Sonata*, for alto saxophone and piano. Coronet 3044.

Tourbillons (1976); *Strophes*, for saxophone and piano (1978). Golden Crest 7098.

Roberts, Megan. *I Could Sit Here All Day* (1976). 1750 Arch Records 1765.

St.-Marcoux, Micheline Coulombe. *Assemblages*. RCI 396.

Doreanes. Dominion S 6900I, vol. 1.

Genesis. SNE-501.

Ishuma. RCI 422.

Mandala I; Moments; Regards. RCI 525.

Quatuor à cordes. RCI 363.

Sequences. RCI 492.

Trakadie. RCI/CAPAC RM 222, vol. 8.

Anthology of Canadian music series will include recordings of the composer's works (projected release).

Scaletti, Carla. *Motet*, for narrator, mezzo, bass clarinet, and harp (1977). Opus One #42.

Schonthal, Ruth. Piano music: *Variations in Search of a Theme*; *Sonata breve*; *Reverberations*; *Sonatensatz*. Orion 81413.

String Quartet (1962). Leonarda LPI 111.

Totengesange, song cycle (1963). Leonarda LPI 106.

Schumann, Clara (1819-1896). *Prelude and Fugue*, op. 16; *Pièce Fugitive*, op. 15, no. 1; *Impromptu*; *Scherzo* in C Minor, op. 14. Pelican 2017.

Songs. Leonarda LPI 107.

Three Romances, for violin and piano, op. 22. Nonesuch 79007.

Trio in G Minor, for violin, 'cello, and piano, op. 17. Phillips 6700051; Vox SVBX-5112.

Variations on a Theme of Robert Schumann; *Two Romances*, op. 21; *Mazurka* in G Major, op. 6. Orion 75182.

Semegen, Daria. *Arc*, music for dancers. Finnadar 9020.

Electronic Composition no. 1 (1971-1972). Odyssey Y-34139.

Electronic Composition no. 2: Spectra (1979). CRI SD 443.

Jeux des quatres, for 'cello, piano, clarinet, and trombone (1970); *Music for Violin Solo* (1973). Opus One #59.

Shields, Alice. *Farewell to a Hill*. Finnadar 9010.

The Transformation of Ani (1970). CRI SD 268.

Wildcat Songs (1966). Opus One #13.

Silverman, Faye-Ellen. *Oboe-sthenics*. Finnadar-Atlantic 90008.

Simons, Netty. *The Pied Piper of Hamlin* (1955); *Puddintame*; *Set of Poems for Children*. CRI SD 309.

Silver Thaw; *Design Groups no. 1*; *Design Groups no. 2*. Desto 7128.

Smiley, Pril. *Eclipse*, electronic. Finnadar 9010.

Kolyosa, electronic (1970). CRI SD 268.

Smith, Julia. Highlights from *Daisy*, opera in two acts. Orion ORS 76248.

Quartet, for strings (1966). Desto 7117.

Spektor, Mira J. *The Housewives' Cantata*. Original Cast Records.

Spiegel, Laurie. *Appalachian Grove* (1974). 1750 Arch Records 1765.

Patchwork; *Old Wave*; *Pentachrome*; *The Expanding Universe*. Philo Records PH 9003.

Szymanowska, Maria (1789-1831). Piano music: *Etude* in F Major; *Etude* in C Major; *Etude* in E Major; *Nocturne* in B-flat Major. Avant Records 1012.

Tailleferre, Germaine. *Ballade*, for piano and orchestra (1922). Turnabout 34754.

Concertino, for harp and orchestra (1927). DG 2543806 (In *Women's Orchestral Works Performed by the New England Women's Symphony*). Galaxia.

Pastorale, for flute and piano. Stolat 0119; Leonarda LPI 104.

Six Chansons Françaises (1930). Cambridge 2777.

Talma, Louise. *Alleluia in Form of a Toccata*. Avant Records 1012.

Corona (Holy Sonnets of John Donne). CRI SD 187.

Six Etudes, for piano (1953-1954). Desto 7117.

Sonata no. 2, for piano (1955). CRI SD 281.

Three Duologues, for clarinet and piano. CRI SD 374.

Toccata, for orchestra (1944) (In *Orchestral Music by Women Composers*). CRI SRD 145.

Tashjian, B. Charmian. *Resan*, for solo contrabass, viola, English horn, amplified harpsichord, and seven percussionists (1978). Capriccio Records (projected release).

Tate, Phyllis. *Sonata*, for clarinet and 'cello (1947). Chantry CH T004.

Themmen, Ivana. *Ode to Akhmatova* (1977). Opus One #54.
Shelter This Candle from the Wind. Louisville LS-767.

Thome, Diane. *Anais*, for piano, 'cello, and tape (1976). CRI SD 437.

Tower, Joan. *Hexachords*, for flute (1972); *Breakfast Rhythms I and II* (1974-1975). CRI SD 354.
Movements, for flute and piano. Advance FGR-24S.
Prelude, for five players (1970). CRI SD 302.

Toyama, (Françoise) Michiko. *Waka* (1958); *Japanese Suite*; *Voice of Yomatu* (1937); *Aoi No Ue*; *Two Old Folk Songs*. Folkways 8881.

Ulehla, Ludmila. *Elegy for a Whale*. Leonarda LPI 104.

Van Appledorn, Mary Jeanne. *Communique*, song cycle; *Set of Five*, for piano. Opus One #52a.
Matrices, for saxophone and piano. Golden Crest 7101.
Set of Five, for piano. Northeastern 204.
Sonnet, for organ. Opus One #43.

Van de Vate, Nancy. *Concertpiece*, for violoncello and small orchestra (1978) (In *Women's Orchestral Works Performed by the New England Women's Symphony*). Galaxia.
Music for Viola, Percussion and Piano (1976). Orion ORS 80386.
Sonata, for piano (1978) (In *Music by Women Composers*, Rosemary Platt, pianist). Coronet 3105.
String Quartet no. 1; *Sonata*, for viola and piano. Orion Master Recordings (projected release).

Vellère, Lucie (1896-1966). *String Quartet no. 3* (1951). Leonarda LPI 111.

Vercoe, Elizabeth. *Fantasy*, for piano (1975) (In *Music by Women Composers*, Rosemary Platt, pianist). Coronet 3105.

Viardot-Garcia, Pauline (1821-1910). Songs. Leonarda LPI 107.

Warren, Elinor Remick. *Abram in Egypt* (1961); *Suite*, for orchestra (1954). CRI 172.

Weigl, Vally. *Dear Earth*; *Brief Encounters*, for wind quartet; *Songs of Love and Leaving*. Orion ORS 80393.
Four cycles of vocal and instrumental chamber music. Musical Heritage Society MHS 3880.
Nature Moods (1956); *New England Suite*. CRI SD 326.
Songs of Remembrance; *Songs Newly Seen in the Dusk*; *Requiem for Allison*, for mezzo and string quartet. Orion 81410.

Witkin, Beatrice. *Beatrice Witkin, Vol. 1: Prose poem*; *Contours*, for piano. *Chiaroscuro*; *Duo*, for violin and piano. Opus One #10.
Beatrice Witkin, Vol. 2: Breath and Sounds, Parameters, for eight instruments; *Triads and Things*; *Interludes*, for flute. Opus One #12.

Wylie, Ruth Shaw. *Psychogram*, for piano (1968). CRI SD 353.

Young, Jane Corner. *Dramatic Soliloquy*, for piano. CRI SD 183.

Zaimont, Judith Lang. *A Calendar Set*, for piano (1972-1978); *Chansons nobles et sentimentales*, for tenor and piano (1974); *Nocturne*, for piano (1978). Leonarda LPI 101.

The Magic World, for baritone, percussion, and prepared piano. Leonarda LPI 116 (projected release).

Sunny Airs and Sober; Three Ayres; Greyed Sonnets; Songs of Innocence. Golden Crest 5051.

Two Songs, for soprano and harp (1978). Leonarda LPI 106.

Ziffrin, Marilyn. *Four pieces*, for tuba. Crystal S-391.

Trio, for xylophone, soprano, and tuba (1973). Capra 1210.

Zwilich, Ellen Taaffe. *Chamber Symphony* (1979); *String Quartet* (1974); *Sonata in Three Movements*, for violin and piano. Cambridge 2834.

Einsame nacht, song cycle for baritone and piano. Leonarda LPI 120 (projected release).

Passages, for soprano and chamber ensemble. Cambridge (projected release).

COLLECTIONS—JAZZ

Jazz Women: A Feminist Retrospective, vols. 1 & 2. Stash Records ST 109.

The Ragtime Women. Includes rags by May Aufderheide, Charlotte Blake, K. Craig, Louise V. Gustin, Julia Lee Niebergall, Muriel Pollock, Adeline Shepherd, M. Tilton, and G. Yelvington. Vanguard VSD 79402.

Vaudeville, songs of the great ladies of the musical stage. Nonesuch H-71330.

Women in Jazz, 3 vols. Vol. 1, all-women groups; vol. 2, pianists; vol. 3, swing-time to modern. Stash ST 111-113.

INDIVIDUAL COMPOSERS—JAZZ

Akiyoshi, Toshiko. *Kogun*, from *Road Time.* RCA CPL2-2242.

Long Yellow Road. RCA AFLI-1350.

Minamata, from *Insights.* RCA AFLI-2678.

Notorious Tourist from the East. Inner City IC 1066.

Toshiko Akiyoshi—Lew Tabackin Big Band. RCA AFLI 3019.

Alive! *Alive!* Wise Women Enterprises WWE 84.

Call it Jazz. Redwood Records RR 8484.

Bley, Carla. *Dinner Music.* WATT-6.

Escalator over the Hill. Jazz Composers Orchestra Assoc. EOTH.

European Tour 1977: The Carla Bley Band. WATT-8.

Musique Méchanique. WATT-9.

Social Studies. WATT ECM-11.

¾, for solo piano and chamber orchestra. WATT-3.

Tropic Appetites. WATT-1.

Bloom, Jane Ira. *Second Wind.* Outline 138.

We Are. Outline 137.

Brackeen, JoAnne. *Prism.* Choice CRS 1024.

Snooze. Choice CRS 1009.

Bradfield, Polly. *Solo Violin Improvisations.* Parachute 008.

Brown, Marion. *Poems for Piano*, performed by Amina Claudine Myers. Sweet Earth SER-1005.

Solo Saxophone. Sweet Earth SER-1001.

Crothers, Connie. *Solo* . . . . Jazz Records 4.

Gorill, Liz. *I Feel Like I'm Home.* Jazz Records 2.

McIlwaine, Ellen. *Everybody Needs It.* Blind Pig Records BP-1081.

McPartland, Marian. *Ambience or Ambiance: An Encompassing Atmosphere.*
    Halcyon Records HAL 102.

A Delicate Balance. Halcyon 105.

Interplay. Halcyon 100.

Now's the Time. Halcyon 115.

Portrait. Concord Jazz CJ 101.

Solo Concert at Haverford. Halcyon 111.

Moses, Kathryn. *Music in My Heart.* P.H. Records PHR-017.

Myers, Amina Claudine. *Song for Mother E.* Leo Records LR 100.

Tintomara (Swedish ensemble). *Tintomara.* Abra Cadabra 2013.

Lek. Amigo 838.

Williams, Mary Lou. *The Asch Recordings.* Folkways 2966.

From the Heart. Chiaroscuro 103.

The History of Jazz. Folkways 2860.

Live at the Cookery. Chiaroscuro 146.

Mary Lou's Mass. Mary Records 102.

Zodiac Suite. Folkways 32844.

Zoning. Mary Records 103.

Part II
ESSAYS

1

Donne in Musica

PATRICIA ADKINS CHITI

In 1979 while performing with Rome's Teatro dell' Opera, I was interviewed by *Paese Sera* and asked about my research into Italy's musical patrimony. The interviewer was most surprised when I spoke about the great number of Italian women composers that I was unearthing during my work. She was amazed to learn that not only had Italy produced *compositrici* (female composers) but that there were *compositrici* anywhere. She then informed the provincial committee of the Unione Donne Italiane (UDI), the Union of Italian Women, our oldest and most militant women's organization, about my research, and they in turn invited me to collaborate with them.

During the course of our first meeting—once the committee realized how many women were, and had been, composing music—they felt that they had to do something to make everybody else in Italy aware of this fact. We decided together that the best form of publicity for the composers would be to run an annual festival in which music from the past and present could be presented. The festival—to be called "Donne in Musica," that is, "Women in Music"—was to be held as soon as possible after the eighth of March, "Women's Day."

As artistic director I have been given a free hand by UDI from the start. In theory I can recommend for performance whatever I like, but in practice I am limited by a financial budget that varies from festival to festival. Finance, or rather the granting of financial subsidies, is a very complicated business in Italy. UDI has a subsidy from the Rome City Council and from the Provincial Council of Lazio (the region of which Rome is the capital city) and also applies for assistance to other government departments as well as to the Ministry of Tourism and Culture. Approval of our application depends in turn on the annual allowance for musical activities granted by the Ministry of Finance. If the passing of the Annual Finance Bill is delayed, so are the grants to the various ministries; consequently, our applications may be authorized as late as one month before the festival begins or, as has already happened, up to six months after the festival has taken place. Therefore, although theoretically I can program opera performances and· concerts of contemporary music with full orchestra, in practice I must limit my programming to a sum that UDI feels it can reasonably expect the Rome city fathers to provide. Payment from all official bodies is only made after a festival is over and all accounts have been settled. To date payments from official sources have arrived up to ten months after the final concert in a festival.

UDI, a highly political organization, has left me completely free as far as contacts and relations with foreign bodies, embassies, and composers are concerned. Never, at any time, has there been a question of discrimination toward a composer of any nationality for political reasons, nor has there been any discrimination as far as musical genres are concerned. I believe this to be extremely important: many European festivals, especially those concerned with contemporary music, do in fact apply a sort of censorship with regard to stylistic schools, streams, and even nationalities.

During the first festival in 1980 we presented music from eighteen countries and from five centuries, and in 1982 the fourth festival presented works by sixty-five composers from twenty-eight nations. (As of 1982, four festivals have taken place, three in Rome and one in Venice.) The oldest known composer represented in 1982 was the Venerable Cassia, a Byzantine nun, who composed during the reign of the Emperor Theophilus (A.D. 829-842), while the youngest was Annie Fontana of Milan, born in 1955.

We have programmed music for solo instruments, chamber ensembles, string orchestra, and symphony orchestras; for singers, choirs, and opera groups. Many works have been given their first performance in modern times, and many more have been given a *prima assoluta*.

Music arrives from many different sources throughout every month of every year, and I usually try to dedicate a full fortnight each August (when I am finally on holiday and not on tour or under contract in a theatre) to reading scores, listening to tapes and records, and to spending hours at the piano playing through works that interest me. So far I have tried to balance the musical content of the festival between works from the past (pre-1900), already-performed works written in this century, and works that are to be given a first performance. It is obviously useful to be able to read a score while listening to a tape, but many works, even if they have been performed, have not been recorded, and I firmly believe that the artistic direction of a festival involves being able to choose music after reading it in score and not just from listening to a recording. Furthermore, to rely on music that has previously been performed or recorded would mean that I would have to disregard about 60 percent of all the material that arrives from different parts of the world. Surely, the whole point of running a festival for women composers is so that their music can be heard, and therefore we must always be prepared to consider fully each work eligible for a first performance.

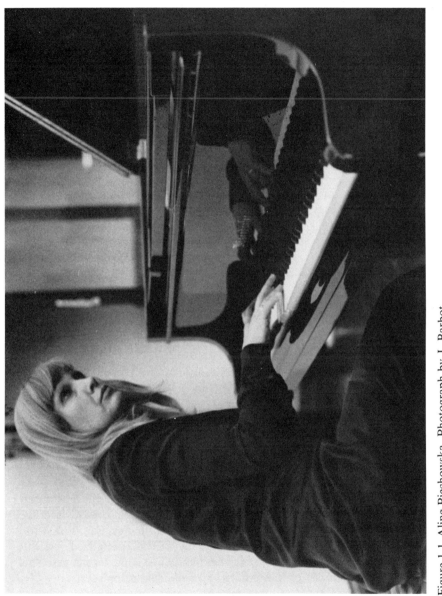

Figure 1.1 Aline Piechowska. Photograph by J. Barbot

Figure 1.2 Leopoldine Blahetka

Many of the recordings that I receive do not do justice to the works performed. Very often scores are accompanied by tapes that only underline
how scantily the work had been prepared for performance. Sad to say, too
many societies and musical organizations try to run specialized festivals
without paying sufficient attention to the quality of the performances. This
is where the question of programming and financing resurfaces.

I am well aware that our festival could sometimes pay for a larger
ensemble with the money that is instead used to pay for a string quartet, but
we never begrudge paying good fees to top quality musicians because these
are the people on whose performance the music will be judged. The avail-

ability of a particular performer or ensemble may well determine, to some extent, the individual works to be programmed. We believe that a good musician asking for a high fee is more likely to dedicate time to study and prepare a performance of a new work than a less expensive musician will, who has to take on three or four jobs in the same period. High quality performances are essential if we want our public and the critics to fully understand the music they hear. Not by chance have all our programs been recorded and televised by one or other of the RAI-TV (Radio Italiana) networks. The programs have been broadcast and rebroadcast, and this is most important for a composer. In 1982, when RAI-TV was plagued with union problems, we arranged for professional recordings to be made of every concert, and these will in due course be broadcast by local radio networks.

In 1981 we were able to program most of Francesca Caccini's opera *Ruggiero sull'isola d'Alcina* because the opera group that had previously mounted this work (Il Centro Italiano di Musica Antica, conducted by Sergio Siminovich) was free during the period in which our festival took place. The 1982 festival included a concert of music for violin and piano because Tomotada Soh, prize winner in the Paganini, Geneva, and Thibaud competitions, was available.

This is the reason why I sometimes write to a composer asking for a work for a particular soloist or ensemble. If I have liked the works that a composer has submitted but we don't presently have the right soloists or ensemble, we try to include something else by the same author.

At a certain point in the planning the choice of music and performers falls into place, and it is then possible to draw up a budget. It includes the cost of renting the Braschi Palace; the building of a platform and lighting columns; booking of instruments, chairs, tuners, cleaners, and security guards; and the payment of an overall insurance policy for artists, instruments, and public. A program is designed, and I then hand over notes for this to UDI's standing committee for Donne in Musica. Together we decide on dates, times, rehearsal schedules, a press conference (usually held ten days before the festival opens), press bulletins, and the exhibition of photographs and scores that accompanies the festival.

The reaction of the Italian press toward our festival was at first one of mild amusement, then surprise as the festivals continued; they now take us for granted—in other words, they believe we have come to stay. Rome has over twenty-four daily newspapers and three evening papers, plus an enormous number of weekly and monthly magazines, and nearly all have, at one time or another, sent a journalist to one or more of the concerts. The major newspapers have all run important articles but have tended to give more space to Saint Hildegard von Bingen or Clara Schumann than to composers living and working today. On the other hand, we have always had carefully written reviews for the concerts of contemporary music, above all from three different directions—from a left-wing paper, from a main-party paper, and from the Vatican daily. A press book is kept each year and the amount of space accorded to the festival seems to be constant from year to year. Like any other festival in Italy, once the novelty has worn off the press prefers to cover only unusual events. This year we ran a full-day workshop dedicated to the performance and presentation of string quartets, most of which were being given first performances. This, for example, not only brought in various critics and most of Rome's musical *intelligenzia* but also formed the basis for a series of radio and television interviews.

Some critics have suggested that after three successful years the time has come to program music by women composers in the regular seasons and not just in a once-yearly festival! We are, of course, completely in agreement but continue to point out that three years ago very few people in the Italian musical world had heard of even ten *compositrici*, let alone the hundred-odd that we have to date programmed.

Most of our performers tend to reprogram the works that they prepare for Donne in Musica. I Solisti Dauni, a chamber ensemble from Foggia in the south of Italy, have presented more than thirty times the program they originally played in 1980. Others, including myself, have recorded their programs for foreign radio stations, included the music by women composers in other recitals, or included the works in commercial recordings. As a result of the interest shown in Clara Schumann's lieder, it was possible to convince the Italian record company EDI-PAN to produce a commercial LP entitled *Donne in Musica* with songs by C. Schumann, Maria Szymanowska, Adelina Patti, and Gilda Ruta.

To return for a moment to the question of musical criticism, it is necessary to underline that, apart from some articles written by junior reporters or by women interested in feminist problems, our concerts have consistently been reviewed by well-known music critics. They would appear to be rather more at home writing about contemporary music but have suggested that they would find it easier to judge music by women of the past if they could hear these works in concerts with music written by known male composers of the same periods. This is a direction toward which we shall probably move—but only for music written before this century.

Italian critics appear to be particularly interested in first performances and, finances permitting, this is another area we should like to develop further. We feel that a very tangible way of helping women composers, apart from performing their works, is to commission (for a fee) and then pay for copyist's expenses or, in case of composers living out of the city where the work is to be performed, to cover travelling expenses so a composer can supervise rehearsals and the first performance of her work. We are convinced that once a work has been given a first performance it is easier to find a publisher. At the same time the possibility of supervising rehearsals and performance (or performances), enables the composer to develop the art of composing much more quickly.

Donne in Musica has already made many composers known to the Italian public, and, naturally, we hope to be able to present many more in the future. We find that certain concert formats attract a particular audience and that certain concerts pull in people who do not normally attend performances of classical music. The 1981 performance of Saint Hildegarde von Bingen's liturgical hymns packed the hall, not just with the general public, but with a very large number of nuns and priests.

The 1982 program for brass instruments, soprano, and piano brought in a large number of school-age music students, most of whom were studying the trumpet or the saxophone. Many members of the Japanese community in Rome came especially to hear a work by "their" composer, Kikuko Masumoto. But whatever the program and whatever the weather, we manage to fill the concert hall; more importantly still—especially in a city like Rome—we have built up a public of regulars who have attended all our concerts since the first festival. In addition, many people who can't travel to Rome for the concerts write in to buy copies of the festival program.

Plans are currently under way to repeat the 1982 festival in different parts of Italy—as happened in 1981 when we took the festival to Venice. This depends, as always, upon the allocation of local funds.

Donne in Musica has not really been so difficult to run—or so we say as each festival and all the problems and sleepless nights come to an end. When the festivals started, performance materials came largely from my private collection and music passed on by friends and colleagues and a few embassies; now the flow of music arriving never stops. Correspondence begun in 1979 with international organizations, unions, guilds, museums, publishers, musicologists, private collections, and the composers themselves means that we now have sufficient music to continue programming for another five or six festivals without any difficulty.

Beginning with the first festival, women composers have travelled to Rome from all over Italy, from Germany, Denmark, Spain, Switzerland, the United States, South Africa, and Korea, aided by private grants and subsidies from their unions or from their governments. So far we have been unable to help with these expenses, and we are extremely grateful to those organizations that have made such visits to Rome possible.

Donne in Musica is a project, an idea, an ideal that could have been planned and programmed by any one of our major musical organizations—but it wasn't. Not even the Italian musicians' unions had thought that a problem existed for women who compose. The Unione di Donne Italiane, born as an antifascist organization during the troubled years of World War II, has for many years been active on behalf of Italian women in many battles for social and professional equality. It has fought for and obtained better schooling, kindergartens, equal pay for women workers in all fields, equal work possibilities, and changes in the family laws and has now decided to help women in that most difficult of musical professions, the field of composition. This battle is being conducted with the same

Figure 1.3 Composers Birgitte Alsted (Denmark) and Kyung-Sun Suh (Korea) at a Rome concert, 1981. Photograph by Bruna Polimeni

enthusiasm mustered to try to convince local authorities to set up family guidance centers. The UDI battles for funds and harrasses city council members in such a way that for them to deny financing becomes awkward.

The hard work has paid off. Today the name "Donne in Musica" is known throughout the Italian musical world, is at home on radio and television, and has also been given to one LP and one book. Certainly, if Donne in Musica continues to grow and expand its activities with more seminars, musicological conferences, first performances, commissions, and perhaps publications, I believe that in a short time it will be easier for women composers to be represented when orchestras, theaters, and concert soloists sit down to plan their seasons. Perhaps the day will come when there will be no need for anyone to ask, *"Ma ci sono compositrici?"* (But *are* there women composers?")

CONCERT PROGRAMS—ROME, 1980

Music in the Courts (March 16)

Anne Boleyn, Queen of England	O death, rocke me asleep (1536)
Leonora Orsina, Duchessa di Segni	Per pianto la mia carne (1570)
Francesca Caccini	Dal "Primo Libro delle musiche a 1 e 2 voci" (1618)
	— O Chiome belle
	Aria della Sirena dall'opera "La Liberazione di Ruggiero dall'isola d'Alcina" (1625)
	— Chi nel fior di giovinezza
Barbara Strozzi	Lacrime mie
	Soccorrete, luci avare
	Spesso per entro al petto (1650)
Elisabeth Jacquet de la Guerre	"Pièces de Clavecin" (1707)
	— Suite in Re minore
	La Flamande
	Double
	Courante
	Double
	Sarabande
	Gigue
	Rigaudon
	Chaconne
Amalie, Princess of Prussia	Sonata per flauto in Fa maggiore
	Adagio
	Allegretto
	Allegro

Clara Schumann and Teresa Carreno (March 20)

Clara Schumann	Andante con sentimento (1838)
	Seven variations on a theme by Robert Schumann in F sharp minor op. 20 (1853)
	Trio per violino, violoncello e pianoforte op. 17 (1843)
Teresa Carreno	Quattro pezzi per pianoforte
	Quartetto in Si minore (European premiere)

Frauenlieder Abend (March 20)

Herzogin Anna Amalia von Sachsen Weimar	Sieh, mich Heil'ger wie ich bin (1776) Das Veilchen (1776)
Josef A. Haydn	"First Set of VI Original Canzonettas" (London 1794) Parole: Anne Hunter — The mermaid's song — Recollection — Shepherd's song — Despair — Pleasing pain — Fidelity
Maria Szymanowska	Da "Six Romances" (1822) Peine et plaisir tout finira Romance du Saule Se spiegar potessi oh Dio
Clara Schumann	Am Strand (1840 circa) Liebst du um Schönheit, op. 12 n. 1 "Sechs Lieder aus Jucunde von Rollet" op. 23 (1856 circa) — Was weinst du, Blümlein — An einem lichten Morgen — Geheimes Flüstern hier und dort — Auf einem grünen Hügel — Das ist ein Tag — O Lust, o Lust

Composers of Today: I (March 21)

Thea Musgrave	String Quartet (1958)
	    Adagio
	    Scherzando
	    Adagio

Irma Ravinale	Improvvisazione per chitarro solo (1978) (first performance)
Ada Gentile	Together for violoncello and clarinetto (1978)
Tona Scherchen-Hsaio	Lien pour alto seul (1973)
Elizabeth Maconchy	String Quartet n. 10 (1971-1972)

Piano Music of Today and of the "Present" Past (March 22)

Ruth Gipps	Themes and Variations op. 57 a (1956)

Nicola LeFanu	Chiaroscuro per pianoforte (1970)
	— Exultate
	— Refrain
	— Sound and Silence
	— Epithalamion
	— Reflection and Cadenza
	— Refrain
	— Scherzo and Epilogue
Anne Boyd	Angklung for solo pianoforte (1974)
Cécile Chaminade	Étude de concert n. 2 op. 35 "Automne"
Rosemary Brown	Intermezzo in E-flat "by" Brahms
	Lyric inspired by Rachmaninov
	"Ninna Nanna" "by" Liszt
	"Woodland Water" "by" Liszt

Composers of Today: II (March 23)

Barbara Giuranna	Adagio e allegro di concerto (1936) (per quartetto, flauto, oboe, clarinetto, fagotto, corno)
Catalina Rodriguez Bella	Movimentos Esquematicos (1960) (flauto, clarinetto, fagotto)
Alice Samter	Kaleideskop (1973) (violino e flauto)
Nancy Van de Vate	Music for viola, pianoforte and percussion (1976)
Therese Brenet	Pantomime pour flûte (1974)
Teresa Procaccini	"Marionette" per pianoforte, dieci strumenti e mimo (1975)
Gloria Coates	Nonett—three movements for instruments (1978)
	— Horizontal
	— Diagonal
	— Back and Forth (2 violini, viola, violoncello, contrabasso, flauto, oboe, fagotto, corno)

CONCERT PROGRAMS—ROME, 1981

Orchestral Concert (March 10)

Maria Rosa Coccia	Sinfonia dell'oratorio "Il Trionfo d'Enea" (1779)
Jenny McLeod	For seven (1965 ca)

| Anna Amalie, Principessa di Prussia | Sonata per flauto (1750) |
| Grażyna Bacewicz | Concerto per archi (1948)
— Allegro
— Andante
— Vivace |

From the Convent to the Court (March 11)

Santa Ildegarda von Bingen	Inno: Canti liturgici
Maddalena Casulana di Mezarii	Madrigali a 4 voci miste: — Ridon or per le piagge — O notte o ciel o mar — S'alcun vi mira fiso — Morir non può il cuore
Suora Isabella Leonarda di Bologna	Sonata V dall'opus 16 per 2 violini, violone e basso continuo (1693)
Francesca Caccini	Selections from the opera "Ruggiero sull'Isola d'Alcina" (1623)

Leopoldine Blahetka and Fanny Mendelssohn (March 13)

| Leopoldine Blahetka | Sonata per violino e pianoforte op. 15
Trio per pianoforte, violino e violoncello op. 5 |
| Fanny Cecile Mendelssohn (Hensel) | Trio in Re minore op. 11 per pianoforte, violino e violoncello |

Early Twentieth Century (March 15)

Lucie Vellère	Troisième Quatuor à cordes (1951) — Allegro — Presto — Andante— Vivo Spiccato
Lili Boulanger	Reflets (1911) Le Retour (1912)
Germaine Tailleferre	Non, La fidélité . . . Les trois présents On a dit mal de mon ami from "Six Chansons Françaises" (1920)
Elsa Olivieri Sangiacomo	Quattro liriche dai Rubaiyat di Omar Kayam (1919) Duermite mi alma da "Tre canzoni" (1918/1919)
Adelina Patti	Il bacio d'Addio
Gilda Ruta	Povero Amore
Teresa del Riego	Homing

Alma Maria Mahler	Hymne
	Der Erkennende
	Lobgesang
	da "Fünf Gesänge" (1920 ca)
Giulia Recli	Quartetto in Fa (1914)
	— Allegro molto moderato —
	Scherzo — Adagio — Finale:
	allegro vivace

Mini-Marathon for Piano and Winds (March 17)

Virginia Pollettini	Marche des Cravates (1900 ca)
Contessa Gilda Ruta	Mesta Serenata (1910 ca)
Maria Giacchina Cusenza	Il Basso Ostinato (1936)
Jean Coulthard	Variations on B–A–C–H (1972)
Gillian Whitehead	Voices of Tane (1975)
Ruth Zechlin	Kontrapunkte (1969/70)
Maria de Lourdes Martins	"Reticencias" op. 24 per flauto e xylo-fono (1961)
Judith Weir	"Out of the air" per quintetto di fiati (1975)
Silvano di Lotti	"Contrasti" per due clarinetti (1976)
Alicia Terzian	Shantiniketan (Dimora di Pace) per voce recitante, flauto e mimo (1974) (coreografia di Alfredo Rainò)
Judith Bailey	Concerto for Ten Wind Instruments (1979)

From Sonnets to "Superman" (March 19)

Phyllis Tate	Songs of Sundrie Kindes (1976)
	(for voice and lute)
	— A description of love
	— The Bell man
	— A love sonnet
	— A religious use of taking tobacco
Maria Margarethe Danzi	Sonata op. 1, n. 1 per violino e piano-forte (1799)
	— Allegro moderato
	— Andante
	— Allegretto
Grażyna Bacewicz	Due Capriccio per solo violinó (1968)
Kyung-Sun Suh	2 Images per soprano, violino e piano-forte (1975)
Cathy Berberian	Stripsody per solo voce (1966)

Ellen Taaffe Zwilich	Sonata in Three Movements (1973/4) — Liberamente — Lento e molto espressivo — Allegro vivo e con brio

Music of Today (March 21)

Verdina Shlonsky	Divertimento for wind quintet (1954) — Allegro — Adagio — Rondino
Mirvana Zivkovic	Pean (1967) per flauto, violino, clarinetto, fagotto e pianoforte
Adriana Hölszky	Pulsationen II (1979) Quintetto per violino, violoncello, contrabbasso e due pianoforti
Alina Piechowska	Aura (1978) per flauto e pianoforte
Joelle Wallach	Quartet Movement (1966) per flauto, clarinetto, violino, violoncello
Birgitte Alsted	Smedierne i Granada (1976) (I fabbri di Granada) per flauto, clarinetto, violino, violoncello, contrabbasso, due pianoforti, percussione, voce recitante

CONCERT PROGRAMS—VENICE, 1981

Two Centuries of Piano Music (April 24)

Maria Szymanowska	Polacche Notturno Studio
Clara Schumann	Andante con sentimento (1838) Romanza (1856)
Cécile Chaminade	Étude de concert n. 2 op. 35 "Automne"
Maria Gioacchino Cusenza	Il Basso Ostinato (1936)
Jean Coulthard	Variations on B–A–C–H (1972)
Gillian Whitehead	Voices of Tane (1975)
Barbara Giuranna	Toccata (1937)
Anne Boyd	Angklung for solo pianoforte (1974)
Ruth Zechlin	Kontrapunkte (1969-70)

From the Convent to the Court (April 25)
repeat of the March 11, 1980, concert

**Music by Teresa Carreno, Clara Schumann
and Composers of the Early Twentieth Century (April 26)**
repeated portions of the concerts of March 20, 1980, and March 15, 1981

From Sonnets to "Superman" (April 27)
repeat of the March 19, 1981, concert

Music of Today
*repeated portions of the concerts of March 21 and 23, 1980,
and March 21, 1981*

CONCERT PROGRAMS—ROME, 1982

Women Sing Music by Women (March 20)

Beatriz de Dia (1160-1212/14)	A chantar m'er de so q'ieu no volria
Louise Reichardt (1779-1826)	Sechs Geistliche Lieder: Dem Herrn; Buss-Lied; Morgenlied; Furbitte für Sterbende; Weihnachtslied; Tief Andacht
Vally Weigl (1889)	Shepherdess moon (1947)
Montserrat Campmany (1901)	Romancillo del Milagro (1949)
Coro femminile	Improvvisazione
Barbara Giuranna (1899)	Due Quartine Popolari Greche (1936)
	— Basilico odora qui . . .
	— Chi prende mille scudi
Giulia Recli (1890-1970)	"Mattutino" da "La collana della madonna" (1936)
	"Dorme una madre" dai "Canti d'amore" (1936)
Nicola LeFanu (1947)	The Little Valleys (1978)
Hilda Jerea (1916)	Quattro madrigali (1973)
	— Hodie Mihi, cras tibi
	— Tomanta inimii
	— Cintec de Leagàn
	— Romantà Apocrifà

Music for Violin and Piano (March 21)

Francesca Le Brun (1756-1791)	Sonata numero 1 in La bemolle maggiore (1780) per pianoforte con accompagnamento di violino

Mademoiselle Campet de Saujon (1800)	Fantaisie et Variations pour le pianoforte sur l'Air della Molinara "Nel cor più non mi sento" de Paisiello opus 2
Teresa Milanollo (1827-1904)	Grande Fantaisie Elégiaque per violino con accompagnamento di pianoforte opus 1 (1888) — Introduzione — Tema — 1ª variazione — 2ª variazione — Grande Fantaisie élégiaque — Finale
Gilda Ruta (1853-1932)	Suite per violino e pianoforte — Allegro Moderato — Adagio — Allegro Vivo
Erzsébet Szönyi (1924)	— Air (1946) — Szerenad, Hajnali Tanc (1948)
Elisabeth Lutyens (1906)	— The Prelude (1979) (per solo violino)
Lili Boulanger (1893-1918)	D'un matin de Printemps pour violin et pianoforte (1917)

The Harpsichord: Yesterday and Today (March 23)

Elisabeth Jacquet de la Guerre (1667-1729)	Suite en Sol majeur — Allemande — Courante — Sarabande — Gigue — Menuet — Rondeau
Maria Anna Martinez (1745-1812)	Sonata numero 3 in La maggiore — Allegro — Rondo — Tempo di Minuetto
Mary Hester Park (1775-1822)	Sonata in Do maggiore opus 4 — Allegro spiritoso — Larghetto — Rondo
Barbara Giuranna	Viola ad Aurea (first performance)

Maria Luisa Ozaita (1934)	Suite in Stile Antico (1981)
	— Preludio
	— Danza
	— Postludio
	— Modulos Canonicos
Margaret Lucy Wilkins (1939)	A dance to the Music of Time (1980)
Joanna Bruzdowicz (1943)	Epitaph en mémoire de mon père (1973)
	(clavecin et bande magnétique)
Irma Ravinale (1937)	Improvvisazione II (1981) per clavicembalo (first performance)

The Age of Romanticism (March 24)

Marjory Kennedy Fraser (1857-1930)	Gradh Geal mo chridh
Harriet Abrams (1760-1825)	The emigrant
	The soldier's grave
Maria Malibran (1808-1836)	Le retour de la Tyrolienne
Clara Schumann (1819-1896)	Trio per violino, violoncello e pianoforte opus 17 (1843)
Emilia Gubitosi (1887-1972)	Colloqui
	arpa, flauto e violoncello
Dame Ethel Smyth (1858-1944)	Four songs per voce, flauto, violino, viola, violoncello, arpa e percussione
	— Odelette
	— The Dance
	— Chrysilla
	— Anacreontic Ode

The Piano in Many Guises (March 25)

Agatha Backer Grøndahl (1847-1907)	Suite "per pianoforte opus 44" La Montagna Blu
	— Notte
	— Nel Salone dei "Trolls"
	— Il grande "Troll"
	— Una ciocca dei capelli di Huldre
	— Canzone dell'Incantato
	— Danza dei "Trolls"
Galina Uvstolskaya (1919)	Grande Duetto per violoncello e pianoforte (1959)
Barbara Kolb (1939)	Solitaire (1971) for pianoforte and tape
Doris Hays (1941)	"Pamp" for pianoforte, tape and bird whistle (1973)

Oh Sook Ja (1941)   Shaman music per pianoforte e
                                                 percussioni (1979)

Colloquium on the Music of Cassia (March 26) Byzantine Chants

String Quartet Workshop (March 27)

Radie Britain (1903)   Musical Portrait of Thomas Jefferson
A. Fontana (1955)   Quartetto n. 1 (1982) (first performance)
A. Gentile (1947)   Diaresis (1981) (first performance)
E. Hayden Pizer (1954)   Interfuguelude (1981)
E. Maconchy (1907)   Quartetto n. 10 (1971-72)
P. Pistono D'Angelo (1938)   Quartetto n. 1 (1982) (first performance)
T. Procaccini (1934)   Quartetto (1979)
Priaulx Rainier (1904)   Quartett for Strings (1947)
M. Zimmermann (1947)   Quartetto n. 1 opus 7 (1979) (first
                                                 performance)

OneTwoThreeFourFive . . . (March 28)

Yvonne Desportes (1907)   Quintetto per ottoni: *Imageries d'Anton*
                                        — L'Appel des Chevaliers
                                        — Mahaut et son Chevalier
                                        — Danceries
Kikuko Masumoto (1937)   Ancient Japanese Songs: Aware —
                                        Hayashi — Shi-te-ten.
Tera de Marez Oyens (1932)   "Trio" "Combattimento Ritmico" —
                                        per basso tuba, percussione e nastro
                                        (1974)
Jennifer Fowler (1939)   Voice of the Shades (2 trombe e clari-
                                        netto)
S. Gubaidulina (1931)   Quattro (2 trombe e 2 tromboni) (1974)
Jeanne Zaidel Rudolph (1945)   Five pieces per quartetto a fiati e
                                        sopran (1976)
Thérèse Brenet (1935)   Tetrapyle: (4 sassofoni e pianoforte)
                                        (1979)

Figure 1.4 Donne in Musica

2

Origin of a Series: Piccolo Spoleto's Minority Artists' Project

DAVID W. MAVES

INTRODUCTION

After concluding the fourth annual series of Minority Artists' Project concerts, the problems and rewards of regularly producing a special-interest performance series are still very fresh in my mind. This chapter will attempt to describe the origin, idea, design, and scope of this series—a still-evolving entity that remains far from a finished product, codified series, or even a polished concept. It will explore what has happened—the harum-scarum potpourri of mistakes and happy accidents that actually went into realizing the programs—with some speculation about what should happen next.

Since 1977 Spoleto USA has been an annual event in Charleston, South Carolina. Modeled on the festival that has been going on in Spoleto, Italy, for twenty-five years, it is, by all accounts, a world-class arts festival composed mostly of concerts but with a good deal of drama, dance, and visual arts events.

Piccolo Spoleto is a kind of adjunct to the main festival, rather like the Edinburgh "Fringe Festival." It has become a very large and now official "outreach" program for the main festival. The Minority Artists' Project is a small part of the total. Once the entire festival gets rolling, it is possible to go to concerts every hour of the day from 10 A.M. until well after midnight. For six of those days, the Minority Artists' Project "Contemporary Festival" has scheduled the noon hour for programming (with few exceptions) the music of living composers.

As director of Minority Artists' Project, I have tried to program almost exclusively the music of women and minority (mostly black and South American) composers. Until 1982 Spoleto USA had, to my knowledge, programmed only one work by a woman composer, an opening fanfare by Sharon Moe Miranda. (Miranda was given credit only after I wrote a review for the local paper and mentioned her name in my article. It took me two hours to find out that she had written it; finally I found an orchestra performer who remembered her name from the orchestra parts.) In 1982 Laura Dean, the dancer/choreographer, was billed on the Spoleto USA festival as a composer, but her main thrust was dance rather than her music.

The College of Charleston, a small (5,000 students) liberal arts college in downtown Charleston, has given me, as chairman of its Fine Arts Department, considerable support for the Minority Artists' Project series. I have been able to use the college recital hall (an attractive hall seating 267) and some of the college's instruments. The college provides about $1,000 in seed money, some secretarial help, and telephoning and duplicating services. Usually I am able to raise another $1,000 that isn't tied to specific works or performers. Considering these modest support services, we have still been able to program an intriguing variety of works, but a lot of the effort remains on a volunteer basis.

As might be expected, finding funds for such an undertaking is almost impossible. Virtually all the other monies received for this series have some kind of strings attached: these funds usually come in the form of small grants to bring in specific performers, and thanks to them, the series has been successful.

The Minority Artists' Project is firmly based on the following manifesto, which I have continually refined and promulgated since its first formulation in the late 1970s:

A PROGRAM FOR WOMEN AND MINORITIES IN THE ARTS

In the twentieth-century world of art, drama, and music, many of the significant achievements of minority artists have not received due attention from publishers, performers, critics, and scholars. And although women comprise 51 percent of the U.S. population, they too are a minority in terms of their share of the serious musical-artistic "pie." A perusal of most contemporary music texts and history books shows a singular lack of attention to women as significant creative artistic figures. Thus, for the purpose of this statement, women too are included as a "minority."

This series of concerts focusing on the music of living composers who are either women or minorities is the beginning of what we hope will be a continuing attempt to redress the aforementioned imbalance. Our objectives: (1) locate contemporary minority artists of merit, collect examples of their works, and make some judgments of their esthetic and historic significance; (2) consider what the position of these works should be in the canon of contemporary art; (3) provide opportunities for research, performance, and documentation (recording) of these works under conditions that hold as closely as practicable to firm professional standards; and (4) try to increase the musical notice and notoriety for minority composers in the areas of public, critical, and scholarly acclaim to that currently accorded their male, mostly white counterparts.

Acting on these thoughts, I began the first concert series in 1979. That year I mounted three concerts to audiences of approximately sixty, twenty, and forty persons, respectively. (Detailed concert programs follow this chapter.) The performers either donated their time or were paid barely enough to meet expenses. By 1982 there were six concerts during the festival, each playing to average audiences of eighty, and a New York City concert took place during the 1982-83 season.

To date there have been a total of ten Piccolo Spoleto concerts, two mid-year recitals in New York (focusing on music performed during the festival), and one special recital (1980) of works by Doris Hays.

I try to use all paid professional performers, but occasionally students and talented amateurs have helped out. On two occasions talented young Spoleto USA Orchestra performers have had to fill in at the last minute. (It has been risky to plan to use regular festival performers since the Spoleto USA Orchestra schedule is very tight and subject to change on short notice, and they are only available during rare breaks in their frantic schedule.)

The performers are usually different each year, but a few have performed in more than one series. They all take great pride in being a part of this series, and the audience response has been enthusiastic. This is especially noteworthy when one realizes that these concerts are composed almost exclusively of contemporary music.

We have had some small success with reviews. Usually the local papers review one of the concerts each year. In 1981 New York writer Allan Kozinn wrote an extended article for a local paper about one of the concerts, a recital by Doris Hays, and two years ago the series received a paragraph in a Spoleto article by Paul Hume in the *Washington Post*. In 1982 I wrote many articles for a special Spoleto newspaper called the *Festival Gazette Daily* and was able to mention the series several times.

As I now recall, the idea for this series sprang in part from a desire to do something significant during the Spoleto Festival. I wanted to be a part of the excitement and contribute to the festival and at the same time do something that would fill a special need.

I had long been aware of the particular problems facing women composers. Although the situation is changing, there remains widespread discrimination on the part of most critics and conductors, not to mention the teachers of composition at the major teaching centers around the world. I also knew that a regular festival of new music would be just another of many such series. Gradually the idea of a contemporary music series featuring mostly the music of living women and minority composers was formed.

Then, in December 1976, I met eighty-five-year-old Vally Weigl, a prolific composer, at an American Music Center meeting in New York. She asked about getting some of her music done at the first Spoleto USA Festival. Over the next two years we corresponded, talked on the telephone, and scrounged up some funds. We recruited a fine mezzo-soprano from New York and performers from Charleston, South Carolina, and Savannah, Georgia, plus a second composer-performer from Montgomery, Alabama. The first funds came from my own pocket, John Weigl (Vally's son), the Xerox Corporation, Piccolo Spoleto, and the college. We had a series.

The second year (1980) we put on four concerts; in 1981 and 1982 six concerts apiece were performed; six more are scheduled for 1983.

Spring of each year marks the beginning of a scramble to get programs together, find performers, arrange housing for out-of-town performers and composers, and assemble the year's production team. Lack of an ample and constant source of funds and a stable and efficient organizing team leads to a climate of ever-present anxiety.

In 1980 I had given up all hope of doing a New York concert. A New York transportation strike two days before the scheduled concert caused a postponement, and I couldn't locate more money to send the performers— five of whom had already gone to New York the first time—north again. Vally Weigl, in less than a week's time, organized an entirely new concert with New York performers who donated their time and was still able to program many of the works we had done in Charleston.

In 1982 everything bad seemed to come together at the last concert in the series: parts were lost, a performer backed out at the last moment (we had to play a 'cello part on the piano—it was that or cancel), and the fire alarm went off several times during the concert—once emptying the building. All this was most discouraging.

It has been consistently difficult for me to coordinate this series. I am by training a composer, by occupation a college teacher and administrator— not a concert producer. However, the improvisatory quality of the series has led to some wondrous discoveries and some very happy occasions. In 1981 the totally unexpected last-minute arrival in Charleston of Alice Doria-Gamilla, the leading woman composer in the Philippine Islands, led to a hurried change of program proofs and a delightful fifteen minutes of her music on the program—and an even more well-rounded series.

Ofttimes, I feel that our failures may have outweighed our successes: many deserving works remain unplayed either because of a lack of good performers or because the performers don't like the works and refuse to play them. A few of the performed works have proven embarrassingly bad. Also, music by black composers thus far has been underrepresented on the programs.

I've come to realize that certain of the ideas in the original manifesto are perhaps too intricate or all-embracing to be implemented as things now stand. For instance, I don't think that Charleston, South Carolina, is the place to try to start a national archive, as I'd once planned, and I need to decide just what to do with the materials (scores and recordings) already at hand. (In actuality, I don't often pick works to be performed. I pass scores on to performers, who decide what they would like to do. And many of the performers are coming up with suggestions of their own.)

The series' successes are genuine and include many good performances of some marvelous works, plus getting a certain amount of publicity for the works we have been able to program. That some of the performers have kept works that they performed in this series in their repertory is also noteworthy.

The concert programs included first performances of seven compositions (one of which was later recorded professionally on Orion Records), and three new works were written especially for this series. I hope we can increase this kind of activity.

At this juncture, after four years of programs, I plan to catalog the works we have performed, perhaps with some kind of critical annotation, and circulate the listing. And while not all of the tapes of all the concerts are of broadcast quality, I have been invited to submit those that are to National Public Radio.

In 1983, having shifted from chairman of the Fine Arts Department to composer-in-residence, I should have more time and energy to devote to the project. Through the years, though, the job has certainly been made easier with the help of many students in a special three-week "Maymester" class at the College of Charleston. The class specializes in learning about the Spoleto USA Festival, and each year many of the students pitch in and help with almost everything: publicity, programs, ideas, transportation, and even housing of visiting artists and composers, plus a lot of moral support. Ellen Dressler, the director of Piccolo Spoleto, has also been an active supporter; the publicity her organization provides is indispensable.

Because we are always looking for new material to program, we offer the following guidelines for anyone planning to submit scores or other materials:

1. Short, relatively easy chamber works have the best chance of being performed. These include works for voice, piano, and/or instrumental parts, music for strings, for winds, or brasses singly or in pairs, and percussion.

2. Include a list of those works we can keep and those which must be returned.

3. Include postage and a properly addressed envelope for the return of anything that you want back.

4. We would like to keep at least one score for the library. Performers are becoming most eager to perform in the Festival; it is convenient to send them to our library to locate music by a particular composer to perform, and scores held over from previous years are here to be

perused. (We try actively to promote year-round performances of all the music, but the Spoleto and New York concerts are the best times.) Recordings, brochures, or reviews can be sent, but decisions are really made from looking at the scores.

5. A short one- or two-paragraph autobiography should be included to be used in program notes if we are able to program your work. In any given year perhaps one in ten works submitted gets programmed, but I have eventually been able to program music by everyone who has sent in scores at one time or another.

6. A few times an organization has sponsored a work or a performance. For example, American Women Composers, Inc. sponsored the first concerts of the 1981 and the 1982 series, selecting the performers and the works performed. In 1980 Sigma Alpha Iota sponsored a performance of a work by Vivian Fine. We welcome this kind of collaboration with responsible organizations.

7. Send scores, recordings, and information to Dr. David W. Maves, Director, Minority Artists' Project, Fine Arts Department, College of Charleston, Charleston, SC 29424.

CONCERT PROGRAMS—1979

Gibbes Art Gallery, Charleston, S.C. (June 1, 12 noon)

David Maves	Woman's Songs (mezzo-soprano and piano)
Vally Weigl	Songs of Remembrance (mezzo-soprano and piano)
Dorothy Rudd Moore	Six Songs from the Rubaiyat (mezzo-soprano and piano)
Vally Weigl	Requiem for Allison (mezzo-soprano and string quartet)
Katherine Hoover	Wings (mezzo-soprano and string quartet)
Vally Weigl	Songs of Carl Sandburg (mezzo-soprano and piano)

Gibbes Art Gallery, Charleston, S.C. (June 1, 6 P.M.)
(Woodwind Quintet Concert)

Persis Vehar	Prelude and Dance
Alberto Ginastera	Flute and Oboe Duo
Vally Weigl	Brief Encounters
Irving Fine	Partita for Woodwind Quintet

Gibbes Art Gallery, Charleston, S.C. (June 2)

Persis Vehar	Aria and Capriccio (bassoon and clarinet)
Vally Weigl	No Loveliness Is Ever Lost (soprano and alto)
	Bold Heart (soprano and alto)
	Adagio for Strings (string quartet)
Jeanne Shaffer	Boats and Candles (voice and string quartet)

CONCERT PROGRAMS—1980

Albert Simons Center for the Arts Recital Hall
The College of South Carolina, Charleston, S.C. (May 28)

Elizabeth Vercoe	Fantasy (solo piano)
Doris Hays	Tunings (string quartet)
Priaulx Rainier	Quartet for Strings (string quartet)

Albert Simons Center for the Arts Recital Hall (May 29)

Morris Land	Ode to Martin Luther King (percussion, tape, and slides)
Imogen Holst	Fall of the Leaf (solo cello)
Jeanne Shaffer	Eternity (soprano and piano)
	On Gardens, Minutes, and Butterflies (soprano, oboe, and piano)
Ruth Crawford Seeger	Chinaman, Laundryman (mezzo-soprano and piano)
Ruth Schonthal	By the Roadside (Walt Whitman) (mezzo-soprano and piano)
Phoebe Knapp	The Bird Carol (mezzo-soprano and piano)

Albert Simons Center for the Arts Recital Hall (May 30)

Vally Weigl	Songs from "Do Not Awake Me" (mezzo-soprano and piano)
	Songs Newly Seen in the Dusk (mezzo-soprano and piano)
	City Birds (flute, mezzo-soprano, and piano)

Ruth Crawford Seeger	Sacco, Vanzetti (mezzo-soprano and piano)
Vivian Fine	Capriccio for Oboe and String Trio (oboe, violin, viola, and cello)
Amy Cheney Beach	Three Settings of Robert Browning, op. 33

Albert Simons Center for the Arts Recital Hall (May 31)
(All solo piano)

Ruggero Lolini	Quaderno di Maria Cristina
Lili Boulanger	Trois Morceaux pour Piano
Louise Talma	Alleluia in Form of Toccata
Arthur Cunningham	Engrams
David W. Maves	Sonata No. 2

Albert Simons Center for the Arts Recital Hall (June 2)

Vally Weigl	Encounters (woodwind quintet)
Julia Stilman	Intensities (woodwind quintet)
Joelle Wallach	Wisps (soprano and piano)
Meredith Wootton	Three Cinquains (soprano and piano)
Ruth Schonthal	By the Roadside (soprano and piano)
Thomas Kerr	Concert Scherzo (piano duo)
George Walker	Sonata for Two Pianos

Donnell Library Center Auditorium, 20 West 53d St.,
New York, New York (October 11)

Roque Cordero	Sonata Brevis for Piano (solo piano)
Alida Vasquez	Electronic Moods for Piano and Tape
Tania Leon	Elegy to Paul Robeson for Piano
Albert Tepper	Suite for B-flat Clarinet and Bassoon
Vally Weigl	Oiseau de la vie for Clarinet solo
	Songs of Remembrance (mezzo-soprano, clarinet, and piano)
David Maves	Three Women's Songs for Mezzo and Piano
Francis Poulenc	Sonata for Clarinet and Bassoon
Judith Dvorkin	From Six Moods (mezzo-soprano and piano)
Max Lifchitz	Elegy for Piano (piano with spoken introduction)

CONCERT PROGRAMS—1981

Albert Simons Center for the Arts Recital Hall (May 27)

Elaine Lebenbom	Sonata for Piano
Jeanne Behrend	Quiet Piece (solo piano)
Haskell Small	A Small Suite (solo piano)
	Sonata No. 2
Amy Cheney Beach	The Year's at the Spring (soprano and piano)
	Night
Mary Howe	O Mistress Mine (soprano and piano)
	Red Fields of France (soprano and piano)
	The Prinkin' Leddie (soprano and piano)
Lyle de Bohun	Winter Song (soprano and piano)
	Sonnet (soprano and piano)
Esther Ballou	Street Scenes (soprano and piano)
Julia Smith	Three Love Songs

Albert Simons Center for the Arts Recital Hall (May 28)

Rose Marie Cooper	Composer's Suite (soprano and piano)
Doris Hays	Water Music (tape, waterpump, and kiddie pool—with slides)
	Saturday Nights (piano and tape)
	Pamp (tape, piano, and bird whistles)
Marga Richter	Requiem (solo piano)
Doris Hays	Sunday Morning (solo piano)
	Sunday Nights (solo piano)

Albert Simons Center for the Arts Recital Hall (May 29)

Keiko Abe	Frogs (marimba)
	Michi (marimba)
Alice Doria-Gamilla	Music (selected excerpts for solo piano)
Judith Lang Zaimont	Soliloquy (from Greyed Sonnets) (soprano and piano)
Emma Lou Diemer	Two Songs (soprano and piano)
An-Ming Wang	Two Songs (from the Song of Endless Sorrow) (soprano and piano)
Doris Hays	Southern Voices (soprano, tape, and narrator)

Albert Simons Center for the Arts Recital Hall (May 30)

Nancy Van de Vate	Letter to a Friend's Loneliness (soprano and string quartet)
Vally Weigl	Beyond Time (seven songs for violin, soprano, and piano)
Doris Hays	For Women (soprano and piano)
Laurie MacGregor	Fitful Sleep (two movements for solo cello)
Juan Carlos Paz	Three Jazz Movements (solo piano)
Wen-Chung Chou	The Willows Are New (solo piano)
Roque Cordero	Tres Piececillas para Alina (solo piano)
Max Lifchitz	Affinities (solo piano)

Albert Simons Center for the Arts Recital Hall (June 1)
(An All Vally Weigl Program)

Old Time Burlesque (cello and piano)
Three Songs for Mezzo-soprano and Piano on American Poems
Three Piano Pieces for Children
Three Discourses for Flute and Cello
Songs Newly Seen in the Dusk (mezzo-soprano and piano)
Five Individual Songs on American Poems (baritone and piano)

Albert Simons Center for the Arts Recital Hall (June 2)
(An All Karl Weigl Program)

Three Songs for Mezzo-soprano and Piano (from Opus 10)
Sonata for Cello and Piano
Three Songs for Baritone and Piano (from Opus 1)
Two Pieces for Cello and Piano
Five Duets for Soprano and Baritone (with piano)

Donnell Library Center Auditorium, 20 West 53d St., New York, New York (October 3)

Keiko Abe	Frogs (solo marimba)
	Michi (solo marimba)
Elizabeth Hayden Pizer	Expressions in Time (piano)

An-Ming Wang   Four Songs from the Song of Endless
                                    Sorrow (soprano and piano)
Nancy Van de Vate   Lullaby (mezzo-soprano and piano)
                                Death (mezzo-soprano and piano)
Vally Weigl   Lyrical Suite (flute, cello, and piano)
Karl Weigl   Love Song (cello and piano)
                                Wild Dance (cello and piano)
Max Lifchitz   Yellow Ribbons #4 (solo bassoon)
Edmund Najera   Three Spanish Songs (mezzo-soprano
                                    and piano)
Vally Weigl   Three Discourses (flute and cello)
Doris Hays   Southern Voices (tape, soprano,
                                    and narrator)

CONCERT PROGRAMS—1982

Albert Simons Center for the Arts Recital Hall (May 26)

Helen Tobias-Duesbert   Sonata in G (cello and piano)
                                — Moderato
                                — Scherzo/allegretto
                                — Lento
                                — Allegro
Judith Shatin Allen   Sursum Corda (cello and piano)
Blythe Owen   Sonata Fantaisie, Opus 3 (cello and piano)

Albert Simons Center for the Arts Recital Hall (May 28)
(A program of the music of Marilyn Shrude)

Music for Soprano Saxophone and
    Piano (1974)
Invocation, Antiphons, and Psalms
    (1977) (percussion)
Solidarnosc (1982) (piano)
Drifting over a Red Place (1982—world
    premiere) (clarinet, dancer, and
    visuals)

Albert Simons Center for the Arts Recital Hall (May 29)

Nancy Van de Vate   Cradlesong (soprano and
                                    piano)
                                Youthful Age (soprano and piano)
                                Two Songs (soprano and piano)

	— Death Is the Chilly Night
	— Loneliness
Judith Lang Zaimont	Greyed Sonnets
	— Soliloquy
	— Let It Be Forgotten
Shulamit Ran	For an Actor: Monologue for Clarinet (1978) (solo clarinet)
Gayneyl Wheeler	Little Suite for Clarinet and Piano (1979)
	— Prime: "Daylight Floods the Earth with Light"
	— Sext: "And Noon with the Blazing Sun"
	— Vespers: "The Setting Sun Turns Our Gaze to Thee"
	— Matins: "The Lord Owns Earth and All Inhabitants"
Dorothy Strutt	Fine Haiku (1975) "Beyond Silver Clouds" (clarinet and piano)
Ryo Noda	Improvisation III (1974) (solo saxophone)

Albert Simons Center for the Arts Recital Hall (May 31)

Elizabeth Hayden Pizer	Expressions in Time (1975) (piano)
Manuel Enriquez	Hoy de Ayer (1981) (piano)
Karl Weigl	Fünf Lieder für eine tiefere Frauen-stimme, op. 10 (1913) (mezzo-soprano and piano)
	— Marchen
	— Jesus
	— Der Toten Mutter
	— Fremd gehich unter Fremden
	— O Nacht du Silberbleiche
Max Lifchitz	Yellow Ribbons #10 (1982—world premiere) (piano)
Miriam Gideon	The Hound of Heaven (1945) (mezzo-soprano and piano)
Bruce Saylor	Psalm Settings (flute and mezzo-soprano)
Vally Weigl	Songs from "No Boundary" (1960) (mezzo-soprano, viola, and piano)
	— Cricket Song
	— Song from the Meadow's End
	— Shell Song
	— New Born
	— April

Albert Simons Center for the Arts Recital Hall (June 1)

Nancy Van de Vate	Preludes (1978) (piano)
Augusta Cecconi-Bates	For Llya (1982) (piano)
Felicia Donceanu	Two Serenades (mezzo-soprano, flute, and piano)
	— Primavara Florentina
	— Ce-nalt e Portalul
Karl Weigl	Variations (piano)
Jean Eichelberger Ivey	Two Songs (1975) (mezzo-soprano, flute, and piano)
	— Night Voyage
	— Illiad
Ruth Crawford Seeger	Study in Mixed Accents for Piano (1932) (piano)
	Chinaman, Laundryman (mezzo-soprano and piano)
Vally Weigl	Songs from "Only the Moon Remembers" (premiere) (mezzo-soprano, oboe, clarinet, cello or bassoon)
	— Lost
	— Fog
	— I Sang to You
	— Calls
	— Sunsets

3

Chronicling Women Composers on Disc

MARNIE HALL

THE HISTORY AND PHILOSOPHY
OF LEONARDA PRODUCTIONS

In 1975 I researched, funded, and produced a two-record anthology of music by eighteen European women composers on the Gemini Hall label, which I founded that year. Leonarda Productions is an outgrowth of that endeavor. As a result of my experience with the Gemini Hall album, I decided it would be better to form a new company that would be a not-for-profit organization rather than to continue to issue records on the Gemini Hall label. Thus, Leonarda Productions came into being, and the first two Leonarda records were released in 1979.

The beginning of my interest in women composers arose from my experiences as a professional violinist. In November 1972 I founded the Vieuxtemps String Quartet. All the members of the quartet were women who were active freelance musicians in New York City; I was the second violinist in the group. During our years together, the quartet made a midwestern tour, played concerts for a number of concert series and at many colleges in the Northeast, and performed for hospitals, senior citizens' groups, weddings and receptions, and parties. We were invited to play at two women's colleges—Lesley College in Cambridge, Massachusetts, and at Russell Sage College in Troy, New York—and at Drew University in New Jersey, where our concert was sponsored by an association of women students.

A few women began asking if we played music by women. We had not, and I decided to see what was available. The first thing I did was to go through *Baker's Biographical Dictionary of Musicians* to pick out the women composers. I began my actual search for music at the Lincoln Center Library for the Performing Arts with a list of names culled from Baker's in hand. In addition, I spent several days of intense music collecting at the Library of Congress. Most of this music was older music and in the public domain. I also got music publishers' catalogs and some new music too, but I was reluctant to spend a lot of money on new music—not only because I did not know what I would be getting, but also because some of the newer music takes a great deal of rehearsal before a nonpianist such as myself can get the slightest idea of what the music sounds like. My attitude was like that of many other performers and listeners: the past interested me more than the present because of my primary affinity for music of the past. (My personal tastes lay with Bartók, Prokofieff, Beethoven, Brahms, Bach, Haydn, Mozart, Ravel, and the generally acknowledged "greats.") The research did not uncover much string music by women before the twentieth century, but I was fascinated by what I did find.

In addition to unearthing a great deal of music from several centuries, I began to learn about the obstacles women composers had faced. Most of the music I found by pre-twentieth-century women composers featured voice or piano, though there were operas, symphonies, and chamber music as well. The reason was simple: women could perform most of this music themselves. Why was this so important? It was important because women composers faced many obstacles in getting their music performed, published, and reviewed and because women were not given the same opportunities as men in the areas of education and employment. Lastly, women were not generally given the same encouragement as men. However, some women, despite the obstacles they faced, did excel as composers. Arthur Elson considered two of these women in his *Woman's Work in Music*:

Carlotta Ferrari is undoubtedly the greatest of the Italian women composers. Born at Lodi in 1837, she soon began her musical studies, completing them with the best masters of the Milan Conservatory. When she tried to enter the lists in dramatic work, she found theatre managers unwilling to give her any encouragement because of her sex. Feeling sure of her ability, however, she was brave enough to hire a theatre and produce her opera, "Ugo," at her own expense. The result justified her hopes, for the work was an entire success. Since that time she has had no trouble in dealings with the managers, who may well feel ashamed of their early fears. Her later operas, "Sofia" and "Eleonora d'Aborea," were as warmly received as her first attempt.[1]

Coming nearer to our own times, Elizabeth Stirling, who died in 1895, was considered one of the very best of English organists. . . . In 1856 she tried for a musical degree at Oxford, presenting an orchestral setting of the 130th Psalm; but, although the work won high praise, no authority existed for granting a degree to a woman.[2]

In *Music and Women* Sophie Drinker also notes some of the problems women composers encountered. Because men, for a long time, did not accept women into their ranks, women formed their own performing groups.

But women's choruses did not perform on the public stage. . . . Even in the United States, where women had so much personal liberty, a public concert by a woman's chorus in 1888 received sarcastic comment. A well-known critic wrote that were the choir composed of angels and led by St. Cecilia, it would still be musically unsatisfactory.[3]

[And] when the women's organizations [orchestras] first appeared, they were met by the critics with a conspiracy of silence. In 1896, for instance, the concerts of the Women's String Orchestra of New York were never reviewed by the press. Later, sarcasm was employed. Patronizing remarks about women's orchestras are still [1948] the rule rather than the exception. It is the reporter's favorite joke to compare women players to sirens or angels [4]

The celebrated violinist Erica Morini, in an article published in 1940, points out that until women became able to support themselves, few had control of money. Serious musical education was virtually denied them. (Morini herself was consistently refused admission to the violin department at the Vienna Conservatory, but when Ottokar Ševčik heard her play, he took her under his wing.) She comments:

Later, during the War, when I found myself in need of money to continue my lessons, I applied for a State Prize. Playing in a public competition, I was voted the award. Before I was able to collect it, however, it was pointed out that the wording of the terms of the award specified its being given "to the man who—" and for this reason the Prize Committee felt itself obliged to withhold the bestowal.[5]

The British composer Dame Ethel Smyth (1858-1944), in *Female Pipings from Eden* (1933), discusses the expense of music publishing. She states that publishers of large compositions, such as choral works, have little chance of getting back the money they must invest unless the work is a huge success. To be a success, it must be performed, and it is conductors and boards of directors who make decisions about what works are performed. Conductors and their boards are often as cautious as the music publishers, however. As Smyth observes, women frequently have not had the support of an inner group consisting of publishers, conductors, performers, music patrons, heads of colleges, university men, and so on, which is necessary to the composer.

In summary, women were historically denied the same access as men to employment in all areas of musical production. It was more difficult to get performances, to get published, and in more recent times, to get recorded. Conductors and critics were almost always men, largely interested in championing the works of composers they knew, and the same largely holds true today. Add to this the fact that women had the responsibility of bearing and rearing children, and one gets a better picture of why there have been no women Beethovens.

Today's composers—just as those of the past—need long, undivided periods of time to devote to composition. When we consider how large the average family of the past was, with all its attendant responsibilities, is it any wonder that the number of men who pursued composition vastly exceeded the number of women?

Historians, by ignoring the contributions of women, led us to believe that there were no women composers. (Indeed, arguments still persist as to whether women *can* compose!) This was, and still is, a gross misrepresentation. It is my hope that Leonarda Productions will help correct this misrepresentation by documenting the music and lives of historical women composers and by assisting living composers in getting their works known.

"Woman's Work," the Gemini Hall two-disc anthology, was the first of its kind. The music spans 300 years—from 1625 to 1925—and includes works by Francesca Caccini (ca. 1587-1640); Elisabeth Jacquet de la Guerre (ca. 1664-1729); Anna Amalie, Princess of Prussia (1723-1787); Anna Amalia, Duchess of Saxe-Weimar (1739-1807); Maria Teresia von Paradis (1759-1824); Louise Farrenc (1804-1875); Fanny Mendelssohn Hensel (1805-1847); Maria Malibran (1808-1836); Josephine Lang (1815-1880); Clara Schumann (1819-1896); Pauline Viardot-Garcia (1821-1910); Ingeborg von Bronsart (1840-1913); Elfrida Andrée (1840-1929); Louise Héritte-Viardot (1841-1918); Cécile Chaminade (1857-1944); Poldowski (Irene Wieniaska Paul) (1880-1932); Germaine Tailleferre (1892-1983); and Lili Boulanger (1893-1918).

Most of the criticism the album received was not only fair, but sympathetic. Most critics gave credit where it was due, that is, they acknowledged that such an anthology was something which had been overlooked by every other record company and was long overdue. Certain technical aspects of the album were not as well done as the subsequent recordings on the Leonarda label, but the album has sold more than 3,700 copies to date, and orders still trickle in.

It cost $16,000 to make 2,000 two-record albums, to promote them, and to sell the first 280 sets in the fall of 1975. This included performers' fees, engineering and editing, manufacturing the discs, jackets, and an accompanying booklet, postage, direct mailings, photocopying of music (which alone cost $1,000), retaining a public relations firm, and so on. Where did I get $16,000? I invested my savings from a 1971-1972 nine-month road tour with a Broadway musical and with that investment, I formed Gemini Hall Records.

Of course, I thought the Gemini Hall album would be a financial success. At that time I knew nothing of record sales statistics. I was, after all, a violinist and somewhat of a speculator at heart. But at the same time I was looking beyond financial reward because I felt I had discovered something that was important to do, and I was happy it was something I could do, something which would utilize my particular talents. I must admit now that I was very naive about the record industry and classical sales. But I do not regret my venture in the least, for I seem to have found my niche, even if it has not paid off financially at this point. Because so much was spent on

Figure 3.1 Marnie Hall. Photograph by Sandra Padernacht

direct mailings, among other things, I lost most of the money invested in ''Woman's Work''; in 1977 I stopped promoting the album.

According to a 1979 survey by the Recording Industries Association of America, the average classical record must sell 17,000 units to make back the original investment, and only 6 percent of classical records sell 17,000 units over a four-or five year recoupment period.

Thus, most, if not all, of the major record companies' classical records are subsidized by their popular records. Many classical releases are licensed from around the world to be sold in the United States, which means that a U.S. company does not incur the expense of making the tape and starting from scratch, but instead pays royalties to a foreign owner for the use of the tapes, metal parts, color separations for album covers, and so on. Thus, although an American company may release quite a few records annually (which usually includes a number of reissues announced as new releases), few of these releases are current American recordings. And most of the new recordings, unfortunately, are recordings from the standard repertoire. Profit-oriented companies, by and large, look for prestige from their classical releases. They would rather record a superstar performing classical ''favorites'' than promote unknown music, however meritorious.

I decided to form Leonarda, a new company that would be nonprofit and tax-exempt, because I realized that any venture of this kind would never earn a real profit. At that time, I knew of three record companies that were not-for-profit, so at least there was a precedent. Although public funding of recordings is still a new concept to most corporations, foundations, and individuals, recordings are gradually gaining support. The National Endowment for the Arts instituted a recording category in 1980, and The New York State Council on the Arts began funding recordings in 1979.

As a tax-exempt organization, Leonarda would not be allowed to compete with commercial record companies that pay taxes. Therefore, the company would try not to duplicate the recordings of commercial companies, but would instead focus on women composers, both past and present, and on twentieth-century music by both men and women. Leonarda mostly issues premiere recordings, although occasionally we record works that have been released in other countries and works that have been deleted from existing catalogs. At the time we applied for tax exemption, we also stated that we would occasionally record music by historical male composers and pair them with their female contemporaries. In the event that Leonarda ever makes money, it will be funneled into new projects, and I will hopefully be appointed by the board to a salaried position in the organization.

I had already done an anthology. With Leonarda I wanted to do more in-depth recording, to explore composers more fully by doing many longer and larger works. My experience with Leonarda to date illustrates that, although feminists, schools, and libraries are much more interested in anthologies than in records featuring one or just a few composers, Leonarda records sell better in stores than the Gemini Hall album did. One reason is that stores prefer records from companies with sizable catalogs; they don't want the trouble of ordering a single issue, which most likely won't sell. Leonarda's best outlets have been distributors who sell mainly to retail stores.

Leonarda does not record women composers exclusively. It continues to surprise me, however, that many people continue to associate me only with women's music on the basis of the Gemini Hall album. And how surprised many people are to discover that I don't specialize in women *performers*! Leonarda records appeal to many different groups of people. I do consider the tastes of feminists, historians, performers of various instruments, people who like music from certain eras, and so on, when planning records. I try to zero in on one or more markets for every disc, since I want each record to find its appropriate audience.

I personally have some misgivings about segregating women's music. I think all-women records are fine, but I don't want Leonarda to make only all-women records. There is hostility on the part of some people, both men and women, toward women's music; even more common is the general belief that "if it is by a woman, it must not be very good." These attitudes seem to affect the thinking of even the most well-meaning people (including women). Then too, if we record only women's music, many people will assume the music is second-rate because we were not free to choose from all music.

I want to gain a wide audience for Leonarda records; and I expect to gain this audience for both the company and for women's music by not recording women's music exclusively. My goal has never been to isolate women's music, but to bring it to the attention of both men and women—to make it available to as many people as I can. I suppose that above all, as a musician, I consider that it is the music that counts most, not the sex of the composer.

Although I am most committed to unearthing the musical history of women, I know how difficult it is for men and women writing music today to get their music performed, published, and recorded. They have extensive copying and duplicating costs for the preparation of scores, and many do not show even a small profit from composing. All composers need assistance in getting recorded. Often a composer cannot obtain even a performance tape of his or her work because the musicians have not been paid recording scale (which in the U.S. is well in excess of $100 per player for 15 to 45 minutes of music, depending on whether it is a commercial, symphonic, or chamber music session) in addition to the fee for the concert and rehearsals.

Composers should also be aware that many record companies prefer to supervise the entire recording process themselves and are accustomed to working with their own engineers and recording spaces. (Trying to piece together existing master tapes made by various engineers can present technical problems, and most surely will result in unmatched recorded sound.) Often too, a record company will make the decision as to which works should be paired on a disc. For these reasons, I would discourage composers and performers from submitting copies of edited master tapes to record companies for consideration, although they should be encouraged to record performances of their music, for such tapes can be sent to publishers, record companies, conductors, and so on, as demos.

Chamber and solo recordings of concert music are usually made in concert halls and churches (a high ceiling is a must) because by recording in two-track stereo in a live acoustical setting, the best sound can be obtained, and it is not necessary to add echo or to do a mix-down.

After a tape is made and edited, it is mastered. This is the process in which the recorded sound is impressed in the grooves of the lacquer; the master lacquer is then immediately electroplated. When one expects to repress records, it is best to do what is called the three-step process in order to avoid mastering a second time. The three steps are: father (a negative), mother (a positive), and stamper (a negative). Leonarda also orders safety mothers. The father cannot be used again, but a mother can make about 50 stampers, which each can press about one thousand records. Stampers may be reordered as needed for additional pressings. Today's cost for mastering, plating (the three-step process with safety mothers), and pressing one thousand discs is approximately $1,250. Recording costs vary considerably, and editing costs vary even more because some records take ten hours to edit, while others may take one hundred hours. At Leonarda we have the luxury of spending whatever time is needed on editing, since I do it myself.

Our manufacturing costs for a record jacket and text insert usually run between $450 and $900, exclusive of design, typesetting, and art work.

A number of independent record companies are vanity presses. I know of one company that charges $2,500 and requires a master tape, or $3,400 plus any performers' fees, if they make the tape. Some companies charge considerably more. The sad truth is that sales from recordings of concert music do not generate enough income for record companies to sustain themselves financially.

Leonarda has no set policy regarding the funding of recordings. At times Leonarda has put forth all the monies needed with the help of grants and my personal loans; now that Leonarda is an established recording company, however, I am gradually withdrawing my personal support.

We continue to receive more and more funding from the artists themselves. The financial support from artists—either composers, performers, or both—is a source of support we cannot do without because recordings are such low priorities with most foundations and corporations, and government grants to record companies tend to be much less than those given to many other types of arts organizations. Funds from universities are another source of support, and these are sometimes available to a university chorus or other ensemble, faculty composers, performers, and/or music historians.

When Leonarda first started, I solicited tapes from composers and received more than I could handle, although all were eventually heard and returned. An occasional work has been selected this way, although one difficulty of this procedure lies in pairing up the music for a recording. For example, if I discover a string quartet I want to record, I look for another string quartet to be its mate; in my opinion, pairing two quartets by different composers is better than combining works for different instrumentations by the same composer, unless that composer is already quite well known. Even if the composer is well known, I prefer to pair his or her work with the music of a lesser-known composer in order for that person's music to be heard. After all, the composer may not be known just because his or her music has not been heard.

It is usually easier to deal with a performing group, which has the potential to present a variety of pieces, than to deal with a composer who is looking for an entire disc of his or her music, no matter what the music is scored for. I think composers should think in terms of being recorded along with other composers on the same disc. If a composer were to present me with works by several composers for the same instrumentation, and the works and styles complemented one another, it might make the music selection an easier matter.

While I do accept tapes (return postage is very important), I am usually very slow in listening to them, and I hate to write rejection letters. I know that composers and performers are aware that a very small number of works submitted for consideration to any record company is accepted, but this doesn't make it any easier for them or for me. How much better it is to discover a composer's music on the radio or at a concert and to be able to approach that composer about a recording! Also, I cannot deny the importance of "the grapevine." A casual endorsement by someone in the field will frequently lead me to make a special effort to hear another person's music.

Recordings of historical works by women composers have more often been generated by Leonarda itself, rather than by the performer. As a result of the records I have produced, I have met and corresponded with many musicologists with a special interest in historical music by women, and my musical library and Leonarda's has consequently expanded to include many rare items from which to choose. For instance, I offered Leonarda's library of vocal music by Clara Schumann, Fanny Mendelssohn Hensel, Josephine Lang, and Pauline Viardot-Garcia to the two singers featured on the lieder record (LPI 107), and they, along with their accompanist, made the choices for the record.

Back in 1975, I must confess that my attitude was that "if it is contemporary music, it is probably not worthwhile." That was before Leonarda was formed and before I knew the music of the contemporary composers that Leonarda has recorded since that time (or for that matter,

Figure 3.2 *Lieder* album cover art

before I had even heard of nearly all the composers themselves). It was before I knew of many fine works that we may yet record, or may never record. Above all, it was before I knew that composers were writing in so many different styles.

At first I had thought Leonarda's music selection would be made by a distinguished panel. But as I found myself spending more and more of my own money and time to establish Leonarda and to produce recordings, I decided that I would only record music that interested *me*. The logic of this decision became more apparent as time went on.

Several years ago I was a member of a committee that was formed to select music for a radio series. Most of the other members were composers. I began to realize then—and am fully convinced now—that music is a very subjective thing. Composers whose music I respected could not themselves agree on the merits of many pieces. There seemed to be little in the way of "right" and "wrong." I was fascinated that composers were so concerned with structure and that they could often determine before I could what pieces might "wear well." But if I am not as aware of musical structure, I am highly aware of what the music does for me emotionally, and in the end I decided that I was just as qualified to judge music as they were.

I believe there are often vast differences between the listening tastes of critics, composers, performers, and nonmusicians, particularly when it comes to contemporary music. Critics hear so much (at least some of them do), that very often they pan anything bearing the least resemblance to a style they have heard before. It seems to me that a search for novelty is a part of the problem—as novelty is praised for its own sake, more composers fashion their works accordingly. Never before has such an emphasis been placed on being different just for the sake of being different. Earlier styles are, by this definition, unpopular: we hear of "worn-out Expressionism" and the like. Although a critic may have "heard it all before," much of the public has not—and neither have many performers.

With only 3 to 5 percent of the listening public interested in concert music in the first place, I do not wish to splinter this small group further, but I do want to get that 3 to 5 percent to listen to contemporary and women's music in addition to the standard repertoire. I am every bit as hard to convince as the general audience when it comes to new music and new composers; although I am not a "distinguished panel," my tastes have been developed through education and experience as a professional musician, and they are in general agreement with the music-listening public regarding great composers of the past. If I find music that convinces *me*, maybe I will be able to convince the public, which follows its own taste. I believe that the listening public wants to be moved by music and that it is perceptibly less preoccupied with structure, new forms, the most originality, various schools of thought, and so on, than are many composers, critics, and grant-givers. If I produce music that affects me personally, that says something to me, perhaps others will buy Leonarda's records, will explore women's history and women's music, and will integrate contemporary music into their listening habits.

I applaud the many independent record companies and publishing houses as well as the various foundations, corporations, and state and federal agencies that promote contemporary and other little-known music. The more music that is recorded and published, the more diversity we will have, and this diversity is what will assure us that more voices will be heard. Future generations may determine what music will last, but chances are that music that is not recorded and published in this generation will not survive to the next, no matter how good it is.

NOTES

1. Arthur Elson, *Woman's Work in Music* (Boston: L. C. Page & Co., 1903; Third Impression, Colonial Press, 1908), pp. 212-13.

2. Ibid., pp. 133-34.

3. Sophie Drinker, *Music and Women* (New York: Coward-McCann, 1948), p. 256.

4. Ibid., pp. 239-40.

5. Erica Morini, "Women as Musicians," *Who Is Who in Music* (Chicago: Lee Stern Press, 1940), pp. 576-77.

Figure 3.3 Leonarda Productions logo

RECORDINGS OF LEONARDA PRODUCTIONS, INC.

A catalog may be obtained by writing Leonarda Productions, P.O. Box 124, Radio City Station, New York, NY   10101-0124.

Living Composers—Women

Aderholdt, Sarah. *String Quartet* (8:53). LPI 111.

*Garwood, Margaret. *Japanese Songs* (5:00), soprano, clarinet, piano. LPI 119.

Hoover, Katherine. *Sinfonia* (10:54), four bassoons. LPI 102.

    Trio (18:04), piano, violin, and cello. LPI 103.

    Princess Isabelle (3:04), flute and piano. LP 104.

    Divertimento (11:39), flute, violin, viola, and cello. LPI 105.

Rainier, Priaulx. *Quartet for Strings* (17:57). LPI 117.

Schonthal, Ruth. *Totengesänge* (23:35), soprano and piano. LPI 106.

    String Quartet (13:22). LPI 111.

Tailleferre, Germaine. *Pastorale* (2:38), flute and piano. LPI 104.

Ulehla, Ludmila. *Elegy for a Whale* (10:36), flute, piano, cello, and taped whales. LPI 104.

Zaimont, Judith Lang. *A Calendar Set* (26:38), solo piano. LPI 101.

    Nocturne (7:07), solo piano. LPI 101.

    Chansons Nobles et Sentimentales (12:50), tenor and piano. LPI 101.

    Two Songs for Soprano and Harp (10:04). LPI 106.

    The Magic World (25:30), baritone voice, percussion, and piano. LPI 116.

Zwilich, Ellen Taaffe. *Einsame Nacht* (song cycle) (11:00), baritone voice and piano. LPI 120.

Living Composers—Men

Brehm, Alvin. *Colloquy and Chorale* (6:53), four bassoons. LPI 102.

*Freeman, John. *Elizabethan Love Songs* (4:30), soprano, clarinet, and piano. LPI 119.

*Hoiby, Lee. Selected songs (18:00), baritone, soprano, and piano. LPI 120.

*Hovhaness, Alan. *O Lady Moon,* op. 139 (4:30), soprano, clarinet, and piano. LPI 119.

Husa, Karel. *String Quartet No. 1* (23:02). LPI 117.

*Lane, Richard. *Elegy* (4:30), soprano, clarinet, and piano. LPI 119.

*Mayer, William. *Enter Ariel* (14:00), soprano, clarinet, and piano. LPI 119.

Nelhybel, Vaclav. *Concert Etudes for Four Bassoons* (10:29). LPI 102.

Palmer, Rudolph. *Contrasts for Four Bassoons* (13:11). LPI 102.

Rorem, Ned. *Last Poems of Wallace Stevens* (24:08), soprano, cello, and piano. LPI 116.

Schickele, Peter. *Last Tango in Bayreuth* (2:24), four bassoons. LPI 102.

Souster, Tim. *Sonata* (31:48), cello, piano, seven wind instruments, and percussion. LPI 114.

    Driftwood Cortege (7:09), computer generated. LPI 114.

Historical Composers—Women

Beach, Mrs. H.H.A. (Amy Beach) (1867-1944). *Theme and Variations,* op. 80 (20:57), flute and string quartet. LPI 105.

    Quartet for Strings, op. 89 (14:43). LPI 111.

*Projected release.

Boulanger, Lili (1893-1918). *Nocturne* (2:29), flute and piano. LPI 104.
   D'un Matin de Printemps (4:46), flute and piano. LPI 104.
   Clairières dans le Ciel (33:35) (song cycle), soprano and piano. LPI 118.
Clarke, Rebecca (1886-1979). *Trio* (22:30), piano, violin, and cello. LPI 103.
   *Selected songs (24:00), baritone, soprano, and piano. LPI 120.
Farrenc, Louise (1804-1875). *Trio in E Minor*, op. 45 (22:59), piano, flute, and
   cello. LPI 104.
   Nonetto, op. 38 (24:08), violin, viola, cello, double bass, flute, oboe, clarinet,
   bassoon, and horn. LPI 110.
Hildegarde von Bingen (1098-1179). *Kyrie* (3:44), women's choir. LPI 115.
LaGuerre, Elisabeth Jacquet de (c. 1664-1729). *Samson* (14:44) (cantata), voice,
   unison strings, bassoon, and continuo. LPI 109.
   Le Sommeil d'Ulisse (15:13) (cantata), voice, strings, flute, and continuo. LPI 109.
Lang, Josephine (1815-1880). "Wie, wenn die Sonn' aufgeht," "Der Winter,"
   "Frühzeitiger Frühling," "Wie glänzt so hell dein Auge," "O sehntest du dich
   so nach mir" (11:46), voice and piano, LPI 107.
Leonarda, Isabella (1620-1704). *Messa Prima, op.* 18 (41:36), choir, two violins, and
   continuo. LPI 115.
Mahler, Alma (1879-1964). *Vier Lieder* ("Licht in der Nacht," "Waldseligkeit,"
   "Ansturm," "Erntelied") (14:26), mezzo and piano. LPI 118.
Mendelssohn Hensel, Fanny (1805-1847). "Die Nonne," "Im Herbste," "Du bist
   die Ruhe," "Vorwurf," "Nachwanderer," "Rosenkranz" (13:37), voice and
   piano. LPI 107.
   Sechs Lieder, op. 1 (15:20), tenor and piano. LPI 112.
Reichardt, Louise (1779-1826). *Tre Canzoni* ("Giusto amor," "Notturno," "Vanne
   felice rio"); "Die Blume der Blumen," "Hier liegt ein Spielmann begraben,"
   "Betteley der Vögel," "Bergmannslied," "Heimweh," "Duettino" (19:44),
   tenor and piano. LPI 112.
Schumann, Clara (1819-1896). "Warum willst du And're fragen," "Er ist gekommen
   in Sturm and Regen," "Liebst du um Schönheit," "Ich stand in dunklen
   Träumen," "Was weinst du, Blümlein," "Die stille Lotosblume," "Das ist ein
   Tag, der klingen mag" (15:45), mezzo and piano. LPI 107.
Vellère, Lucie (1896-1966). *String Quartet No. 3* (16:30), LPI 111.
Viardot-Garcia, Pauline (1821-1910). "Des Nachts," "Das Vöglein," "Die Besch-
   wörung" (7:35), baritone voice and piano. LPI 107.

Historical Composers—Men

Bartók, Béla (1881-1945). *Quintet for Piano and Strings* (43:51). LPI 108.
Courbois, Philippe (fl. 1710). *Dom Quichotte* (15:37) (cantata), voice, strings, oboe,
   trumpet, bassoon, and continuo. LPI 109.
Foote, Arthur (1853-1937). *A Night Piece* (7:57), flute and string quartet. LPI 105.
*Paer, Ferinando (1771-1839). *Beatus Vir* (9:00), soprano, clarinet, and piano.
   LPI 119.

*Projected release.

Reger, Max (1873-1916). *Piano Concerto in F Minor*, op. 114 (38:58). LPI 113.

Rheinberger, Josef (1839-1901). *Nonet,* op. 139 (32:40), violin, viola, cello, double bass, flute, oboe, clarinet, bassoon, and horn. LPI 110.

Schubert, Franz (1797-1828). *Die schöne Müllerin* (67:04), tenor and piano. LPI 112.

Weill, Kurt (1900-1959). *Frauentanz* (11:36), soprano, flute, clarinet, viola, bassoon, and horn. LPI 106.

4

Women Composers' Upbeat: Arsis Press

CLARA LYLE BOONE

Arsis Press, affiliated with Broadcast Music, Inc., publishes serious contemporary music by women composers. The company began as a small operation in July 1974; by 1982 it was publishing the music of thirteen women composers, and it continues to add new composers each year. Recognizing that a good composer may come from anywhere, we currently publish composers from nine states and the District of Columbia, distributed from Hawaii to Massachusetts. We publish music of any style that is acceptable for concert performance. Our one criterion is that a composition must express artistic wholeness. Arsis Press is a standard publishing firm paying double the usual royalties plus providing one hundred printed copies for the composer's own use. All costs are borne by Arsis Press. We market through out-of-state direct sales, through retail music stores in the United States and abroad, and through wholesale distributors.

As its founder, I have brought certain skills to Arsis Press. My basic music training has been in piano and voice. I majored in piano and theory at Centre College of Kentucky and performed my own piano composition at my senior recital. My theory professor, Samuel Siurua, a native of Finland, first oriented my thinking toward composition. I later studied composition at Harvard with Walter Piston, who greatly expanded my sense of the possibilities in musical expression. Wherever I happened to be—as a teacher "learning" the country—I composed.

Darius Milhaud helped me particularly to believe in myself. At least, I had truly found my individual voice by the time that I came under his influence at the Aspen Music School. I am fond of graceful contrapuntal lines, which I call my "wind-in-the-pine-trees" style. I expect my music to "speak"—if it does not, into the wastebasket it goes.

My inner compulsion is not necessarily to write great quantities of new music myself: rather, I have sworn to create new avenues of expression for the many women who have something essential to share with the world. On the basis of their particular need, I founded Arsis Press for women only;

however, I do see it expanding to include male composers, particularly of liturgical music, for we haven't been able to attract enough music of significant quality in this area from women alone.

My teaching career, which provided the funds to finance Arsis Press, began at a small midwestern college. My career as a composer almost ended there after the department head informed me that *he* was the one who wrote music. The academic pecking order was clarified further with the president's far from casual remark, "No idea is a good idea unless I have it."

After teaching in Kentucky, Michigan, and New York, I arrived in Washington, D.C., in 1957. My company-to-be had already been named Arsis Press for *Arsis*, my first composition, and I had decided to use the original French spelling of my family name, Lyle de Bohun, as a pen name to conceal my sex. I already knew music publishing and the entire music industry to be male-dominated, and I intended to cushion my entrance into that world as discreetly as possible. The Italian word *arsis*, meaning "upbeat," expressed the optimism of my commitment to women composers, and my own music in manuscript provided me with the means to acquire working experience in publishing without making all my mistakes on other women's music. To this end, Arsis Press issued its first publication—music by Lyle de Bohun—in July 1974, during my summer recess from teaching fifth grade in Washington, D.C.

By this time, I already had a substantial amount of trade experience, dating back to 1954, when I had served as a G. Schirmer representative at a Music Educator's National Conference in Boston. Looking back, I realize that sharing dinner with publishers who enjoyed the exchange of ideas was a marvelous education without tuition. Unfortunately, none of them ever took me seriously enough as a composer even to look at my music, but I made them content enough by being an appreciative and sympathetic listener. I already was certain of my intention to enter music publishing on my own, but I confided in no one.

Not personally knowing any women composers, I began with faith: "Because I am, there must be more out there like me." The comparative obscurity of women composers and the scarcity of their music in retail stores and libraries became our company's strong argument for promoting special collections. A customer needs to be able to find in one location samples of a store's entire listing of women's concert music. We offered a 50 percent discount on these collections, and the first one was started at the Joseph Patelson Music House in New York City in July 1979. Some stores bought our complete catalog to open a collection and then added music from additional publishers. Unfortunately, I have found that male music clerks are not always aware of the existence of any such collection, while a female employee can lead one straight to it. Many women have reported experiences similar to mine. Most difficult for our budget is the retail music stores' fairly standard practice of selling reference copies and never reordering unless a customer makes a specific request. Our music has to be seen to be bought. Concert music by women composers constantly circulates through the mail in manuscript copies because it is often difficult to lay hands on a suitable composition either in a library or in a store.

In the beginning information spread mostly by word-of-mouth. Ruth Lomon found some Arsis Press music in Boston music stores and sent her manuscripts to the company for possible publication. We published her *Soundings* for piano duet and *Dust Devils* for solo harp in 1976. She passed the word to Elizabeth Vercoe, and we took three of her scores. We are still publishing the music of these two talented composers.

After an announcement about Arsis Press appeared in an issue of the *International League of Women Composers Newsletter* in December 1977, the company never lacked for music to review for possible publication. Arsis welcomes advice about manuscript choices for publication from anyone who feels experienced enough to offer it. Final decisions are mine alone, as I am the one who must keep the budget in the black.

Figure 4.1 Arsis Press logo

The company's continuity has been assured by the savings I accumulated during a full career of teaching until my retirement from the classroom in 1977. As the publishing affiliate of the International League of Women Composers, Arsis Press is also eligible to receive tax-deductible contributions through the League to promote the music of women composers.

Having joined the Music Publishers' Association of the United States in 1975, I received warmly extended practical suggestions from officers and committee chairmen. My experience as a lobbyist in Washington, dating from 1956, made me feel that I could give as well as receive, and that attitude has allowed me to be my feminine self in the essentially male preserve of music publishing.

In 1976 Arsis Press had entries in three categories of the Paul Revere competitions in graphic excellence, sponsored by the Music Publishers' Association. (The competitions are held in conjunction with the association's annual meeting in New York in June.) We received three awards in the bicentennial year, more than any other company. *Mirrored Love* took first prize for quarto sheet music, *Thou Shalt Light My Lamp* won third prize for octavo sheet music, and *Songs of Estrangement* won third prize for orchestrations. This was a great encouragement, for during that entire year we had no income from sales. (One music dealer had placed an order, but no payments had come in. It was no surprise to us, but the Internal Revenue Service was suspicious, and why not? However, I detected a growing sensitivity to our circumstances in the IRS review process, and we were assured that we could continue to file returns as a business enterprise.)

As I look back on all the obstacles that only increased my determination to start a music publishing company in the first place, I must feel at the same time ultimately blessed because only the kindest and gentlest pople have been my associates in the day-to-day operation of the business.

When I was teaching in Michigan, a small Detroit firm published one of my piano compositions. The engraver was Carl Nulsen of Fort Thomas, Kentucky, where I had graduated from high school. When I was ready to organize Arsis Press, I asked him to recommend a firm for engraving and printing. He had already retired and readily named the Otto Zimmerman & Son Company, which has printed all our music. Ernest S. Zimmerman, executive vice-president, has personally supervised the processing of every publication.

Arsis Press covers, which have generated much comment, are the result of both persistent research and blessed happenstance. As an example of the latter, I will mention the afternoon I stood on the sidewalk admiring an unusual shade of impatiens growing in a neighbor's garden. The basement tenant, a total stranger, stepped outside at that moment and was soon offering me seeds and an invitation to come inside for a cup of tea. My acceptance meant that I was promptly face to face with her wall collection of photographs. The cover photograph for the choral composition *Thou Shalt Light My Lamp* was discovered on that basement wall, and I left, not just with impatiens seeds, but with the address of the photographer in Montana. His picture, graciously released to us, helped to account for one of the Paul Revere Awards.

Although Arsis Press is a sole proprietorship, it can accurately be labeled a "neighborhood bicycle circuit." Within the neighborhood east of the Capitol, known as Capitol Hill, are our cover designer, catalog and stationery printer, our bank, our two photographers, typesetter, and a post office.

John and Claudette Best have a print shop on Pennsylvania Avenue, and they have placed an indelible mark on Arsis Press. After reproduction fees are paid to museums and artists for the original art work, Claudette designs the covers for our publications. She is the company's exclusive designer, and her husband continues to be an invaluable adviser. His cover negatives were used for all three of our award-winning publications.

The major portion of the company's original budget was needed to create a catalog and find sales outlets for the music. The fact that we were publishing works that would be lasting contributions to the concert repertoire attracted valuable friends.

Through a good friend in the Music Division of the Library of Congress, I was introduced to Jane Van der Sluys, founder of C. T. Wagner Music Publishing Company, who reprints music of colonial America. Jane typeset an updated catalog for us, combined our mailing list with hers, and distributed 7,000 copies of our catalog along with hers.

SUITE FOR SOLO VIOLIN

BIRD I
by Daniel Ruben Wynn

by Nancy Van de Vate

Figure 4.2 Cover art from Sisra Publications (Arsis Press ASCAP affiliate)

Although our sales have increased each year, we did not sign a contract with an exclusive distributor until the fall of 1981. Plymouth Music Company, with offices in Florida, is now the exclusive distributor for Arsis Press. We have a unique arrangement, which provides computer services and an excellent promotional staff. When retail music dealers can order through a wholesale distributor, they save on shipping and order processing costs. At the same time, publishers acquire personalized representation over an extended geographical area, which they could not otherwise afford.

Basically, Arsis Press is dealing with the natural ignorance and indifference of a buying public that goes to concerts and to church without hearing any music by women composers. Generally, the public has concluded there aren't any women composers whose works merit performance. As we screen manuscripts, we have become aware that the best composers quite often are not the best promoters of their work. Some music is being presented by women composers that does nothing to enhance the reputation of women, while at the other extreme are women who have exquisite compositions but had done nothing about their music until it came to the attention of Arsis Press. In my own lifetime I hope to see women achieve a renewed faith in themselves through the creative success of their sisters. Any notable commercial success for my company is truly beyond my wildest dreams, but I do dream that one day women will think female, buy female, and perform female until the standard publishing firms can afford to do no less than give the woman composer her due. At that time, Arsis Press would then be appropriately out of business.

Women have much to say through music that the world needs to hear and that men cannot say for them. Arsis Press will continue to seek this music and encourage its creation. Consequently, we go beyond the usual rejection slip and try to provide constructive evaluation and practical advice. Sometimes a composer discovers that she can write better than she thought she could, and through our guidance and suggestions a promising score becomes a published score.

ARSIS PRESS CATALOGUE

Instrumental and Vocal Chamber Music

de Bohun, Lyle. *The Americas Trio for Flute, Clarinet and Bassoon* (4:30).
  Songs of Estrangement, for string quartet and soprano voice, score and parts (6:45).
  Art Songs (piano accompaniment unless otherwise indicated): "Beyond the Stars," "Celestia," "Fantasia," "Goodnight Kiss," "Lovely Heart," "Mirrored Love," "Sea Thoughts," "Sonnet," "Time Cannot Claim This Hour," "When Songs Have All Been Sung," "Winter Song," "Slumber Song" with melody instrument (ca. 2:30-5:30 each).

Bolz, Harriett. *Capitol Pageant*, for piano duet (4:00).
  Episode for Organ—Autumn Joy (3:00).
  Floret—A Mood Caprice for Piano (3:42).
  Narrative Impromptu for Harp (5:30).
  Two Profiles for Piano (3:30).
Brockman, Jane. *Tell-Tale Fantasy*, for piano (4:43).
Diemer, Emma Lou. *Toccata for Piano* (6:40).
Donahue, Bertha Terry. *The Castle Yonder,* a cycle of songs for soprano with
    piano accompaniment (7:30).
Frasier, Jane. *Festivous Sonata for Piano* (14:30).
Lomon, Ruth. *Dust Devils for Solo Harp* (7:40).
  Five Ceremonial Masks, for piano solo (14:40).
  Five Songs After Poems by William Blake, for contralto and viola (6:00).
  Soundings, for piano duet (6:50).
Van de Vate, Nancy. *Six Etudes for Solo Viola* (7:45).
  Suite for Solo Violin (9:00).
  Trio for Strings (14:40).
Vercoe, Elizabeth. *Balance—Duo for Violin and Cello,* score only (19:20).
  Fantasy for Piano (10:00).
  Herstory II, thirteen Japanese lyrics for soprano, piano, and percussion (20:00).
  Three Studies for Piano (3:00).
Walker, Gwyneth. *Sonata for Flute and Piano* (12:00).
Weigl, Vally. *Dear Earth—a Quintet of Poems for French Horn, Violin, Cello,
    and Piano with Medium Voice* (15:30).

Sacred Choral Music

de Bohun, Lyle. *Alleluia*, SATB a cappella.
  Meditation, SATB a cappella.
  Thou Shalt Light My Lamp, SSATB a cappella.
Bolz, Harriett. *How Shall We Speak?* SATB with keyboard.
  Sweet Jesus, SAB with keyboard.
Callaway, Ann. *Agnus Dei I*, SSATB a cappella with soprano solo.

5

Grażyna Bacewicz: Evolution of a Composer

During the past decade of renewed interest in women composers, several recurring questions confront the serious scholar: "Why have there been no great women composers?" or "Who are the great woman composers?" or "Can a woman be a great composer?" One answer comes from a composer herself. Grażyna Bacewicz wrote the following:

Nature has bestowed on me a certain talent and also a little something that enables me to use this talent. Deep inside I possess a minuscule, invisible motor that allows me to accomplish a task in ten minutes that would take others an hour or more. Thanks to it I run, not walk; I speak fast; even my pulse beats faster than normal, and I was born two months premature. I have no patience for slow and phlegmatic people. I was born for action, not for empty talk, so I hate any sort of meeting with those never-ending speeches which try to dazzle with their eloquence. I have always hated any sort of interview with the same questions repeated by some silly journalists. Questions like: "Can a woman be a composer?" "Can a woman be a real full-blooded composer?" "Should a woman composer get married?" "Should a woman composer have children?" I used to run away from them, but privately I will tell you: a woman blessed with musical talent *can* be a serious composer. She can get married, have children, and concertize extensively all over the world. There is only one little essential needed—she must have that little motor ticking away. Without it, she'd better not bother at all![1]

Grażyna Bacewicz was slight of stature and rather fragile in appearance, but her energetic pace resulted in a large compositional output: over two hundred compositions, including four symphonies, seven violin concertos, seven string quartets, five sonatas for violin and piano, concertos for piano, two pianos, viola, and cello, plus numerous works for chamber orchestra and for symphony orchestra. Her compositional life started when she was thirteen in Łódź, Poland, and only ended at her premature death (she was not quite 60) in 1969.[2]

Previous attempts to place her creative output into a variety of often arbitrary divisions have not been successful because hers was a slow and subtle evolutionary process. There was a consistency and unity in her life's work that is best comprehended by following the internal and external events surrounding her life in the order in which she experienced them.

To place her in proper perspective as an outstanding twentieth century composer, it is necessary to examine the social, cultural, and even political environment in which she worked as well as the influences which helped shape her musical language.

Born on February 5, 1909, to a musically oriented and close-knit family, Bacewicz was encouraged from a very early age to study music; her father was her first teacher.[3] She had an immediate affinity for the violin and played chamber music at home with her two older brothers, Kiejstut and Witold. Grażyna was especially close to Kiejstut. She followed him to Warsaw after she had graduated from high school in Łódź and later, as a concert violinist, she premiered many of her own sonatas with Kiejstut at the piano.

At the Conservatory in Warsaw she studied violin and piano as a step toward fulfilling her childhood proclamation that she would be a composer. Her very first compositions were a piano prelude and some miniatures for violin and piano.

A major influence in Bacewicz's life, one shared with other young Polish composers, was meeting Karol Szymanowski (1882-1937) at the Conservatory. Whereas in the past Poles sought the culture and musicality of Germany (as did Szymanowski, himself), his own travels and exploration into other European cultures—especially the time he spent in Paris—made him a proponent of a French musical education. His direction of the Conservatory students led Bacewicz and others to the Ecole Normale de Musique and Nadia Boulanger. (Bacewicz's Paris studies were made possible by a scholarship from Ignacy Paderewski [1860-1941], the Polish virtuoso and composer.)

She graduated summa cum laude in 1932, having studied violin with Joseph Jarzebski and composition with Kazimierz Sikorski (b. 1895). For her graduation examinations, she composed works for large and small ensembles, which were presented at a special concert at the Conservatory.

In Paris during 1932 and 1933, she studied the violin with André Touret and composition with Nadia Boulanger. The *Wind Quintet* of 1932, a model of neoclassicism, was her first composition to win a prize—first place in a competition for young composers.[4]

She left Paris to concertize as a violinist in Spain and Majorca but returned at the end of 1934 to study with Carl Flesch, the distinguished violinist. She found him to be a stern, but exacting, teacher. During the time she studied with Flesch, she composed the *Partita for Violin and Piano* (1934). It was first performed upon her return to Warsaw in 1935 and met with critical success:

This composer has no need for sensational effects and is to be commended on the beauty and seriousness of the work. There is a sense of youth in the composition while simultaneously there is a high degree of maturity. The musical impressions will overwhelm you and the musical thoughts will absorb you. She has a lot to say, and she already knows how to say it well.[5]

Bacewicz appeared to have found in neoclassicism a basic style and creative aesthetic that suited her musical temperament. From the *Wind Quintet* through the *Overture* of 1943, she clarified and expanded these stylistic affinities while perfecting her craft. For example, her 1935 *Trio* for oboe, violin, and cello (which received a prize from the Young Composer's Competition) is reminiscent of the earlier *Wind Quintet* but contains more interesting complex polyphonic textures.

In 1936 the most gifted young instrumentalists were invited to join the Polish Radio Orchestra in an effort to upgrade it to the level of the Warsaw Philharmonic. Bacewicz accepted the position of principal violinist and toured with this orchestra for two years. This not only sharpened her orchestration skills but provided the opportunity for performances of several of her own orchestral works.

The *String Quartet no. 1* was one of six compositions written in 1938—an indication of the speed with which she worked.

I think to compose one has to work very intensely. One has to pause between composing different works, but interruptions shouldn't be made when you are in the middle of writing a piece. I'm capable of working on one composition for many hours daily. Usually I take a break in the middle of the day but even during the break my brain keeps on working. I like to get very, very tired. It's sometimes then that I suddenly get my best ideas.[6]

The same year that Bacewicz joined the orchestra, she married Andrzej Biernacki, a physician and amateur pianist. (Their only child, Alina, born in 1942, now lives in Warsaw and is an accomplished sculptor.)

In the spring of 1939, Bacewicz returned to her adored Paris to supervise a special evening of her own works, which took place at the Ecole Normale de Musique. She returned to Warsaw just two months before the start of the war.

As they did for millions of Europeans, the war years of 1939-1945 proved difficult for Grażyna Bacewicz and her family. The musical life of Poland was greatly curtailed, but concerts were given, often in private homes or coffee houses. Despite the vicissitudes of these years (including the nursing of her wounded sister and the temporary displacement of the family—first to a camp in Pruszkow and then to the city of Lublin where they waited out the end of the war), she managed to compose a number of works, including the *Overture* for orchestra (1943), which had its premiere at the first "Festival of Polish Music" held in Cracow just after the war. It immediately placed her among the best Polish composers of the time.

At the end of 1945, Bacewicz and her family returned to the rubble that had been Warsaw. With renewed strength, she approached composing. Her first sonata for violin and piano and the *Violin Concerto no. 2* were completed that year. She also resumed concertizing and began serving on numerous international juries for violin competitions. In addition, she became a member of the Polish Composers Union.[7]

Though she personally objected to the categorizing of her music as "neoclassic," it is difficult to avoid the use of the term in describing her works. Perhaps one reason for her adherence to this basic style can be attributed to the social, cultural, and even political climate in which she lived and worked.

The years 1945-1955 represent a significant, fascinating, and important era in Polish music. As in other European socialist countries, there was a general nationalizing of artistic institutions. The government's first music publishing house, Polish Music Publishers (Polskie Wydawnictwo Muzyczne —PWM), was established in April 1945. Though a few private companies had started publishing after the war, their licenses were revoked in 1950. These creative barriers arose at a time when the Polish people were trying to overcome the emotional barriers that resulted from the war, particularly the feeling of martyrdom characteristically associated with survivors of war.

The nationalizing of institutions, which was announced in 1948, made what would have been a difficult task—that of bringing Poland's musical world back to a life of creative freedom—virtually insurmountable. However, the government did make positive gains in its stated goal of creating a large number of organizations such as philharmonic societies, symphony orchestras, and music schools in which to popularize Polish art. It also began the collecting, categorizing, and classifying of folklore—folklore becoming synonymous with nationalism. There were, however, negative aspects in terms of the thwarting and controlling of artistic creativity. The doctrine of "social realism" was used to discriminate against many works of art. Witold Lutosławski's first symphony was the first important musical work to be accused of being "formalistic"—government terminology for something opposed to social realism—and was removed from the concert halls for many years.

Social realism required artists and composers to incorporate folk music and themes in their works. In this atmosphere, the universal aspiration of composers of postwar Poland was to find "a synthesis between a contemporary musical language and the elements of native tradition within a framework of individual, stylistic categories."[8] It was inevitable that the Poles would be drawn to and would borrow from the music of Bartók.

In spite of the restrictions placed on them, some composers—for example, Witold Lutosławski (b. 1913) and Artur Malawski (1904-1957) —fought the oppressive doctrines. They defended a more modern musical language and incorporated it into their music, paving the way for younger

Figure 5.1 Grażyna Bacewicz

musicians who later would flourish under new and better conditions. Thus Polish music did develop, though at a much slower pace than it might have in a freer environment. In the decade after the war, some works were written without any folk elements, such as the *Overture for Strings* (1949) of Lutosławski, the *Symphony no. 2* (1956) and *Piano Trio* (1953) of Malawski, and the *Violin Concerto no. 4* (1952) of Bacewicz.

Clearly, in spite of the creative and cultural vacuum that existed in Poland during the decade after the war, some composers were able to pursue their inner calling and their craft. Of the excellent works that emerged (though understandably not as radical as the music then being written elsewhere), the compositions of Bacewicz were in the forefront.

By a quirk of fate—her birth in 1909—she was thirty years old at the start of the war, an age that should be a time of flexibility and growth for a composer; by the end of the war, she was thirty-five years old. Had she lived in a Western European country, she could once again have absorbed, synthesized, and created. However, she lived in a country that immediately imposed artistic controls. By the close of the period of isolationism, she was a mature, forty-six-year-old woman and artist. Since her creativity was in part controlled and stifled by outside circumstances, the fact that she composed with any originality at all at this time becomes proof of her innate musical genius.

The quantity of creative output once again points to her unquestionable drive. In 1948, an especially rich year, she produced many works, including her *Violin Concerto no. 3*, the first composition to show some folk influence; the *Olympic Cantata*, written for the London Olympics; and the most important of her works in the strict neoclassical style, the *Concerto for String Orchestra*. This work confirms the success of the earlier *Overture* and received the National Prize in 1950. In 1952 it had its American premiere in Washington, D.C. Critic Milton Berliner wrote:

Last night in Constitution Hall Grażyna Bacewicz's *Concerto for String Orchestra* was performed for the first time in America. There is nothing female in the work—it pulses with rhythmic, monumental, building, thematic material—just like a man's [*sic*]. The concerto is not conservatively classical or radically modernistic. It was well worth listening to.[9]

In 1949 she produced two major works that met with immediate success: the *Piano Concerto*, which contains elements of folk music (the finale being an *oberek*), and the *Sonata for Violin and Piano no. 4*, which proved to be another gem in the neoclassical tradition.[10] Reviewer Jules Wolffers wrote:

The *Sonata no. 4* by Grażyna Bacewicz was performed in the United States for the first time. This piece was the most impressively touching and controversial on the whole program. The composer is a master of melody, which challenges the listener in the way it is expressed.[11]

Nineteen forty-nine concluded with Bacewicz receiving the Warsaw Prize, given by the city of Warsaw for both her compositional abilities and her charitable and humanitarian efforts. (During the war years, her home often had been a refuge for the hungry and a sanctuary for the continuation of Polish culture.)

Concertizing and serving on competition juries occupied a great deal of her time in the early 1950s. A significant work from this period is the *String Quartet no. 4* (1951), which received first prize in the International Composer's Competition in Liège, Belgium. In 1953 this piece became a required piece for competitors in the International Quartet Competition in Geneva, and it continues to be chosen for performance in the United States and abroad.

This was a period of great recognition and acclaim. In 1952 she again received the National Prize, this time for three works: *String Quartet no. 4, Violin Concerto no. 4,* and *Sonata for Violin and Piano no. 4.*

The *Symphony no. 4,* her last effort in this form, was written in 1953. This same year she premiered her *Piano Sonata no. 2,* which quickly became a favorite work and was added to the repertoire of many international pianists.[12] During this year she also turned to a new creative form and completed her first ballet, *The Peasant King,* based on a comedy by the seventeenth-century writer Piotr Baryka. Although it was popular enough to have excerpts frequently aired over Polish Radio, Bacewicz was unenthusiastic about this work.

In 1954 she wrote the *Polish Overture,* which virtually closed the period of folk influence in her work, and also the *Violin Concerto no. 5,* first performed by Wanda Wilkomirska and the Warsaw Philharmonic Orchestra.

She had already begun to withdraw from concertizing, and by 1955 had ended her career as a violin soloist in order to devote all of her creative time to composition.

At the end of June 1956, the stirrings of political and social unrest that had been evolving over the years erupted in Poznan. The Polish working class rioted against the Russian regime of political terror and low standards of living. The result was a more liberal Polish Communist Party rule, which allowed increased religious and cultural freedom. The Warsaw Autumn Festivals served as a musical symbol of this new freedom. The first of these festivals, designed as a platform for contemporary music, took place in October 1956. Three of Bacewicz's compositions were performed at this festival (*String Quartet no. 4, Concerto for String Orchestra,* and the *Overture*)—a measure of her preeminent role in Polish music. Her works were subsequently performed at every festival from 1956 until the year after her death.

In the ensuing months, as the long period of isolation from Western musical trends came to a close, the Poles heard for the very *first* time works of Arnold Schoenberg, Alban Berg, Anton Webern, and also Olivier

Messiaen. Polish composers were inundated with the musical avant-garde. In addition to the composers of the Second Viennese School, the music of Karlheinz Stockhausen, Pierre Boulez, Luigi Nono, and even electronic music permeated the Polish musical psyche.

This input was most advantageous to those younger composers who had not yet fully formed their own musical style. Mature composers, such as Sikorski or Piotr Perkowski (b. 1901), did not have much interest in the new idiom. For Bacewicz, the gradual evolution of style and technique that had always been her trademark would again undergo subtle changes. Though she did not approve of explaining her own compositional process, she did speak out on her beliefs as they applied to contemporary music:

The diversification of today's music and the tempo of its growth is inspiring. This is not only experimentation or an endeavor to find new forms as some are saying. In contemporary music there are some genuine and great composers. The so-called avant-gardists, no doubt, influence mainstream composers who find it attractive. At times, a more traditional composer crosses over to the avant-garde. I disagree with those who maintain that once a composer develops her own style, she should stick to it. I find such an opinion totally alien; it impedes further development and growth. Every composition completed today will belong to the past tomorrow. A progressive composer should not repeat herself. A composer should not only deepen her creation and improve upon it but should also expand its scope. I believe that in my music, even though I do not consider myself an innovator, a certain trend of progression is discernible.[13]

The first perceptible changes in her artistic craft occur along three paths: (1) departure from tonality; (2) greater attention to instrumental color; and (3) enrichment of rhythmical patterns. These are noticeable in the *String Quartet no. 5* (1956), the *Violin Concerto no. 6* (1958), and particularly in the *Symphonic Variations* (1957).

The *Ten Etudes* composed in 1957 became very popular with pianists throughout the world. They were played at the second Warsaw Autumn in 1958 by Regina Smendzianka, who subsequently recorded them together with other piano works of Bacewicz.[14] This outstanding pianist virtuoso remarked:

Her *Etudes* are masterly and free from any folkloristic reminiscences, yet they are full of technical difficulties, providing a fine incentive even to concert pianists. They indicate that Bacewicz, a pianist herself, must have been very accomplished. . . . I also feel that the *Small Triptych*, dedicated to me and premiered at Helsinki, will interest many pianists. This piece has some fascinating dynamic and aural effects due to the most interesting use of the sustaining pedal.[15]

A further step in the stylistic development of this composer was realized in *Music for Strings, Trumpets and Percussion* (1958); some critics believed it to be her greatest orchestral achievement. It was performed at the Warsaw

Autumn of 1959 and received third prize from among over sixty entries at the International Composer's Tribunal of UNESCO (Paris, 1960). This composition has proven so popular that through the years six different ballet versions of it have been staged in Europe.

With the completion of this work, Bacewicz entered a contemplative period of reevaluation and analysis that slowed down her usual rapid work pace. She could not ignore the new musical expressions that were taking place around her, yet she was not sure to what extent they could or should be incorporated into her own musical language. Insights into her thinking at this time can be seen from a conversation with her old friend, the composer and critic Stefan Kisielewski, which took place in 1960 while she was in the process of writing the *String Quartet no. 6*:

Kisielewski: Grażyna, what is your reaction to the latest directions in music such as those based on Schoenbergism or the experiments with electronics?

Bacewicz: I am very interested, because in music like in everything else, something new must come along from time to time. The technique itself is very important to me because it provides the necessary rigor and formal technique for the composer. Without this base, improvisation could not be created. As a drawback, I find that often the works that have been written all sound quite alike. In the composition I am now writing—the *String Quartet no. 6*—I want to maintain certain sections in the serial technique, but by the same token I want to give them a different character. I am not interested in pointillism because I believe the road to be too narrow, but I feel directed by the coloring in sounds and the new rhythms of electronic music.[16]

The *String Quartet no. 6* possessed some new techniques, but the real fruit of her deliberations was *Pensieri Notturni* (1961), which ushered in the last phase of Bacewicz's output and is characterized by bolder musical expressions. The *Concerto for Orchestra*, written the next year, continued this new direction. It contains vigorously contrasting sections and some innovative motifs, though it is written in a conventional four-movement form.

The *Quartet for Four Cellos* (1963) was part of the eighth Warsaw Autumn. In her program notes for this performance, Bacewicz said:

I've been thinking of writing a quartet for four cellos for a long time. This was to be different from the *Quartet for Four Violins* which I composed several years ago and which was more of a teaching piece. In writing for four cellos, I was drawn to the richness of sound that is available to the cello. During the process of creating this piece, I came to the conclusion that four cellos in one ensemble is truly a treasure for the contemporary composer. This concept has forced me to discard certain elements that are very characteristic to the cello, as, for example, a broad "cantilena."[17]

Her usual energies were boundless in 1965, when she composed *Musica Sinfonica* in three movements, *String Quartet no. 7, Violin Concerto no. 7, Piano Quintet no. 2, Small Triptych* for piano, *Divertimento* for string orchestra, *Incrustations for Horn and Chamber Orchestra*, and *Trio for Oboe, Harp and Percussion*. *Musica Sinfonica* contains sounds that appear to be achieved through aleatoric devices, but in fact it would go against the basic tenets of this composer to leave anything to chance. The smallest details are carefully defined and written into the score.

Bacewicz's last string quartet, the seventh work in this genre, was internationally acclaimed. Lutosławski said: "The *String Quartet no. 7* is new evidence of the use of certain possibilities that have been hidden in this type of an ensemble, but which have never been utilized. From the time of Bartók very few composers have written in the same manner as Bacewicz, who was able to penetrate the secrets of the string quartet."[18] Tadeusz Zielinski, a leading Polish critic and musicologist, called this string quartet "a masterpiece of contemporary quartet literature."[19]

The pace set in 1965 continued into 1966 with the short *Esquisse* for organ, the powerful and dynamic *Concerto for Two Pianos and Orchestra*, and *Contradizione*, which contains elements of the *Trio for Oboe, Harp and Percussion*. Programmed at the eleventh Warsaw Autumn, *Contradizione* subsequently has been scheduled in numerous concerts throughout the world.

Having written occasionally for the stage during her career—a comic opera, *The Adventure of King Arthur* (1959), and two ballets—Bacewicz was drawn once again to this medium. For six months during 1968 she worked on a ballet entitled *Desire*, based on Picasso's play, *Desire Trapped by the Tail*. She felt it represented a new period of composition for her and placed real importance on it. Unfortunately, she would never see it performed. On January 17, 1969, she died suddenly and unexpectedly.[20]

The overwhelming loss felt by her colleagues as well as her admiring public was beautifully expressed by the composer Tadeusz Baird, who wrote:

The richness and vastness of creativity achieved in such a short life never ceases to amaze me. There is no aspect in music that has not been enriched by her decisive, swift, courageous and experienced pen. Like the maestros of the past, Bacewicz was equally at home when creating a monumental cycle of symphonies, miniatures for instruments, chamber music or music for the stage. The craft of music-making held no secrets for her. An inexhaustible source of inventiveness, technical virtuosity, and a wide breadth of approach suffice for placing the works of her life among those that are most admired. But that is not all. She has been given something more important, more precious, found only among the few, a gift of being different and unique.[21]

It is these gifts which, in an age of quickly fading trends, give one the hope and expectation that Bacewicz's works will survive to be heard and appreciated by future generations.

NOTES

1. Grażyna Bacewicz, *Znak szczegnólny* (The birthmark) (Warsaw: Czytelnik, 1964), pp. 25-26. For their help in translation from the original Polish, I wish to thank Leszek Weres, Wanda Wilk, and Michael Golabek (in memoriam).

2. A list of her works with complete discography are included in Judith Rosen, *Grażyna Bacewicz: Her Life and Works*, one of the booklets in the *Polish Music History Series* to be published by and available (in 1984) from Friends of Polish Music at the University of Southern California, Music Department, University of Southern California, Los Angeles, California 90007.

3. The 1913 birth date previously attributed to her was corrected at the time of her death and also in a letter to this author from the composer's sister, Wanda Bacewicz.

4. All noted composition dates are dates of the work's completion.

5. Feliciana Szopski, *The Warsaw Courier*, no date. Quoted in "Biographical Notes," original typescript in Polish in the possession of Wanda Bacewicz, translated by Wanda Wilk, no date.

6. Stefan Kisielewski, "An Interview with Grażyna Bacewicz," in *Z muzycznej miedzyepocki* (Between musical eras) (Cracow: Polskie Wydawnictwo Muzyczne, 1965).

7. The Union was founded in 1945, a few months after the liberation, at the National Congress of Polish Composers, which was held in Cracow. It pledged itself to the popularizing of Polish music at home and abroad, initiated musical competitions, and in the ensuing years was instrumental in organizing the Warsaw Autumn Festival.

8. Stefan Jarocinski, ed. *Polish Music* (Warsaw: Panstwowe Wydawnictwo Naukowe, 1965), p. 181.

9. Milton Berliner, *Washington Daily News*, December 31, 1952, cited in Stefan Kisielewski, *Grażyna Bacewicz i jej czasy* (Grażyna Bacewicz and her time) (Cracow: PWM, 1963), p. 54.

10. An *oberek* is a Polish dance akin to a mazurka but in a faster tempo.

11. Jules Wolffers, *Christian Science Monitor*, Boston, February 16, 1953; cited in Kisielewski, *Grażyna Bacewicz*, p. 55.

12. About ten years ago, an American pianist, Sister Nancy Fierro, wanted to add the *Piano Sonata no. 2* to her growing performance list of works by women composers. Not being able to obtain it directly from the Polish government, she contacted this author, who through a series of circuitous, but fortunate, events eventually managed to obtain a copy of the score—direct from a piano bench in the Warsaw Conservatory. In the ensuing years, through numerous concerts as well as a recording on the Avant label, Sister Nancy Fierro has helped to popularize this piece in the United States.

13. *Polish Music*, no. 2 (Warsaw: PWN, 1973).

14. The American pianist, Virginia Eskin, has recorded the *Etudes no. 2, no. 8*, and the *Small Triptych* on the Musical Heritage Society label.

15. B. M. Maciejewski, *Twelve Polish Composers* (London: Allegro Press, 1976), pp. 73-74.

16. Kisielewski, "An Interview with Grażyna Bacewicz."

17. "Biographical Notes," p. 20.
18. Ibid. pp. 21-22.
19. Ibid. p. 22.
20. For a more detailed discussion of *Desire* and her death, see Judith Rosen, "Grażyna Bacewicz (1909-1969)," *Heresies: A Feminist Publication on Art and Politics* 10, 1980, p. 28.
21. *Ruch Muzyczny* (The musical movement), No. 7 (Warsaw: PWM, 1969).

SELECTED BIBLIOGRAPHY

Bacewicz, Grażyna. *Znak szczególny* (The birthmark). Warsaw: Czytelnik, 1964.
Bacewicz, Wanda. "Biographical Notes." Translated by Wanda Wilk. Typescript in Polish. No date.
_____. Letters to the author, 1974-1982.
Grove's Dictionary of Music and Musicians. 5th ed. 9 vols. 1956.
_____. 6th ed. 20 vols. 1980.
Jarocinski, Stefan, ed. *Polish Music.* Warsaw: Panstwowe Wydawnictwo Naukowe, 1965.
Kisielewski, Stefan. *Grażyna Bacewicz i jej czasy* (Grażyna Bacewicz and her time). Cracow: Polskie Wydawnictwo Muzyczne, 1963.
Maciejewski, Boguslaw M. *Twelve Polish Composers.* London: Allegro Press, 1976.
Vinton, John, ed. *Dictionary of Twentieth Century Music.* London: Thames and Hudson, 1974.

BACEWICZ RECORDINGS CURRENTLY AVAILABLE IN THE UNITED STATES

Concerto for Viola and Orchestra; Concerto for Two Pianos and Orchestra, MUZA SXL 0875[1]
Divertimento for Strings, MUZA SCL 0586[1]
Piano Quintets no. 1 and no. 2; MUZA SXL 0608[1]
Piano Sonata no. 2: Maly Tryptyk (Small Triptych); *Ten Etudes for Piano*, MUZA SXL 0977[1]
Piano Sonata no. 2, Avant 1012[2]
Small Triptych for Piano; *Etudes no. 2 and no. 8 for Piano*, MHS 4236[3]
Small Triptych for Piano, Turnabout TV 34685
Sonata no. 4 for Violin and Piano, MUZA XL 0505[1]
String Quartet no. 3; *String Quartet no. 5*, MUZA SX 1597[1]
String Quartet no. 4; *String Quartet no. 7*, MUZA SX 1598[1,4]

Available from:
[1]Polish Record Center of America, 3055 Milwaukee Avenue, Chicago, Illinois 60618.
[2]Sister Nancy Fierro, Mt. St. Mary's College, 12001 Chalon Road, Los Angeles, California 90049.
[3]Musical Heritage Society, 14 Park Road, Tinton Falls, New Jersey 07724.
[4]Wladyslaw and Ted Przybyla, 15858 Annellen, Hacienda Heights, California 91745.

Selected scores are available from Przybyla (see above); University of California at Los Angeles, Music Library, Schoenberg Hall, Los Angeles, California 90024; New York Public Library at Lincoln Center, 111 Amsterdam Avenue, New York, New York 10023. Also check your local libraries.

6

Grażyna Bacewicz: Form, Syntax, Style

ELIZABETH WOOD

From her early works to her last, regardless of genre, form, or instrumentation, Grażyna Bacewicz developed a distinctive personal and expressive musical voice. In her large body of works there is consistent intelligence and technical virtuosity. She crafts sound with impeccable skill and scrupulous control. Yet in her very consistency lies a uniformity, a repetitive and at times formulistic quality that both defines and confines her personal imprint. It is perhaps for this reason that her influence, a stabilizing one in twentieth-century Polish music, is slight in comparison with her less prolific but more adventurous contemporaries such as Witold Lutosławski (b. 1913), and the younger Krzysztov Penderecki (b. 1933).

Bacewicz fully embodies the mainstream neoclassical outlook of European musical thought in the 1920s and 1930s, which refurbished and thus revitalized classical forms and older contrapuntal and polyphonic practices through the rhythmic innovations and instrumental colorations pioneered by composers such as Igor Stravinsky (1882-1971) and Claude Debussy (1862-1918). The French connection, through the teachings of Nadia Boulanger, indelibly impressed on Bacewicz and her inherited Polish folk and romantic traditions the eclecticism and sense of musical continuity implied in the music of a Stravinsky or an Albert Roussel (1869-1937). In this, her outlook and her work may be compared with those of her contemporaries, the Czech composer Bohuslav Martinů (1890-1959) and the German Paul Hindemith (1895-1963). They share similar classical forms, motivic techniques, rhythmic energy, a fondness for contrapuntal textures, a constantly variating syntax, and a concentration on instrumental virtuosity. Bacewicz, like Hindemith, developed quite early in her career a meticulous control of tonality, of the tension and ambiguity of dissonance in a fully chromatic style.

Another more lyrical, more subtle influence was that of Béla Bartók (1881-1945), especially on her slow movements and her assimilation of folk music. Polish folk traditions in her work are sufficiently unobtrusive that many writers have underestimated them. Yet they are often present in her rhythms and melodic inflections, sometimes govern her chosen formal design, or at other times are completely integrated in an atmospheric impressionism. That inheritance, more evident in her early works written after her studies with conservative Warsaw composer Kazimierz Sikorski (b. 1895) and contemporary with neoromantic works by Karol Szymanowski (1882-1937), is transcended in her last phase during the 1960s, where a syntactic minimalism and further disintegration of both tonality and of formal symmetry relates her last works to post-Webern musical modernism. However, Bacewicz has never been described as belonging among the avant-garde, nor does she join the ranks of twelve-tone or serial composers, for she never completely discards her neoclassical frame of reference. What is new in these last works is a more spacious texture, a controlled dispersal of sound, a more epigrammatic style. However, in no way do they appear to make a significant break with her previous compositions.

From the start of her career, an important feature of Bacewicz's technique of composition was her orchestration. Unlike the then-contemporary techniques used by Szymanowski, her textures are never thick, never overorchestrated. Her technical virtuosity as a concert violinist and accomplished pianist is evident throughout her work. She composed for all varieties of instruments during her career, but the major works remain her pieces for strings, whether in solo, chamber, concerto, ensemble, or orchestral genres. It appears that stringed instrumentation is where she placed most of her compositional emphasis, whereas her use of brass, wind, and percussion sonorities is more for accompanimental and punctuating effects.

A stylistic cohesiveness binds her work. Its dominating ingredient is a dissonant linearity woven through contrapuntal patterns. Another feature of her musical thought is its binary expression. In her adherence to baroque and classical structures, she presents pairs of contrasting thematic subjects that each invariably contain two parts. These are then contrasted further in two-part, two-subject dialogues that interplay and effect a balance between her two most significant styles: a free, expressive, and flowing linear counterpoint, and a more closed, chordal, or clustered vertical and polyphonic texture that is frequently grave, stern, or emphatic in expression. Grounding these styles and helping to articulate them are her typically angular and forceful rhythms that contrast with a more mobile, fluid, relaxed, rhythmic pattern based on Polish dance and song traditions.

All the foregoing features are already present in a mature manner in the relatively well-known and widely performed *Concerto for String Orchestra* (1948). This firmly classical and tonal work shows the distinct influence of Stravinsky in the outer movements, in its strongly contrasted themes and driving rhythmic momentum, and of Bartók in the evocative, impressionist, and elegiac slow movement. The sections within each movement are demarcated by transitions and linking passages in a free toccata style. Bacewicz's tendency is to understate and control her lyricism, which heightens for the listener a sense of the music's restrained power. That similar features may be discovered consistently throughout her musical output suggests both her strengths (in creating and maintaining a definite personal style honed and perfected through remarkable technical gifts) and her limitations. The latter include a certain conservatism, a wariness of risk-taking and experimentation, and a refinement of intellectual clarity and conviction at, perhaps, the expense of imagination. It must be stressed, however, that within these limits, she remains an interesting, accomplished, and *musical* composer.

The following analysis of two of the seven string quartets demonstrates her method of composition and the manner in which she renewed and matured her style.

The *String Quartet no. 4,* written in 1951 and published in 1952, is in three movements. The first is in sonata form. The opening, binary theme on the 'cello contains semitonal shifts, octave leaps, and an arpeggiated rising phrase which will be exploited later through dense chromatic alterations, oscillating pitch plateaux, and biting motoric rhythms (figure 6.1). The second theme is an eight-bar lilting, folklike melody derived from the six-note "Polish mode" of D–F–G–A–B–C (figure 6.2). Announced by the first violin, it is answered contrapuntally by the second violin before the second of its phrases is gradually broken up. A longer development section follows, which debates and further contrasts the modal, intervallic, and rhythmic features of these expository materials. Tempos alternate between andante and allegro-energico sections, while polyphonically layered ostinatos exchange with free-moving scale figurations that make formal transitions between restatements of the initial motivic elements.

Figure 6.1 *Quatuor No. 4*, violoncello, first movement, measures 1-14. Copyright © 1952 by Polskie Wydawnictwo Muzyczne. Used by permission.

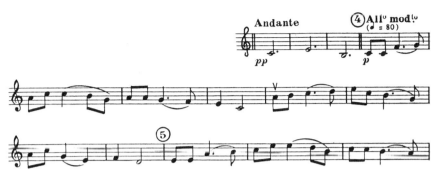

Figure 6.2 *Quatuor No. 4*, violino I, first movement, measures 27-40. Copyright © 1952 by Polskie Wydawnictwo Muzyczne. Used by permission.

The second movement also presents two binary themes whose lyricism and contemplative mood contrast with those of the two outer movements. The former of these two subjects is composed of brief, meandering phrases laid out in fifteen bars and then explored through a series of transpositions and chromatic, contrapuntal, and imitative passages (figure 6.3).

The final movement dominates the work. It is exceptionally finely crafted and cunningly grafts older dance formations to a syntax reminiscent of the baroque. Its principal "jocose" and jaunty theme is an *oberek*, a homely, Polish round dance, which embarks at once on an extended set of repetitions and simple variations in the traditional waltz form of the mazurka.[1] Bacewicz's setting is lively, almost improvisatory, in eight-bar phrases of energetic triple meter that is strongly accented (figure 6.4). On completion of the set of variations, a second, more cantabile theme appears, but this soon adopts and then develops materials from the first, and thus assumes

Figure 6.3 *Quatuor No. 4*, violino I, second movement, measures 1-19. Copyright © 1952 by Polskie Wydawnictwo Muzyczne. Used by permission.

Figure 6.4 *Quatuor No. 4*, violino I, third movement, measures 11-18 (repeated) and 27-34. Copyright © 1952 by Polskie Wydawnictwo Muzyczne. Used by permission.

the function of a development section. Both the original dance theme and a shortened version of the secondary theme return and proceed toward a final recapitulation of the *oberek* and its last turn as an unadorned coda.

This movement, however, is not simply constructed upon dance patterns, even though its succinct rhythmic arrangements retain that characteristic throughout. It conforms, rather, to the notion of an instrumental ricercar, because Bacewicz has alternated her toccata-style passages of interlacing scales with a contrapuntal, imitative treatment of the main theme that employs broad fugal techniques through part-crossings, stretto entries, inversions, augmentation, and diminution.[2] The entire movement is a brilliant example of her grasp of formal schemes that permit flexible variations and an easy interplay of different styles without ever abandoning momentum and thematic unity.

These stylistic and formal approaches are also advanced in the later *String Quartet no. 7*, written in 1965 and published in 1967 at the peak of her powers. Here the first movement is once again in a broad sonata form with two main thematic groups. The first, presented in a severe counterpoint, is punctuated by glissandi, pizzicato, and percussive exclamations. A rich, stunning display of technical gymnastics is thus made as structurally significant as the quite limited range of this subject's melodic and intervallic materials. Ascending and descending chromatic scales flatten out into static oscillating passages, or close into vertical clusters of sounds in a shifting landscape of disintegration and reintegration. Stretto-like entries at the diminished fifth, inversions, and imitative part writing glue the different segments together.

For the slower second subject, spacious diminished seventh chords frame glissandi and tremolo on viola that are underpinned by a pedal drone on 'cello that resembles the *dudy* (bagpipe) of Polish folk dance (figure 6.5). In the development section, the primary themes broaden out into mirror-like counterpoint now offset by the glissandi-drone-trill effects of the second subject and pivoting on an implied F-tonic. However, a series of forte chords accumulates all twelve tones of the scale to disrupt any tonal resolve. Now the development proceeds to disperse all these components, including the vertical clusters, and drives them through taut, nervy, and restless transformations until an extended transition phase restabilizes this section. At the recapitulation, a dualism between rapidly repeated note formations and brief, static ostinatos hastens the movement to its close, once again in toccata-fashion through its alternations of free/horizontal versus closed/vertical passages.

A slow and melancholy middle movement, ternary in form, and somewhat similar to the corresponding movement of the fourth quartet, is reminiscent of the "night music" of a Bartók slow movement. Lacking any strong melodic focus, it develops a lyrical harmonic texture with offsetting free counterpoint in an extension of the musical vocabulary of the first movement.

The finale is a neobaroque rondo constructed on classical sonata principles. There are three couplets that employ variation techniques for both the original 17-bar rondo theme and for its three episodes. Although the movement is stated as a conventional eighteenth-century rondo (R1–A1–R2-B-R3-A2-R4), it is also perceived as exposition (R1-A1), development (R2-B), recapitulation (R3-A2), and after further variation and ornamentation, a final coda (R4). The binary rondo theme, in duple time, is lightly distributed between the four parts, which highlights its lightning-fast and

Figure 6.5 *Quatuor No. 7*, first movement, measures 46-49. Reprinted by permission of the publishers, Moeck Verlag und Musikinstrumentenwerk.

Figure 6.6 *Quatuor No. 7*, third movement, measures 1-17. Reprinted by permission of the publishers, Moeck Verlag und Musikinstrumentenwerk.

airy exuberance (figure 6.6). On its first appearance, the repeat is unaltered. The interrelated episodes (A1, B, A2) are more lyrical, in contrasting triple time, yet contain elements of the rondo theme to enhance an overall sense of cyclic unity. The main interest in the movement is in its exceptional vivacity brought about by the rhythmic energy of the theme and the effortless inventiveness of the variations.

The appearance of twelve-tone passages in the first movement of this string quartet is a natural extension of Bacewicz's technique of continuous variation, rather than an excursion into serial techniques. In fact, the manner in which she constantly explores her motivic materials through repetition, imitative and ornamented counterpoint, and shifting polyphonic textures confirms rather than confuses what is essentially a tonal organization. A modal orientation is also inevitable when Bacewicz integrates folk materials. Their rapid, vigorous, and often abrupt rhythms and their elusive melodies tend to resolve chromatic ambiguities and to smooth dissonance.

By her last prolific decade, Bacewicz's imprint is fully formed. It is antiromantic, precise, clearly defined, logically organized, and, above all, controlled. There is an aural sense of curtailed—even concealed—lyricism, as if there were an inner, passionate, soaring, yearning voice that the composer chooses to sublimate rather than unleash. In these final works, her expressionist tendencies are dramatized by an increasing interest in percussive and fragmentary effects. Bacewicz cultivates a dispersal of densities through an iridescent pointillism in preference to accumulating and intensifying sound.

In the 1960s, Bacewicz began to abandon classical forms. Again, in the orchestral *Pensieri Notturni* (1961), her imprint is unmistakable. More programmatic than is usual in her music, here she is poetic, evocative, and spacious in her texture, although the work is short and extremely succinct. Free-scale passages contrast with clustered sonorities; a mellifluous counterpoint contrasts with fragmented, desiccated punctuations, especially in dry xylophone tones and the metallic timbres of celesta and vibraphone, set against ensemble strings. Bacewicz achieves in this work a greater rhythmic suppleness and fluidity than before.

Contradizione (1966), a two-movement work for a chamber orchestra of fifteen players, is both more intimate, dramatic and spontaneous in expression, and experimental in syntax than *Pensieri Notturni*. It is also pleasantly accessible to modern ears. The first movement, like a Bartók slow movement, is nocturnal and suggestive, where sliding harmonic centers of gravity vie with rapid, nervous, grotesque scale figurations that revel in ingenuity and variety.

The second movement, marked *acuto*, exploits to the full a rich and contradictory tone palette set in strong rhythmic contexts. Sonorities burrow, dissipate, then reappear to explode in sparkling and cascading fireworks that are echoed and answered and reverberated, and occasionally interrupted, by muted string passages. In an earlier work, *Music for Strings, Trumpets, and Percussion* (1958), set in three movements for five trumpets, celesta, xylophone, kettledrum, timpani, and string orchestra, Bacewicz explored echo and answer devices by often grouping brass sonorities against divisi strings as if retrieving old *conçertino-ripieno* traditions from the concerto grosso (figure 6.7). In the last works, however, Bacewicz sculpts

Figure 6.7 *Music for Strings, Trumpets, and Percussion*, third movement, measures 1-5. Copyright © 1960 by Polskie Wydawnictwo Muzyczne. Used by permission.

much more freely-adventurous shapes that dazzle with instrumental virtuosity culled from the entire avant-garde vocabulary: glissandi, dense clusters, harmonics, tremolo, pizzicato, bowing col legno, sul tasto, sul ponticello, saltando, jeté, and detaché. All of these techniques she has used before, but never in such rapid and immaculately precise concentrations.

It is curious that so idiomatic, so dramatic a composer was rarely drawn to word-painting and poetic settings. She wrote few songs or choral works, although there is one short opera and a variety of incidental pieces mainly written for radio performances. She appears not to have required extra-musical stimulus either as a spur to musical thought, as symbol, or as structural scaffolding. In this sense, she is a pure abstractionist whose chosen expression is music, not words or images, yet whose personality, in the written words she has left us, is deeply private and somewhat elusive. What lasts, and should ensure her place in twentieth-century music, is her disciplined and sophisticated assimilation of neoclassicism and Polish folk tradition into new, poised, and wonderfully polished works of art.

NOTES

1. The *oberek*, or *obertas*, is the fastest of the Polish dances that include the *mazurek* and *kujawiak*. Well-known Polish models for this type of adaptation include several by violin virtuoso Henryk Wieniawski (1835-1880), *Oberek*, op. 19, and *Mazurka Charactéristique*, no. 1 for violin. Bacewicz sets the *oberek* in the last movement of her second *Piano Sonata* (1952).

2. The first Polish composer to unite the folk *mazurka* with academic techniques is Chopin in the canon that ends *Mazurka* op. 63, no. 3 in C-sharp Minor (1846). He, too, sets the *oberek* in the Mazurka op. 56, no. 2 in C Major (1843).

7

Louise Talma: Essentials of Her Style As Seen Through the Piano Works

SUSAN TEICHER

The distinguished career of American composer Louise Talma has been characterized by continued success. Among her many honors, Talma has the distinction of being the first American woman composer to have had an opera staged in a major European opera house; the first woman to receive the Sibelius Medal for composition,[1] the first woman to be twice awarded Guggenheim fellowships in music; and, in 1974, the first woman composer to be elected to the National Institute of Arts and Letters. The citation at her induction into the National Institute read in part: "Many of her admirers, who had grown accustomed to seeing or hearing her referred to as one of our foremost women composers, have noticed with pleasure in recent years that she is being referred to more and more often without any qualification at all as one of our foremost composers."

Talma's works for solo piano display essential features of her style and constitute a distinctive group of compositions. Reflections of Copland, Barber, and occasionally even Gershwin are manifest in the unmistakably American nature of her music. Perhaps, due to her birth in France, she was fated to express a kind of dual musical allegiance: although the music is clearly American, French influence is very strong. While Talma's music is largely polyphonic and motivically inspired, it is basically undevelopmental; ideas follow one another or alternate, often for the purpose of mutual contrast. (A characteristic device in Talma's piano music is an abrupt change from material which is very active and even relentless to reflective, often chordal, material.) Consequently, the formal structures that dominate these works contain relatively short sections, more in keeping with a rondo than a sonata allegro form.

The piano works require from the performer a high degree of digital dexterity, a wide palette of contrasting colors, and considerable physical stamina. Her most well-known piano work, *Alleluia in Form of Toccata*, while not the most technically demanding or emotionally dramatic of her

Figure 7.1 Louise Talma. Photograph by Basil Langton

piano works, is one of Talma's most successful ventures in this medium.

The *Alleluia*'s textural lightness and astringency, angular rhythms, and sense of high yet controlled energy are qualities found throughout Talma's piano music. The two piano sonatas are major works and are also among the best of the piano compositions.

Talma, an only child, was born on October 31, 1906, in Arcachon, France. Her mother, Alma Cecile Garrigue, an opera singer who appeared at the Metropolitan Opera House in New York and in companies in Europe, happened to be working in France at the time of Louise's birth. Her father, Frederick Talma, a pianist, died when Talma was an infant. Both parents were American, and Talma has always been an American citizen. After a brief visit to the United States when she was three years old, Talma returned to America during the summer of 1914; with the outbreak of World War I in Europe, she and her mother had no choice but to stay. It was in New York City that Talma grew up, and she has lived there most of her life.

Talma's initial music study was with her mother. In fact, her first formal piano lesson came as a present on her fifth birthday. Coming from such a musical background, she says, "My being a musician was from the very beginning [of life],"[2] Although as a teenager she developed an avid interest in chemistry and considered it seriously as a career, teaching music was, by that time, her living. Her mother became ill when Talma was a teenager, and she did not have the luxury of beginning in a new field.

After graduating from Wadleigh High School in New York City in 1922, Talma attended The Institute of Musical Art from 1922 to 1930.[3] Her original ambition was to be a pianist, and when she first went to the Fontainebleau School of Music in France in the summer of 1926, it was to study with Isidore Philipp. However, it was at Fontainebleau that she came under the profound influence of Nadia Boulanger, and it was Boulanger who convinced her that she was a composer. Talma studied at Fontainebleau every summer from 1926 to 1939, returning again during the summers of 1949, 1951, 1961, 1968, 1971, 1972, and 1976.

During the summers of 1936 to 1939, Talma taught solfège at Fontainebleau, becoming the first American ever to teach there; during the summers of 1978, 1981, and 1982, she taught solfège, analysis, and harmony. She studied basic theoretical subjects in addition to composition and organ with Boulanger, who was adamant that her students develop absolute command of harmony, counterpoint, and fugue. Boulanger insisted that theoretical exercises could never be done merely according to the rules or in an academic fashion—they also had to contain beauty. "I learned more about what composition is really about," Talma says, "from her corrections of my harmony lessons, than from the actual composition lesson."[4] She also learned much about teaching from Boulanger, whose uncanny gift for perceiving weaknesses in a piece of music apparently never failed. In Talma's earliest attempts at composition, she emulated the German romantics, especially Brahms.[5] Later, she explored the more highly chromatic language of Scriabin. (In addition to Boulanger's great musical and pedagogical influence on Talma, she also had a remarkable impact on Talma's religious convictions. Although born a Protestant, Talma was an atheist when she first went to France to study. After hearing Boulanger, during a lecture, list the professions in order of their importance with "priest" in first place, Talma spent three years reading intensively about religion. She converted to Catholicism when she was twenty-eight, and today religion is the basis of her life.)

In 1931, Talma received a Bachelor of Music degree from New York University and, in 1933, a Master of Arts degree from Columbia University. She taught theory and ear-training at the Manhattan School of Music from 1926 to 1928. She was on the music faculty at Hunter College in Manhattan from 1928 to 1979, during which time she wrote two harmony textbooks.[6]

Since 1943, Talma has often been in residence at the MacDowell Colony in New Hampshire, where most of her music has been composed. It was at the MacDowell Colony in the early 1940s that she met and became closely allied with the so-called Boston group of composers: Lukas Foss, Irving Fine, Harold Shapero, Claudio Spiess, and Alexei Haieff. Aaron Copland, in *Stravinsky in the Theatre* (1950), referred to these composers as "a Stravinsky school." Since the time of her first association with Boulanger, Talma has considered Stravinsky to be the greatest and most important composer of the twentieth century; it is thus natural that the style in which she and the Boston group were composing was neoclassical. Neoclassicism represents, according to Talma, "a kind of clarity, transparency, logic; no fuzziness. It's not a pastiche . . . because that's an imitation. The great neoclassical compositions are in no sense imitations, but they employ the same aesthetic."[7] All of Talma's music until 1952 is neoclassical, tonal, and strongly contrapuntal.

In the *Six Etudes for Piano*, written during 1953 and 1954, Talma first used serial technique. The music of the Second Viennese School, with the exception of Berg, has never held much appeal for her. She feels that "one can not cut oneself off from the past and dismiss the whole lower level of the overtone series, because in doing so one denies the very nature of sound."[8] In discussing her triptych for baritone and orchestra, *The Tolling Bell*, based in part on Shakespeare's *Hamlet* soliloquy, Talma wrote: "It seemed to me that the musical equivalent of existence ("to be") was the interval of a fifth, without which music is not. It is the basic, inescapable interval as soon as any sound is made in whatever style or period."[9] Talma's music has always retained the tonal principles expressed in the overtone series, that is, the priority of the intervals of the fifth and the third. Her twelve-tone rows are often created with these intervallic relationships in mind.

The catalyst for her conversion to serial technique was hearing the just-written *String Quartet* of Irving Fine in 1952. Fine was a composer for whom she had enormous admiration; it was a revelation to her that a serially conceived piece could be so beautiful and expressive.[10] After discussing this with Fine, she decided to begin using serial technique; all of her music since then has been woven together from serial and tonal elements.

Arthur Berger wrote in 1955:

It was not, as far as I can judge, Stravinsky's recent concern with tone rows that motivated Fine and Talma. That they should think of using twelve-tone devices at all is, of course, related to the whole general rapprochement between the Stravinsky and twelve-tone schools and the growing acceptance of twelve-tone music. . . . But the fragmentation, permutation, and wide leaps that fascinate Stravinsky . . . are of a variety that seems to have been suggested by Webern. These devices are not particularly evident in the twelve-tone works of Fine and Talma, who have absorbed the row technique into their customary manner.[11]

In adopting serial technique into her compositional repertoire, Talma did not forfeit or negate tonality. Serialism and tonality need not be mutually exclusive, and they are not in her music. She explains: "I like to use serialism as a tool and to incorporate it with the other modes in music. I see no reason for chopping off what has developed simply because something new has come along. I believe in using all the tools available."[12]

Talma's piano compositions are a significant component of an output that includes music for solo voice, organ, chamber groups, chorus, orchestra, and opera. Among her major orchestral works is the *Toccata*, written during the summer of 1944 and dedicated to conductor Reginald Stewart, who premiered the work with the Baltimore Symphony in 1945. Other important orchestral works include *The Divine Flame*, an oratorio; *A Time to Remember*, for mixed chorus and chamber orchestra; *The Tolling Bell*; and *Celebration*, for women's chorus and small orchestra. Frequent inclusion of vocal parts in her chamber works, her deep involvement with literature and religion, and her strong feeling about the relationship between text and music testify to her propensity for vocal expression. She has written many lovely solo songs and works for a cappella chorus, including *La Corona* (John Donne), and *Psalm 84*. No doubt, the most discussed of all her works is her opera *The Alcestiad*, with a libretto by Thornton Wilder; the opera was first performed on March 1, 1962, in Frankfurt with seven subsequent performances that spring.

Talma's output includes two works that highlight the piano but which are not solo works: *Four-handed Fun*, written originally for piano four hands and published later for two pianos; and *Dialogues for Piano and Orchestra*. *Four-handed Fun* (1939) represents one of her earliest attempts at composition; as its name implies, it is lighthearted and technically not very difficult. *Dialogues* was premiered by Grant Johannesen, Lukas Foss, and the Buffalo Philharmonic Orchestra in 1965. The titles of the five sections of the work, "Challenge," "Struggle," "Respite," "Pursuit," and "Peace," reflect Talma's deep concern with moral, ethical, and religious issues. In program notes for the concert, the *Dialogues* are characterized as "permeated by stark, shifting sounds. The piano utterances . . . while requiring a great deal of skill, are more in the nature of an obbligato than a virtuosic display."[13]

Talma's solo piano works span the years from 1943 to 1977. Perhaps because she started out as a pianist and remains an excellent one, her music for the instrument constitutes a significant part of her oeuvre. Joseph Machlis writes of Talma's works that "those for piano display her profound knowledge of the instrument,"[14] exploiting the full capabilities of the instrument and challenging the player technically as well as musically. With the two exceptions of the *Bagatelles* and *Soundshots*, the piano works are virtuoso pieces.

Talma has always been fascinated with the wide range of possibilities the keyboard offers. Her approach to the piano does not include mechanically altering the inside of the instrument, strumming the strings, or using the keyboard and pedals in any other than their conventional manner. She writes, "When it comes to forearm or flat palm clusters, the effect is so limited [that] it has no interest for me. And as for tampering with the inside of the piano, I have much too much respect for the exquisite adjustments of its parts to do that. You might as well ask a surgeon to use his instruments to open a tin can."[15]

Talma's neoclassical piano works consist of: *Piano Sonata No. 1*, 1943; *Alleluia in Form of Toccata*, 1945; *Venetian Folly: Overture and Barcarolle*, 1946-1947; *Pastoral Prelude*, 1949; and *Bagatelle*, 1950. Her works containing serial and tonal techniques are: *Six Etudes,* 1953-1954; *Piano Sonata No. 2*, 1944-1955; *Three Bagatelles*, 1955; *Passacaglia and Fugue*, 1955-1962; *Soundshots*, 1944-1974; and *Textures*, 1977.

The *Piano Sonata No. 1*, winner of the North American Prize in 1947 and published by Carl Fischer in 1948, was written during Talma's first summer at the MacDowell Colony. Although not written on commission, the work is dedicated to Mrs. Edward MacDowell; Talma herself performed the premiere of this work at a League of Composers concert in 1945. Of all the performances of this piece which Talma has heard, Virginia Eskin's recording of it on the Musical Heritage label is, in her opinion, the most satisfying. It is the best, she explains, "because [Eskin] paid attention to what was on the page, and she did not alter anything."[16] Talma is unfailingly meticulous and uncompromising about what she puts down on paper, including detailed instructions for dynamic markings, pedaling, fingerings, and tempo indications. The printed musical score is the final word, and those who perform her music should respect and heed what they see. She never alters the music once she has finished it. "I never look back," she says. "It is inexplicable to me that great composers went back to old pieces and revised them."[17]

This first sonata is, in the words of one critic, "difficult to play until one accustoms oneself to Miss Talma's intricate interlockings of the hands, which are reminiscent of some of George Balanchine's balletic tangles."[18] However, like all of her piano writing, it is never difficult just for the sake of being virtuosic or flashy; the difficulties are always in the service of the musical ideas.

For Virginia Eskin,

Talma's music is reminiscent . . . of certain skyscrapers . . . where the foundation is one basic block, then each successive level is block-upon-block to the spire. In this piece [*Sonata No. 1*] she begins frugally, taking a plain four note block, upon which the entire structure is gradually built. The work is firmly anchored to its foundation, constructed logically yet expressively, thrusting to its finale. It strikes me as American in its naiveté, which contrasts well with the angular, driving rhythmic shapes.[19]

Figure 7.2 *Sonata No. 1*, first movement, measures 1-6. Copyright © 1948 by Carl Fischer, Inc. New York. Used by permission.

The declamatory statement that begins this quasi sonata allegro first movement outlines the notes C, F, D, G—unmistakably indicating a C center. The key signature of three flats and the effect of a pedal point on C throughout the first page further attest to the tonal center. The motive, C, F, D, G, is also stated vertically in various combinations, creating the structural unity to which Ms. Eskin alluded. This introductory Largo is followed by a driving Allegro, molto vivace in C minor, giving way after two pages to a lilting, folklike melody in E-flat major whose simplicity and openness seem distinctly American.

The second movement, a song-like Larghetto, is a pensive, reflective movement that never exceeds a mezzoforte level. The texture is predominantly polyphonic, and the first theme carries memories of the C F D G motive of the first movement (for example, on the downbeat of measure four). The second theme, displaying a rich and delicate use of seventh and ninth chords, illustrates Talma's use of a distinctively wide registral range. The third movement is a galloping Presto, leading the sonata to its intense conclusion.

Figure 7.3 *Sonata No. 1*, first movement, measures 82-89. Copyright © 1948 by Carl Fischer, Inc. New York. Used by permission.

Figure 7.4 *Sonata No. 1*, second movement, measures 1-5. Copyright © 1948 by Carl Fischer, Inc. New York. Used by permission.

Figure 7.5 *Sonata No. 1*, second movement, measures 26-29. Copyright © 1948 by Carl Fischer, Inc. New York. Used by permission.

Alleluia in Form of Toccata, written for Ray Lev, was published by Carl Fischer in 1947 and has been recorded by Şahan Arzruni on Musical Heritage and by Nancy Fierro on Avant Records. Arzruni, who would like to devote a whole album to Talma's piano works, says: "I find a rightness about the music. She really thinks about every note. She takes intuition and molds it with a lot of discipline."[20] Although its continuous and flowing nature set it apart somewhat from her other piano works, the *Alleluia* contains two elements that Arzruni and others find generally characteristic of her music: a propulsive, perpetual motion coupled with a restrained lyricism. This is not a toccata in the style of Bach, but rather—as Schumann and Ravel used this form—a perpetual motion. Like the opening movement of her first sonata, the *Alleluia* opens with a declamatory section before the actual toccata begins. The notes D, F, G, A, and C are sounded repeatedly,

Figure 7.6 *Alleluia*, measures 1-4. Copyright © 1947 by Carl Fischer, Inc. New York. Used by permission.

creating a chime-like atmosphere. One might hear this as pentatonic or even bitonal, since the tones of both the D minor and F major triads are present. However, since the piece is in B-flat major and the D in the opening bars sounds like a pedal point, it is simply a prolonged mediant area. The toccata itself begins and ends very much in B-flat major with practically constant running eighth note motion. A contrasting theme also present in the toccata seems to harken back to the D minor of the introduction.

The *Pastoral Prelude* was written as an introduction for the *Alleluia*, although it may also be played independently. It was premiered by Brooks Smith at Town Hall in 1950 and was published by Carl Fischer in 1952. This work is a three-page, lyrical piece in ABA form. It clearly begins in C, albeit in a pandiatonic rather than a functional way. That is, since we can

Figure 7.7 *Alleluia*, measures 12-15. Copyright © 1947 by Carl Fischer, Inc. New York. Used by permission.

Figure 7.8 *Alleluia*, measures 67-71. Copyright © 1947 by Carl Fischer, Inc. New York. Used by permission.

not functionally analyze or label a chord made up of B, C, and D, the tonal center is determined by the particular diatonic tones used. The piece ends in D major. This is the first time in a piano piece that Talma ends in a different key from that in which she began. The conclusion in D serves as a tonal connection between the *Prelude* and the *Alleluia*. In listing the *Pastoral Prelude* in his book on contemporary piano music, Stanley Butler comments that it "makes no concession to an easy appeal, thereby gaining [an] awesome attraction."[21]

The *Venetian Folly: Overture and Barcarolle* is an unpublished piano work written as incidental music for a play by Carlo Goldini. The music is dedicated to Otto Zoff, who translated the play into English and asked Talma to write music for it. Unfortunately, the play was not performed at the MacDowell Colony that summer of 1947 in which the music was completed; consequently, the music remains unperformed. Other than *Soundshots*, this "Italian Suite" is Talma's sole venture into programmatic piano music.

Both the *Overture* and *Barcarolle* are in ABA form and are quite overtly tonal. In the *Overture* a Phrygian mode in C-sharp occurs with the hands playing in unison for two octaves. (Interestingly, traces of the Phrygian mode also occur in the opening of the first piano sonata, in the descending bass line in measures four to five, and in the avoidance of the leading tone. These allusions to modality in no way compromise the fundamental diatonic structure inherent in all of Talma's music until 1953.)

The *Six Etudes* were written in response to a request in 1952 from composer John Edmunds, who was at that time director of a new music group in San Francisco; Talma wrote them for the pianist of the group (which apparently disbanded soon thereafter). The first performance was given by Beveridge Webster at Carnegie Recital Hall on April 18, 1955; he later recorded the etudes on Desto Records. The composer notes:

The etudes were written to challenge the pianist, technically and musically. For this I chose six pianistic problems which, with the exception of the staccato one, no. 2, had not been the subject of previous etudes, at least of those known to me. I have tried, first of all, to make them pieces of music, and only secondarily pieces of virtuosity. I am not at all interested in writing etudes which are merely display pieces.[22]

In a review of the *Six Etudes,* Irwin Freundlich commented: "In my opinion the entire set demands serious consideration by pianists searching for 'playable' and 'listenable' works from the contemporary American repertoire. In addition to their intrinsic musical and pianistic substance, the six pieces are meticulously pedaled and expertly fingered."[23]

In addition to their innate musical and pianistic worth, the *Six Etudes* are significant in Talma's output because they contain her first serial writing. Each etude is based on a different twelve-tone set. Perhaps because they are her first serial compositions, they are sometimes stricter in that regard than her later serial works. From the beginning, however, she uses serial technique in her own, unique way, never applying the method dogmatically in a textbook manner.

The first etude is dedicated to Thornton Wilder, who had originally suggested writing an etude for the study of pianissimo. This Talma did, making the etude more difficult by interpolating "a few fortissimo passages, since it is much harder to pull back to pianissimo from fortissimo, than it is to keep on all the time pianissimo."[24]

After its initial statement, the set appears in inversion, retrograde, and retrograde inversion. She also presents the set in vertical arrangements, canonic imitation, and, at one point, using half the set at a time. The set

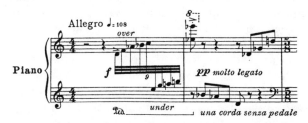

Figure 7.9 *First Etude,* measures 1-2. Copyright © 1962 G. Schirmer, Inc. All rights reserved. Used by permission.

itself contains tonal remnants; as early as the second measure, before notes eleven and twelve of the set have even appeared, notes one through four are repeated, outlining a B-flat dominant seventh chord. In view of the E-flat which precedes this chord, a tonal connection to an E-flat tonal center can be drawn.[25] The etude ends with a minor third, D and F, the opening two notes of the set. The allusion to D minor is supported by an A in the bass voice immediately before the last chord. Such intimations of tonality in her very first serial piece support her contention that "any new form of expression must be an extension of what has been in the past."[26] Indeed, many of her twelve-tone constructions contain implicit tonal relationships in the form of perfect fourths and fifths, major and minor thirds, and triadic sections within the set.

The second etude is a study in staccato, marked *sempre senza pedale*. As Ravel did when he wrote the *Piano Concerto for the Left Hand* for his friend, Paul Wittgenstein, who had lost his right arm in World War I, Talma wrote this etude for an excellent student of hers, Estelle Hershler, who lost her right leg in a car accident. One is therefore to take the *senza pedale* very literally. The piece is highly effective.

The third etude is dedicated to John Edmunds in thanks for his commission. The only pedal utilized in this etude is the sostenuto pedal, for the study of which the etude is written. Talma assumed that since most European pianos have no sostenuto pedal, no etudes from that part of the world would have been written dealing with it. This etude is strikingly original and exciting.

Etude number four is a study for wide skips in both hands in opposite directions. Talma got the inspiration for this from a difficult passage in the piano part of Paul Nordoff's *Sonata for Violin and Piano*. She had experienced great difficulty when she played it and decided to compose an etude based on the same kinds of skips she had encountered. The etude is dedicated to Nordoff. Marked *senza pedale*, the uncompromising writing requires of the pianist a fleet and precise command of the keyboard. From first notes to last, there are constant skips with no place to rest.

The fifth etude is a study for frequent hand-crossings. Talma was inspired here by the sonatas of Scarlatti, which involve this technique. It is dedicated to Talma's good friend Guiomar Novaes, "who played those sonatas so beautifully."[27] This is an attractive and extremely difficult etude. Except for two measures, where there are specific pedaling instructions, *senza pedale* is again the general indication. The tempo is quick, and the note patterns are irregular.

The final etude confronts the problem of steadiness of pulse. A passacaglia-like *molto adagio*, it is written for an increasing number of notes per beat, beginning with one note per beat and ending with twenty-four. The dedication is to Beveridge Webster, an important proponent of contemporary piano music in general and of Talma's works in particular.

Talma's *Piano Sonata No. 2* was started in 1944, but not completed until 1955. Talma explains:

My second piano sonata was composed to unite tonal and serial elements in one work. In August 1944 I wrote the first nine measures and measures thirty-six through thirty-nine of the first movement, and the first seven measures of the second movement. This beginning I had to set aside to do other things. In January 1952 I took it up again. By then I had become interested in serial writing and did not wish to return to an exclusively tonal style. But I liked those twenty measures, which are tonal, and wanted to use them. So I decided to combine them with a serial continuation and see what I could make of that. All the movements employ this procedure in some form or other. After another interruption of three years, the sonata was completed, August 22, 1955, at the MacDowell Colony.[28]

The sonata is dedicated to Thornton Wilder; it has been recorded on C. R. I. by Herbert Rogers and was published by Carl Fischer in 1972. Rogers says of this sonata: "It is one of the best contemporary sonatas of that ilk [American, mid-century], and certainly one of her best pieces. It is a piece that is so hard technically that if you don't have a very fine piano, it just doesn't work. The nature of the music is such that it has to be played accurately in order for the lines to come out. It is not at all vague."[29] He goes on to compare her music with a Beethoven sonata or Chopin etude in the sense that one must approach it both technically and interpretively as one would approach the standard piano repertoire of the eighteenth and nineteenth centuries. He finds Talma's piano writing typified by very sharp, intricate patterns, contrasted with chordal, consonant writing. Representations of such traits are readily found in the second sonata.

The opening movement displays a rhythmically sharp and accented first theme which continues unabated until measure thirty-six, at which point a lush, gentle theme appears. Throughout the movement, the two contrasting characters alternate, ending with the lento, lyrical theme.

Figure 7.10 *Sonata No. 2*, first movement, second theme, measures 36-39. Copyright © 1972 by Carl Fischer, Inc. New York. Used by permission.

The second movement, marked Tranquillo, is a five-voiced, song-like movement. This is followed by a scherzo-like Allegro molto vivace, a very effective movement somewhat reminiscent in character of the second movement of Samuel Barber's *Piano Sonata*. Being motivically and harmonically very clever, this movement serves as a nice complement both to the lyrical second movement, and to the dramatic Allegro energico that follows and which requires great physical endurance from the pianist.

The use of either tonal or serial elements is never systematic or academic, but rather as Talma has said: "All these things are determined by what the music needs. It responds to something I want. I always know what I don't want."[30]

Talma's two piano sonatas have both striking similarities and differences. The fast sections of the second sonata have a motoric, clipped, somewhat inflexible character (for example, the opening measures and the third

movement), while the first sonata is more driving, rhythmically less predict-
able, and in a sense more dramatic. The second sonata begins with a kind
of Alberti bass in the left hand and in other ways as well conveys a classical
orientation. Although consciously emulating the antiromantic style of
Stravinsky, Talma expresses some romantic gestures in the first sonata,
albeit tempered by a classical sense of proportion and clarity. It is the third
movement of the second sonata which characterizes the piece as a whole and
which distinguishes it from the first sonata. The character of this scherzo
movement—whimsical and dry—does not appear in the first sonata, which
remains straightforward and direct. (The first sonata is minus a scherzo
movement altogether.)

The *Bagatelle*, written in 1950, should be included in performance with
the *Three Bagatelles* of 1955. The earlier bagatelle is a delicate, sparse work
with frequently changing meters. Although the key signature has four flats,
the piece ends in C minor. The relationship between A-flat major and C
minor here is reminiscent of the tonic/mediant relationship in the *Alleluia*.
Common tones of the tonic and mediant allow for a fluid transition from
one key to the other. (The later bagatelles are, like the *Sonata No. 2* and the
Passacaglia and Fugue, dedicated to Thornton Wilder; this group of three
was, in fact, written as a present for him.)

Bagatelle No. 1, based on a twelve-tone set stated in the first two measures, is a delicately polyphonic work reminiscent of certain of J. S. Bach's
keyboard inventions.

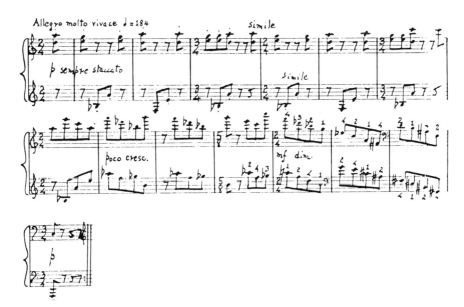

Figure 7.11 *Sonata No. 2*, third movement, measures 1-14. Copyright © 1972 by
Carl Fischer, Inc. New York. Used by permission.

Bagatelle No. 2 employs two contrasting materials in alternating sections in an ABABAB form. Elements of both set technique and tonality coexist in this rhythmically arresting work. *Bagatelle No. 3* is a strongly tonal work in a bouncy perpetual motion. A major/minor triad (that is, a triad with both the major and minor third sounding simultaneously) appears with enough regularity to warrant calling it a basic sonority.

All four bagatelles taken together comprise a lovely group of pieces on a smaller scale and of a less intense nature than most of Talma's other piano works. They were composed between the *Piano Sonata No. 2* and *The Alcestiad*, much like Beethoven's *Six Bagatelles*, op. 126, which were composed after the Ninth Symphony and before the first of the late string quartets. Like the Beethoven, Talma's *Bagatelles* contain basic seeds of her style, a distillation of larger gestures.

Talma began composing the *Passacaglia and Fugue* in 1955 while she was in Rome on a Senior Fulbright Research Grant to compose *The Alcestiad*, but she did not complete it until 1962 in Florence. The twelve-tone set that is the basis for both parts of the passacaglia and fugue is constructed so that the interval between each of the six pairs of tones is a consonant, tonal interval: a major third, perfect fifth, or perfect fourth.

E-flat G F C D B-flat B F-sharp E A G-sharp C-sharp

In addition, each group of four notes contains a triad and, in the case of the second two groups, a seventh chord. Talma uses these groups within the set as chords, as illustrated by the opening of the piece. The use of these inner groups also occurs when the set is inverted or transposed. In fact, the inverted and transposed sets are sometimes in striking relation to one another. For example, the inverted form of the set is: E-flat B C-sharp

Figure 7.12 *Passacaglia*, measures 1-16. Used by permission of the composer.

F-sharp E G-sharp G C D A B-flat F; the transposition on E: E G-sharp F-sharp C-sharp D-sharp B B-sharp G F B-flat A D. Each half of both of these sets contains the identical pitch material as the same half of the other set, although the notes are in a different order. Different forms of the set can occur simultaneously, creating a kind of polyserial texture—sometimes with strong tonal implications. For example, in measure fifty, the right hand plays the inversion on E, and the left hand plays the inversion on C-sharp: the resulting intervallic relationship of a minor third between the two sets produces the marked sensation of a particularly prepared final tonic.

Soundshots is a group of twenty short, descriptive pieces. The first, second, and twentieth were written in 1944, the remainder in 1974. The dedication is to Şahan Arzruni, and it was he who played the first performance on WNYC radio (1974). The work was published by Hinshaw Music in 1979.

Although not written necessarily for children, these pieces can, like Schumann's *Kinderszenen*, be played by children. Many of the pieces are inspired by natural and animal sounds with titles such as "Duck Duet," "The Clocks," "Whirling Pins," and "The Robin." These are whimsical, charming, and imaginative little works that cover a wide musical and technical gamut. From a pedagogical vantage point, *Soundshots* makes challenging and interesting teaching material for the intermediate piano student.

Talma's most recent solo work for piano is *Textures*, written in 1977 in tribute to Beveridge Webster on his seventieth birthday. It was commissioned by the International Society for Contemporary Music, and was premiered by Webster in 1978 at an ISCM concert at Carnegie Recital Hall.

Textures is a sectional, fantasy-like virtuoso piece concerned with the exploration of contrasting spatial layouts and tone colors. It begins with an arpeggiated section marked "rhapsodically," which covers an extremely wide pitch range, followed by a section marked "without inflection." Two more sections succeed, the last one resuming the character of the opening.

The piano works of Louise Talma form a varied yet cohesive body of compositions. Although her style and technique developed over the course of thirty-four years, the music is always distinctively her own and certainly well worth the attention of serious pianists.

NOTES

1. The Sibelius Medal for Composition from the Harriet Cohen International Awards; London, England, 1963.
2. Personal interview with Louise Talma, March 31, 1982.
3. The Institute of Musical Art became incorporated with The Juilliard School of Music in 1946.

4. Personal interview with Louise Talma, March 31, 1982.

5. None of Talma's piano solo works written before 1943 are available. In fact, the earliest work she lists in her curriculum vitae is *In Principio Erat Verbum* for chorus and organ written in 1939. *Two Dances* for piano solo, written in 1934, is included as part of her piano output in some sources. However, Talma no longer considers it part of her mature work and does not wish that it be seen.

6. *Harmony for the College Student*, 1966, and *Functional Harmony*, written in collaboration with James Harrison and Robert Levin, 1970.

7. Personal interview with Louise Talma, February 13, 1982.

8. Ibid.

9. Elaine Barkin, "Louise Talma, 'The Tolling Bell,' " *Perspectives of New Music* 10, no. 2 (1972): 150.

10. Personal interview with Louise Talma, February 13, 1982.

11. Arthur Berger, "Stravinsky and the Younger Composers," *Score* no. 12 (June 1955): 44.

12. David Ewen, *Composers Since 1900, First Supplement* (New York: Wilson, 1980), p. 296.

13. C. Wesley Steiner, *Buffalo Philharmonic Notes*, December 12, 1965, pp. 24-26.

14. Joseph Machlis, *Introduction to Contemporary Music*, 3d ed. (New York: W. W. Norton, 1979), p. 592.

15. Talma to Julia Anne Morris, June 15, 1980. Ms. Morris wrote to Talma on March 30, 1980, requesting information about the *Six Etudes* for a proposed thesis on etudes by American composers.

16. Personal interview with Louise Talma, March 31, 1982.

17. Ibid.

18. Robert Sabin, "New Piano Pieces in Various Styles," *Musical America* 69, no. 1 (January 1949), p. 32.

19. Album Jacket Notes, *Piano Music by Five Women Composers,* Pianist, Virginia Eskin, Musical Heritage Society, 4236.

20. Personal interview with Şahan Arzruni, April 20, 1982.

21. Stanley Butler, *Guide to the Best in Contemporary Piano Music: An Annotated List of Graded Solo Piano Music Published Since 1960*, vol. 2 (Metuchen, N.J.: Scarecrow Press, 1973), p. 64.

22. Talma to Ms. Morris, June 15, 1980.

23. Irwin Freundlich, "Louise Talma: Six Etudes," *Notes* 20, no. 4 (1963): 582.

24. Talma to Ms. Morris, June 15, 1980.

25. This is discussed in Elizabeth Mruk Stevens, "The Influence of Nadia Boulanger on Composition in the United States: A Study of Piano Solo Works by Her American Students" (Ph.D. diss., Boston University, School of Fine and Applied Arts, 1975), pp. 91-93.

26. Personal interview with Louise Talma, February 13, 1982.

27. Talma to Ms. Morris, June 15, 1980.

28. Album Jacket Notes, *Piano Sonata No. 2*, Pianist, Herbert Rogers, C. R. I., SD 281.

29. Personal interview with Herbert Rogers, April 12, 1982.

30. Personal interview with Louise Talma, February 13, 1982.

THE SOLO WORKS FOR PIANO OF LOUISE TALMA

Published

Alleluia in Form of Toccata. Carl Fischer, 1947.
Bagatelle No. 3 (from *Three Bagatelles*). Published in Kurt Stone's *100 Pieces for Piano*, Scribner, 1955.
Pastoral Prelude. Carl Fischer, 1952.
Piano Sonata No. 1. Carl Fischer, 1948.
Piano Sonata No. 2. Carl Fischer, 1972.
Six Etudes. Schirmer, 1963.
Soundshots. Hinshaw Music, Inc., 1979.

Unpublished (available from the composer)

Bagetelles.
Passacaglia and Fugue.
Textures.
Venetian Folly: Overture and Barcarolle.

BIBLIOGRAPHY

Adcock, Joe. "Concert Today at Civic Center." *Philadelphia Sunday Bulletin*, February 10, 1974, p. 5.
Alvarez, Aida. "Daily Closeup." *New York Post*, March 1, 1974, Magazine Section, p. 37.
Anderson, Ruth E. *Contemporary American Composers: A Biographical Dictionary*. Boston: G. K. Hall, 1976.
ASCAP Biographical Dictionary of Composers, Authors and Publishers. 4th ed. New York: ASCAP, 1980.
Baker's Biographical Dictionary of Musicians. 6th ed. Edited by N. Slonimsky. New York: Schirmer, 1978.
Barkin, Elaine. "Louise Talma, 'The Tolling Bell.' " *Perspectives of New Music* 10, no. 2 (1972): 142-52.
Berges, Ruth. "The German Scene." *The Music Magazine* 164 (May 1962): 33-34.
Block, Adrienne, and Carol Neuls-Bates, comps. *Women in American Music: A Bibliography of Music and Literature*. Westport, Conn.: Greenwood Press, 1979.
Bull, Storm. *Index to Biographies of Contemporary Composers*. Metuchen, N.J.: Scarecrow Press, 1974.
Cohen, Aaron I. *International Encyclopedia of Women Composers*. New York: R. R. Bowker Co., 1981.
Cohn, Arthur. *Recorded Classical Music: A Critical Guide to Compositions and Performances*. Riverside, N.J.: Schirmer Books, 1981.
Emerson, Gordon. "Ms. Talma on Women and Wilder." *The New Haven Register*, March 14, 1978, p. 1D.

Ericson, Raymond. "Celebrating Louise Talma." *New York Times*, February 4, 1977, p. C22.

Ewen, David. *Composers Since 1900*. First supplement. New York: H. W. Wilson Co., 1980.

Goss, Madeleine. *Modern Music Makers*. New York: Dutton, 1952.

Hixon, Don L., and Don Hennessee, comps. *Women in Music: A Bio-bibliography*. Metuchen, N.J.: Scarecrow Press, 1975.

Le Page, Jane Weiner. *Women Composers, Conductors and Musicians of the Twentieth Century: Selected Biographies*. Metuchen, N.J.: Scarecrow Press, 1980.

Meggett, Joan M. *Keyboard Music by Women Composers*. Westport, Conn.: Greenwood Press, 1981.

Moor, Paul, "Louise Talma's 'The Alcestiad' in Premiere at Frankfurt Opera." *New York Times*, March 2, 1962, p. 25.

The New Grove Dictionary of Music and Musicians. 6th ed. Edited by Stanley Sadie. London: Macmillan, 1980.

Reis, Claire. *Composers in America*. New York: Macmillan, 1947; reprint ed., New York: Da Capo, 1977.

"The Singing Greeks." *Time*, March 23, 1962, p. 54.

Thompson, Oscar, ed. *The International Cyclopedia of Music and Musicians*. 9th ed. New York: Dodd Mead, 1964.

Vinton, John. *Dictionary of Contemporary Music*. New York: Dutton, 1974.

8

Invisible Theater:
The Music of Meredith Monk

GREGORY SANDOW

In one of her recent theater pieces, Meredith Monk used a Dutch actress and let her speak only Dutch, perhaps because it was the language the actress spoke best or because speaking Dutch was something nobody else in the cast could do. Monk treats herself as a composer in more or less the same way. Just as she sees no reason for a Dutch actress to speak English, she sees no reason why she herself should use the standard range of compositional techniques. Instead she speaks her own brand of musical Dutch: like many experimental composers she sticks to a few characteristic procedures that work well for her. These can be heard on *Airwaves,* a two-record set she shares with thirteen other experimental musicians and sound artists (One Ten Records OT 001/2), and on her four solo discs: *Our Lady of Late* (Minona Records MN 1001); *Songs from the Hill/Tablet* (Wergo SM 10 22); *Key* (Lovely Music LML 1051); and *Dolmen Music* (ECM-1-1197). Only the last two are currently available.

Her compositional procedures include a variety of unusual vocal techniques; simple repetitive keyboard accompaniments, clearly derived from her early experience with folk music and rock; equally simple but often subtly varied, often modal melodies and melodic cells; and additive, more or less improvised, musical forms in which basic ideas are repeated with constant small variations and/or alternated with other material, which in turn is usually repeated, again with small variation. Both the musical ideas and the way they are handled are reminiscent more of birdsong than of composed music; Monk's solo pieces sound more like a kind of repeated personal cry than like any structured compositional entity.

And why not? Her main instrument, after all, is her own voice. Everything else in her music functions almost as an extension of it, or at least as an extension of herself. When she has written for other singers, she has trained them in techniques very like her own. *Our Lady of Late* uses Collin Walcott's glass percussion, but apart from that, her instrumentation is limited to jew's harp (almost an alter ego for her voice) and keyboards, both of which she plays herself; soprano recorder, which found its way into *Tablet* because a member of Monk's vocal ensemble knew how to play it; and cello, which is incorporated in *Dolmen Music* for the same reason. Her use of instruments, in other words, is a matter not so much of compositional choice as of opportunity.

What she does with her voice is as idiomatic as her use of instruments; singing isn't quite an adequate word for it, though in some ways she sings very well. A phrase from her theater piece *Quarry* is typical of what a vocal traditionalist would say lies well for her:

Figure 8.1 "Procession" from *Quarry*. Copyright © 1976 by Meredith Monk. Used by permission of the composer.

It is typical also of her modal melodies and her simple, pop-like accompaniments. In an exceptional passage from *Tablet*, she blends registers and glides in portamento over a register break with a skill any classical singer would envy:

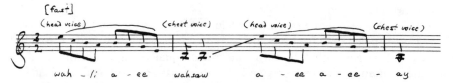

Figure 8.2 From *Tablet*. Copyright © 1977 by Meredith Monk. Used by permission of the composer.

But from a classical point of view, her vocal technique is actually rather limited. She says she has a four-octave range, but she doesn't have access to each register on every vowel and at any dynamic, as classical voice technique would prescribe. The extremes of her range have their own, apparently unchanging, character. Her highest sounds are bright, sometimes wispy, never full; they're produced, oddly enough, on an "ee" vowel, which classically trained sopranos would rather avoid in their high range. Her gloriously wine-dark bottom register is much more open; even the "oo" vowel, which she often uses there, sounds much more relaxed than it would, say, on Maureen Forrester's bottom notes. Monk almost never changes register without a pause (which is why the passage from *Tablet* is so exceptional). Most of her phrases lie—regardless of the octave they're in—within a very narrow compass.

But why should she care about classical voice technique? Her field is experimental music; she's interested in finding new ways to sing. "Over the years I have developed a vocabulary and a style designed to utilize as wide a range of vocal sounds as possible," she says in liner notes to *Dolmen Music*. Or, as Robert Palmer quotes her in the liner notes for *Songs from the Hill/Tablet:* "I've been trying to extend the voice in as many ways as possible, utilizing as many resonating chambers, different kinds of syllables, positions of the mouth, the inside of the mouth, the tongue, the lips, and breathing techniques [*sic*]." The results are extraordinary. Yet I wonder—even though I know she thinks about how she makes each sound— whether she has really extended vocal technique in any extraordinary way. Or, to put it differently: are her achievements really new techniques? Mostly not, I think. She is able to emphasize one overtone or another as she sings, producing a filter-like, quasi-electronic effect, or sometimes (by strongly bringing out one or another overtone) intones two notes at once. These things are techniques, because in principle, at least, anyone could learn to do them and then use them for expressive ends in ways that had nothing to do with Monk. (Actually, Monk herself doesn't use these techniques much. Karlheinz Stockhausen mandates a much broader control of overtones for anyone performing *Stimmung;* in *Eight Songs for a Mad King* Peter Maxwell Davies requires a pinpoint control of vocal multiphonics that Monk may not have. Strictly as a performer, she'd be unlikely to be in demand to sing anyone else's music, assuming she'd want to.) She works with microtones; this seems as if it might be a musical effect rather than a vocal technique, but her most characteristic use of them may best be termed a "musical effect tied to the voice": an irregular glide down from a sustained pitch. This is truly a technique, since anyone could learn to do it, although its expressive uses seem more limited.

The rest of what Monk might call her techniques strike me as being simply sounds—wonderful sounds, but still just sounds. They're very much her own—it's possible that no one else could produce them—but in principle they're nothing new. She colors, modulates, and alters her voice, but so do pop, jazz, and rock singers and the very few opera singers who are genuine vocal actors. Monk thins her sound to a wisp without losing control; so did Maria Callas, when on the Angel recording of Bellini's *I Puritani* she made each of the downward scales at the end of "Vien, diletto" more and more ghostly and mad. Callas needed technique to do that, but she wouldn't have called the process itself a "technique." Probably she'd have called it acting, and in the same way, the most wonderful of Monk's sounds seem not so much vocal or even musical achievements, but rather a strange and haunting kind of musical drama.

That's most obvious in many of the *Songs from the Hill,* where titles like "Insect" or "Old Woman's Song" show how impressively specific her vocal imagery can be. After only a few moments of "Prairie Ghost"—wispy and relaxed, but at the same time insistent; wistful, but also good-humored—it's clear that she's a great actress; she remains one elsewhere, even when her imagery isn't overt (it usually isn't), or even when she's mannered or childish. (That happens all too often: compare her cries, "I still have my hands!" "I still have my me-mo-ries!" on side one of *Dolmen Music.* It is at once aloof, cloying, and fey, though I'd never have thought such a combination possible.) I could argue that she's limited as a composer. The unaccompanied *Songs from the Hill* strikes me as her best work; next are the songs with keyboard, buoyed by their accompaniments, but also a bit dragged down by them because the keyboard licks seem conventional and because the vocal lines dovetail with them too predictably. *Our Lady of Late* is a special case, a timbral exercise more in a generalized early-1970s experimental idiom than in Monk's personal style; I don't find it especially convincing. Lowest of all I'd rank the ensemble pieces, which don't seem to do enough with the ensemble possibilities Monk's specially trained singers ought to offer. In *Dolmen Music,* for example, despite her talk of working with "the unique quality of each voice," she doesn't do nearly as much with the three men in her ensemble as with the three women. Perhaps this is due to compositional inexperience; perhaps she understands women's voices better because she's worked so much with her own. Another problem with the ensemble works is that they tend to be long: she's not good with large-scale form. *Tablet* could very well end several times before its actual conclusion. But at least it's held together by the same kind of keyboard accompaniments that hold many of the solo songs in place; with no ostinato, *Dolmen Music* seems to lack a musical spine and wanders.

But so what? When I think of Meredith Monk, I think of what she does well, above all of the opening song from her theater piece *Quarry* pouring forth in mournful stasis from an old-fashioned radio near the center of the expansive performing area (which the audience surrounded, like spectators at a football game). And I've always thought that the theater works (which have toured the United States, Canada, and Europe) are her best compositions, not because the songs in them are any better than the songs written separately, but because here the interrelated sounds, movement, words, and imagery flow into one another with all the assurance her purely musical composing doesn't always have. *Key,* she says, is not so much a record as, in her words, "invisible theater," an audio version of what she does on stage. In the same way, I'd call *Quarry* and other works like it—which move from point to point with perfect emotional grace, even if their meaning is not entirely clear—not theater, opera, dance, or even performance art, but, to use a transformation of Monk's own phrase, visible music.

9

Women Composers of Electronic Music in the United States

BEVERLY GRIGSBY

This chapter is part of a larger study on women composers in North America. The second part, on composers in Canada, will appear in the next edition of *The Musical Woman.* Composers are grouped according to stylistic affinity, specific compositional technique, use of the electronic medium, or by other factors held in common. Each woman's work is analyzed individually and at length. Quoted extracts are from correspondence or interviews with the author. A selected discography, organized alphabetically by composer, completes the chapter.

* * *

Some forty women composers of electronically generated, processed, or manipulated music (using both analog and digital computers) working in fifteen states have brought to their neoteric art a renewed spirit of humanism, extraordinary powers of invention and originality, and a vivacity of imagination that well merits the many grants and awards they have been accorded. They hold a variety of distinguished positions in the academic world and also in the commercial world of television, theater, and recording.

About half of these women hold professorships at leading universities that support electronic and/or computer music studios, and therefore they are actively involved in the teaching as well as in the creation of the art. Fifteen women are directors of these studios and, of these, six are founders (Ruth Anderson, Hunter College, New York; Jane Brockman, University of Connecticut, Storrs; Emma Lou Diemer, University of California, Santa Barbara; Beverly Grigsby, California State University, Northridge; Jean E. Ivey, Peabody Conservatory, Baltimore, Maryland; Pauline Oliveros, Mills College, Oakland, California).

Some women composers have been involved in equipment design (Ruth Anderson, Joan La Barbara, Maggie Payne, Daria Semegen), some in designing instruments (Laurie Anderson), and some have been commissioned by major electronic industries, such as Texas Instruments, Apple

Computer, and New England Digital, to devise either hardware or software packages (Suzanne Ciani, Laurie Spiegel).

The coveted Composer Fellowships, awarded by the National Endowment for the Arts, have been received by some twenty American women, about half of all those composing for the electronic medium. In some cases, multiple awards have been won (twice by Doris Hays, Joan La Barbara, and Priscilla McLean; three times by Laurie Anderson; and four times by Daria Semegen). In addition, many of the composers have been Rockefeller, Guggenheim, and Fulbright fellows. Their music has won them gold records (representing one million dollars in gross sales), BMI, CAPS, ASCAP, Armstrong, Clio, and Golden Globe awards, as well as Meet the Composer and Ford Foundation grants. They have received recognition from the National Federation of Music Clubs and the American Composers Alliance and have won awards at the international level (Prix de Rome, Barbara Kolb) or at their local or state levels to carry on research and study. The MacDowell Colony and Yaddo are havens in which they write, and the number of commissions awarded to them is far too extensive for this introduction.

These noted women have studied with a variety of acknowledged twentieth-century masters, such as Arnold Schoenberg, Béla Bartók, Paul Hindemith, Ernst Krenek, Edgard Varèse, Milton Babbitt, John Cage, Hugh Le Caine, Hans Barth, Nadia Boulanger, Pierre Schaeffer, Vladimir Ussachevsky, Otto Luening, Witold Lutosławski, and others. Some of the women themselves have been mentors to other women discussed here: Jeannie Pool has studied with Ruth Anderson, Megan Roberts with Emma Lou Diemer, Patricia Zanardi with Beverly Grigsby, Alexina Louie with Pauline Oliveros, and Anne LeBaron with Daria Semegen. Many more have been producer-organizers of programs, broadcasts, and festivals and/or writers on the subject of women in music: Beth Anderson, Tommie Carl, Marcia Cohen, Joan La Barbara, Priscilla McLean, Ann McMillan, Elizabeth Pizer, and Jeannie Pool.

As composers they move in a variating complex of stylistic directions. The two extremes of mathematical postserialism and classical Cagian indeterminacy (which often sound the same in aural perception) are well represented; but the music of certain of these composers eclectically interweaves somewhere between the totally controlled and aleatoric realms, while the works of others stand completely outside these schools. Most avow their humanistic tendencies and a determination to communicate, be it through participatory pieces leading to meditation and healing (Ruth Anderson, Kay Gardner, Annea Lockwood, Pauline Oliveros, Alice Shields) or through pure commercialism (in the best sense of the word) enlivened with an originality that raises it far above the mundane and trivial (Laurie Anderson, Suzanne Ciani, Dika Newlin).

These composers embrace a variety of aesthetics from the traditional attitude—which considers the sound all important—to a concept of performance as "process"—which holds that the way the sound is made is as relevant as the sound itself. Some are minimalists, some use citation and symbolic action. Some structure and color their compositions according to their own virtuosity and hence tend to expand the capacity of their instrument as well as the literature written for that instrument. Laurie Anderson and especially Joan La Barbara's live and electronically altered vocal ventures and Emma Lou Diemer's flights of keyboard and electronic virtuosity are good examples. There are those who prefer live electronics, those that cleave to environmental or nature sounds alone or in combination with electronics until they merge into an imago-abstract of sonic articulation (the list is long in both categories), and those who lean toward text-sound with electronic processing (plus, in some cases, electronic generation through computers and vocoders). Most of the women are interested in and have worked in multi-media; quite a few have written electronic film scores, some for major producers (Ciani for Lily Tomlin, Grigsby for Francis Ford Coppola). Video tape and computers have been of particular interest to Ciani, Payne, Roberts, and Spiegel. Creating electronic music for ballet has attracted composers such as Marcia Cohen, Barberi Paull, Maggie Payne, and Laurie Spiegel.

These artists work out of all sorts of studios with a variety of equipment, ranging from the oldest analog synthesizers to the latest computerized ones. Some composers, such as Ciani, have home studios that may be envied by most universities; others, such as Jeannie Pool, work with any equipment they can find and in any condition. They have been influenced by Eastern philosophies, political polemics, jazz, rock, new wave, new diatonicism, new romanticism, new modalism, impressionism, improvisation, surrealism, and "kitsch," but most of all, they have been influenced by the electronic medium itself and a desire to create in it. Composers such as Dika Newlin have moved through the gamut in influences from pure Schoenbergian dodecaphonicism to new wave, country, ragtime and blues; travelling from academia to pop turf, from concertizing pianist to *musique concrète* to analog synthesizers to computer-generated sound to singing her own ballads: "I may be the first 59-year-old rock star [most others being either dead or burned out well before that age!]" Others, such as Emma Lou Diemer, have moved, as she says, from writing for acoustical instruments in a neoclassic vein ["with much more sympathy for and empathy with twentieth-century French and Russian music in this genre than with the Second Viennese School serialists"] to an interest in expressing themselves through computers. Often, the impetus for these composers to move into or out of the field is the access to equipment (or the lack of it) and a friendly place to work. However, once exposed to the medium, there is virtually no escape from its sonic impression, which forever afterward permeates their acoustical writing as well as the overall way in which they think about the parameters of sound.

Whatever their directions—which zigzag across the cosmos of the electronic universe—these composers have made an impact that needs to be recounted. Their work exerts an influence not only on this decade, through such commercial successes as Suzanne Ciani in television and Laurie Anderson in recording, but will extend its influence into and across the next century through the teaching and training that they bring to their pupils, and beyond, in a never-ending cross-fertilization of ideas and concepts.

In this compilation of forty women, I attempt to let them speak for themselves as much as possible. I thank them for their generous communications; in most cases composer's quotations have been taken from these communiques. I dedicate this article to their genius and celebrate their musical achievements.

THE COMPOSERS

Beth Anderson (New York, New York)

Laurie Anderson (New York, New York)

Ruth Anderson (Hunter College, New York, New York)

Jane Brockman (University of Connecticut, Storrs)

Tommie Carl (McLean, Virginia)

Suzanne Ciani (New York, New York)

Marcia Cohen (St. Petersburg, Florida)

Frances Danforth (Ann Arbor, Michigan)

Kay Gardner (Stonington, Maine)

Emma Lou Diemer (University of California, Santa Barbara)

Janet Gilbert (St. Olaf College, Northfield, Minnesota)

Beverly Grigsby (California State University, Northridge)

Doris Hays (New York, New York)

Jean Eichelberger Ivey (Peabody Conservatory, Baltimore, Maryland)

Barbara Kolb (New York, New York)

Joan La Barbara (California Institute of the Arts, Valencia)

Anne LeBaron (Odenville, Alabama; State University of New York, Stony Brook, Long Island)

Annea Lockwood (Hunter College, New York, New York)

Priscilla McLean (Austin, Texas)

Ann McMillan (New York, New York)

Joyce Mekeel (Boston University, Massachusetts)

Dika Newlin (Virginia Commonwealth University, Richmond)

Gladys Nordenstrom (Palm Springs, California)

Pauline Oliveros (Zen Art Center, Mt. Tremper, New York)

Barberi Paull (New York, New York)

Maggie Payne (Mills College, Oakland, California)

Sylvia Pengilly (Loyola University, New Orleans, Louisiana)

Elizabeth Pizer (Three Mile Bay, New York)

Jeannie Pool (Los Angeles, California)

Sally Johnston Reid (Abilene Christian University, Texas)

Megan Roberts (Houston, Texas)

Daria Semegen (State University of New York, Stony Brook, Long Island)

Alice Shields (Columbia University, New York)

Pril Smiley (Columbia University, New York)

Laurie Spiegel (New York, New York)

Helen Stanley (Jacksonville, Florida)

Diane Thome (University of Washington, Seattle)

Ruth White (Los Angeles, California)

Beatrice Witkin (New York, New York)

Patricia Zanardi (Reseda, California)

Jeannie Pool, Doris Hays, and Beth Anderson have worked with text-sound/sound poetry and tape. JEANNIE POOL (b. 1951), a music historian, author, lecturer, radio producer, and founder and national coordinator of the International Congress on Women in Music, earned a B.A. in music from Hunter College (1977), where she studied composition and electronic music with Ruth Anderson.* Pool did graduate work in historical musicology at Columbia (1977-1979), specializing in women musicians throughout history. Although she has written *concrète* works such as *Basic Piano 101* (1977) and *From the 19th Floor* (1981), a fourteen-minute piece created from the sound of a single brass bell with only four edits, over thirty of her works are vocal pieces with tape manipulation of texts.

I play with sounds as an inventor, as a discoverer . . . my operable aesthetic relates to total exploitation of minimal elements. I hesitate to use ''minimal'' because I do not consider myself to be a minimalist, but a maximalist—one who maximizes all of the materials, all of the possibilities of a single element, or a small group of elements.

*Asterisks are used throughout this section to indicate composers who are given fuller treatment elsewhere in the section. Where a composer is discussed at length, her name initially appears in capital letters.

Figure 9.1 Beverly Grigsby. Photograph by Amanda Blanco

In text-sound this means placing five words in a maximum number of meaningful configurations; in tape pieces, as many different sounds from a single brass bell as I can get. In addition, I stay away from tons of equipment, the latest of this and that. . . . I am satisfied to work a long time with a single piece of equipment and often my best efforts come in maximizing the potentials of broken or malfunctioning equipment.

Like Dika Newlin,* Pool does not believe in becoming inhibited by or a slave to the equipment with which one surrounds oneself.

Some of my best pieces have been created with lousy tape, poor quality microphones and under seemingly impossible conditions. . . . I am challenged to figure out how to . . . make a fifteen minute piece with seventeen minutes of tape.

She has been working mainly with texts and text sound/sound poetry and tape for the past few years. Typical works are *For the Love of Mankind* (1981-1982), a text-sound muti-media work, and *Life in All* (1981), for mixed chanting chorus on tape. She describes her compositional technique:

I write them, tape them, listen to the tape forever, then revise the written version and make a new tape until I am satisfied with how it sounds. . . . I play the sounds as many times as I can before I start to work with them. One thing about living in Los Angeles, you have to do a lot of driving and with a cassette recorder in the car I am able to do this kind of listening while at the wheel. I am learning more and more how to use my own voice as an instrument and to use texts with other sounds.

DORIS HAYS (b. 1941) is a very prolific composer-pianist and recording artist who has moved musically from pure electronic to *concrète* to voice processing techniques. After studies at the University of Chattanooga (Bachelor of Music, 1959), she was awarded a grant which gave her three years of study at Munich's Hochschule for music. It was in Munich that she began to concertize, and she performs internationally to this day. Returning to the United States, she earned her Master of Music (1968) from the University of Wisconsin.

Her studies in electronic music were taken at the Center for New Music at the University of Iowa, where she worked with Richard Hervig. After her move to New York in 1969, she worked for several years as guest composer at Queens College's Electronic Music Studio, producing thirty-five electronic works. This included twenty-two electronic music pieces for radio and film (including a score for a science-fiction feature, *The Invasion of the Love Drones*) and five electronic pieces for a children's music text commissioned by Silver Burdett Company.

A great deal of my music-making with tape in the past ten years has been with *concrète* methods, though the first music I made for tape was pure four-channel layered electronically generated sound, which I sold to the Southern Library of Recorded Music in 1971. That was an enormous boost to me, fresh as a composer using the tape and synthesizer equipment, to be able to support my cultural vices with the vice itself. It didn't happen again like that, for I soon got away from conventional contrapuntal layering up, into lots of splicing, miles of experiments with processing acoustic signals from piano or voice through modifying equipment, and very satisfying experiments with tape reverb.

Works out of this technique include *Awakening,* a short piece using the voice of Paul Ramsey processed into a "tapeized poem." *PAMP* was created during the summer of 1973 and she describes

having recorded on piano some of the material which forms the live piano performance part of the piece, and then processing this recorded piano sound for filtering, ring and amplitude modulation and then per instinct splicing many, many times to make the seven-minute tape part, with a few processed bird-call whistles thrown in. The piece is a fantasy piece, on my ear's recollection of the sonic aura of traditional piano literature I like best . . . Chopin, Ravel . . . because they used the overtone, ringing possibilities very well on the keyboard.

Hays's first version of *Sensevents* (for five instruments and tape), her largest multi-media piece, was premiered in 1976 in Atlanta. She spent 1970-1971 working on the design, sculptures, and music using

Buchla generated sequences on endless cassette tapes of twenty seconds up to two minute durations. . . . There are eleven movements to the *Sensevents Suite* and each is accompanied by a different cassette with material similar in pulse and imagery to the live music for strings and winds. The cassettes are always playing, but are only heard when a foot switch is stepped on by a member of the audience or one of the dancers (in the dance version), so the occurrence of these fragments within the movements is indeterminate.

Another version of *Sensevents* (for Lincoln Center) was premiered in 1977.
    She has recently returned to using speech manipulations, first in the tape portions of a suite for dance (*UNI*) and again in *Southern Voices*.

The tape solo in *UNI* is for a scene of urban citizens at home, asleep and dreaming, rather nightmarish, about what makes them happy. I interviewed Georgians, asking them what makes them happy, and ran the answers into my Buchla Electric Music Box. I also used tape loops, speed changes, and a UREI Filter when I began doing similar things with the voices of the *Southern Voices* project. I interviewed people all over the South, asking them where they were born, how long they had lived in their present community, and what they might change about where they lived. I used the voice rhythms to trigger selected electronic signals on the Buchla and interspersed these abstract rhythmic lines with the true voices. With ring modulation and filtering, the voice inflections became abstract melody.

Her *Southern Voices* for tape "is a mixture of montage techniques known to our ears from radio and television, plus more complicated mixing techniques from tape music of the past thirty years." Hays calls the work text-sound documentary music because "many of the voices can be heard literally, so an attitude is voiced, though the context is music-compositional." The work has been heard over National Public Radio in Beth Anderson's* "Poetry Is Music" series.
    A particular technique used by Hays is the utilization of tape to cue singers. This is done in the "choral tape piece from *UNI* called 'Uni's Dream' a four minute piece [for] SATB, in which the tape runs all the way through the performance with constant drone tones changing only in amplitude or range, with occasional filigrees of other sounds on top of the drone. The chorus has approximate entrances in the four minute drone line." Hays works in a studio at home.
    BETH ANDERSON (b. 1950) refers to herself as an "avant-garde,

romantic composer-performer-artist-astrologer.'' She is one of the major new creative personalities on downtown New York's artistic scene through her activities there as a writer-composer-performer.

A church organist and pianist since the age of ten, she studied piano and theory at the universities of Kentucky and California at Davis (B.A., 1971) and was awarded an M.A. in composition from Mills College in Oakland, California, in 1973. Upon Anderson's arrival in New York in 1975, she

became involved in text-sound and in solo performance situations as a direct response to the economic conditions of downtown artistic life in New York. My recent works could be described as "cut-ups": arrangements of material—some composed, some found, some generated by a process. Unlike the collage writing of the past, the intention is to make the diverse elements into a harmonious whole. As a professional astrologer, I am always involved with ideas of harmony, cosmic wholeness and over-all-sense-making. These concerns, together with a fascination with numerology, produce a work of patterns, secret clues, boxes within boxes. Nevertheless it would be a mistake to assume that these works are dry or mathematical. Quite the contrary; the aim is to create and sustain strong emotional/dramatic states, and my work is full of very intense personal and psychological resonances.

As a performer-composer, Beth Anderson combines two strands of contemporary artistic endeavor: "the formalistic and the confessional." Various of her text-sound scores are published in *Heute Kunst, Flash Art, Dramatika, Ear Magazine* (of which she was coeditor and publisher from 1973 to 1979), *Assemblings,* and others. Eight of her instrumental scores, including the quartet version of *Skaters' Suite* and *Eighth Ancestor* (which was chosen for performance at the ISCM Contemporary Music World Days in Belgium, 1981), are published by Joshua Corp./General Music. Others appear in anthologies and *Ear.*

Her work in electronic music ensued mainly from her studies at Mills, which has remained one of the leading electronic studios since its establishment in 1966 when Pauline Oliveros,* one of its founders, became its first director. Anderson's tape works realized there include *Tulip Clause and Buchla Bird Hiss Down the Road of Life* (tape), *Recital Piece* (tape/piano), and *Tower of Power* (tape/organ), all written in 1973. The latter is a large graphic score with the organ part resembling a "wide paint brush stroke" on a five-line staff. The most dense portion calls for the greatest sound production, and as the brush runs out of paint, so the sound diminishes to silence. *Good-bye Bridget Bardot or Hello Charlotte Moorman* (cello/tape), 1974, the last piece written in California, was her farewell to Hollywood. It features experimental singer Pam Sawyer using vocal multiphonics on the vowels and contour of "Bye-Bye Blackbird"; this is layered on eight tracks at various speeds and mixed down to form a forty-five-minute stereo piece. The cello part, mainly a guided improvisation in

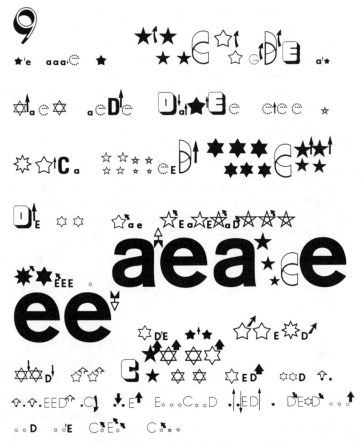

Figure 9.2 Page 9 of *Tulip Clause and Buchla Bird Hiss Down the Road of Life*, for tape/tenor/chamber ensemble (1973) by Beth Anderson. "The pitches on the score page are decoded from the text of the recorded speech [a ring modulated lecture on Jupiter] and the arrows are for quarter tones either up or down, depending on their direction. Stars indicate a free choice of pitch for the player. . . . chance is used to determine which instruments play and which pages and in what order each player plays. CELLO – has five letters and would therefore have five score pages and since the 'LL is present – two of those pages would be consecutively the same. An instrument such as the STRING BASS would have many more pages and therefore would have to play much faster than an instrument such as the ORGAN. Fewer letters = slower pace." (Notes by the composer.) Reprinted by permission of the composer.

octaves or fifths, acts as a bas-relief to the tape-mix. Other tape works include *Ode* (tape, 1976) and *Promised Church Beautiful River* (trombone/tape, 1977), a meditative guided improvisation on hymns played on a pump-organ.

In 1977 Anderson recorded her oratorio *Joan* (produced in 1974 at the

Cabrillo Festival in Northern California) as a piano mix on fifteen tracks. In the original, Joan's voice is a ring-modulated, multi-channel, live mix-down. (*Joan* and her opera *Queen Christina* [1973] are works concerned with women and their social situation.) Other works using tape are the multi-media *Morning View and Maiden Spring;* the environmental work *Hallophone;* the "sculpture music" written in collaboration with Paul Cotton, *The Bridegroom Is Hear* (1974); and *Skate Suite* (1979) for tape, violin, and cello.

In 1980 she composed a score for Sunrise Films entitled *World Honeymoon.* And in 1981 her ballet, *Manos Inquietas,* was written for Bonnie Scheibman and troupe. Anderson's continued interest in dance has been another influence upon her style, "making it more rhythmic, more popular, more romantic." *Manos Inquietas* is a good example, employing "rock-and-roll harmonies, cut-up techniques, and sweet lyricism in a classical frame." Although in 1975 John Rockwell of the *New York Times* considered her work "decidedly non-academic, experimental, post-Cagian," today she is turning to a more conservative and modal style and toward pure acoustical instrumentation, as in her musical comedy *Nirvana Manor* (book and lyrics by Judith Morely). What is causing her to turn away from electronics may be the high cost of equipment or equipment rental and fewer friendly places to work in this tight economy. At any rate, Anderson is one of a number of composers who are turning toward a more commercial vein of composition.

Another electronic composer who has moved into the commercial world of music is LAURIE ANDERSON (b. 1947), whose hit album *Big Science* is leading "pop music into the 80s," according to Robert Hilburn writing in the May 30, 1982, Sunday Calendar of the *Los Angeles Times.* Laurie's music, as Beth's, is not purely electronic, but uses multi-track methods and voice distortion. Very original, highly intellectual, sometimes profound, always amusing, many of her works are social commentaries with elaborate imagery in the accompaniment conjured up by her novel texts. The literary aspect of her art is an important one, just as it is for various other composers, including Jean Eichelberger Ivey.* The texts, in original prose or poetry, are entertaining accounts of some happening, usually personal. Although sometimes cryptic, they and their musical setting have a warmth and wit that quickly catch the ear and imagination.

Since 1973 she has climbed rapidly to become a leading performer-composer of tremendous impact. At first she utilized museums such as New York's Whitney and Modern Art, California's La Jolla Museum, and Berlin's Akademie der Kunst to perform her film-sound-electronic-talking pieces. In 1976 The Collation Center (Witterborn Art Books, N.Y.) published her *Notebook,* a collection of scores and photographs of her performances, and in 1977 the Holly Solomon Gallery in New York City released a recording of her work. The Gallery still represents her visual output.

Figure 9.3 Laurie Anderson. Photograph by Marsha Resnick

In performances throughout the United States, Canada, and Europe, Anderson utilizes such musical paraphernalia as a violin with an audio head from a tape recorder mounted on its body rather than strings, and a bow that has recording tape instead of horsehair. As the bow is drawn back and forth across the body of the violin, words recorded on the tape literally retrograde: "yes" becomes "say," and "no" becomes "one." (She has played the violin since childhood.) Another of her unusual instruments is the "Handphone Table," used in a Project Series at the Museum of

Modern Art in 1978. Participants at that performance became sound conductors by leaning their elbows on the pine table and placing their hands on either side of their head. Stereophonic music was transmitted from concealed audio tape in the table up through their forearms into their skulls. Anderson comments:

I designed the table to combine vibrations, depression, meditation, the sense of electrocution, and sound that seems remembered rather than heard. What I call Orthophonic sound has been used in many of my performance works—tuning the room so that sound can be felt as well as heard . . . a kind of spatial music.

Other electronic accoutrements used in her performance works include a Farfisa organ, Vocoder, Casiotone keyboards, and Harmonizers 910 and H949. These, combined with film, slides, and her own natural and electronically modified speaking-singing voice, create a unique media-mix that combines electronic, *concrète* and choral music.

Some of her fanciful compositions of the 1970s are *If You Can't Talk about It, Point to It,* a stuttering vocal track modified by frequency shifting; *It's Not the Bullet That Kills You—It's the Hole,* a syncopated, rock-calypso piece dedicated to the conceptual artist Chris Burden, whose own macho performance of his work called for a bullet to be shot through his arm; *New York Social Life,* a parody of artists' conversations to the strumming of a tamboura; and *Time to Go (for Diego),* a musical and dramatic portrayal of a guard at the Museum of Modern Art at closing time.

Her work today stems around a four-part, eight hour multi-media show (opera!) filled with electronic techniques. Entitled *United States Pts. I-IV,* it is a social critique of transportation, politics, money, and love, in that order and somewhat minimalist in style. Songs from all four parts may be heard in her most recent record release, *Big Science.* John Rockwell writes (*New York Times,* October 1980):

Anderson has . . . won attention from connoisseurs ranging from punks to European opera directors to intellectuals of the avant-garde. But ultimately what makes her performance noteworthy even to those who stand outside such categories is the sheer charm and energy of her work: she is a powerful creator and a powerful performer, and such phenomena don't come along all that often.

Other composers who have worked in the commercial vein are Megan Roberts,* Joan La Barbara,* Dika Newlin,* Beatrice Witkin,* Marcia Cohen,* and Suzanne Ciani.* MEGAN ROBERTS (b. 1952) recorded in the mid-1970s with the rock group "Novak," who featured her pop song "Oh, Farrah" on their first single. This collaboration with William (Bill) Novak (a former assistant director of the electronic studio at the State University of New York in Albany), inspired *I Could Sit Here All Day* (1976), a concert prelude for drums/Moog synthesizer/bird recordings/tape/vocalist; a live performance was given at the 1976 Cabrillo Music

Festival in Aptos, California. This six-minute, twenty-two-second work, with its intense rhythmic drumming and wild African/Indian chant, draws from rock's tenacious beat and screaming vocals. It is important to note here that the sheer wail of the human voice is more significant and relevant to the style than wit or profundity of text (another feature drawn from rock). The composition uses foreground/background fields with the persistent drums always up front and the maniac vocal yells and whoops afar; somewhere in between are the electronic insect and water sounds that assert themselves at several points. This effective piece sets its powerful mood and closes with the fading of the ubiquitous drums.

The work was realized at Mills College's Center for Contemporary Music, where Roberts obtained a Master of Fine Arts in electronic music, composition, and experimental media (film and video) in 1977. Undergraduate work in theater and music was pursued at the University of California, Santa Barbara (1970-1972), where she studied composition with Emma Lou Diemer.* Her B.A. was granted in 1976 from Humbolt State University, Areata, California.

Several other electronic works with provocative and witty titles were realized by Roberts in 1976: *Applause for Small People, a Pygmatic Function* for amplified vocal/percussive pigmy chant with resultant cello solo; *Support Stocking; No One Cares About Me Anyway,* from "Songs for Television," with live percussion/vocals and tape; *I Had to Make This Tape;* and *Cerealized Music.* Most of these works show influences of the rock culture but remain in the domain of the avant-garde.

In a similar mode, JOAN LA BARBARA (b. 1947) has done jazz, rock, folk, and commercial singing, but it is her innovative vocal techniques and exploration into multiphonic singing that characterize her unique music of voice and electronics. Her work "has expanded the sound spectrum of the vocal instrument, exploring its vast possibilities in solo/ensemble works, and in combination or modification with electronics." She, as Laurie Anderson, has performed throughout the United States and enjoyed broad European exposure including performance at the Akademie der Künste in Berlin; Centre Culturel du Marais, La Chapelle de la Sorbonne in Paris; Louisiana Gallery in Denmark; and in centers in Bonn, Amsterdam, Milan, Naples, Rome, and Stockholm. She has participated as composer/performer in various international festivals since 1977, including the First Festival of Electronic Music held in Brussels in 1980. La Barbara conducts workshops on her extended vocal techniques and compositions at numerous universities and at present is on the faculty of the California Institute of the Arts in Valencia.

La Barbara began working with electronic music in the late 1960s, while still an undergraduate, using the large Moog system at Syracuse University. In 1970 she began her investigations and explorations into the myriad possibilities of vocal color; four years later she purchased electronic modification devices including the Roland Space Echo tape delay unit, a

Frequency Analyzer that she used for ring modulation, and a MXR Phase 90 phase shifter that "mixed a kind of white noise at variable speeds with the voice signal." These she used in her solo concerts to further extend her voice by "working on the textural orchestration possibilities" of the voice. The devices were also used in several works with instruments: *Thunder* (1975) for six tympani and voice with electronics; *An Exaltation of Larks* (1976) for voice with electronics, ARP 2600, Moog drum, and electronic percussion; and *Chandra* (1978) for solo voice with electronics, five male voices, and chamber ensemble.

Her *Cyclone* (1976-1977 Cyclone/Wind/Tornado Piece), a sound-sculpture environment, was chosen for an International Jury Award by the International Society for Contemporary Music (ISCM) League of Composers and presented at the World Music Days in Bonn in 1977.

The tape is a sixteen-track recording of layers of voices, percussion, ARP, Moog synthesizers, and electronic instruments including tape delays and electronic drums. These sounds were mixed to a monaural tape, and I conceived a special panning device, designed and built for me by Ralph Jones, which combines two types of panning, one a knob which could control four sets of speakers, and one a set of four light-sensitive cells operated with a light pen so that the speakers were turned on when the light hit the cells. The light-panning part was also sensitive to the intensity (amount) of light hitting the cells so that dynamic changes were directly proportional to the proximity of the light source to the cell.

The composition creates the swirling and unpredictable movement of a weather cyclone with all its real and psychological terror. In the same year (1977), she recorded *Twelvesong* on a commission from Radio Bremen, Germany. It is her first layered tape piece using her own voice as the sole sound source. This led to a series of works using this technique, that is,

making a sonic canvas in which most of the information is presented in the first few moments and then details are brought forward as one listens longer, much like when one first observes a painting, receiving most of the data at first glance and then noticing details of structure, form, and content as one looks longer.

In 1978 she moved to California from New York to join her husband, pioneer electronic composer Morton Subotnick, and began to use the Buchla systems, working at the California Institute of the Arts. The first work to use the Buchla, *Autumn Signal* (1978), was premiered at Metamusik 3 Festival in West Berlin. It is a quadraphonic "soundance."

I thought of the sounds as three-dimensional forms moving in space like dancers . . . while one sound walked around the perimeter of the space defined by the speaker, others would swoop and glide overhead or along diagonals. *Autumn Signal* uses the voice as the sound source and the Buchla system was used to locate and move the sounds. . . . this was also my first composition to use a text (my own), a word transformational work.

One of La Barbara's latest works is *Erin* (1980), commissioned by VPRO radio in Holland. This beautiful work is a fantasy of Ireland that creates "a series of characters in overlaid textures, a melody constructed by additive process and a rich, multiphonic choir in which overtone melodies are developed." The additive process is used by many composers to create rich, dynamic, and beautiful textures. Laurie Spiegel* utilizes it in her gorgeous and meditative *Expanding Universe,* (1975), a computer generated piece; Maggie Payne,* in her exquisite *Ling,* (1981), an analog (voltage-controlled) sound source (Moog III). La Barbara achieves the technique by layering ten-tracks of multiphonic voices (her own) in which specific midrange frequencies are rolled off and the upper and lower extremes are emphasized.

La Barbara is presently moving into computer music and now works with the Buchla 300 system.

In contrast and still parallel to Laurie Anderson* and Joan La Barbara,* DIKA NEWLIN (b. 1923) is now moving away from electronic music and into pop. Newlin, who in the early 1970s realized several computer pieces at Bell Labs (Murray Hill, N.J.), where she was resident visitor in acoustic research from 1973 to 1976, dislikes

being dependent on the schedules of labs and the vagaries of equipment. I like just to be with my paper and pencil with which I can write anywhere, anytime. I feel more and more the need to communicate to many people. I think pop doesn't have to be junk! It can serve higher artistic/spiritual needs. I love to work with a lyrical partner and also to write my own lyrics when so moved. My lyrical partners have been, are, or will be: Ray Mabry, Julia Morrison, Shakespeare, Tom Moore, Tom Merton, Pope John Paul II, and many more. Dear friends in the flesh (the first two) plus great writers of the past and present who have captured my imagination—many of whom you might not think of as typical pop lyricists.

Coming from an intellectual, widely travelled, and musical family (her father was a professor of music at Michigan State University), she began the study of piano at six and composing soon followed. One of her first compositions (written at age eight) was orchestrated by Valdimir Bakaleinikoff, assistant conductor of the Cincinnati Symphony and performed by that group in December of 1935. Her precocity continued as she entered high school at eight, Michigan State University at twelve (B.A., 1939), and began her studies with Arnold Schoenberg at the University of California at Los Angeles at sixteen, which resulted in one of the first M.A.'s in music presented by that school (1941, composition). Her university and private studies with Schoenberg are recounted in her book *Schoenberg Remembered* (New York: Pendragon Press, 1980). Newlin went on to Columbia University in 1941 to receive her Ph.D. in musicology four years later, the first one ever granted by that institution. Her dissertation was the now famous study, *Bruckner-Mahler-Schoenberg* (King's Crown

Press, 1947; rev. ed., Norton, 1978). She has taught at several universities, including founding and chairing the music department at Drew University, Madison, New Jersey, from 1965 to 1973. At present she is a professor at Virginia Commonwealth University, Richmond.

Her *Big Swamp* (1973), a computer simulation of nocturnal swamp sounds, and *Purr* (1973), the purring of a single cat treated in *musique concrète* fashion, fall under the category of nature sounds and/or natural sounds found in the music of Megan Roberts;* Annea Lockwood* (*World Rhythms,* 1975; *Tiger Balm,* 1970, a ritualistic piece with some powerful cat purring); Priscilla McLean* (*Beneath the Horizon* I, II, III, 1977-1978 for whale ensemble plus tuba[s]); Ann McMillan* (*Solar Winds; Amber* 1975; *Gateway Summer Sound; Whale* I, II, 1973); Sylvia Pengilly* (*Three Moments of Agony,* 1975); Beverly Grigsby* (*Preludes,* 1968; *Morning at Seven,* 1982); Janet Gilbert* (. . . *out of the looking glass,* 1975); Barberi Paull* (*Asylum,* 1973, a ballet—the aural material is sounds from life); Alice Shields* (*Coyote,* 1980, a powerful, ritualistic work); and Helen Stanley (*Rhapsody* for orchestra and tape with bird calls, 1972).

Both *Big Swamp* and *Rose Pedal Rhapsody* (1973) also call for audience participation in ritual fashion. In the former, the audience, seated or moving about, performs on animal or bird-call instruments, while in the latter, rose scent is sprayed and petals or confetti are scattered. This genre of composition (participatory piece) is also used by Ruth Anderson* (*Participatory Sound Environment,* 1975, with Lockwood); Annea Lockwood* (*Tripping,* 1974; *Singing the Earth,* 1975); Pauline Oliveros* (*Sonic Meditations,* 1970-   ); Kay Gardner* (*A Rainbow Path,* healing music); and Doris Hays* (*Help Compose,* for audience and pianist).

Newlin's sense of the humor/drama component in life and art is demonstrated in her music. *Friday Night Rumble* (1973) makes use of parody (quoting) in the computerized intonation of the *Dies Irae.* An atmospheric piece, it is performed in total darkness with occasional lightning-like flashes piercing the gloom while rumbling, sinister sounds prevail. An early satiric *concrète* work, *The Dr. Dika and Newlin School of Music* (1971), is constructed of taped practice-room sounds plus a totally incompetent live piano performance ("or voice or violin if you prefer"). Her sense of humor and directness remain when she discusses her pop styles: "Ballad, cabaret songs, country, ragtime, blues, torch, rock, gospel—you name it, I write it. Some call it punk, new wave, or whatever. I'm not so interested in the labels—I just DO it! My work is humanist, not feminist."

Another humanist is MARCIA COHEN (b. 1937), producer for cultural affairs programming WSRE-TV public television in Pensacola, Florida, and past director of the Department of Cultural Affairs for that city.

She holds a Master of Music in composition from Northwestern University (1969) and in the 1970s managed the Electronic Music Studio for the school of the Art Institute of Chicago. A dynamic woman, she makes things happen. An example is her determination to enhance twentieth-century music's accessibility, especially to young people, by taking it out of the university and into the main stream. The year before she left Chicago, she assembled a multi-media production that incorporated pop, experimental theater, and video, and through ingenious advertising succeeded in attracting youth to a concert they might have otherwise ignored. Her interest in pop continued after the move to Florida, where she produced *In Record Time,* a thirty-minute documentary on the recording of a rock album, for PBS. Rock has also affected her style. "The longer I write electronic music, the closer it gets to avant-garde rock."

Her earliest work utilizing electronics is *Finnegan's Wake* (1968), for two female voices/two male voices/trombone/cello/piano/electric guitar/four percussions/electronic tape/conductor. Others written between 1969 and 1978 include *Zodiac Cast* for flute/tape; *Double Play* for two dancers/tape and *STOPGO* for dance troupe/sculpture/tape—both created for the Columbia College Dance Center in Chicago for which she was composer-in-residence; *Chess Set* for percussion/tape; *A*R*P* (Any Reliable Preparation), a linear and timbral study in varying speeds for tape alone; *Devonshire Air; Beginning* for soprano/tape and *Santa Rosa Sound.*

Most of her works are approximately ten to fifteen minutes in length. *Santa Rosa Sound,* fifteen minutes in duration, utilizes contrasting materials arranged spatially, often in beating tremolos. She writes poetically of her music:

Santa Rosa Sound was composed in the fall of 1978 with an ARP synthesizer and Echoplex in my studio overlooking beautiful Santa Rosa Sound, a tributary of the Gulf of Mexico on Santa Rosa Island, Florida. I had spent a good deal of time watching the play of light and wind on the water and began to imagine how it looked and sounded from underneath instead of over the water. Thus the ideas for this piece took shape. The work is composed as though the composer and listener lived under the water and from there experienced the sunlight, moonlight, and darkness as well as the breeze, the winds, and the calm. Raindrops echo as they fall on the surface of the Sound, and furious storms lash the ears of the underwater denizens. Sound upon sound resonates thickly through the density of the water.

Although she has moved in many musical directions, Cohen is at present studying law at Stetson University's College of Law in St. Petersburg, Florida. Her goal? Art law. Her intentions? "[To specialize in] copyright and protection of intellectual property, especially electronic and computer music, and video disks."

Two women working in music for television commercials and television film are Beatrice Witkin and Suzanne Ciani.* BEATRICE WITKIN (b. 1916) composed for the series *Wild, Wild World of Animals* as well as logo music for the Home Insurance Company on a Buchla synthesizer and on an electric harpsichord during the early 1970s. In 1970, her composition

Glissines won the *High Fidelity Magazine*'s Electronic Music Contest. Two more serious works followed in 1971 and 1972-1973: *Breath and Sounds* for tuba and tape, and *Echologie* for flute and tape. The former, a nine-minute work in four movements, explores the relationship between the electronic and acoustical instruments, including the innovative feature of having the performer's breathing imitated by synthesized breath.

Witkin, who studied piano with Edward Steuerman and composition with Roger Sessions and Stefan Wolpe, studied electronic music techniques as a graduate student at New York University. She presently works out of her home studio in New York.

SUZANNE CIANI (b. 1946) also works out of her New York apartment. She is a composer-producer-arranger and specialist in electronic music for television commercials and film scores. Her company, Ciani/Musica Inc., founded in 1974 when she came to New York, has turned out "jingles" for over thirty famous commercial clients (Atari, Coca-Cola, Lincoln-Mercury, Chevrolet, Eastern Airline, Bulova, Crest, General Electric, and so on), earning the Clio and Golden Globe awards for excellence and originality.

Her at-home studio is an enviable collection of the finest components: Buchla analog synthesizer, Synclavier II digital synthesizer with terminal (CRT), Prophet V, Voice Box, Vocoder, and an Otari (MTR-90) twenty-four-track tape recorder; processing equipment includes a Marshall Time Modulator, Eventide 949 Harmonizer and Delay Unit, Ursa Major SST 282 Space Station, and a Poly Fusion Frequency Follower.

Ciani's music is often scored for concert-size orchestras as well as electronics. The jingles are not always thirty-second spots: she has written a fifteen-minute suite for strings, horn, and synthesizer for one of her clients; an electronic score for a full-length film; and reworked the electronic portions of Menotti's opera, *Help, Help the Globolinks!*

She is an outstanding technician, often designing sound packages and redesigning chips. Besides programming electronic microchips for Xenon (a pinball-machine manufacturer) to produce a synthetic voice and designing a system with New England Digital (the Synclavier people) to integrate sound with pictures, she has recently been commissioned by Texas Instruments, a leading developer of microchip technology, to develop sound for its products.

Trained as a classical musician, Ciani received her B.A. in 1968 in music from Wellesley College, where she first came into contact with computers and synthesizers through association with the work being done at Massachusetts Institute of Technology (MIT). She went on to study at the University of California at Berkeley (M.A., 1970), but she began to spend more time at Mills than Berkeley after taking a course with Max Matthews of Bell Labs (renowned father of computer music) and renting studio time and space for five dollars an hour at Mills. Special postgraduate studies in computer music followed at Stanford's Artificial Intelligence Laboratory. After graduation from Berkeley, she went to work for Donald Buchla as a technician in his factory to learn how to build a synthesizer when she found it impossible to get time in the overcrowded Mills studio. Eventually, using the studio workshop synthesizer at the Buchla factory, she turned to commercials in order to earn enough money to buy her own equipment.

She recently electronically scored Lily Tomlin's *Incredible Shrinking Woman,* a full-length major motion picture, accomplishing the task in three weeks. Prior to Tomlin's film, she contributed to another feature film (*Stepford Wives*), logos (among them, Columbia Picture's film logo), shorts, film strips, and the television series *The Search.* She has made guest appearances on television's *Omni* and *Wonderama.* Ciani received a gold record for composing and performing the electronic effects on Meco's noted *Star Wars* recording and received praise for her new electronic score to *Help, Help, the Globolinks!* For the past few years, she has worked arduously at electronically orchestrating "classically inspired music." The result appears in her recent album, *New Waves.*

Several other composers such as Pril Smiley,* Ruth Anderson,* Laurie Spiegel,* and Maggie Payne* have been interested in film, television, and especially theater and have composed extensively for these mediums. PRIL SMILEY (b. 1943) has specialized in electronic music for theater and film and has created scores for about forty major productions. From 1968 to 1974 she was the electronic music consultant to the Lincoln Center Repertory Theatre in New York but also wrote scores for the Cleveland Playhouse, Cincinnati Theatre-in-the-Park, as well as other productions in Baltimore, at Tanglewood, and at the Stratford Shakespeare Festival of Canada. Some of the Shakespeare productions called for glorified sound effects, some productions utilized more *concrète* sounds or modified instrumental music, but most of the scores were realized on the Buchla system at the Columbia-Princeton Electronic Music Center, where she is an associate director with Alice Shields.* In 1963 she was hired at the center as an apprentice to Vladimir Ussachevsky, pioneer composer in the electronic medium. At this time he was working on several film and theater scores:

From the start, I became acquainted with the composing methods required for those media, as well as the techniques used within the more academic style of composing. . . . I continue to enjoy working in both the academic and nonacademic world simultaneously: each requires different intellectual and technical skills, and so is distinctly challenging. To verbalize just one of the differences: theater music can involve a very exhilarating *collaborative* creative effort (the sum of the individuals involved equalling more than the parts); "straight" electronic works exemplify a very personal and individual expression—especially since the composer is also the performer in electronic music.

Smiley has about ten films to her credit including the feature-length *Premonition* (1975), *Incredible Voyage* (1969) for CBS-TV, and *Can You Hear Me* (1967) for ABC-TV. Her "straight" electronic works include

Figure 9.4 Pril Smiley. Photograph by Manny Warman

Eclipse, the 1968 winner of the First International Electronic Music Contest; *Kolyosa,* 1970; and *Trip,* the first finalist in the Currents First International Contest for Electronic Music and Film, 1974. *Eclipse* is a quadraphonic tape utilizing both *concrète* and electronic (Buchla) procedures, which are interspersed throughout the work. The *concrète* material consists of voice and percussion, and the synthesized material contrasts with midrange wood timbres, low gong, and high glassy sounds that dovetail and sometimes completely interrupt each other (hence *Eclipse*). *Trip* (1971), is the electronic score to a film by Istvan Ventills; however, in this case the filmmaker spliced the film to fit the music, which was prearranged. The *Trip* is a physical trip from California to New York's Times Square shot from the windshield of a car. The film is ten minutes spliced out of four hours with sections speeded up ten times. The result is an abstract version of the trip with a highly structured visual tied to a five-part musical form:

City	to	Country	to	City
L.A.	to	Yellowstone	to	N.Y.
Dawn		to		Night

Kolyosa (1970) is the Russian word for 'wheels,' and the structural idea for this composition deals with wheels and circles that move through space and never end where they have begun. Space and location are invoked through the Doppler effect, foreground-background perception, and an abstract hypocycloidial concept of whirling, spinning forms. The entire piece is a large circle with each of its five (not clearly defined) sections containing phrases and motives that are circular.

Interestingly, MAGGIE PAYNE (b. 1945) has written several works dealing with the same concept. *Spirals* (1977), *Spheres* (1977), and *Circular Motions* (1981) all are concerned with spatial location and modulation. This technique is "accomplished during the original recording process with phase, amplitude, and frequency matching techniques." Payne's compositional procedures "involve extensive multi-tracking with layering, and premixing of material" most frequently generated by a Moog III system and layered onto thirty-six tracks at one time. Great attention is paid to timbres, which are often delicately and continuously manipulated. Structurally, the pieces are "clearly defined, with large areas of clearly differing textures, frequently with very subtle transitions." As Payne goes on to explain:

I think I get more influenced by ideas. . . . Ideas such as Varèse's idea of crystallization . . . and technical ideas of how to move sounds in space vertically (tricky to do) and doppler-shifts for the two-axis are very intriguing to me. When I work musically, I am working typically with a visual idea of where I want a sound to originate and where and how I want it to move.

Her interests also lie in the presentation of visual material in conjunction with her music. Usually abstract, the visuals range from complicated oscilloscope imagery to photomicrography; 16mm film, 35mm slides, and video tapes are integral to concert presentation of her music.

A graduate of Northwestern (B.A., 1968), Payne studied electronic music and audio engineering at Mills College and received a Master of Fine Arts in those fields in 1972. She is now on the faculty at that institution, where she often collaborates with colleagues in the building and design of video equipment and audio techniques. Payne has composed electronic music for the Ashland Shakespearean Festival, the Merce Cunningham Dance Company, and the Moving Space Dance Company. She also composed the music for *Voices,* a one-hour play for KQED-TV, which won a 1974 Emmy Award, and performed and/or synthesized material for several pop disks (Country Joe McDonald's album, *Goodbye Blues;* Blue Gene Tyranny's album, *Out of the Blue,* and so on). Her *Ling* (1981) for quad electronic tape and photomicrographic slides won the second prize in the Third International Luigi Russolo Competition for Young Composers of Electronic Music. Payne's latest compositions—*Circular Motions* (1981), *Io* (1982), and *Crystal* (1982)—all incorporate three-quarter-inch video tape. She is moving more and more into digitally manipulated and controlled visuals in conjunction with electronic music.

LAURIE SPIEGEL (b. 1945) also has written for dance extensively, for theater, and for video synchronization of computer-generated images and music. She has composed soundtracks for satellite cable television, for commercials, for educational film, and for the feature film *Emma*, produced and directed by Jean-Pierre Mahot (1975). She has the distinction of having a galaxial reputation, as her *Harmony of the Planets* (a computer realization of Kepler's *Harmonica Mundi*) was included on NASA's record *Sounds of Earth* produced by Carl Sagan for inclusion on the *Voyager* spacecraft launched in 1977.

Some of her dance commissions have been from the Elliot Feld Ballet, the Juilliard Dance Ensemble, Kathryn Posin Dance Company, the Netherland Dance Theatre, the Utah Repertory Dance Theatre, and national PBS broadcasts of her *Music for Dance*. Music for theater includes incidental music for Quog Music Theater, Mercer Art Center, George Gershwin Theater, and the Gene Frankel Workshop, all of New York.

She studied at Oxford University in 1967 and took private studies in classic guitar with John Duarte in London. In 1969 she studied electronic and instrumental composition at Juilliard and New York University and obtained her M.A. in composition from Brooklyn College in 1975, working there and in private with Jacob Druckman. Two years earlier she had become a resident-visitor at Bell Labs and worked in computer music with Max Matthews and Emmanual Ghent and in computer graphics with Kenneth Knowlton. Spiegel has been director of the Electronic Music Studio at Bucks County Community College in Newtown, Pennsylvania, as well as instructor in electronic music for the Aspen Music Festival. At present she works exclusively in computer music and acts as a consultant to various corporations (IBM, Rutt Electrophysics, Syntonic Research). She is an adjunct instructor of music and director of the electronic music studio of Cooper Union for the Advancement of Science and Art.

Some of her most beautiful works were done on the now defunct GROOVE system at Bell Labs: *Appalachian Grove No. 1* (1974), *Patchwork* (1976), and *Expanding Universe* (1975). The latter is a striking example of slowly evolving overtone melodies that blend into a multiphonic texture without losing their identity by emerging and fading back into an undulating matrix which itself is everchanging in color and texture. The effect is mesmerizing—a half-hour work of beauty, peace, and deep reflection. The richness of tone color continues in her later works such as *Voices Within* (1979), a fourteen-minute analog piece, and the half-hour-long computer generated videotape and music *Voyages* (1979). All of Spiegel's work is intensely humanistic and sensual.

Designer and installer of the first operative electronic music studio within the City University of New York system in 1968, RUTH ANDERSON (b. 1928) is also the founder and director of the Hunter College Electronic Music Studio at the City University of New York, where she has been on the faculty since 1966. She holds the distinction of being the first woman admitted to the Princeton University Graduate School in 1962. In 1966 she entered Columbia University to study electronic music at the Columbia-Princeton Electronic Music Center, having previously earned her B.A. and M.A. from the University of Washington (in 1949 and 1951, respectively).

For many years, Anderson orchestrated for NBC-TV and CBS-TV—the first woman to do so—and for the Rodgers Library and the Lincoln Center Theater. From these endeavors came orchestration assignments for several major shows: Broadway's *Annie Get Your Gun* (1966), Lincoln Center's productions of *Showboat* and *Sound of Music,* and television's *Du Pont Show of the Week* and *Armstrong Circle Theater.*

Although Anderson has written for traditional instrumental and vocal forces, we will discuss only her tape pieces, which include *concrète*, electronic, and text-sound techniques. Written in 1973, the collage *SUM (State of the Union Message)* incorporates patches of television commercials intermingled with Nixon's presidential address. According to Anderson, "the various noises, sounds, words, phrases were collected on tape, cut into succinct lengths, hung in rows for consideration and then spliced together." Some of the accidents that occurred in splicing together the work were left in and create several funny and provocative sections. On the whole, the piece is basically social commentary and criticism "saying as little, and by omission, as much as the president [said]." At about the same time, another collage, *DUMP*, was written for an intermedia presentation. Centered around Buffy St. Marie's refrain "My Country 'Tis of Thy People You're Dying," it contains fragments of folk song and popular music interwoven with electronically generated sounds. (It was created for an outdoor event which included—along with films, slides, poetry, and dance—works by the artist Tania who incorporated debris and other items collected from the East Hampton dump.)

Other early 1970s tape pieces are *So What #1, #2; Studies #1, #2, #3,* and, from the late 1960s, *The Pregnant Dream* and *ES II. Dress Rehearsal, Conversations,* and *Points* were written in the mid-1970s. The latter is built from pure sine tones which she tells us:

[are] a single-frequency focal point of high energy. In this work, such points occur on various arcs which float in and out of one another. Separate sine waves enter at five-second intervals, accumulate in a long veil on one channel while another set of sines then is introduced on the second channel, and continue this way with veils of sound shifting in and out of each other. The high focus of energy of a sine wave, the outsized breathing interval of five-second entries, the calm of the veils and timeless quality are some of the elements I can isolate which have made this a healing piece, one that consistently generates in listeners a sense of repose and quiet energy.

Her recent compositions have evolved from a holistic concept and use of sound and music. From research in this area of psychoacoustics, she creates text pieces which are meditations, tape music designed to reduce stress, interactive biofeedback works, and participatory pieces. *I Come Out of Your Sleep* (1980) is one such text-sound piece. On a poem by Louise Bogan in which a "dual self is described in mirror images," the composition reconstructs these images through their vowel sounds. Some of the vowels form melodic contours, others are steady-state tones of varying qualities on different pitches. Whispered and elongated, the tones interact in four canonic lines to form melodies and changing harmonies near the threshold of hearing. Hugh Davies has said on the record jacket notes (Opus One, 1980), "these sounds touch very deep preconscious memories which we are rarely if ever able to retrieve on our own."

With the composer Annea Lockwood* Anderson developed a series of hearing studies and listening techniques. Her interest in electronics persists not only in *Centering*, a composer-performer piece written in 1979 for dance and live electronics, but in her recent experimental computerized environmental control system built for a colleague afflicted with a paralyzing illness.

Anderson's interest in meditation and healing is paralleled not only in the work of her colleague Annea Lockwood* but in the work of other composers such as Pauline Oliveros,* Kay Gardner,* Patricia Zanardi* and Alice Shields.* ANNEA LOCKWOOD (b. 1929) attempts to "make each

Figure 9.5 Annea Lockwood wearing "Sound Hat," a wearable sound sculpture. Photograph by Peter Elgin

piece as direct a realization of the philosophical idea which underlies it, as possible.'' This has resulted in a number of environmental works with a meditative spirit. Such compositions as *World Rhythms* (1975), *Singing the Earth—Singing the Air* (published, 1978), *Malaman* (1971), and *Spirit Songs Unfolding* (1977) are examples.

Graduating with a Bachelor of Music from Cantebury University, New Zealand, in 1960, Lockwood has studied at various electronic music studios in England, Germany, and Holland. In 1972 she was the codirector of Experimental Music in London for the International Carnival of Experimental Sound, Inc. She produced a series of programs for BBC radio on trance music of many cultures, and her music has been performed in galleries, concert halls, and over television and radio stations in England, the United States, Sweden, Austria, and Germany. At present she is an adjunct associate professor at Hunter College and, in collaboration with Ruth Anderson,* has created *Participatory Sound Environments*—an activity held in a two-room studio equipped with audiovisual stimuli designed to heighten awareness. Anderson and Lockwood combine their knowledge of music with physics and Eastern philosophy to create healing through electronic and vocal sounds.

This is similar to the holistic healing through music practiced by composer-conductor-performer KAY GARDNER (b. 1941). Her major multi-media work, *A Rainbow Path* (presently in progress and five years in the planning), explores sound and color and their power to heal specific areas of the human organism. The realm of healing through the powers of music continues to occupy her thoughts.

I've studied modal expressions and the powers of particular modes and intervals to affect healing in the human organism. I travel extensively performing my own music and teaching "Music and Healing" workshops. My "style" has evolved but retains modal expressions. Avant-garde accompaniment figures are used now as provokers of mood and/or duplications of natural sounds, e.g., flutes blowing gently into X mouthpieces to create "snow" or a cello slide or gliss to create "moaning," etc. Repetition, similar to what might be called minimalism, becomes chant-bass over which melodies happen, often totally improvised by the musician(s).

Her earliest compositional style was influenced by American folk music and the blues and has grown more varied through the years as elements of jazz, Hindu ragas, and electronic device have been absorbed. Although her basic forms are cyclic with improvisational interpolations, her musical architectures are varied, ranging from pure meditative chant, to classic structures, to aleatoric principles. She has used electronic music "to accompany acoustic expression, to provoke and evoke moods, and to transform aural space," and although she has never worked exclusively in the medium, she plans to continue its use in her "recordings as a technique to bring the excitement of theater to disc in place of the excitement of live

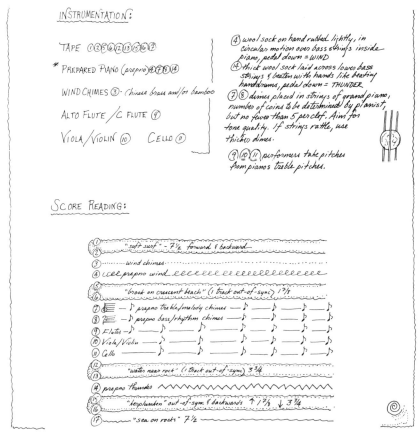

Figure 9.6 Notation explanation chart for *Atlantis Rising*, by Kay Gardner. Reprinted by permission of the composer.

performance.'' Her introduction to the medium came in 1973 through an association with Marilyn Ries, who has been recording engineer on three of Gardner's records.

I've used electronic expression consciously in subtle ways: . . . there are elements of *musique concrète* technique . . . [in the use of] ocean sounds collected from my favorite coastal meditation spots. . . . In "Mermaids" rocks thrown in the lily pond are played at quarter speed to represent mermaids diving. In "Atlantis Rising" . . . I created a collage of transformed sounds including in-studio feedback.

Another composer who has written for films is BEVERLY GRIGSBY (b. 1928), a professor of theory, composition, and music history at California State University, Northridge. After helping to establish and develop that institution's Electronic Music Studio in the early 1960s, she founded its computer music studio in 1976, and has since served as director of the school's programs in computer music composition and computer assisted instruction in music (CAI). In 1980 she cofounded the State of California Consortium for Computed Assisted Instruction in Music and has been the chair of its Southern Section since that time.

Grigsby switched from premedical studies to music composition after meeting and becoming a composition student of Ernst Krenek at the Southern California School of Music and Arts in 1947. After a seventeen-year marriage and the rearing of two daughters, she returned to school and received Bachelor of Arts and Master of Arts degrees in composition from San Fernando Valley State College in 1961 and 1963 respectively, and she earned her doctorate in 1971 from the University of Southern California. In 1976 she worked in computer music with Leland Smith and John Chowning at Stanford University's Artificial Intelligence Laboratory in Palo Alto, California.

Although Grigsby's compositional technique was originally based on manipulating tones contrapuntally in a strict serial fashion, she has used free atonality and modality, aleatoric and stochastic techniques, and, increasingly, a more minimalist, meditative approach that features timbral contrast as a form-building element. In some instances pure chant becomes the basis for a piece, reflecting an influence and interest she has maintained for two decades, reinforced by her continued studies with the monks of the Abbey St. Pierre, in Solesmes, France.

Her pre-synthesizer electronic compositions include *The Awakening . . .* (1963), inspired by the last three lines of T. S. Eliot's *The Lovesong of J. Alfred Prufrock.* Realized at the San Fernando Valley State College Electronic Music Studio, it was constructed from both electronically generated sound sources (banks of oscillators) and *musique concrète* material (voice reverberating off piano strings). The work received its first performance in 1963 at the International Society for Contemporary Music Concert held in Los Angeles. In 1964 she composed the music score to Francis Ford Coppola's feature film *Ayamonn the Terrible*, using similar sound source materials. A montage of scene sequence music from the film was adapted by the composer for concert performance and received its premiere at a concert of the National Association of Composers, USA, in 1964.

By 1966 Grigsby had built a private studio with one of the first Buchla synthesizers, an Ampex 360 and Sony 777 stereo recording units, and related peripherals. *Preludes on Poems of T. S. Eliot* (1968), for soprano, tape, and lighting, utilized this equipment and was first performed at a 1968 concert of the National Association of Composers, USA. Her 1976 computer work realized by direct synthesis on a PDP11, *A Little Background Music*, was premiered at the First International Computer Music Conference, held in Boston in conjunction with the International Society of Contemporary Music's World Music Days. Grigsby's most recent computer music composition was written in 1982 using a Nova 3/12 computer powering a NED digital synthesizer as its sound source. The work, entitled *Morning at Seven*, for flute and quadraphonic tape, is a whimsical study in sonic layering of overtones, spatial location of delicate timbres, and contours of electronic bird calls and twitterings. It is in three movements and calls for alto and bass flutes as well as a standard C flute. (A second version of this work, entitled *Shakti (Divine Light)*, uses for the tape component a *concrète* tape that manipulates pitches played on alto and bass flutes, and piccolo. *Shakti* was first performed in New York in 1983.) Grigsby's *Concerto* for piano and orchestra (in progress) also includes a computer-generated tape.

Grigsby has lectured extensively on all aspects of twentieth-century music, especially electronic and computer music. In 1982 she presented a month-long discussion and performance of electronic music featuring the women of this article on radio station KPFK-FM in Los Angeles, and she has, for the past three years, presented concerts of electronic and computer music at California State University, Northridge.

PATRICIA ZANARDI (b. 1949) is most interested in the meditative effects she can conjure through her work in computer music. She is also involved in writing film scores and has studied with David Raksin (film composer and professor of film music at the University of Southern California) and Don B. Ray (musical director for CBS and professor of film music at the University of California at Los Angeles). Zanardi has been intrigued with the challenge of creating scores that can stand on their own and still not detract from the visual image.

Film music is only meant to enhance the visual image, to bring out the emotional qualities of what is being shown on the screen. Because of this, the unusual sound qualities that can be created by the computer or electronic sound synthesis lend themselves beautifully to film background. Because of the poor economic health of the film industry of Hollywood, composers who compose a soundtrack primarily from an electronic and/or computer studio are going to have an advantage in finding work. This economic change can already be seen with composers such as George Moroder [*Midnight Express*] and Vangelis Papathanassiou [*Chariots of Fire*]. I believe we will be seeing many more "one-man operations" in the near future. In this area of sound synthesis for film music, composers have only begun to explore the possibilities of what can be done, and I believe that given the potential of the computer, a whole new sound world can be introduced into films. Already, many composers have utilized synthesizers and electronic effects, and special effects people have used electronics and *musique concrète* techniques for sound effects. There are already computer-generated visuals and audio being used. As these systems become more commonplace, there will be more opportunities for people to create, using these tools. I would like to explore these possibilities more fully.

Zanardi received her B.A. from California State College, Sonoma, in 1977 and is completing her M.A. in composition at California State University, Northridge, where she is studying computer music composition with Beverly Grigsby.* Zanardi's *Mandala* (1981) was recently premiered at the Second International Congress of Women in Music at the University of Southern California. A computer-generated piece for tape and dancer, the work symbolizes the religious significance associated with the design, "basically a circle within or surrounding a square, or a circle containing four points creating a cross used in Eastern religions as a focus for meditation." The dance performed in conjunction with the tape brings forth the concept of the Mandala, that is, "a representation of the cosmos in its connection with divine powers, or in Jungian philosophy, the symbol of human wholeness."

One could not move from the subject of meditation and human wholeness without a discussion of one of the most respected and influential composers of the twentieth century, PAULINE OLIVEROS (b. 1932). Her "compositions are experiences of total sound communion." Having developed her sonic meditations slowly over the years since 1970 through guided improvisation in carefully thought out practice with "musicians and non-musicians throughout the world," she creates "a unique environment in which musical differences and personal distinctions blend to provide an unforgettable sonic mandala."

In 1960 Oliveros cofounded (with Ramon Sender) SONICS, the center for *concrète* and electronic music at the San Francisco Conservatory of Music, which became the model for the San Francisco Tape Center established in 1962 by Morton Subotnick and Sender. Her *Bye Bye Butterfly* (1965) was realized at the Tape Center, and John Rockwell, writing in the

Figure 9.7 Pauline Oliveros

May 1980 issue of the *New York Times*, considers it "one of the most beautiful pieces of electronic music to emerge from the 60's. . . . Madam Butterfly's entrance aria is subjected to ever increasing electronic 'distortion.' The result does not so much obliterate Puccini as transform his music into an eerie celestial song." Other tape pieces of the 1960s, *Big Mother Is Watching You* (1966), *Beautiful Soop* (1967), and *I of IV* (1966), are typical of her attempt to use lengthy drones. At this point in her career, she was founding director of the Mills College Electronic Music Studio (Tape Music Center), but *I of IV* was created at the University of Toronto Electronic Music Studio, where she studied briefly with Hugh LeCaine. This work is an important composition for its time because it is one of the first real-time studio performance compositions, that is, a work that is created without editing and is produced by direct performance. In this case the direct performance was by twelve generators (oscillators), eleven of which were set at above 20K and one generator below one cycle per second. The combination tones created by the eleven generators above 20K were further modified by the reverb and tape loops of eight-second delay and the pulse modulation of the subaudio oscillator; thus, steady-state drones were modified and modulated to create a dynamic and undulating texture with an ever-changing sonance—a technique much simplified by today's synthesizers and computers but nevertheless unique in its time and concept and the precursor of multiphonic sonic contours.

In 1967 Oliveros left Mills for San Diego and the University of California at La Jolla, where she remained for the next fourteen years. Today she resides in the Zen Art Center at Mt. Tremper, New York, where her current work continues the meditational music she began in the 1970s with its conceptual and participatory style. Whether or not she returns to writing electronic scores (and she might), her mark has been set upon the art.

ALICE SHIELDS (b. 1943), associate director of the Columbia-Princeton Electronic Music Center, received her B.S. (1965) in music and her M.A. (1967) and Doctor of Musical Arts (1975) in composition from Columbia. She undertook further training in music therapy, and she is presently active as a music therapist.

Shields has developed a theory of strong and specific relationships between the progress of a melodic line and the effect of that line on the listener's subconscious (see her article "Music in an Expressive Therapy" in *Expressive Therapy*, ed. A. Robbins, Human Sciences Press, 1980). Whether in the tape manipulations of the voice with its animal-like wails in the *Transformation of Ani* or in the chilling demonic snarls of the Shaman as he turns himself into a coyote and then back again (in the tape "Coyote" from the opera *Shaman*), Shields practices her psychology of sound in order to produce an emotional response in the listener. Microtonal movement up and down in the latter work does increase tension and produce a sense of fear, in contrast to the piece's more stable sections. Here we have procedures that fall somewhere between music therapy, environmental sound/natural sound, and brilliant word painting.

Other composers such as Ann McMillan,* Priscilla McLean,* and Helen Stanley* create compositions using natural or animal sounds. HELEN STANLEY (b. 1930) uses live bird songs interwoven with electronically generated sound and modified natural sounds in her *Rhapsody for Electronic Tape and Orchestra.* ANN MCMILLAN (b. 1923) has often utilized nature sounds and particularly animal sounds as the main material for her works. Abstracted and structured animal sonances become the tape part of a piece for three solo flutes and small orchestra, *Solar Winds* (1982). Earlier works such as *Animal Studies* I (1972) and *Whale* (1973) also use the technique of abstracting and restructuring the original sounds in a manner analagous to cubist techniques in visual art.

PRISCILLA MCLEAN (b. 1942) has a deep affinity for another art technique—surrealism; she and her composer-husband Barton often draw analogies between their music and this type of construct.

Surrealism is the use of opposition and juxtaposition of sound events which seem unrelated but are placed strategically so that one evokes the feeling of the other, often retaining its own integrity. Opposite qualities of sound are merged as well, as for example in live instruments versus synthesizers. Perhaps a central idea in all of this is the creation of an illusion of wholeness from disparate elements through surrealistic means.

McLean's *Beneath the Horizon* (1978) for tuba solo and whale ensemble tape is an example of the surrealist technique; in it contrasting materials are in continuous "fluctuation between merging together on one hand and stating their individual ideas on the other, resulting in a quiet tension."

Her principle of imago-abstract sound—fully discussed in "Fire and Ice: A Query," in the Fall-Winter 1977 issue of *Perspectives of New Music*—deals with the blurring of planes of reality by removing sound several degrees from its obvious source onto a more abstract level of perception. This may be done by altering "the original drastically so as to obliterate any direct reference to it, or by synthesizing a musical event reminiscent of an environmental sonority on its own level of abstraction" and moving these contrasting but related elements in and out of the extremes of their domains and through all of the degrees between.

A work that uses *musique concrète* and synthesizer to express the imago-abstract is the three movement *Invisible Chariots* (1975-1977). The title of this beautiful work is from Carl Sandburg's poem *Isle of Patmos* and refers "to the intuitive creative force that shapes a work, often in direct conflict with one's 'external' judgments, which have to be obeisant to the voice within."

ELIZABETH PIZER (b. 1954) achieves an almost surreal atmosphere in her *Under & Overture* (Version II), 1979, as the manipulated and modified tape sections contrast with sections of clearly recorded band music, which

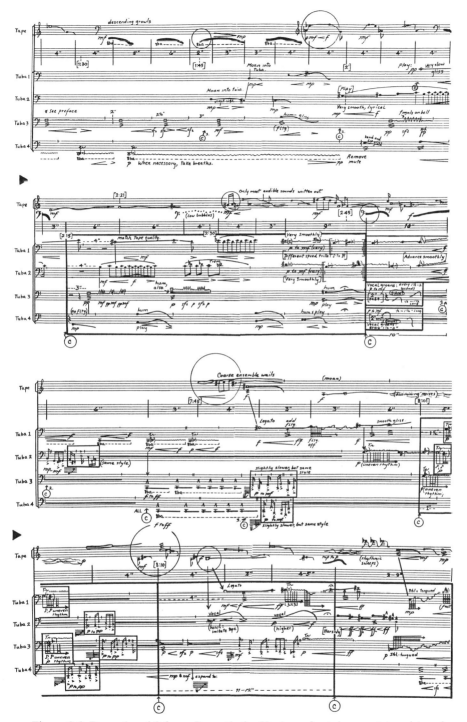

Figure 9.8 Pages 4 and 9 from *Beneath the Horizon*, for tuba quartet and taped whale ensemble, by Priscilla McLean. Reprinted by permission of the composer.

was prepared by the composer from an actual performance. The fairly straightforward tonal composition is perceived in a new way as the blurring of the planes of sound create a distinct way of experiencing the band: at times clearly, at times through a veil. *Sunken Flutes* (1979), in contrast, is a multi-track recording with the composer at the ARP Synthesizer creating various flute timbres in flute-like modal scale passages. The piece illustrates a type of improvisation used in multi-track layering: a single melodic figure is used in various dimensions, experienced through layering and multi-tracking. Although the texture remains fairly dense throughout, it thins somewhat at the end; various figural entrances and exits maintain interest through timbral differences and shifts.

An interesting work by ANNE LEBARON (b. 1953) is *Quadratura Circuli,* 1978 (The squaring of a circle? Shades of mandala!). Two main contrasting timbres pervade the composition; one is a bell tone that modifies itself in various ways, beginning as a high pitch; the other is comprised of unpitched percussion timbres that intersect and cause the bell to mutate. In the center of the work, a gong-like timbre reverberates between the speakers, which at the end has modified itself from an ear-piercing sound, to a gong, to a clear and peaceful chime. Assuming that the bell symbolizes the circle and the percussive elements the square, the resulting aural representation of geometric figures is an interesting compositional construct creating some tricky problems in space and location (as Maggie Payne* describes it in her *Circular Motions*).

SARAH JOHNSTON REID (b. 1948) creates another spatial geometric in her eight-minute and thirty-second *Gyro-Space* for quadraphonic tape. It too opens with a bell-like muted tone that acts motivicly and returns at various points in the work. As a contrast, brass-like harmonic progressions build to orchestral dimensions but eventually recede to the rising figures. The work was realized at the Abilene Christian University Electronic Music Studio on an ARP. (The studio owns both the ARP 2600 and an ARP AXXE along with various TEAC mixers and recording units and is seriously considering purchasing various computer systems now available.) Reid, who is not only the director of the studio but chair of the department, did not begin working in the field until 1976, when regular access to the studio became a reality. She received her Ph.D. in Music Theory in 1980 from the University of Texas at Austin, where she worked with Thomas Wells and Gary Kendall in electronic music in 1972 and developed an interest in the medium.

Other works by Reid are *The Eagle Is Born to Soar* (1980), a sequence of a figure that is used thematically throughout; and *Celebration in Sound and Space* (1981), which utilizes ascending and descending figures of varying timbres. "In this work I was more free in my expression and less concerned with the nature of the sounds themselves. Instead, I selected them for their unrestrained qualities. The idea was to create a work of uncontrolled celebration almost orgasmic in tone." Reid is now working on a series of ten miniatures for quadraphonic tape in which a single contrasting timbre, motive, or texture will be explored.

Another studio founding director is JANE BROCKMAN (b. 1949) of the University of Connecticut, Storrs. She studied at the University of California at Santa Barbara and received her Doctor of Musical Arts in 1977 from the University of Michigan. Notable among her awards is the 1973 Sigvald Thompson Prize for orchestral composition. She is the first woman to be so honored. Her works for chamber ensembles, orchestra, and electronic media have been performed throughout the United States and Europe, and in 1978 the Rhode Island Festival of the Arts commissioned her *Metamorphosis,* a seventeen-minute multi-media work for dance, quadraphonic electronic tape, and lighting. The work was composed with the ARP 2500 synthesizer and inspired by Franz Kafka's short story. The abstract adaptation that she uses explores various psychological states of mind experienced by the protagonist after his discovery one morning that he has somehow been transformed into a giant cockroach. Conceptually, the work moves between a calm, meditative spectrum of sound, and frenetic, echoic sounds rhythmically beating out the dance of the beetle. Opening on sonorities built of complex spectra centering on a fundamental pitch of F, the complex slowly moves microtonally to G, producing the meditative, introspective, calm section. In contrast a clicking, percussive timbre pervades the contrasting rhythmic portion of the work, which undoubtedly symbolizes the roach. Interestingly, the work closes with a recapitulation a fifth higher, moving microtonally from C to D, thus suggesting a move to the dominant without, in reality, effecting any tonal reference. Brockman comments:

As many composers of electronic music, I feel that the tape piece alone is not a sufficient performance vehicle. It must be accompanied by some closely integrated visual element: live performers, dance, film, etc. The "drama of the unexpected" cannot be duplicated in any other way. In collaboration with other art forms, electronic music has much to contribute; how else is it possible to obtain such a vast palette of timbral possibilities by such economical means?

Another of her works is the twelve-minute *Descent into the Maelström* for electronic tape and percussion written in 1981 and utilizing as primary sound source the Synclavier II, a highly accessible computer-controlled keyboard instrument created by New England Digital (NED). Brockman, among other electronic composers, is delighted as well as perturbed by the sophistication of sound palettes an up-to-date studio is able to produce.

A number of prominent composers have forecast the demise of the electronic medium. With the recent introduction of digital synthesizers, it is my opinion that the future of electronic music has never looked more promising. However, we must guard against the use of impressive technology as a compositional end in itself. It is now easy to produce music in which immediate "surface" events disguise the absence of deeper structural meaning. In the past, composers of electronic music struggled to obtain the elegant timbral effects which are now easily available on digital synthesizers. Compositional aspects of the work may now receive full attention.

A similar work in concept to Brockman's *Maelström* is *Into the Vortex: Dialogue for Timpani and Tape* by FRANCES DANFORTH (b. 1903). An effective study of white and colored noise, glissandos on complex harmonic spectra, violent sonic bursts, and timpanic virtuosity, the piece was realized at the University of Michigan's Electronic Music Studio in 1975 and was inspired by the report of an adventurer's ride over the falls at Niagara:

I imagined the barrel bumping into rocks, tree stumps, and small whirlpools at its base. I imagined the still-intact barrel being sucked down into the big whirlpools' depths, then being whirled upwards until it was spewed still spiralling outward into space. . . . All the sounds [of] both timpani and the tape are to effect the mood [of that experience].

One of the most honored electronic composers is DARIA SEMEGEN (b. 1946), associate director of the Electronic Music Studio at the State University of New York at Stony Brook. A student of Witold Lutosławski, she also studied with Bülent Arel at Yale and Vladimir Ussachevsky at Columbia. She describes her *Spectra* (Electronic Composition No. 2) (1979) as a work whose

thematic material is presented as short motivic bursts in the minute-long exposition and is subsequently developed into interacting layers generating their own phrase contours through increasingly complex superimpositions. This compositional approach differs from the conventional use of thematic elements bound to specific rhythmic patterns in a skeletal frame. In *Spectra,* the fast-flowing thematic groups are combined in various successions to generate new structures which are different from the characteristics of their original components. Several untempered tonal motives emerge from time to time, recurring in a diffused manner, but always in their unaltered state in contrast with the accompanying layers of activity, which are subject to constant variation and development. The work's rapidly changing sound colors are the result of the superimposition of many sound layers, each having its own individual timbre.

The densely mixed and precisely edited work combines a rich palette of timbral colors realized on the Buchla Series 200 synthesizer system. In contrast to *Spectra, Arc: Music for Dancers* (1977) opens with waltz-like, rhythmically pulsating patterns that return and evolve through timbral change. Commissioned by the Mimi Garrard Dance Theatre, the work was composed "following the choreographer's detailed diagrams in which each count of the dance was indicated along with details of the dancers' motions on stage, combined with a plan of synchronous lighting effects." The formal structure of the music is in five sections with a pentad arrangement of themes and tempos (A B C B A), hence the "Arc" title. Each of the sections forms a smaller arc: a b c, and is orchestrated with individual timbres.

The ballet has held attraction for many composers of electronic music: Spiegel's* *Waves* for nine acoustical instruments and prerecorded tape (1975); Sylvia Pengilly's* *The Pi Man* for orchestra, violin, percussion soloists, quadraphonic tape, and laser projections (1979); Ann McMillan's* *Gateway Summer Sound*, choreographed by Eva Zapfe for the Forion Ensemble, Mexico City, and her *Whale II,* also choreographed by the Forion Ensemble and performed in Mexico City in 1981. Another composer of ballet is the director of Boston University's Electronic Music Studio, JOYCE MEKEEL (b. 1931). Three of Mekeel's ballet scores are not electronic, but *Feast* (1970) is a ceremony for tape and dancers.

BARBERI PAULL (b. 1946) realized the score for her ballet *Time* (1973) on the equipment available at the Columbia-Princeton Electronic Music Center. The work was placed in the repertoire of the Joffrey Ballet Company in New York and in the National Ballet of Norway.

Time was made from a choral composition which I composed and taped and then altered electronically according to standard development techniques of fugue, theme development, and contrast. Of course these so-called standard development techniques are very much expanded by the capabilities of the machines. Rhythms, pitches, instrumentation can each be changed in some very tender and dramatic ways.

Paull wrote another work for dance during the same year. Choreographed by Lorraine Persson in Paris, this stunning piece about madness is entitled *Asylum* and uses environmental sound ("sounds from life") for its original material.

A student of Jacob Druckman in electronic music at Columbia, Paull's early works in electronic music were "of a theatre nature" using tapes, projection, film, live performers; they tended to have unifying themes and to approach the mix-media format. Eventually Paull formed the Barberi Paull Musical Theatre, which toured the United States from 1972 to 1975. She has written other works: *Mass* (1976) for tape, projections, and two percussionists won the Segall award and requires a ceremonial dance-like manner of the percussionists; *TBPMT,* a mixed-media event; *Antifon* for piano and tape won the Delius composition award in 1975. A neoromantic work, the latter utilizes tape imitation of piano thematic elements, jazzy rhythms, nostalgic waltz-like figures, and timbral interchanges between tape and piano.

Some of DIANE THOME's (b. 1942) earliest pieces are for dance. *Caprice* (1957) is an original children's ballet score and story, while *In My Garden* (1956) is scored for soprano, baritone, dancers, and small instrumental ensemble. A student of Milton Babbitt at Princeton, Thome is the first woman to receive a Ph.D. in music from that institution. Her music has been presented throughout the United States, in Europe, and in

Australia, and she is currently on the faculty of the University of Washington's School of Music in Seattle.

My use of the electronic medium may be divided into three general categories: (1) that which uses synthesized sound alone, such as *January Variations* for computer tape (1973); (2) that which combines synthesized and live instrumental sound, such as *Anais* for cello, tape, and piano (1976); and (3) that which utilizes recorded instrumental sound, live instrumental sound, and electronically-synthesized sound, such as *Alexander Boscovich Remembered* for viola, tape, and piano (1975).

Anais is an analog tape that was realized at the Electronic Music Studio of the State University of New York in Binghamton. Dedicated to the memory of writer Anais Nin, it is a very introspective work in which Thome uses the tape as a member of the ensemble. Passages of melodic or timbral imitation (or both) occur throughout. Her *Winter Infinities* (1980) explores further the rich compositional possibilities of pairing the live and the electronic medium. Written for seven performers and stereo tape, it is scored for flute, clarinet in B-flat, viola, cello, piano/celeste, and percussion I and II. In *January Variations* the relationship between pitch and timbre is structured; it is a dark piece with sombre wind timbres, which "represent vertical, 'frozen' manifestations of the interval relationships which underlie the work and which are subjected to various degrees of internal temporal and pitch modulation." *Los Nombres* (1974) for computer, percussion, and piano is a brilliant virtuoso vehicle where the computer is a member of a small ensemble "whose timbral, spatial, and gestural characteristics are distinct from, yet extending of, the compositional materials given to the live instruments."

There are several composers who like to combine live performers with electronic music because they believe the visual is extremely important in the ritual of the concert. JEAN EICHELBERGER IVEY (b. 1923) is one who sees a "complex human interaction between the audience and player(s)." Although she has written pure electronic works, such as *Continuous Form* (1967), *Pinball* (1967), and *Cortege—for Charles Kent* (1969), it is in works rich in symbolism and literary themes that her true talent arises. The monodrama *Testament of Eve* (1974) is an example. The work, written on her own text, is a debate between Lucifer and Eve, for mezzo-soprano, tape, and large orchestra, in which the tape becomes the disembodied voice of Lucifer. In *Hera, Hung from the Sky* (1973) the tape becomes part of the ensemble. This work is based on a poem by Carolyn Kizer in which Hera, the wife of Zeus, is punished for presuming to be the equal of her husband by being forever suspended in the heavens as a constellation. Again the powerful theme of confrontation allows Ivey full range of her orchestrative talents and she word-paints with abrupt contrasts of mood to fit the text. The libretto itself is set generally syllabically with the words clearly and easily heard. Written for mezzo-soprano, seven winds, three percussion, piano, and tape, the text is often interrupted and dotted throughout with instrumental and electronic interludes of various lengths that help to underline and punctuate it. The tape, created at the Peabody Conservatory Electronic Music Studio where Ivey has been founding director since 1969, adds a stunning dimension to the powerful swinging pendulum effect and chaotic swirls of the final section based upon the text: "I have lost the war of the air: Half-strangled in my hair, I dangle, drowned in fire."

Ivey's interest in Shakespeare's *Tempest* is demonstrated by two works based upon that play: *Prospero* (1978), a scene for bass voice with horn, one percussionist and four-channel tape, enacts the last speech of the last act of Shakespeare's last play—a farewell to his magical powers and his attendant spirits. The second work is *Sea-Change* (1978) for orchestra and 4-channel tape, in which the tape creates the effect of a magic isle with its fairy voices, nature sounds, and wordless singing. The electronic component interacts with the orchestral setting to conjure up a world of blithe spirits.

SYLVIA PENGILLY (b. 1935), director of the electronic music studio at Loyola University in New Orleans, is another composer who enjoys "composing for a wide variety of media from mixed instrumental chamber ensembles to full orchestra." Pengilly adds, "I am particularly interested in the coloristic possibilities of combining electronic sounds with live instrumental performers." Her *Three Moments of Agony* (1975) is an example that combines flute and bass clarinet with a tape created entirely from natural sounds. *Incantation,* written in 1978, combines synthesizer, solo percussion, and laser projections. "Electronic music, to my great delight, appears to be attempting to combine the visual with the aural to the greater enrichment of both." Her most recent pieces are more conservative. *Premonitions* (1982) for flute, cello, piano, and tape is based on the Gregorian chant, *Victimae paschali laudes,* and *The Flower Seekers* (in progress) will involve tape loops, real time distortion of the singer's voice, and a different method of laser projection. "It is not my intent, however, that these devices be used merely for effect. I must say what I have to say musically, using the most appropriate tools available."

BARBARA KOLB's (b. 1939) work with tape combines live instruments with prerecorded instrumental sound. In *Looking for Claudio* (1975) a solo guitar concerts itself with a prerecorded tape of six guitars, a mandolin, chimes, vibraphone, and three human voices. The work opens with a soft tremolo on E-flat, and the vibraphone and mandolin enter from afar with the vibes sounding as soft chimes in the distance. The piece builds as the interactions of live and taped instruments break through the barrier of each other's domain via a loop-like repetitive figure, out of phase. All fades away after this climax to an ever-retarding fragment in the vibraphone succeeded by a far-away hum, which grows into a melancholy, chant-like tone until the chimes come and chant us into silence.

The use of guitar/vibraphone/chimes also appears in *Trobar Clus* (1967); in *Spring River Flowers Moon Night* (1974) the three again appear with the mandolin, a combination which begins to create a special Kolb sonance. In the latter work, two pianos in real-time are accompanied by a prerecorded tape of mandolin/guitar/chimes/vibraphone/marimba/and Carl Orff instruments. The composition is based upon a poem written by Chang Jo-Hsu in the eighth century. The piece moves from serene nocturnal moods to greatly agitated sections. The affect of a koto is created by playing the strings inside the piano, and a persistent, soft tremolo on the marimba in the opening of the work produces a mantra-like beginning. Another work of the 1970s, *Soundings* (1972), has been written in two versions: the first is for double sextet/harp/chimes/prerecorded tape, and the second is for full orchestra.

JANET GILBERT (b. 1946) has written extensively in the electronic medium, realizing her works by both analog and digital generation of sound. She studied in Italy at the Pisa Computer Center and later at the University of Illinois's Experimental Music Studios. In 1979 she was awarded a Doctor of Musical Arts in composition from that institution but continued her studies in computer music with Charles Dodge at the Bregman Electronic Music Studio, Dartmouth College, in Hanover, New Hampshire. During this time (1979-1980), she taught electronic music and supervised the studio at Middleburg College in Vermont. She has been active in various experimental theater and vocal groups and now teaches electronic music at St. Olaf College in Northfield, Minnesota, where she also heads the St. Olaf Verbal Workshop, a group of six professional musicians "devoted to exploring the contemporary possibilities of verbal improvisation controlled by musical/poetic structures."

Gilbert's . . . *out of the looking glass* for tape/visuals was written in 1975. It is a work in eight sections, based on the Lewis Carroll book: "Falling pool of tears," "Lullaby," "White Knight," "Dialogue w. Humpty D.," "Checkers I," "Caucus Race," "Growing," and "Checkers II." The various sections follow one another with no real breaks and are depicted by timbral and textural changes that range from a variety of string effects (pizzicato, ponticello, and so on) to bell-like tones, percussive attacks, raspy glissandos, to wonderful children's voices slowly becoming less electronically abstract and more of this world; the total effect is one of coming out of a dream into reality. Especially notable are the techniques used in "Checkers I" and "Checkers II": the first section represents an electronic version of a checkers game with its clicking, percussive attacks, while the second (and concluding section of the entire work) brings the game, the children's voices, and the piece back into reality and "out of the looking glass."

Oenone (1976) is an equally effective, though shorter, work for quad tape and visuals. It depicts the tale of the Greek nymph, Oenone, who is the abandoned wife of the Trojan, Paris.

Figure 9.9 Janet Gilbert at the St. Olaf College Electronic Music Studio. Photograph by Henry Kermott

Other works were realized at Illinois in 1977. One, *Paisaje con dos tumbas* for soprano/tape (10 minutes) is a modal and impressionistic setting of Garcia Lorca's text. Weaving around the tritone motif of the vocal part, the electronic tape forms a rapturous accompaniment to the voice. Gilbert's last work realized at Illinois is also on a text, this one by Mallarmé. *Un coup de dés* (20 minutes) (1979) is a chant for chorus/tape/readers/visuals.

Although her earlier pieces incorporated much *musique concrète*, her most recent pieces are computer-generated, being realized on a Synclavier. *Revelation* (1981) combines computer-animated film with tape, and *Fusions* (1981) utilizes dance, computer visuals, film, and tape. Both are again longer works, running fifteen and twenty minutes, respectively, and were created at the Middlebury studio.

One of the most prolific composers, electronic or otherwise, is EMMA LOU DIEMER (b. 1927), professor of composition at the University of California at Santa Barbara (UCSB). Director of UCSB's Electronic Music Studio, which she founded in 1973, Diemer has written over one hundred works in the traditional medium (including many for her own instrument, the organ). She credits herself with between fifteen and twenty electronic compositions on two- or four-channel tape written between 1978 and 1981.

She received her Bachelor of Music (1949) and Master of Music (1950) in composition from Yale School of Music, where she studied composition with Richard Donovan and Paul Hindemith. She later studied with Howard Hanson and Bernard Rogers at Eastman (Ph.D. 1960). It was in 1970, while attending a workshop at Catholic University in Washington, D.C., conducted by Emerson Meyers, that she first took an interest in electronic music; participants there were introduced to such equipment as the Putney VCS-3 synthesizer along with other electronic devices. But it was not until 1973 that she began to explore the sounds generated and processed by synthesizers:

[I began] to come to terms with what sort of sound and structures I might create using [them]. I felt in the early 70s that an expansion of my style was necessary and that working in the electronic medium would influence this expansion. I wanted not only to experiment with new sounds, new timbres, but to find alternatives to the attractions of my comfortable use of free tonality, somewhat regular rhythmic patterns, linear melodic concepts.

From 1973 to 1978, UCSB's Electronic Music Studio began to acquire a few synthesizers, such as the electrocomp 101 and the 401 sequencer synthesizer, along with a quadraphonic recording system.

Patchworks, Diemer's first major electronic composition, was realized in 1978.

I was determined to "turn the tables" and bring to electronic music composition some of the qualities I felt were lacking in much of it, qualities that were in my works in other mediums: a definite feeling for structure, melodic patterns that were more home-based than pointillistic, rhythmic ideas that had some semblance of organization, all contributing to more dynamic contrasts of mood (joy, even!) than I was hearing in some of the Eastern establishment creations.

A four-movement work, *Patchworks* combines "sequenced percussive timbres with keyboard interpolations and uses from four to sixteen overlays of sound with glissandos and loud percussion entering to create a climax," which ends, as she says, "very quickly, harmlessly." She tells us that she developed a specific technique for building this composition which she has since used in all her other electronic works.

[There was] much searching for patches that were unlike those I had heard in other music and that had a timbral "life of their own" and that would contrast well in an extended composition. I planned which combinations would be used in each movement of the work and then recorded one channel at a time, improvising at the keyboard of the 101 and the controls of the 401, modifying the sounds as I went along, listening to what had been recorded before, and interacting with it. Since much of my composing has come about through keyboard improvisation, this was the most natural way for me to use the electronic medium.

Another synthesizer, Prophet 5, was added to the studio in 1980. As Diemer describes her use of it, this instrument can

hold forty separate programs (patches) at one time and has a five-octave, five-voice keyboard. Rapid switching from patch to patch is possible, and I set up each of the programs in such a way that would allow timbral similarity as well as contrast: for each of the eight programs, I created five banks of like-sound (five kinds of harpsichords, five kinds of percussion, and so on). In my first programming of the Prophet, only the harpsichord sounds were equal-tempered, the others being more concerned with varying timbral activity and uses of frequency and amplitude modulation. My other equipment, in addition to the quad recording system, was the ever-present mixer with reverb (I have no affinity whatsoever for unreverbed electronic sound!), and a 256-stage sequencer.

The majority of her electronic works came from this procedure, most of them written in 1980: *Harpsichord Quartet, Presto Canon,* and *Of the Past* are examples. They are highly structured, usually with returning sections, and are influenced, in most cases, by her organ/piano virtuosity.

Her *Add One* series was written in 1981. It is more original in timbres and less organ-like in sound than the earlier compositions, representing a distinct move away from acoustical orientation. In each of the three works written thus far in the series, the "add one" denotes the use of another electronic device in live performance with the four-track tape. The first of the series and the shortest (8:41), *Add One #1,* utilizes an electronic piano. *Add One #2* (11:30) calls for live improvisation on synthesizer, while *Add One #3* (14:50), may use either the synthesizer or electronic piano for live improvisation with the four-channel tape. Both *#2* and *#3* may also be performed by tape alone. Since 1981 Diemer has begun to develop ideas on a microcomputer system and will soon be composing in this medium.

RUTH WHITE (b. 1925) who studied at Carnegie Mellon Institute and with George Antheil, has written a number of works dating from the late 1960s and early 1970s. GLADYS NORDENSTROM (b. 1924), wife of Ernst Krenek, has used electronics in combination with a solo instrument in her work *Signals from Nowhere* (1973) for organ and tape. And TOMMIE CARL, president and founder of American Women Composers, Inc., composed a number of works from 1974 to 1975, including *Illusions, Chromosynthesis* (a quasi-toccata for synthesizer), *Futurama I, Futurama II, Sands,* and *Bells.* The realization of these pieces in quadraphonic sound is an important element in their structure. Carl describes her work as follows:

I conceived and executed these [pieces] working alone as performer-engineer-composer. The works are not spliced, as are those of many composers working with tape, but are all whole with the exception of small edited parts.

As with many others, Carl also feels "that it would be somewhat more satisfying to incorporate live sound with tape," and she is doing so in two of her latest works, which are still in progress, *Deux Poems Electronic* and *Fantasy: When Johnny Comes Marching Home*. At present, she composes out of her own home studio in Virginia with a four-channel TEAC tape deck, four speakers, and an ARP 2600 Synthesizer.

* * *

In preparing this study, I began to discern several ideas that thread their way across and between individual esthetic points of view and appear to be held in common by many of the composers profiled: First, there is a movement away from academia or academically conceived intellectual schools of music toward a more accessible, humanistic, communicative style of composition. I do not mean that the music is simplistic; in fact, there is a deep and profound intellectualism in the works of the humanists and naturalists. What is most evident is a growing disinterest in music that is based on either serialism or pure chance. Second, there is a stress on strong ties to nature, apparent in music whose method or purpose invokes healing, audience participation, and meditation. This emphasis involves greater interest in tone colors, in melodies and/or harmonies derived from added overtones and timbral changes, and in forms and structures primarily related to timbral contrast. Third, this study also points up a growing trend to combining electronics with other elements—film, video, ballet, live performance, or multi-media—if the music is to be used in a concert hall. This also suggests that music for tape alone works best in a nonlive-audience context: for recordings and radio broadcasts, where quadraphonic tapes may be experienced more fully.

Finally, the study demonstrates the tremendous force of activity that is at large today in this country, coming from America's core group of highly motivated, extremely active, talented, and trend-setting women composers of electronic music.

SELECTED DISCOGRAPHY

Anderson, Beth. *10 + 2 + 12 American Text-Sound Pieces.* "Torero Piece." 1750 Arch Records No. 1752.

Anderson, Laurie. *Airwaves.* "Song for Juanita," "Is Anybody Home?," "Ethics Is the Esthetics of the Future," "It's Not the Bullet That Kills You—It's the Hole." 1-10 Records.

   It's Not the Bullet That Kills You—It's the Hole. Holly Solomon Gallery, NY (45 rpm).

   New Music for Electronic and Recorded Media. "New York Social Life," "Time To Go (For Diego)." 1750 Arch Records No. 1765.

   O Superman. "O Superman," "Walk the Dog." Warner Bros. Records.

Big Ego. "Three Expediencies." Dial-A-Poem Series.

Big Science. (Songs from "United States Pt. I-IV"). Warner Bros. Records BSK 3674.

Anderson, Ruth. *State of the Union Message.* "Dump," "SUM (State of the Union Message)," Opus One No. 70.

New Music for Electronic and Recorded Media. "Points." 1750 Arch Records No. 1765.

I Come Out of Your Sleep. "I Come Out of Your Sleep," Opus One No. 63.

Ciani, Suzanne. *New Waves.* Victor Musical Industries.

Gardner, Kay. *Emerging.* "Atlantis Rising." Urana Records WWE-83

Mooncircles. "Lunamuse." Urana Records WWE-80.

Hays, Doris. "13th Street Beat," "Syn-Rock," "Arabella Rag," and thirteen other electronic pieces. Southern Library of Recorded Sound MQLP38.

Southern Voices. "Southern Voices (speech/synthesizer)." Folkways Record.

Ivey, Jean Eichelberger. *Electronic Music.* "Pinball." Folkways Record FMS 33436.

Music by Jean Eichelberger Ivey (voices/inst/tape). "Terminus," "Aldebaran," "Three Songs of Night," "Cortege—for Charles Kent." Folkways Records FTS 33439.

Contemporary Music: New Vocal Music. "Hera, Hung from the Sky." Composers Recordings CRI-SD 325.

"Prospero Scena." Grenadilla Enterprises, Inc.

Kolb, Barbara. *American Contemporary Instrumental Music.* "Looking for Claudio," "Spring River Flowers Moon Night." Composers Recording Inc. CRI SD 361.

La Barbara, Joan. *Reluctant Gypsy.* "Autumn Signal," "q-/-votre petites bêtes." Wizard Records RVW 2279.

Voice Is the Original Instrument. "Vocal Extensions." Wizard Records RVW 2266.

Tapesongs. "Cathing," "Thunder." Chiaroscuro Records CR 196.

LeBaron, Anne. *Raudelunas Pataphysical Revue.* "Concerto for Active Frogs." Say Day-Bew Records. No. 1.

Lockwood, Annea. *New Music for Electronic and Recorded Media.* "World Rhythm." 1750 Arch Records No. 1765.

"Tiger Balm." Opus One No. 70.

McLean, Priscilla. *Electro-Symphonic Landscapes.* "Invisible Chariots." Folkways Records FTS 33450.

Electronic Music from the Outside In. "Night Images." Folkways Records SFPX 6050.

American Contemporary: Electronic Music. "Dance of Dawn." Composers Recording CRI-SD 335.

McMillan, Ann. *New American Music.* "Whale I," "Carrefours." Folkways Records 33904 Vol. IV.

Gateway Summer Sound. "Amber '75," "Syrinx," "Episode," "Gateway Summer Sound," "Gong Song." Folkways Records FTS 33451.

Oliveros, Pauline. *New Sounds in Electronic Music.* "I of IV." Odyssey 32 160160.

Electronic Essays. "Jar Piece." Marathon Music MS2111 (Canada).

Extended Voices: New Pieces for Chorus and for Voices Altered by Sound Synthesizer and Vocoder. "Sound Pattern." Odyssey 32 160156.

New Music for Electronic and Recorded Media. "Bye Bye Butterfly." 1750 Arch Records No. 1765.

Payne, Maggie. "Lunar Dusk," "Lunar Earthrise." Lovely Music Record.

Roberts, Megan. *New Music for Electronic and Recorded Media.* "I Could Sit Here All Day." 1750 Arch Records 1765.

Semegen, Daria. "Electronic Composition No. 1." Columbia/Odyssey Y 34139.

Satan's Sermon and Other Electronic Fantasies. "Electronic Composition No. 2: Spectra." Composers Records CRI 443.

Electronic Music for Dance. "Arc: Music for Dance." Atlantic/Finnadar SR 9020.

Shields, Alice. "Farewell to a Hill." Atlantic Records.

Columbia-Princeton Electronic Music Center Tenth Anniversary Album. "Transformation of Ani." Composers Records CRI SD 268.

Smiley, Pril. "Eclipse." Vox: Turnabout 34301.

Columbia-Princeton Electronic Music Center. "Kolyosa." Composers Records CRI SD 268.

"Eclipse" (four-track version). Finnadar QD 9010.

Spiegel, Laurie. *New Music for Electronic and Recorded Media.* "Appalachian Grove 1." 1750 Arch Records 1765.

The Expanding Universe. "The Expanding Universe," "Patchwork," "Old Wave," "Pentachrome." Philo Recordings No. 9003.

Sounds of Earth. "Harmony of the Planets." NASA Record.

Thome, Diane. *American Contemporary.* "Anais." Composers Records CRI S-437.

New Directions in Music. "Les Nombres." Tulsa Studios TS 78-208.

White, Ruth. "Variations on Couperin's Rondeau," (Synthesizer). Angel S-36042.

Witkin, Beatrice. "Breath and Sound for Tuba and Tape" Opus One No. 12. "Echologie for Flute and Tape." Belwin Mills (cassette).

10

Women Jazz Composers
and Arrangers

JILL McMANUS

Women jazz composers have had few, if any, female role models. As men have dominated instrumental jazz, so have they called the tunes while the ladies generally cheered from the sidelines. But there are a handful of women who happened to be at the right place at the right time (for example, they managed to have a male friend or relative in jazz), took score paper in hand, and began composing simply because someone nearby needed music and they could write it. Some, by their persistence and talent, have made unique and recognized contributions. This chapter will cover some of the most noted and recent female composers of the instrumental music that falls under the heading of jazz—such as Lil Hardin Armstrong, Mary Lou Williams, Melba Liston, Toshiko Akiyoshi, Carla Bley, and JoAnne Brackeen—but it is not intended to be a complete survey. It will not emphasize the many composers of popular songs, which grew from American Negro slave field chants, spirituals, and blues to become an acknowledged and often-discussed part of jazz history.

At this point it might be helpful to discuss the context and history of jazz composition. The distinctive component and the challenge of jazz as an art form is improvisation. Therefore, the jazz composer has two considerations: to build a framework of melody, chords, and rhythms that will stimulate the creativity of the soloist; and to produce written material that itself sounds like the highest level of improvisation so that the transitions are nearly seamless. The best improviser, equipped with a well-developed ear for choice of notes as well as a sense of architecture, actually "composes" chorus after chorus until a gleaming tower of sound of such graceful proportions arises, that it hovers long afterward in the memory of the listener.

The foundations of jazz were in the field chants, blues, and spirituals, where call and response, repetition, and slurred vocal notes were characteristic. When more than six or seven horn players got together, they had to be organized into sections playing as one voice or in harmony, and early arrangements were "riffs"—short, rhythmic, repeated phrases—with spaces where gifted players could "glisten" on their own. Eventually, the breaks became the most exciting aspect, and solo playing was put in the spotlight in modern jazz with the ensemble in a supporting role. By contrast, rags and written-out pieces sounded set and European, while the new style called for on-the-spot daring by the soloist, which was similar to being confronted by all the hazards and choices of daily life compressed into a schematic problem.

As soloists became more adept, the tunes became more complex, until, during the be-bop revolution in the mid-1940s, they were like obstacle courses whose sharp turns, patterned progressions, and chromatic inclines had to be taken in stride. Rhythms were strongly related to African (and later Afro-Cuban) polyrhythms, and streams of eighth notes were displaced in various ways to produce off-beat accents. Later, composers tried to bring European elements—extended phrases, thicker harmonic textures, longer forms, and atonality—to fuse with jazz (the "Third Stream" music of the 1950s and 1960s), but little of it retained the gut feeling of original jazz. There may still be some possibility of integrating these ideas for composers who are knowing improvisers.

One of the first of the unusual, energetic women to become known in jazz as a composer as well as an instrumentalist was Lovie Austin, a pianist from Chattanooga, Tennessee. She led an orchestra and composed and arranged music for the Blues Serenaders' shows. This was often done under last-minute pressures, so that she would sit cross-legged at the keyboard, writing parts and smoking a cigarette and conducting. Austin also provided organic accompaniment for cornetist Tommy Ladnier, clarinetist Johnny Dodds, and trombonist Kid Ory on tunes that she wrote in the boogie romp style of the day—such tunes as *Steppin' on the Blues, Traveling Blues,* and *Frog Tongue Stomp.*

One of the earliest women to have a significant career as a jazz writer was pianist Lil Hardin, who was active in Chicago in the late 1920s. In 1924 she married Louis Armstrong and played in his group, the Hot Five. She also arranged and wrote material for them, such as *Lonesome Blues, Skid-da-de-dat,* and the popular *Struttin' With Some Barbeque.* She is given joint credit, as either lyricist or composer, for *Knock Knee'd Sal, Everything's Wrong, Ain't Nothing Right,* and *Safely Locked Up in My Heart*—songs recorded while working on her own after separating from Armstrong. Due to publishing practices at that time, it may be difficult to pin down all that she did compose.

Little Mary Lou Burley, a gifted, rather lonely child whose sensitivities bordered on the psychic, was a prodigy who later became known as Mary Lou Williams, the leading lady of jazz piano and a central figure in jazz history from the 1930s on. As a small girl, she sat entranced on her brother-in-law's lap in a Pittsburgh theater one night watching Lovic Austin perform and never forgot that vision of versatility. Williams had perfect pitch, could "hear around corners," and developed a strongly swinging two-handed style expressed with a Tatumesque touch.

When her first husband joined Andy Kirk's band in the late 1920s, Williams quickly learned from Kirk how to sketch arrangements and eventually put together a whole book of tunes for the band. One night the regular pianist did not show up for a date; Williams filled in and later copped the piano chair, technically joining the band in 1931 and staying with it until 1942. Two of her best compositions from this period are *Froggy Bottom,* a boogie twelve-bar blues with eight-bar sections interposed, and *Walkin' and Swingin',* with a cheery, innovative chorus scored for trumpet with three saxophones, a sound that became one of the hallmarks of her style in the 1930s. She arranged her tune *Roll 'Em* (1937) for Benny Goodman's swing era band to perform, and it is a boogie-swing classic. Constantly on the prowl for new sounds, Williams always kept just a bit ahead of the changing styles. When she settled in New York in 1942, she became a spiritual anchor for several of the founders of be-bop, such as Thelonious Monk and Bud Powell. She helped many musicians crystallize their ideas and tunes, often working late into the night with them with arrangements spread all over the floor of her apartment. She spent six months arranging for Duke Ellington and came up with such gems as *Trumpets No End* (her version of *Blue Skies*). Her playing projected a deep sense of peace and control which perhaps did not always accurately portray her state of mind. In 1954, the chaotic state of the world and the demands of a travelling life overcame her, and she dropped out of the playing scene altogether. After converting to Catholicism and dedicating herself to helping indigent musicians, she gained the strength to reemerge as a performer and in 1964 made a welcome comeback at the Hickory House in New York. During the 1960s, Williams composed a religious piece for vocal choir called *St. Martin de Porres* (*Black Christ of the Andes,* 1963) with rich-textured, shifting minor voicings, and *Mass for the Lenten Season. Music for Peace,* commissioned by the Vatican in 1969, later became known as *Mary Lou's Mass;* it was arranged for a children's choir in 1975 and became the first jazz mass to be performed at St. Patrick's Cathedral in New York City. A revised version was successfully choreographed by Alvin Ailey for his dance company's repertoire.

Her piece called *A Fungus Amungus* (1963) begins with a melodic line that dissipates into the dissonant and jagged sounds of the avant-garde; it expressed William's foreboding that those developments would bring an end to the blues/gospel/swing basis of the jazz tradition. Shortly before her death in 1981, this dichotomy was explored in a rather extraordinary joint concert she gave at Carnegie Hall with Cecil Taylor, one of the "farthest out" pianists on the scene. Called "Embrace" and conceived as a mutual admiration venture, the concert actually set Williams's proclivity for serene swinging at odds with Taylor's free-form lyricism and intense scurrying outbursts, and the "embrace" became a standoff.

As for composing, Williams describes her feeling thus: "The basic thing is the piano because I can do so many things on the piano, switching and changing. . . . My arranging and composing comes while I'm playing piano. . . . I think of a melody . . . and get a copyright and then work from that."[1] When writing the *Zodiac Suite* (1945), which she later played with the New York Philharmonic, she wrote out arrangements for the first two pieces and composed the remainder while playing it through for a recording.[2] This is a prime illustration of the jazz player's facility for instantaneous composition—the discipline of craft married to a flow of pure creativity on the instant.

Trombonist-arranger Melba Liston, from Kansas City, Missouri, who belongs to the next musical generation, pays tribute to Williams, referring to her as her "New York spiritual mother."[3] Liston came up in the 1940s playing in the big bands, such as those of Count Basie and Dizzy Gillespie, and became a respected arranger writing for Ellington, Basie, Gillespie, singers Tony Bennett and Abbey Lincoln, and the Buffalo Philharmonic Orchestra (in 1967). In the 1960s, she freelanced in the Los Angeles studios and later took a job in Jamaica teaching general popular music courses. In 1979 the organizers of the Kansas City Women's Jazz Festival invited Liston to lead an all-star group, and that appearance heralded her return to the U.S. and to performing.

Even now that she is embarking on a new round of compositional efforts, she considers herself primarily an arranger. Among her best-known tunes are *Len-Sirrah,* a medium-tempo jazz waltz built on minor chord structures written in the early 1960s (and first played by Mary Lou Williams); *We Never Kissed,* a ballad with lyrics; and *Just Waiting,* another ballad with a satiny, meditative melody. As far as influences, Liston says, "Ellington was my everything, but I also love Ravel and the pretty French composers." She feels that she found her own voice in her arrangements for pianist Randy Weston; while doing a half-dozen albums for him, she researched African music in order to be able to incorporate its sounds authentically.

In spring of 1982, Liston completed a work with a carnival flavor for seven-piece ensemble, brass choir, and stage band that was performed in concert at Northeastern University. There are other long pieces that she has worked on bit by bit over many years which she is determined to finish—one of these is a salute to the be-bop of the late 1940s, in which she hopes to evoke the excitement that Dizzy Gillespie brought to the music and to amplify the beautifully-woven lines that were Charlie Parker's contribution to the style. Liston has formed a group of her own and plans to compose for them in her practiced style of joining attractive orchestral colors with robust, bluesy, swinging sounds. Hopefully her works will be recorded.

British jazz pianist Marian McPartland has been a regular on the jazz scene since she came to the U.S. in 1946. Best known for tasty reharmonizations of standards and loving treatments of friend Alec Wilder's music, she has also written lilting ballads such as *Ambiance, A Delicate Balance,* and *Twilight World* (recorded by Tony Bennett). Her tunes have well-crafted contours and sail under a flag of elegance, yet there is warmth and tenderness in her ruminative probings. She has often included standards written by women composers, such as *Willow Weep for Me* (by Anne Ronell), in her repertoire at the Cafe Carlyle in New York, and she has also put together an all-woman band for a recording (*Now's the Time,* Halcyon 115). While writing, lecturing, and teaching at clinics around the country, McPartland has also discovered and encouraged young female jazz players.

Toshiko Akiyoshi was born in Manchuria, studied piano in Japan, and became interested in jazz, forming her own trio in 1952. Oscar Peterson heard her there and helped make it possible for her to record and later come to the U.S. to study at the Berklee College of Music in Boston. Early compositions, such as *Between Me and Myself,* already show her interest in interplay between instruments and have a pensive Oriental flavor; these were vehicles for her percussive be-bop style, heavily influenced by Bud Powell. In the fall of 1967, Akiyoshi organized her first big band concert and aired a few of her own compositions. At that time she met her second husband, saxophonist Lew Tabackin, and in 1972 they moved to California to put together a sixteen-piece band.

Akiyoshi has command of a large palette of colors, strong propulsive rhythms, and a special ingredient—inspiration from traditional Japanese music—which led her to blend sounds from Noh drama with contemporary jazz. Of her composition *Kogun* (1974), she says, "Using traditional Japanese *tsuzumi* drums was never done before—it was a revolutionary thing for me. I had always wanted to because my father was a student of Noh. I thought it would be criticized in Japan because the jazz fans are very traditional there, but it was received very well." The cries of the Noh singer and the curious drooping nasal resonances of the drums against the brass section create a startling introduction that eventually gives way to a piano solo, a building ensemble, and a haunting hilltop sound of flute (in a fine solo by Tabackin).

Perhaps Akiyoshi's most important work is the suite *Minamata,* which was named Best Album of the Year by Japan's *Swing Journal.* It begins with a few lines chanted by her daughter, a sunrise of suspensions (sustained by staggering the horns), and waves splashed by the drummer on his cymbals. A furious swinging section follows where punching rhythmic figures jab the soloists forward; this changes to a sinister undertow of low brass, a hint of frenzy, and the disturbing intoning of the Noh singer and drums (made eerier by the changing speeds of the tape). Finally, the music degenerates into discomfiting huffs from the brass while the saxes play a forlorn, disjointed line that seems to be in a different time zone. It is strong music and it gets its point across—it is about a peaceful village being poisoned by the pollution from encroaching industrial development.

Influenced by Ellington and Mingus, and inspired by some painters she admires, Akiyoshi says that for her "the feeling is the main thing and the techniques come second. I'm interested in incidents that happen to individual people that catch my heart."

A more eclectic innovator is Carla Bley, a keyboard player who came from Oakland, California, to New York in the late 1950s and worked for a while at Birdland as a cigarette girl. Her early pieces, such as *Ictus* and *Batterie,* were irregular ditties—frameworks for free-jazz improvisations. She gained recognition with a longer work for vibraphonist Gary Burton called *A Genuine Tong Funeral* (1967). It expresses her emotions toward death with passages of melancholic dread, painful chords of finality, and limping dirges built over moving tritone and minor third intervals in the bass; the vibes float melodically or hold anxious exchanges with guitar and saxophone. Here Bley captures all the shades and nuances of loss and anxiety with great inventiveness. "Up 'til then I had been writing tunes for jazz musicians without knowing if I liked the way they sounded," she says, "but I wrote this for myself."

Bley went on to write *Escalator over the Hill,* a three-album-length "opera," in collaboration with Paul Haines; it won the Melody Makers

Figure 10.1 Carla Bley. Photo by Roger Ressmeyer/WATT/ECM

Jazz Poll's Top Album of the Year Award in 1972. All kinds of sounds were wrapped into this giant project, which took four years to complete—Western dance music, Eastern chants and wails, circus music, jazz, avant-garde music, and cacophonous trips through the unconscious. Bley likes emotive trombone and low brass textures. One sound that frequently recurs in her music is a sort of Kurt Weillish, seedy, beer-hall dance band; it keeps popping out of the attic with the acridity of mothballs and loneliness. She remembers taping Satie's *Parade* as a child, a piece with a circus-like sound. "That might be one reason. Or it might have been something I heard accidentally that stuck in my mind." Some of the abrupt changes of mood in Bley's music come with the capriciousness of scenes from dreams, while some pieces, like *Floater* and *Copyright Royalties,* have a more cohesive jazz feel. Her tune *Sing Me Softly of the Blues* became popular with many jazz performers, and the noted pianist Keith Jarrett played the piano solo when her piece *3/4* was performed at Alice Tully Hall in 1974.

Having tried several grooves, Bley is settling into a functional one for the present. Her aim is to write fresh material for her successful ten-piece band, which has already toured Europe and will go back for the summer festivals. Future assignments include producing one album for her husband, trumpeter-composer Mike Mantler (with whom she manages the Jazz Composer's Orchestra Association); another for her fifteen-year-old composer daughter (who has some ideas that Carla says she finds inspiring); music for three French films ("I'm popular in France"); and arrangements for Charlie Haden's New Liberation Orchestra. Her own album *Live,* recorded at a San Francisco concert, was released in 1982, and she calls it "all instrumental and incredibly conservative, but I'd like to feel that it's as good as it gets for a ten-piece band. No one else has a ten-piece band, so I guess I won't fail."

Bley recently finished *The Piano Lesson*, a short piece with a plot—"I play a stern music teacher teaching scales; three players start a mutiny and I end up joining it"—but there are no lyrics. For her, composing is "very satisfying but not enjoyable. My system is to spend a lot of time. If you work all day every day, inevitably something comes out. It makes each day of life worth living or dying."

JoAnne Brackeen, an impressive, mostly self-taught pianist from Ventura, California, made her name playing in the bands of Art Blakey, Joe Henderson, and Stan Getz. In the mid-1970s, she turned to creating her own music, which would intimidate all but the most technically well-equipped keyboard players. Her tunes are often built from segments of intense rhythms, with percussive chords and patternlets doing counterpoint dances, or on lyrical, free lines with highly irregular phrasing. Changes of tempo within a tune seem to serve as breathers between bedazzlements of virtuosity, tumbling landslides, rumbles and tremolos. A piece like *Einstein* consists of avant-garde lightning bursts in the manner of Cecil Taylor;

Figure 10.2 JoAnne Brackeen. Photograph by Giuseppe Pino

Brackeen's lines cascade, prance, or march with such energy that a swinging momentum is built up. Her work connects with the roots of all music—"naturalistic sounds of the essence of the planet earth and the fullness of the human spirit," as she expresses it.

I compose all the time, and the tunes are all different. Each one is the emanations that come from the life I'm living at the time. *African Aztec,* the most recent tune, holds the most fascination for me right now. I'll put on the tape recorder and a tune sometimes comes out in order, or I change the order. Usually, there's some feeling that I want to write, but that's about the extent of it. It ends when it feels like it's ended.

Among Brackeen's most lyrical creations are *Lost or Found* and *Golden Garden,* while *El Mayorazgo* starts with an eight-bar strut, moves into sixteen bars of a Spanish vamp over a descending bass line with skittering chords in the right hand, repeats the eight-bar strut, and then moves into a freer section of fifteen bars. *Ancient Dynasty* opens with twenty evenly dealt-out chords and goes into a quick-step series of phrases that stop short, build in intensity, scurry over a brief pedal point, and jump back to the chords again. She manages to improvise on her tunes by retaining the original form but shifting metric gears, allowing implicit 4/4, 6/8, 8/8, or other meters to prevail at various points along the way. *Haiti-B* is a dance over uneven ground, with an ostinato bass line in 7/4, which her left hand states with the bassist; she then leaves him to carry the insistent pattern while she continues freely above. Occasionally a tune such as *Remembering* will be as darkly reflective as an evening pond and then turn to rapid eddies of sound in the improvisations.

Brackeen plans to "expand immensely on what I'm doing. My main satisfaction now is in playing the compositions, and it's even more exciting with the proper rhythm section. It would be interesting to hear an orchestra play them."

Beside these now-recognized women composers, there are others also beginning to be heard. One is saxophonist Jane Ira Bloom, a graduate of Yale Music School in composition and arranging. She has brought out two albums of mostly original music and has written two charts for fifteen pieces and one for twenty pieces that have been performed in New Haven. A whimsical player who likes to provoke both playful and thoughtful instrumental exchanges, she is also writing solo sax pieces that will capture the sounds that she can make while "in motion" and responding to a dancer.

Sharon Freeman, who plays the piano and French horn, is a composer, arranger, and sometime bandleader. Amina Claudine Myers, also a pianist, has so far written mostly in the gospel, earthy vein rather than jazz, but she is equipped to do more in the jazz area. Julie Cavadini, a Berklee graduate and protégée of composer Bill Finegan, has written three or four arrangements for the Mel Lewis Orchestra; Lewis plans to record her ballad, *A Simple Wish,* on his next album. Ellen Rowe, a student at the Eastman School of Music, won the 1982 *down beat* student award for best original jazz composition with a work entitled *Passages,* written for piano feature with jazz band and strings. There are many more women who have not yet received enough exposure to be counted in this chapter, but they will certainly be heard from in the near future.

Several of these composers have had common experiences. They have often produced their own albums or started their own record companies to get their new music recorded: Akiyoshi plans to release her own records from now on, McPartland owns the Halcyon label, Mary Lou Williams recorded her religious music on Mary Records, Bley (who, incidentally, owns all her own works) releases her material through JCOA or WATT, and Bloom releases hers on Outline. The record industry apparently has little or no interest in jazz or experimental new music; only Brackeen currently has a contract with a major company.

While these women say that being a woman has had no negative effect on their careers, several thought that it might have slowed their progress somewhat. All of them felt compelled to write music no matter how painstaking the process or what hardships it imposed on their family life. Musically, most of them were striving to find the best way to represent their feelings with spontaneity rather than through the use of specific methods or techniques.

In jazz composing, as in all the arts, drive, determination, and ingenuity are as important as talent. The jazz composer starting out today will be fortunate if she has a group of friends or students to perform her music. Otherwise she (or he) may have to set up and finance rehearsals as well as create opportunities for performance. Obviously, the more instruments involved, the more planning that will be necessary. A small group is always easier to assemble than a large one. Another possibility for a composer who wants to be played is to tailor arrangements to the needs of an existing group. The personal element in jazz performance demands a knowledge of each player's individual "sound," reading capabilities, availability, and price. The musical concept and players' styles must be carefully matched, since rehearsals will, for the most part, be nasty, brutish, and short. Actual performances may be called on short notice, be slated as "one-time only" events, or, at best, be intermittent engagements.

For the established composer, more regular outlets may open up, such as providing arrangements for school bands, writing for radio orchestras, or being a regular contributor to a permanent outfit. The composer often assists at rehearsals and has to be ready to conduct, play out specific parts, and convey the concept to be expressed. It is important that a good rapport be quickly established with the players as people, since most jazz performers are inspired by good feelings, not by just getting the job done.

Despite the difficulties, it should be said that those with talent and unshakable self-confidence will doubtless get their music played and make their contribution to the course of musical expression. Here are some comments from the women who have already done it.

Bley cautions: "I started out writing in a good time. Musicians were looking for music and someone like me could be depended on to pull out something they could use. Now people write their own tunes and none of them become standards. I don't think there's a field to go into, no demand.''

Akiyoshi says: ''Whenever you do something in a pioneer field there will be things that hold you back—they come with the territory. If you can't deal with it, you can't accomplish anything.'' And she adds to would-be composers, ''Give yourself a lot of chances, be patient.'' Bley suggests, ''If you do write something, make sure your handwriting is so clear that you don't have to be there when it's played. If it does get played and changed, try to be graceful enough to like it for how it has changed.'' Brackeen encourages young writers to ''really listen to what you are attracted to, get to know it inside and out, and keep on writing with no limitations.''

NOTES

1. National Endowment for the Arts Oral History Project, Rutgers Institute of Jazz Studies, interview with Mary Lou Williams, pp. 170-71.

2. Williams, Oral History interview.

3. All other quotations in this article are from interviews with the author in the spring of 1982.

A SAMPLE DISCOGRAPHY

Akiyoshi, Toshiko. *Between Me and Myself,* from George Wein Presents, Storyville STLP 912, recorded c. 1954.*
Long Yellow Road, RCA AFLI 1350, 1975.
Kogun, from *Road Time,* RCA CPL2-2242, 1976.
Minamata, from *Insights,* RCA AFLI 2678, 1976.
Toshiko Akiyoshi-Lew Tabackin Big Band, RCA AFLI 3019, 1978.
Austin, Lovie. *Steppin' On the Blues, Traveling Blues* (recorded November 1924), *Frog Tongue Stomp* (recorded April 1926) on Fountain, Vintage Jazz Series FJ105 reissue.
Bley, Carla. *Ictus, Batterie,* from *Barrage,* Paul Bley Quintet, ESP 1008, 1964.*
A Genuine Tong Funeral, Gary Burton, RCA Victor 3988, 1967.
Escalator over the Hill, JCOA, 3-album box set, 1972.
European Tour, WATT 8, 1977.
Floater, Copyright Royalties, from *Social Studies,* ECM W11, 1981.
Bloom, Jane Ira. *We Are,* Outline 137, 1978.
Second Wind, Outline 138, 1980.
Brackeen, JoAnne. *Haiti-B,* from *Tring-a-Ling,* Choice CRS 1016, 1977.
Lost or Found, Golden Garden, from *Prism,* Choice CRS 1024, 1979.
El Mayorazgo, from *Keyed In,* Tappan Zee, JC36075, 1979.
Ancient Dynasty, Remembering, from *Ancient Dynasty,* Tappan Zee, JC36593, 1980.

*Out of print.

Einstein, from *Special Identity,* Antilles (Island), 1982.

Hardin, Lil. *Lonesome Blues, Skid-da-de-dat* (recorded 1926) CBS 62471, V.S.O.P. vol. 2, reissue.

Knock Knee'd Sal, (Randolph-Armstrong), *Everything's Wrong, Ain't Nothing Right,* (Armstrong-Evans), (recorded 1938) Decca 2542.*

Safely Locked Up in My Heart, (Armstrong-Avon), (recorded 1938) Decca 2234, Swingfan 1014, reissue.

Liston, Melba. Sev. Liston arrs. on *Birk's Works,* Dizzy Gillespie, Verve MGV 8222 (recorded April 7, 1957).*

We Never Kissed, from *Lonely and Sentimental.* Gloria Lynne, Everest LPDR 5063, (recorded February 25 and March 10, 1960).*

Just Waiting, from *Big Band Bags,* Milt Jackson, Milestone 47006, reissue, (recorded August 5, 1963).

Len-Sirrah, from *And Then Again,* Elvin Jones, Atlantic 1442, recorded Feb. 1965.*

Tanjah, Randy Weston, composer Liston, Polydor 5055, 1973.

McPartland, Marian. *Interplay,* Halcyon 100, 1969.

Ambiance, Halcyon 103, 1970.

A Delicate Balance, Halcyon 105, 1971-72.

Portrait, Concord Jazz CJ 101, 1979.

Myers, Amina Claudine. *Song for Mother E,* Leo Records LR100, 1979.

Williams, Mary Lou. *Froggy Bottom, Walkin' and Swingin!* on *Andy Kirk and His Twelve Clouds of Joy,* Parlophone 60865A, (recorded March 1936).*

Roll 'Em, Folkways FA 2966 reissue, (2 discs) Asch 450-2, (recorded 1944-47).

Zodiac Suite, Folkways FTS 32844, reissue, (recorded June 29, 1945).

St. Martin De Porres, A Fungus Amungus, Folkways FJ 2843, reissue, (recorded October 9, 1963).

Mary Lou's Mass, Mary Records 102, 1969-70.

From the Heart, Chiaroscuro CR 103, (recorded June 8-9, 1971).*

Live at the Cookery, Chiaroscuro CR 146, October 1965.*

Zoning, Mary Records 103, 1974.

My Mama Pinned a Rose on Me, Pablo 2310-819, December 27, 1977.

Special thanks to the Staff of the Jazz Archives at Rutgers Institute of Jazz Studies for their assistance.

*Out of print.

11

Living British Women Composers: A Survey

VALERIE O'BRIEN

It is now relatively gratifying to be a woman composer in Britain. In their own perceptions of professional opportunites and successes, British women composers possess an uncommon peace of mind. The socialist system supports the arts, and it is within the government's power, due largely to its control of the British Broadcasting Corporation, to hold sway over the part composers play in society. This it does generously. By virtue of the way government funding sources in Britain make their decisions, it is also possible to infer that the socialist system fosters equality between the sexes. Positions of power are always changing, with different men and women chosen to decide specific questions—of commissioning and programming, for example—based on their particular expertise and accomplishments.

The composers surveyed in this chapter are of varying opinions on the question of sex discrimination in the music profession in Britain. Some say there is no sex discrimination, others claim there is, and a few are unwilling to talk about it. No doubt such a range of reactions could be gotten from any group of women composers of any nationality. What is telling is that there are no women composers' organizations in Britain at a time when the presence of such groups is felt in many other countries, including West Germany, Japan, and the United States. The only women composers' organization ever to exist in Britain, the Society of Women Musicians, disbanded with a gala concert in 1972 because its members felt they had met their goal of ending discrimination. It had been formed in 1911 to encourage and organize the programming of women's music and to award the Cappiani Prize for Women Composers. In 1948, when men were admitted as associates, the society numbered five hundred members. Today the Cappiani Prize is one of the few vestiges left of its activities. Most of the living women composers covered in this survey said that the society had outlived its need, intimating a belief that for present-day women composers to band together is both unnecessary and a sign of professional inferiority.

In the first quarter of the twentieth century, the simultaneous emergence of a national music and women's rights took place. In an essay entitled "An Open Secret," Dame Ethel Smyth, the noted opera composer and suffragette, attributed England's two hundred-year dearth of a national music to "the price we pay for becoming the greatest colonising power the world had seen except Rome."[1] She was concerned with the effects of the Empire's tendency to look toward "material worlds" at the sacrifice of "listening to inner voices and building edifices of sound." Whatever the explanation for British music's long silence, the fact was that British women were not in a position of having to pit themselves against a preexisting patriarchy of British music. Men had the advantage legally as voters and in other social areas, but as composers they were at about the same place as women: the beginning.

World War I was one of the factors in delaying women's suffrage. From 1914 to 1918, even the suffragists' energies were diverted into supporting their country during this unprecedented national crisis. Many women were performing tasks and fulfilling functions they had never had the opportunity to try before. But men returning from service were given deferential treatment, so that, for example, as the male musicians of the Hallé Orchestra returned from the war, women with wartime positions as orchestra members were roundly sacked. (Smyth decried the action, claiming it was taken purely on grounds of sex, with no regard for individual instrumentalists' ability.)

Yet enlightenment did follow. An important by-product of the Great War was that Great Britain was forced to take stock of itself. For so long it had been a world empire with an outwardly directed gaze; now had come a time, as Ethel Smyth put it, of "listening to inner voices." And with its inward look, Britain initiated a sweeping movement of public service that was to have a profound effect on the future of the nation's arts.

As far as the future of composers, the single most important public service to come out of Britain's social reform was the establishment of the government-run British Broadcasting Corporation. At first a company run by a group of wireless manufacturers, the BBC was established in 1927 as a corporation under Royal Charter. As such, it was inexorably tied to the public good, having clear specifications as to quality and variety of programming, and being required to allow ample time for broadcasting the works of living composers. The BBC, in the exercise of this mandate, became the life source of the arts in Great Britain. Now it is a publisher, reference library, live music program sponsor, and is responsible for commissioning and broadcasting hundreds of composers' works each year. Composers often present their own programs, and at one time or another most composers serve the BBC as committee members or administrators. The BBC has four symphony orchestras. Of its several stations now broadcasting throughout the United Kingdom, the BBC's Radio 3 is devoted almost solely to "serious" music, much of it broadcast live. With the presence of the BBC permeating all of British society, music education developed into a serious topic of study in public schools, music funding sources and festivals burgeoned, and the level of public and private support for the arts throughout the country became one of the highest in the world. Even when government funds are scarce, Britain's composers are not outcasts in the sense that, for instance, United States composers are. The difference is that British composers are formally recognized by their government where American composers are not. Perhaps because public acceptance and government support make it possible for them to pursue their craft with a sense of worth, British composers have resisted grouping themselves along lines of sex.

The status of women composers is not easily isolated from the whole of the composers' community in Great Britain, and, for someone not resident in that country, it is therefore difficult to tell how women are faring in relation to men. In 1972 Francis Routh published the results of his exhaustive study on works played in the major British music establishments during a three-year period.[2] The study showed that much British music had been played during that period, and that very little of it was by women. But a lot has changed in ten years' time, and no current study on the subject is available. Remember too that it was over ten years ago that the Society for Women Musicians disbanded; were it still active, the society might be a source of information on women composers.

An additional hindrance to doing research about living British women composers is reflected in the discography that accompanies this chapter. Scores and articles may be found, but very few recordings of these composers are in print. In a time when recordings are clearly crucial to a composer's basic survival, not to mention widespread acknowledgment and serious evaluation, the dearth of recordings would seem to indicate that British women composers are not yet seen as being as vital a musical force as certain of their male colleagues (Peter Maxwell Davies, Michael Tippett, and so on). Certainly the scarcity of recordings does not encourage independent research and discussion of these women's works.

Though Britain's mark on musical history is generally attributed entirely to its male composers, British women composers today participate vigorously in its creation, as they have from the beginning of the century.

Some of the women who took part in creating the new tradition of British music can be traced to a group of composers and performers from the London area of Chelsea-Kensington who, in 1931, decided to do something about the plight of unknown composers by forming a concert series. The series, still in existence today, is the Macnaghten Concerts.[3] At the beginning it was led by violinist Anne Macnaghten, composer Elisabeth Lutyens, and conductor Iris Lemare. Macnaghten, Lutyens, and Lemare stirred the music community not by calling attention to women but to all living composers, because they saw all as equally neglected. The cooperative nature of the Macnaghten effort was crucial in setting the tone for the generations of British composers that followed. Other composers closely involved with the inception and early years of the series were Elizabeth Maconchy, Alan Rawsthorne, Patrick Hadley, and Grace Williams. Ralph Vaughan Williams, a teacher of Maconchy, was supportive as patron and guide, and he helped the group to obtain funding. In September 1932, Vaughan Williams wrote to Anne Macnaghten, "You are doing great work and putting the BBC and T. Beecham to shame."[4]

Several of the composers introduced as veritable unknowns on the Macnaghten Concerts would come to be of major importance in British music. Lutyens and Maconchy became members of the vanguard of their generation, their works being played with first performances of those of Benjamin Britten, Michael Tippett, and Gerald Finzi. In the fifties there were new names, such as Richard Rodney Bennett and Priaulx Rainier. Performances were presented of music by two other women composers, who, like Maconchy, were Vaughan Williams students: the Irish composer Ina Boyle, and Dorothy Gow.

Lutyens* and Maconchy, still active today, were in their early twenties when they took part in organizing the Macnaghten Concerts in 1931. Both came from nonmusical backgrounds, married, and had families, but they continued to compose fairly regularly throughout their lives. Along with Priaulx Rainier, who is roughly the same age but whose name did not appear on the Macnaghten programs until later, they make a statement quite apart from their contemporaries Britten and Tippett. Possessed of distinctive individual styles, they each ultimately embarked boldly on fresh musical terrain with individual voices, forswearing imitation or distillation of the styles of their male contemporaries.

ELISABETH LUTYENS was born in 1906, a daughter of the renowned British architect Edwin Lutyens. In her autobiography, *A Goldfish Bowl,* Lutyens recounts a privileged but stifled upbringing.[5] Her mother was a theosophist, who held prayer meetings in the house and whose ideals Lutyens found impossible to live up to. Her father favored one of Elisabeth's sisters and was not home enough to give her the kind of recognition and intellectual exchange she desired.

As a child Lutyens was introduced to music through violin lessons. She resolved at the age of sixteen to become a composer, a decision from which she absolutely could not be dissuaded, though her mother tried. Her serious musical studies began with a year (1922-1923) at the Ecole Normale de Musique in Paris. From 1926 to 1930 she studied composition with Harold Darke and viola with Ernest Tomlinson at the Royal College of Music.

The second of Lutyens's two marriages was to Edward Clark, a conductor who was behind innovative, contemporary music programming at the BBC. Lutyens herself was involved in another aspect of the business,

*Lutyens died in April 1983, after this essay was written.

writing music for radio productions. In this capacity and as a writer for film, she enjoyed working with producers, directors, and editors. But as far as there being a relationship between her music for film, which she calls "journalism," and her other music, she claims there is none. Lutyens writes in her autobiography: 'Both film and radio music must be written not only quickly, but with the presumption that it will be heard only once. Its impact must be immediate. One does not grow gradually to love or understand a film score like a string quartet."[6]

In terms of her serious music, Lutyens probably can be credited with introducing serial procedures to British music. Anthony Payne points out that she was using a tone row with some effectiveness in the 1930s; one piece he cites in illustration is the *Chamber Concerto no. 1* of 1939. The fact that Lutyens was even toying with serialism at that time is noteworthy when one considers that music of the Second Viennese School was virtually unknown in Britain. She apparently thought she was making the discovery on her own. A bit later Lutyens heard a performance of Webern's cantata *Der Augenlicht* at an International Society for Contemporary Music (ISCM) festival in London and wrote, "Here was a composer with a musical mind and an almost Mozartian ear that could only belong to a human being of utter integrity."[7] In England, meanwhile, atonal music was regarded as immoral and improper, and Lutyens was alienated for her serialist persuasion. Her determination not to be cowed by popular derision and her experimental eclecticism during the period of World War II were qualities that earned Lutyens the reputation of being a "radical."

Beginning with a time before this when she wrote in the romantic idiom, Lutyens's development consisted of impulsive jags of composing, publishing, and then withdrawing works. For example, of her six string quartets published between 1938 and 1952, nos. 1, 4, and 5 were withdrawn. She also withdrew all of her works preceding the 1938 *String Quartet no. 2.* This and the 1939 *String Trio,* she claimed, were the first of her worthy compositions. Lutyens did not entirely come to terms with her craft until some years later.

In an article in *The Listener,* the magazine of the BBC, Anthony Payne speaks of Lutyens's "stylistic crisis" of around 1953. Payne writes: "The conservative twelve-note usage was becoming increasingly unsatisfactory for an imagination that was demanding realization in terms of an acute dissonance and increasing rhythmic complexity that owed little to traditional processes." Lutyens's solution to the problem, and a turning point in her composing, he says, was to sustain "the notes of her widespread melodies beyond their duration as part of the melodic span."[8] Thus she could better coordinate the melodic and harmonic functions of certain tones. This chromatic density is what sets Lutyens apart from other British composers of her generation.

Lutyens stands as an extremely prolific composer—in stage, choral and vocal, orchestral, and chamber genres—even after taking into account the works she has withdrawn. Other marks of her mature style are the use of palindromic structures and a progressive paring down of materials and gestures. One of the first works to achieve a balance of the latter is the vocal-orchestral *Quincunx,* completed in 1960. She structured her 1967 orchestral work *Novenaria,* written for the Leicester Arts Festival, on the motto of the city of Leicester arranged in a palindromic arch: in the second half of the work, melodic lines used in the first half are reversed. *Essence of Our Happinesses,* a setting of poems of Abu-Yasid, John Donne, and Arthur Rimbaud for chorus (1968), achieves a timeless effect through the subtlety of its musical events, spareness of images, and repetition. Some of Lutyens's stage works are to libretti she wrote herself, and in 1967 she completed a very successful opera entitled *The Numbered,* based on the text of Elias Canetti's *Die Befristeten.* In 1969 Lutyens was made a Commander of the British Empire (C.B.E.) and was honored with the City of London Midsummer Prize.

ELIZABETH MACONCHY is of Irish descent but was born in England in 1907. She began writing music at the age of six and in her teens went to study at the Royal College of Music with Ralph Vaughan Williams and Charles Wood. She first received public attention for her works in 1930 with performances of her *Piano Concertino* and her suite *The Land.* She married the poet and novelist William LeFanu the same year. One of their two daughters is the composer Nicola LeFanu.

A presaging period of study with Karel Boleslav Jirák in the 1930s exposed Maconchy to expressionism and to the music of Bartók. Many of her works were first heard at the Macnaghten Concerts and at ISCM festivals in Prague and Paris. In spite of a very serious bout with tuberculosis in 1932, she did not stop composing. Maconchy was the first woman to serve as chairman of the Composers Guild of Great Britain, and she won the London County Council Prize in 1953 for her overture *Proud Thames.* Among her other honors, she was made a C.B.E. in 1977.

Maconchy has written for opera, orchestra, chorus, and chamber and instrumental ensembles. Some of her work has the sweet diatonicism of her contemporary Benjamin Britten. Examples are her 1978 choral setting of Gerard Manley Hopkins poems, *The Leaden Echo and the Golden Echo,* and the lush, impressionistic, dramatic cantata, *Héloïse and Abelard,* written in 1979 to her own text, which was well received. She has also been noted for her works for children.

But of all her compositions—by both her own and general critical opinion—Maconchy's string quartets comprise her ultimate statement. There are twelve of them, spanning the years from 1933 to 1979.[9] The strongest apparent influence at work in the quartets is Bartók, with Maconchy's writing being contrapuntal in her use of line, motive, and rhythm. The language is highly chromatic, and she is concerned with the transformation of short motives rather than with drawn-out development of material. Maconchy's nearly fifty years of quartet writing show a

Figure 11.1 *String Quartet No. 5*, Elizabeth Maconchy, first movement, Molto lento, measure 1. Copyright 1950 by Alfred Lengnick & Co. Ltd. Used by permission.

Figure 11.2 *String Quartet No. 5*, Elizabeth Maconchy, second movement, Presto, measures 1-4. Copyright 1950 by Alfred Lengnick & Co. Ltd. Used by permission.

Figure 11.3 *String Quartet No. 5*, Elizabeth Maconchy, fourth movement, Allegro, measures 1-4. Copyright 1950 by Alfred Lengnick & Co. Ltd. Used by permission.

tightening and perfecting of the use of these elements. Each quartet tends to get shorter and starker so that, finally, its simplest gestures are nearly bursting with the assimilation of so many levels of background.

The fifth quartet was written in 1948 and won the Edwin Evans Prize that same year. All of the work's ideas are derived from the canon that opens the first movement. The canon, built of alternating half and whole steps, is drawn upon for purposes of melodic inversion, rhythmic transformation, and for exploration of the expressive possibilities of contrasting its two basic inflections. Octave transposition is used freely. Accumulated texture and intensified elaboration on the basic arch shape of the germ bring the quartet to a climax in the fourth movement.

In 1972 Maconchy wrote: "Is it still harder for a woman than for a man to impress the impresarios and powers-that-be who keep the gateway to success? Yes—I think it is."[10] She recalls in the same article that when as a young woman she expressed an interest in the coveted Mendelssohn Scholarship, Sir Hugh Allen told her, "If we give you the scholarship, you will only get married and never write another note."

But Maconchy's daughter, NICOLA LEFANU, born in 1947, was destined for a different experience as a composer. The house in which LeFanu grew up had to have been always strewn with new scores and various tools of the composer's trade and filled with the sounds of music being put to paper. The people who came and went as part of Maconchy's life as a composer and administrator were leading figures in their fields. Since the source of musical life in the household was her mother, Nicola never doubted her own ability, or, more important, the acceptability of being a woman who wrote music. "It wasn't very good, but it was natural," she says of her earliest attempts at composing. LeFanu's musical exposure throughout her teens consisted of hearing "more new music than old music," and within this, "all the newest music of the sixties."[11] She went to St. Hilda's College, Oxford, and to the Royal College of Music. LeFanu never studied with her mother: her teachers in Britain were Jeremy Dale Roberts and Egon Wellesz, and in 1968 she was awarded a scholarship to study with Goffredo Petrassi in Italy.

There was a time when LeFanu denied that her pursuing composition as a profession had had anything to do with her mother. When she took on composition students of her own, however, she began to recognize her mother's influence. LeFanu noticed in many conversations with her women students that they would claim it was crucial to their development to have a woman teacher, that they even doubted they would have persevered with composition studies without the example of a woman composer. The statistical gains made by women composers in twentieth-century Britain are for these women not quite enough; tangible proof of one's possible achievements, in the presence of a woman who has already received a good measure of success and recognition, is often the missing element. LeFanu herself had grown up with it. Her mother's example had surrounded her with a musical environment of achievement so natural that she actually took for granted the simple joy of discovering composition and developing her craft.

LeFanu won first prize in the BBC Composers' Competition in 1971 for a work composed in 1968, *Variations for Oboe Quartet*. In 1972 she was the recipient of a Gulbenkian dance award and of the Mendelssohn Scholarship, the latter an award her mother never did get. While on a Harkness Fellowship at Harvard University during 1973-1974, LeFanu studied with Earl Kim. Meanwhile she began lecturing widely, broadcasting, and conducting her own works. She now lectures at King's College, University of London.

Her closest influences are Harrison Birtwistle, Anthony Gilbert, and her husband, Australian composer David Lumsdaine. Their way of thought, a preoccupation with the use of time in music and an equal exploitation of all the aspects of a given work, has had a considerable effect on younger British composers. LeFanu is emphatic about her admiration for Birtwistle's work, which she claims is unjustly neglected.

LeFanu's earliest music is characterized by serial organization and a simple linear style. The more recently composed works reveal a more complex use of line and a tremendous range of instrumental expression. LeFanu's works are extremely colorful and simple on the surface, yet they yield a background of rich complexity on repeated listening. Gerald Larner says, "The later style is particularly well suited to theater pieces such as *Antiworld* and *The Last Laugh*."[12] Both were written in 1972. *Antiworld* uses poems of Russian dissidents and is a reaction to the lack of a world partnership between countries and between peoples.

The Same Day Dawns (1974), a setting of fragments from Oriental poems, is stylistically among the simplest of LeFanu's works. It is scored for soprano and a five-member mixed ensemble that uses exotic percussion instruments. The voice carries the line, but all instruments make equally important contributions in their own way, and the work makes a statement of immense breadth using the sparest of effects. About the piece LeFanu has written: "I have always admired the concentration of Chinese and Japanese art: an art apparently simple, yet rich in implicit meanings. A few brush strokes can conjure up a magical landscape for us. It was towards this economy and intensity that I aspired in the music for *The Same Day Dawns*."[13]

One of LeFanu's personal favorites is *The Old Woman of Beare,* a monodrama composed in 1981 and based on an Irish poem dating from the ninth or tenth century. Using several English translations and the original three hundred-word Gaelic version, LeFanu compiled and elaborated to make her own thousand-word version. She used a pitch matrix to derive permutations as a basis for generating material but did not utilize strict serialism. LeFanu's particular use of the matrix here results in harmonic language that moves freely from diatonic to chromatic. Characteristic of her works, the structure of *Old Woman* is established by changes in pitch and rhythm, not by a preexisting outline. The work is scored for amplified soprano and thirteen players, calling on the full virtuosic capabilities and dramatic effects of winds, brass, strings, and percussion. A crack of the claves begins and ends the piece, providing a frame. In it the highly inflected voice of a medieval woman, stranded on a craggy island off the west coast of Ireland with a group of nuns, speaks of her youth when suitors came from miles around to make love to her. But as the old woman whispers, cackles, and coos, the young woman lives. LeFanu says that, rather than experiencing nostalgia, the old woman "is the person she was. . . . It is a poem in which past, present, future are one. So the medium had to be music, which of all the media is the one that can transcend time."[14]

In contrast to Lutyens's dark atonality and Maconchy's many-faceted contrapuntal refinement, PRIAULX RAINIER's music is earthy and primitively rhythmic. Rainier's childhood was spent in Howick, Natal, South Africa, where she was born in 1903. There she was in the constant presence of a predominantly Zulu population, African instruments and music, and a tropical climate with the intoxicating colors and sounds of indigenous birds and wildlife.

Rainier had her early training in harmony and violin at the South Africa College of Music under W. H. Bell and at Cape University. A scholarship to the Royal Academy of Music took her to London in 1920 where she studied composition with J. B. McEwen. Rainier has lived in England ever since, and in 1942 she became a professor at the academy.

Having developed into an excellent violinist, Rainier performed extensively in professional string quartets. During the 1930s she appeared regularly in one such group with Guilhermina Suggia, the same cellist that British violist and composer Rebecca Clarke performed with for many years.[15] It was not until she was seriously injured in a car accident in 1935 that Rainier turned exclusively to composition. Sir Arnold Bax encouraged her, and in 1937 she was awarded a scholarship that enabled her to study with Boulanger in Paris.

Little of Rainier's language is derived from the currents of twentieth-century compositional progress. She is said, instead, to glean compositional concepts from actual scenes in her memory, for example, "the visual insights of [Barbara] Hepworth and [Ben] Nicholson, with both of whom she had contact."[16] Rainier composed music for *Figures in a Landscape,* a film about Barbara Hepworth's sculpture. She has consistently denied any attempt to duplicate African style in her music, saying, "It is not imitative, but some instinct in my ear."[17] But such works as *Phala-Phala* and *Cycle for Declamation* (one of her commissions from Peter Pears) are pointed to as examples of a primitive style that cannot be explained other than by the influence of her early environment. Aside from her primary trademark—

coarse asymmetric rhythms undergirded by pedal points or ostinatos— Rainier makes liberal use of augmented fourths and very little use of themes. Her early works favor block harmony; the later ones have more horizontal interest.

Her first major work, the 1939 *String Quartet,* drew quite a bit of attention. The quartet was not performed until 1944, and in 1951 it was recorded by the Amadeus Quartet. Although this was a 78 r.p.m. recording and is now out of print, Leonarda Productions, Inc. (USA) plans to issue a new performance by the Alard Quartet in the near future.[18] A four-movement piece, the quartet offers a fantastic range of emotions and an especially raucous and brutal finale. José Limon heard it and became so interested in dancing the work that he urged the renowned Doris Humphrey

Figure 11.4 *String Quartet*, Priaulx Rainier, fourth movement, Presto spiritoso, measures 1-6. Copyright by Schott & Co., Ltd., 1947. Used by permission of European American Music Distributors Corporation, sole U.S. agent for Schott & Co. Ltd.

Figure 11.5 *Barbaric Dance Suite*, Priaulx Rainier, third movement, measures 1-4. Copyright 1950 by Schott & Co. Ltd., London. Used by permission of European American Music Distributors Corporation, sole U.S. agent for Schott & Co. Ltd.

to choreograph it. The result was "Night Spell," premiered by Limon in New London, Connecticut, in 1951. It is telling to note that in August 1951, as Humphrey worked and exchanged ideas with Rainier by letter about putting the quartet to dance, the main complaint the composer had about the way things were going was, "[But it is] the general feeling more than anything i.e. too Romantic not primitive enough [sic]"[19]

Ten years after the composition of the String Quartet, the third movement of Rainier's Barbaric Dance Suite for piano shows characteristic asymmetric rhythmic propulsion, this time stressing intervals of the second, seventh, and ninth. Other elements of her late style are heightened textural contrast and a more prominent use of melody, evident in such works as Declamation and the Requiem for solo tenor and unaccompanied choir.[20] In one critic's summation:

What modulations there are pass almost unnoticed because the composition is not concerned with harmony. Counterpoint has rarely more than two parts and the texture is fascinating but spare; it is music of sinew which sometimes tends to gristle. The impression gained from listening to this music is that it more nearly resembles architecture or sculpture than painting.[21]

While some critics call Priaulx Rainier the third figure of the three foremost British women composers of the mid-twentieth century (along with Lutyens and Maconchy), others say that PHYLLIS TATE holds that place. Tate's music is characterized by a basic simplicity and accessibility to which are applied unlikely combinations of instruments. As Mosco Carner has observed, "Selecting elements from several sources, English and continental (chiefly French and Stravinskyan), she has, in a gradual process of amalgamation, succeeded in fusing them into a style of distinctive personal features."[22] She works with subtle effects, favors small forms, and is not a prolific composer; for the first reason in particular, Tate tends to be overshadowed by Rainier.

Phyllis Tate was born in England in 1911. As a child she improvised at the piano, writing her own words and music to the current popular dances. Harry Farjeon was her composition teacher at the Royal Academy of Music, where she wrote and produced an opera, Policeman's Serenade, and she also studied piano and timpani. In the 1940s, Tate destroyed all her early works.

Her first work to reach a wide public was the Concerto for Alto Saxophone and Strings, composed in 1944 as one of her many BBC commissions. Norman Kay relates that "with its hornpipe, tarantella, and hints of other dance forms, one suspects that it preserved a few links with the works that had just been destroyed."[23] But the concerto also had moments of the classical clarity and intriguing timbral quirkiness that are now considered Tate's strongest points. A later work, the 1953 String

Quartet in F, is a telling harmonic statement in that, though Tate "took the trouble to define the tonal centre of the work, it actually moves about with great chromatic freedom, taking up the position approximately similar to the music of another distinguished contemporary, Alan Rawsthorne."[24]

There is an absence in Tate's music of such popular contemporary techniques as serialism, athematicism, complex use of rhythm and meter, and clipped motivic material. Her major challenge was to come to terms with her linear instinct, and in doing so she wrote most of her works for voice. "In her settings of texts Miss Tate manifests, like most modern English composers, a subtle ear for verbal inflexions and the prosody; yet where she differs from her fellow-musicians is in the fact that frequently she conceives her vocal lines in quasi-instrumental terms," says Carner.[25] Tate's mature works are intensely, inevitably lyrical for the voice, even as she employs leaps and articulations of an instrumental nature.

The Lodger, an opera composed in 1960, is the first work in which Tate reconciled her quasi-instrumental bent with what the human voice can do. Built around the legend of Jack-the-Ripper, *The Lodger* exhibits Tate's flair for dark, ominous sonorities. Preceding and following composition of *The Lodger,* Tate experimented with numerous songs and choral works, both unaccompanied and to accompaniments by various instrumental combinations.

The manner in which Tate combines her lyric impulse with other-worldly sonorities makes for a mesmerizing effect in a 1968 work entitled

Figure 11.6. *Apparitions,* Phyllis Tate, first movement, "Evocation," measures 1-4. Reprinted by permission of Oxford University Press.

Apparitions. This is a setting of four traditional ballads and laments from British localities, scored for tenor, harmonica, piano, and strings. Piano and strings are used to create two stunningly contrasting moods, sounded simultaneously, in the opening "Evocation." For each text, a new mesh of tonal areas and timbres is called upon to fuse suggestions of the present and past and of voices recalling stories and mourning the dead. Tate's use of the harmonica in three of the pieces is particularly effective as a quietly unsettling background to the vocal line; it occasionally emerges to magnify the meaning of the text. The postlude, *Envoi,* is a variant of the *Evocation.*

ELIZABETH POSTON, another living British woman composer born in the first decade of this century, is known for quite different reasons than are Lutyens, Maconchy, and Rainier. Poston was born in 1905 in Highfield, Hertfordshire, where her neighbors were the English novelist E. M. Forster and his family, and she grew up in the same locale Forster depicts in *Howard's End.* (Later she would write the score for a film based on Forster's *A Room with a View.*) Poston is probably as well known as a pianist and broadcaster as she is for her compositions. One reason for this is that since setting a Thomas Vautor text for her *Sweet Suffolk Owl* in 1925, Poston has resisted publishing her works, preferring to keep control over their performance. The result is that her music is not well known outside Britain. Too, Poston has written little serious music for the larger forms; much of her output consists of works based on historical models of style, and in some cases she has written for early instruments.

Poston's early musical training was sketchy, but she was a natural at the piano and published several songs before she was twenty years old. As a teenager, she studied piano with Harold Samuel. At the Royal Academy of Music, she studied composition under Sir Henry Wood. Poston has said that Samuel taught her to play repertoire within the capability of her small hand so that she could always play exceptionally well, and that she applied this principle to what she composed as a student of Sir Henry Wood with rewarding results.

Poston then pursued several careers. First, she temporarily shelved composing to study art in Italy. But while in Italy she became fascinated with its folk songs and was compelled to give them the type of musical codification Bartók had given Hungarian folk melodies. Her experiment with the idea produced *Sei Canzoni: Six Italian Folk Songs* (1950). Upon returning from Italy during World War II, she was made music director of the European service of the BBC. As a pianist, Poston appeared many times at the London National Gallery and in performance on her own broadcasts, including a series of lecture-recitals on the songs of Peter Warlock.

Songs would always be Poston's favorite for their miniaturist form and for the inherited British lyrical tradition she brought to them. She was deeply affected by her contact with Warlock, and there is more than a suggestion of similarity between their styles. Warlock's music looked to Frederick Delius (with too much dependence, Poston has said) and harked back stylistically to the Elizabethan period. Joan Littlejohn says, "Her [Poston's] musical influence she describes as nursery rhymes (their intensity of rhythm), Delius, the early contrapuntalists and plainsong."[26] Poston herself claims: "I'm only a littlemonger, you know, I dislike the Kolossal, never wanted to write any big works and never have. My loves are folk song, carols, nursery rhymes, the English lyrical tradition . . . Blake's 'world in a grain of sand.' (Fellow-feeling with dear E. M. Forster. Interviewers: Why didn't you write more, Mr. Forster? EMF: Didn't want to.)"[27]

The bulk of Poston's compositional activity has found its way into choral works, anthems, and folk songs, most visibly in anthologies of songs for children and adults. An early wish was to lead a reform of hymns and carols—codifying, transcribing, amending, and arranging—and Poston, having studied briefly with Vaughan Williams at the Royal College of Music, discussed with him in detail the possibility of their collaborating on such a project. Vaughan Williams was amenable to the plan but died before they could carry it out, so Poston has continued steadily on her own. She edited and compiled two volumes of Christmas carols, both important standard works whose contents are available on recordings, and several other recordings of hymns and suites with first-rate performers.

Poston went to the United States to study jazz and blues after World War II but was soon called back to Britain to fill a position with the BBC's Radio 3. Her return coincided with the BBC's first plunge into serious music programming. Poston was approached with commission after commission to write incidental music for generously financed dramatic productions, from fourteenth-century plays to contemporary drama. In fulfilling these assignments, she availed herself of the orchestra to an extent she previously had not. Joan Littlejohn says that Poston's best orchestra writing is "embedded" in these works and quotes the composer as saying: "I love the opportunities and the techniques afforded by the medium of incidental music ('my journalism,' she calls it); the fact that it is word-oriented and that one is working alongside voices and can experiment continually, catching moods and setting them, getting one's effects without *longueurs*."[28]

Her new exercise in orchestra writing may have been the reason for what is regarded as the broadening of Poston's style in this period. She worked on instrumental and vocal works, one of the latter being a group of songs with string orchestra entitled *A Garland of Laurels,* and a bevy of pieces for early instruments. Then came more work on folk songs, this time making use of her exposure to blues, in the form of *The Penguin Book of American Folk Songs.* Poston has published several other songbooks of all levels of difficulty. One that stands out as the kind of work she and Vaughan

Williams had intended to do together, *The Cambridge Hymnal* (London: Cambridge University Press, 1977), is credited with bringing certain hymns into common use in Britain.

The generation of British women composers born in the 1920s includes two composer-performers. One of them, RUTH GIPPS, was born into a musical family at Bexhill-on-Sea in 1921. Her mother, Hélène Gipps, was principal of the Bexhill School of Music, where Ruth had her first private training. Gipps made her performing debut at four and had a piece of music published when she was eight years old. A number of her early works were first performed by the Society of Women Musicians. At one point Eric Blom remarked of Gipps, "How often does musical history show a case of so remarkable a symphony (no. 1 in F minor) written by a girl of twenty-one—or for that matter by a boy?"[29]

Gipps attended the Royal College of Music, studying composition with R. O. Morris, Gordon Jacob, and Vaughan Williams, piano with Arthur Alexander and Kendall Taylor, and oboe with Leon Goossens. She also studied privately under Tobias Matthay himself at the Matthay Piano School. As a student, Gipps won many prizes, including a Caird Travelling Scholarship. The oratorio she wrote in 1947 as a requirement for her doctorate at Durham University, *The Cat*, is a setting of poems about cats by A. C. Swinburne, Christopher Smart, and others. She eventually returned to the Royal College of Music as a professor and also had a position at Trinity College, London. Like Maconchy, Gipps served as chairman of the Composers' Guild of Great Britain. Ruth Gipps was given the honorary title of Member of the Order of the British Empire (M.B.E.) in 1981.

The clarinetist Robert Baker and Ruth Gipps married in 1942. Their son, Lance Baker, is coprincipal hornist of the English National Opera and plays what she considers to be the "definitive performance" of her virtuosic 1968 *Horn Concerto*. Gipps is the composer of some eighty works, four of them symphonies. The early ones reflect a strong Vaughan Williams influence, and the 1948 *Piano Concerto,* premiered with the composer as soloist, is a good example. In later works such as the *Horn Concerto,* she breaks away into a "brilliant and vigorous manner."[30]

Increasingly Gipps has turned to conducting. She was the first woman to conduct a performance of her own symphonic work on the BBC (the *Third Symphony*), and, when consistently denied interviews for full-time conducting jobs, she formed her own orchestras. In 1955 Gipps founded the London Repertoire Orchestra, a body of students and young professionals led by a paid conductor and concertmaster. Two other organizations exist under Gipps's founding and music directorship, one of which was established to serve the other. The Presentation of New Artists Society is a nonprofit or "legal charity" organization that raises funds to present the fully professional London Chanticleer Orchestra. Both orchestras regularly play music by living British composers.

THEA MUSGRAVE, now just in her fifties, is a composer of international reputation and certainly the most commercially successful of the currently active British women in her field. Her development as a composer follows clearly discernible stages in which, by putting herself into positions where her vision could be realized only by solving some difficult problems, Musgrave's voice evolved from a gingerly conservative handling to where her music now speaks naturally and with an element of surprise.

Musgrave was born in Scotland in 1928. After studies at Edinburgh University under Hans Gal and Mary Grierson, she studied from 1950 to 1954 with Nadia Boulanger. Even while she was in Paris with Boulanger, Musgrave's works were being discovered and acclaimed in Scotland. Before completing studies in Paris, Musgrave wrote *A Suite O'Bairnsangs,* in fulfillment of a commission from the Scottish Festival at Braemar, and *Cantata for a Summer's Day* for the Scottish BBC. She was the first British composer to win the Lili Boulanger Memorial Prize. Musgrave's other prizes include the Donald Francis Tovey Prize, a Koussevitzky Award, and a Guggenheim Fellowship.

In 1973 Musgrave presented a series of eight broadcasts over the BBC's Radio 3 for the purpose of exploring electronic music. She also served on the Central Music Advisory Panel for the BBC and is very well known in Britain as a lecturer and by the many performances of her works. At times when she is cited as a "woman composer," or when her works are performed on programs of all-women's music, Musgrave insists that she does not align herself with the feminist movement. Her argument is that not just the women among them, but all composers have a rough time making a living. Musgrave now lives in the United States and is active on both the East and West Coasts. It was while teaching at the University of California at Santa Barbara that she met the violist Peter Mark. They married, and now spend much of their time in Virginia, where Mark is artistic director of the Virginia Opera Association. Musgrave has written a viola concerto and several other solo works for her husband.

Musgrave's earliest compositions, including a few written after her studies in Paris, employ a melodic and diatonic style; after that, her harmonic language becomes increasingly chromatic and the idiom, abstract. Francis Routh, in his chapter about Musgrave, says that a summer of William Glock's lectures at the Dartington Hall School in 1953 introduced Musgrave to the techniques of Schoenberg, Webern, and Ives, and that it was at this point that Musgrave's harmonic style turned toward chromaticism.[31] In 1958 Musgrave was at Tanglewood in the presence of Copland and Babbitt. As reflected in her String Quartet of that year, free chromaticism and highly-charged expressionistic gestures had by then become part of her vocabulary. Generally, however, Musgrave's pre-1960 music was controlled and without much experiment, and the mid-1960s saw a broadening of her musical scope. The change is most evident in her second opera, *The Decision*, composed in 1964-1965. The one opera Musgrave produced before this, *The Abbot of Drimock* (1955) is scored for chamber orchestra; *The Decision* is the first work she wrote for full orchestra.

Part of the reason for Musgrave's growth as represented by *The Decision* was the particular dramatic challenge posed by her subject. But she also found, in her work with the Scottish poet Maurice Lindsay, that writing the music and poetry together increased possibilities for their interplay. In her scoring of the opera, Musgrave had foremost in mind the idea of using music to give life to dramatic questions. Her characters have their own themes, and whenever she talks of musical language and technique, it is the dramatic situation that is paramount.[32] These points are not new in themselves, but they were fundamental in Musgrave's growth, particularly in her writing for instruments. As observed by Stephen Walsh, "*The Decision* forced an extroversion which these [pre-1965] earlier works had generally lacked, and the benefit is apparent in most of Musgrave's subsequent work."[33]

What Musgrave finally hit upon was a desire to write dramatically conceived works for instruments alone. Her term for the concept is "dramatic-abstract"; "dramatic" because instruments take on dramatic functions in relation to one another and in monologue; "abstract" because this is achieved without a program. The idea began innocently enough in her work with *The Decision*. But once Musgrave felt the need to establish the voices of instruments as characters in themselves, without the help of words or the frame of a plot, she had the challenge of her career on her hands—a challenge that, once addressed, was to yield an imposing result.

Two main problems are posed by Musgrave's dramatic-abstract concept. One is that the orchestra must be released from its dependence upon the

The following diagram shows the suggested seating for the orchestra, ⊗ indicating the various positions for the solo clarinet.

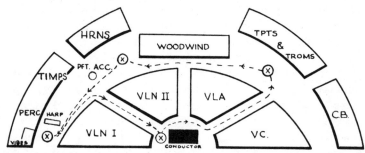

Figure 11.7 Orchestra seating diagram from *Clarinet Concerto*, Thea Musgrave. Used by kind permission of J&W Chester/Edition Wilhelm Hansen London Ltd.

Figure 11.8 *Clarinet Concerto*, Thea Musgrave, p. 22. Used by kind permission of J&W Chester/Edition Wilhelm Hansen London Ltd.

conductor so that instrumentalists are more flexible and responsive to one another. Musgrave's solution is to provide a series of points in the score at which one soloist cues another soloist or section to stop or begin. Acting as characters, instruments or instrumental factions must have their own rhythm and pace. The other problem, then, is how to allow for soloists or units to be metrically independent of one another. To make this possible, Musgrave coordinates a variety of barrings. In explaining how the same procedures apply to a work from 1974, *Concerto for Orchestra,* Musgrave has written that she "wanted them [the instrumentalists] to have moments of freedom of expression without the texture of the whole lapsing into anarchy."[34] Musgrave continued to apply dramatic-abstract procedures in such works as *Night Music* (1969), the *Horn Concerto* (1971), *Memento Vitae* (1970), and the *Clarinet Concerto* (1968).

Another procedure Musgrave employs in the *Clarinet Concerto* is designed to give the soloist intimacy with concerto grosso groups that periodically emerge from the instrumental texture. As shown in a diagram on the facing page of the score, the clarinetist is instructed to move through the orchestra during the performance, stopping at specified positions to play with featured groups, finally ending up back at the conductor's podium by the close of the piece.

There were other operas after *The Decision.* From 1972 to 1973 Musgrave composed a chamber opera in three acts entitled *The Voice of Ariadne.* Ariadne's voice is on tape; the heroine is never seen on stage. In 1977 she completed *Mary, Queen of Scots,* scored for full orchestra, nine singers, and chorus. *Mary* has been the most popular of all the operas, and a recording of the Virginia Opera Association production is available. Both *Ariadne* and *Mary* have been controversially received. While commending Musgrave's "intelligence" and "integrity," critics are split over their assessment of her vocal writing. Some say that it does not "sing" as it should for opera and that her scores need more textural variety. Others applaud her precisely for the power of texture and lyricism in her works. Andrew Porter, for instance, writes that "dramatic and musical pacing, transitions, variety of tension, of texture, and of density, contrasts of expansive lyricism and quick-moving music are controlled in a masterly way."[35]

MARGARET LUCY WILKINS, born in Surrey in 1939, considers herself part of a generation of women composers that broke new ground socially more than in any other way. Though Wilkins acknowledges a few occasions when she felt a hint of prejudice, she also points out that her success was swift, with more performances and broadcasts than most composers, and that men were almost invariably in the positions of judgment where her works were being evaluated. In response to a query letter, Wilkins wrote: "I've had great support and encouragement from men composers and performers, and all my commissions have originated from a masculine source." A feature of the current economic conditions, says Wilkins, is that composers of Great Britain, in spite of the opportunities open to them, generally cannot support themselves on what they earn as composers. They tend to compete individually for those opportunities, and the concept of a women composers' organization is not in keeping with the individual mode of conduct they have established.

After a strong, early exposure to music and after completing music degrees at Nottingham University and the Royal Academy of Music, Wilkins devoted several years exclusively to raising children. She did not actually pursue composition professionally until she was thirty-one years old. Meanwhile the family had moved to Newfoundland and then to Scotland, and this is where she began her career in 1970.

Wilkins entered several competitions and immediately secured a number of performances. In 1971 she won the Cappiani Prize for Women Composers with *The Silver Casket* and had her *Witch Music* premiered at a Society for the Promotion of New Music composers weekend. Finding that she enjoyed being in control of the business aspects of getting her music published, disseminated, and performed, Wilkins founded her own publishing firm, Satanic Mills Press.

Stylistically and conceptually, Olivier Messiaen, Pierre Boulez, Luciano Berio, and Karlheinz Stockhausen have had the greatest influence on Wilkins's music. Her twenty-four published works include *musique con-crète* written for an outdoor exhibition of modern sculpture, and a work for electronic tape. Her first computer-synthesized piece is now being completed. Wilkins has also employed contemporary performance techniques with acoustic instruments. *Etude,* a string trio written in 1975, is an organically generated study in the fine points of rhythm, pitch, and syntax. However complex their application becomes, however, these techniques are meant only to exploit the range of natural capabilities of stringed instruments.

A pronounced vein of religious symbolism runs through Wilkins's work. *Witch Music,* composed in 1971, is one of Wilkins's most popular works and a good example. A setting of the texts of actual witches' cures, it is scored for mezzo-soprano, clarinet, trumpet, and double bass. The eight movements go by titles such as "Cure for a Toothache" and "Cure for Staunching Blood." Wilkins's way of establishing theological symbolism is to have the singer double in two movements on triangles and finger cymbals hung from the four points of a six-foot high cross. Another religious-symbolic work is *Ave Maria,* a setting of fourteenth- and fifteenth-century English texts commissioned by the New Music Group of Scotland in 1975. Here Wilkins evokes the path leading from temptation to redemption by contrasting texts dealing with two main biblical women, Eve and Mary. The first three texts are concerned with Eve, the fourth is a pivotal text that symbolizes the transformation of evil into good, and the last three are texts about and spoken by Mary. The apple tree and the cross are textually and visibly established as counterparts. Refrains between each text setting use the identical isorhythmic pattern, which in itself is symmetrical. The balance of this symmetry points up the contrast between the grotesque music of Eve and the benevolent music of Mary. One review of the work observes that "the perverse quality of this music, poised between the childlike and the unbalanced, brings to mind some of the pieces of Peter Maxwell Davies."[36]

JENNIFER FOWLER, born in Australia in 1939, has been active internationally and now lives and works in Britain. Her early training was at the University of Western Australia with John Exton. She spent 1968 at the Electronic Music Studio at the University of Utrecht under G. M. Koenig on a Dutch Government Scholarship and moved to Britain in 1969.

The prevalent use of aleatoric operations, be they applied with regard to rhythm, tempo, dynamics, or pitch, is a mark of Fowler's work. In *Ravelation,* composed in 1971 and revised in 1980 (the version referred to here), she employs approximate accidentals. Players are told to play, for example, between a given natural pitch and its sharp, but "not necessarily precisely half way." Two levels of notation are used in the score: large notes indicate precise pitch, while small notes stand for approximate pitch. The work is freely atonal and continuous and sets up contrasts between what Fowler describes as "on the one hand, static, unchanging or slowly-moving elements without directional pull; on the other, a directional movement or 'tendency.' " The title of the work is based on the word "to ravel," a term which, through common usage has come to have two meanings clearly in opposition to one another. It can mean to make something complex, to "tangle," or it can also mean to clarify or "disentangle" something. In *Ravelation* Fowler reacts to this contradiction in musical terms.

The chance concept has taken on a number of guises in Fowler's works. A collage piece composed in 1971 entitled *Chimes, Fractured*[37] is an experiment in giving musical structure to the combined bagpipe, bell, and organ sounds she heard during a visit to the new Liverpool Cathedral. As Fowler walked and positioned herself in different relationships to the festivities of a Scottish wedding, the sounds of an organist practicing, and the peal of church bells, she was struck by the way each sound was modified, or "fractured," by the others. Fowler says that she does not think of *Chimes, Fractured*—scored for winds, organ, bagpipes and percussion—as an effort to re-create what she heard that day but as an exploration of the musical possibilities the event suggested to her.

In both *Piece for an Opera House* (1973) and *Voice of the Shades* (1976-1977), Fowler provides several alternate instrumentations for performance. *Ring Out the Changes* (1978) is a play on the art of change ringing, in which the object is to exhaust all the possible permutations of a given melodic figure without repeating a change. The work is scored for two bell players and strings: the bells play a variant of change ringing, and the strings act as a resonating chamber, heightening the bell sonorities.

Jennifer Fowler's fourteen published works span the last twelve years. With no apparent penchant for a single genre—her works include those scored for orchestra, mixed timbres sometimes in conjunction with tape, vocal combinations, solo piano, but no opera—Fowler reveals an open-mindedness of expression. Maureen Radic says that "vigorous imagination and ironic wit are notable features of her work."[38]

The following brief mentions barely touch upon the activities of the youngest women composers presently active in Britain; by all indications, there are other figures emerging whose work is certain to be worthy of note.

A foreign-born composer who is now closely associated with British music, ODALINE DE LA MARTINEZ was born in Cuba in 1949. Martinez received her Bachelor of Fine Arts degree at Tulane University in 1972 and thereafter studied at the Royal Academy of Music on a Marshall Scholarship from the British government. She then spent several years at the University of Surrey doing work in electronic music, during which time a Watson Fellowship made it possible for her to carry on related research in Europe. Martinez has won several prizes and fellowships, including a U.S. National Endowment Composer/Librettist Award and a Guggenheim Fellowship. Her works have been heard in several countries and include two pieces for electronic tape alone and several for electronics scored with acoustic instruments. She is a familiar figure in Britain not only as a composer but as a pianist and founder, in 1976, of the contemporary music ensemble Lontano. (It was Martinez and her ensemble who gave the world premiere of Nicola LeFanu's *The Old Woman of Beare* on the fiftieth-anniversary series of the Macnaghten Concerts in 1981.)

JUDITH WEIR was born in Cambridge, England, in 1954.[39] Hers is a musical family of performers from Aberdeen, Scotland. Weir did her early composition studies with John Tavernor. During the 1970s, she studied briefly with Barry Vercoe at the Massachusetts Institute of Technology and spent three years as a student of Robin Holloway at King's College, Cambridge. On a 1975 Koussevitzky Fellowship at Tanglewood, Weir worked with Gunther Schuller. Her first mature work, the wind quintet *Out of the Air*, (1975) won the Greater London Arts Association young musicians' composition award in 1976. Weir served as composer-in-residence to the Southern Arts Association in England from 1976 to 1977. She is currently teaching composition at Glasgow University, where she is the first woman to hold a Cramb Fellowship.

Although British women composers may find no complaint with their status, the music of the women who worked beside Michael Tippett, Benjamin Britten, Alan Rawsthorne, and Gerald Finzi as vital shapers of the new musical tradition in the 1930s is now, half a century later, nowhere near as well known as is the music of their male peers. With the exception of Thea Musgrave, not one of the recordings of women composers discussed in this chapter is presently listed in American record catalogs.[40] Yet many of their male contemporaries—including all those mentioned in connection with the first Macnaghten Concerts—are represented in the same catalogs, sometimes by voluminous listings of works. Only by seeking out, playing, and writing about the work of these women can we hope to appreciate the truth of Britain's twentieth-century musical self-discovery.

NOTES

1. Ethel Smyth, "An Open Secret," *Streaks of Life* (London: Longmans, Green and Co., 1921), p. 234.

2. Francis Routh, *Contemporary British Music* (London: MacDonald and Co., 1972), p. 387.

3. The series also went for some time under the name "Macnaghten-Lemare Concerts" and in 1978, under new management, became "The New Macnaghten Concerts."

4. Anne Macnaghten, "The Story of the Macnaghten Concerts," *The Musical Times* 100 (September 1959):460-61.

5. Elisabeth Lutyens, *A Goldfish Bowl* (London: Cassell, 1972).

6. Ibid., p. 171.

7. Ibid., p. 76.

8. Anthony Payne, "Lutyens's Solution to Serial Problems," *The Listener* (December 5, 1963), p. 961.

9. For a brief summary of the styles of the first ten quartets, see Hugo Cole's article, "Elizabeth Maconchy," *The New Grove Dictionary of Music and Musicians,* 6th ed., 20 vols., ed. Stanley Sadie (London: Macmillan, 1980), 11: 448-49.

10. Elizabeth Maconchy, "A Composer Speaks," *Composer* 42 (Winter 1971-1972):25-29.

11. From a lecture delivered by Nicola LeFanu at Harvard University's Payne Hall on April 20, 1982.

12. Gerald Larner, "Nicola LeFanu," *The New Grove Dictionary of Music and Musicians,* 12:604-5.

13. Nicola LeFanu, record jacket notes for *The Same Day Dawns,* performed by Jane Manning and the Gemini ensemble (Chandos ABR 1017, 1980).

14. LeFanu, Harvard Lecture, April 20, 1982.

15. Rebecca Clarke's *Trio* may be heard on recording in a performance by violinist Suzanne Ornstein, cellist James Kreger, and pianist Virginia Eskin (Leonarda LPI 103, 1980).

16. Ian Kemp, "Priaulx Rainier," *The New Grove Dictionary of Music and Musicians,* 15: 546-47. Kemp refers to two British artists, the painter Ben Nicholson and the sculptress Barbara Hepworth.

17. Priaulx Rainier, "The New World of Modern Music," *Ideas of Today* 15 (April 1967):108.

18. The new Leonarda release of Rainier's 1939 String Quartet is included in the discography appended to this chapter.

19. Letter from Priaulx Rainier to Doris Humphrey dated August 6, 1981, folder C-670, The Doris Humphrey Collection, Dance Division of the New York Public Library of the Performing Arts, New York City.

20. Timothy Baxter, "Priaulx Rainier: A Study of Her Musical Style," *Composer* 60 (Spring 1977):23.

21. John Amis, "Priaulx Rainier," *The Musical Times* 96 (July 1955):354-57.

22. Mosco Carner, "The Music of Phyllis Tate," *Music and Letters* 35 (April 1954).128.

23. N. Kay, "Phyllis Tate," *The Musical Times* 116 (May 1975):429.

24. Ibid.

25. Carner, "The Music of Phyllis Tate," p. 131.

26. Joan Littlejohn, "Elizabeth Poston (Part 1)," *Composer* 56 (Winter 1975-1976):15-18.

27. Ibid.

28. Joan Littlejohn, "Elizabeth Poston (Part 2)," *Composer* 57 (Spring 1976):27-32.

29. Eric Blom, concert review, *The Birmingham* (England), March 26, 1945.

30. J.N.F. Laurie-Beckett, "Ruth Gipps," *The New Grove Dictionary of Music and Musicians,* 8:404.

31. Francis Routh, "Thea Musgrave," *Contemporary British Music* (London: Macdonald & Co., 1972), p. 121.

32. Thea Musgrave, "The Decision," *The Musical Times* 108 (November 1967):988-91.

33. Stephen Walsh, "Thea Musgrave," *The New Grove Dictionary of Music and Musicians,* 11:797-99.

34. Thea Musgrave, record jacket notes for *Concerto for Orchestra,* performed by N. DelMar and the New Philharmonic Orchestra (Decca Headline 8).

35. Andrew Porter, "Mary in Virginia," *The New Yorker,* May 1, 1978, p. 136.

36. "Ave Maria," *The Scotsman,* January 1, 1975.

37. Fowler reports that a recording of *Chimes, Fractured* may be available in Australia on Festival Records: Australian Festival of Music Vol. 10.

38. Marueen Therese Radic, "Jennifer Fowler," *The New Grove Dictionary of Music and Musicians,* 6:736.

39. Martin Dreyer, "Judith Weir, Composer," *The Musical Times* 122 (September 1981):593-96.

40. Musgrave is an exception, too, because she is now much more active in the United States than she is in Great Britain.

DISCOGRAPHY

This listing contains recordings of music by living British women composers in print and available in the United States and Great Britain as of September 1982.

LeFanu, Nicola. *The Same Day Dawns* (1974); *But Stars Remaining* (1970); *Deva* (1979). Jane Manning, soprano, and the Gemini Ensemble (*The Same Day Dawns*). Jane Manning, soprano (*But Stars Remaining*). Christopher

Van Kampen, cello, and the Nash Ensemble (*Deva*). Chandos ABR 1017.

Lutyens, Elisabeth. *This Green Tide* (1975), for clarinet and piano; *This Green Tide* (1975), for basset-horn and piano; *Valediction* (1954), for clarinet and piano. G. Dobree, clarinet, and M. Pert, piano. Chantry CH T005.

Five Bagatelles (1962); *Five Intermezzi* (1943); *Piano e forte* (1958); *Plenum 1,* for piano (1972). R. Deering, pianist. Pavilion/Pearl SHE 537.

Plenum IV (What Is the Wind, What Is It) (1974), for voice and organ duet. S. and N. Cleobury. Gamut/Vista VPS 1039.

And Suddenly It's Evening (1966), for tenor and eleven instruments (wds. Quasimodo). H. Handt, tenor, the BBC Symphony Orchestra with Handt conducting. Decca/Argo ZRG 638.

Stevie Smith Songs (1948), for voice and piano. M. and P. Dickinson. Trans-atlantic/Unicorn UNS 268.

Maconchy, Elizabeth. *Proud Thames,* Overture (1953). London Philharmonic Orchestra, V. Handley conducting. Lyrita SRCS 57.

Serenata Concertante, for violin and orchestra (1962); *Symphony,* for double string orchestra (1953). M. Parikian, violinist (*Serenata Concertante*), London Symphony Orchestra, V. Handley conducting. Lyrita SRCS 116.

Musgrave, Thea. *Chamber Concerto* no. 2 (1966). The Boston Musica Viva, R. Pittman conducting. Delos DEL 25405.

Mary, Queen of Scots (1977). A. Putnam, soprano; Virginia Opera Association, P. Mark conducting. 3-MMG 301.

A Christmas Carol (1979). Virginia Opera Association, P. Mark conducting. 3-MMG 302.

Concerto, for clarinet and orchestra (1967). G. de Peyer, clarinetist; New Philharmonic Orchestra (London), N. Del Mar conducting. Argo ZRG 726.

Concerto, for horn and orchestra (1971); *Concerto,* for orchestra (1967). Barry Tuckwell, hornist (*Concerto,* for horn and orchestra); Scottish National Orchestra, T. Musgrave conducting. Decca Head 8.

Rorate Coeli (1973), for SATB Chorus (wds. Wm. Dunbar). B.B.C. Northern Singers, Wilkinson conducting. Abbey LPB 798.

Rainier, Priaulx. *String Quartet* (1939). Alard String Quartet. Leonarda LP1 117.

Tate, Phyllis. *Sonata,* for clarinet and cello (1947). G. Dobree, clarinetist and J. Kirsten, pianist. Chantry CH T004.

12

The Woman Opera Conductor: A Personal Perspective

DORIS LANG KOSLOFF

In the contemporary world of American opera, the opportunities for women as performers have perforce always been great. Ever since the demise of the castrati (c. 1824), roles written for female voices have been sung by women. Despite such strong participation in specific areas of performance, women have unfortunately made very little crossover into the multifarious "off-stage" jobs that exist in opera—most particularly in conducting.

In understanding the ascent of women to the podium, it is important first to understand the hierarchy of the musical and administrative positions within a typical opera company.

The general director has the most powerful position because, usually with the advice and consent of a board of trustees, he or she determines the basic philosophy and budget requirements for the company. The general director also has the overall responsibility for hiring and firing artistic and managerial personnel. This position naturally carries with it an enormous amount of both power and responsibility.

Below the level of general management are several other staff positions of varying importance and power (depending on the specific organization). The most important of these are: (1) the artistic director (sometimes the same as the general director), who is responsible for the selection of the repertoire, soloists, stage directors, set and costume design, makeup and wig masters, and conductors; (2) the music director (sometimes the same person as the artistic director), who is chief consultant to the artistic director in regard to repertoire planning, selection of soloists and conductors, and who usually conducts at least one opera each season; (3) the production director, who coordinates the various nonmusical aspects of opera—selection of set designers, renting of sets, hiring and supervision of carpenters to build new sets, collection of measurements to be submitted to the costumer, and hiring of stage crew personnel; and (4) the stage manager, who is in charge of directing the stage crew during rehearsals and performances, supervising the "load in" and hanging of drops, setup of scenery and striking of the set, cuing entrances and calling the light cues as well as mediating any differences between artistic and technical personnel. An opera staff also includes rehearsal pianists, a chorus director, and various technical personnel specializing in makeup, set design and construction, costuming and lighting, and the stage crew.

In addition to the stable positions listed above, there are many artists who are hired on a per-show basis: singers, directors, choristers and—conductors.

Prior to the 1970s, operas produced in the United States were frequently reproductions of European operas, most often Italian. Such "reproducing" included importing singers, directors, set designers (sometimes entire sets), costumes (to a lesser degree), and—almost always—conductors. In fact, even lesser musical positions, such as chorus master/mistress, were often filled with talent imported from Europe.

In order to enter this world of European-American opera production, American artists usually began with the position of rehearsal pianist. This relatively invisible role became a springboard to advancement for many female and male pianist/conductors.

In the European school of training, the rehearsal pianist starts off as a skilled keyboard person who progresses, when the requisite talents are there, from pianist, to chorus director, to assistant conductor, to conductor. Along the way, traditional repertoire is ingrained to such a degree that it is fairly easy to conduct a first *Traviata* or *Aida* after having previously prepared it five or six times.

The same process is common in this country, the biggest difference being that often the rehearsal pianists who work their way up are women—still an extremely rare occurrence on the European continent.

The progression from rehearsal pianist, to coach, to chorus mistress, to assistant conductor, to conductor and music director of a major opera company is the basic outline of my own career.

Like many conductors, I have a very strong keyboard background. I did extensive recital work and concertizing from the age of eight on. During my college and graduate years, in addition to the normal complement of academic courses that are expected of music majors, I found myself increasingly drawn to the then-mysterious world of the singer. Playing through opera scores (just for the gratification of doing so) began to be a regular part of my daily routine.

I received a B.A. in music from Queens College of the City University of New York (1967) and a Master of Music from Boston University, School of Fine and Applied Arts (1969) with a major concentration in piano and minor concentration in vocal coaching and accompaniment. As an undergraduate I studied the basics of conducting, and as a graduate student

I mentally began to translate piano-vocal scores back to the orchestration, to modify piano reductions to be more realistic, and to understand the art of "orchestral" piano playing.

Playing any score orchestrally is an art in itself. Some of the very best pianists find that they cannot adapt themselves to the particular differences between learning a Chopin étude and learning to play *La Forza del Destino*. An opera pianist has to be able to augment piano reductions as needed as well as to eliminate pianistic idioms that are unnecessary or cumbersome to the singer's ear. Learning to forego playing every note on the printed page is difficult for many pianists, but it is essential to the art of the coach/accompanist.

The opera pianist must also have a great sensitivity to the human voice, which is the most unreliable of all instruments. The vocal mechanism, totally reliant on constantly building and maintaining a supported technique, is subject to the slightest whim of a cold or muscle strain and has to be slowly and carefully reenergized every singing day. The opera pianist must recognize and know how to anticipate and adjust to any kind of variation of production or phonating that a singer might experience on any given day. This experience translates directly from the coaching studio to the orchestra pit, where the conductor must always be totally attuned to the unexpected nuances of live vocal performance.

From rehearsal pianist ("singer's pianist"), many American women have made the next advance in the European pattern by becoming a coach and/or chorus mistress. These two positions often work well together—in fact, it is hard to imagine a well-schooled opera chorus director who could not also function as an effective coach.

The role of an opera coach requires definition. First of all, a coach is a skilled keyboard person—most often a graduated rehearsal pianist. Having played the repertoire many times enables the coach to work with singers in an advisory capacity, concentrating on musical and stylistic ideas rather than on any pianistic problems of the score. Staff coaches often have a great deal of power over the molding of the musical product and become a conduit through which the singer's and conductor's ideas pass to one another.

Good comprehension of the languages of the operas is also a must for every opera coach. (This is the reason that for so many years Italian coaches were imported to this country). Young American coaches, both men and women, have learned quickly that an excellent knowledge of Italian, as well as a good ability to pronounce and understand French and German, is a prerequisite for coaching. Even with the trend to opera in English in this country, advanced language skills are an absolute necessity for a coach.

In addition to keyboard and language skills, the coach must also possess a good sense of the various performance traditions associated with varying style periods in opera and be able to impart these differences and nuances within the context of a studio lesson while, at the same time, retaining vigilance over the basics: pitch, rhythm, diction, and phrasing.

The last of the coaching basics is especially important in the development of a conductor—cuing. The opera coach must be prepared to sing every cue to a singer (on pitch and, whenever possible, in proper register). There should be little concern with what a coach's singing sounds like; the cue is the thing, and not worrying about "la voce."

The most complete preparation for conducting an opera is to have coached the major roles, prepared the chorus, and played the entire score. Knowing a score intimately from these varied perspectives makes the transition to the orchestral preparation a creative job rather than a technical one.

There are several women who have gained great prominence in the field of operatic coaching, usually specializing in operas from one particular country. A quick look at the *prime donne* of the coaching studios reveals a smorgasbord of nationalities.

Just as Italian opera dominates the repertoire, Alberta Masiello dominates the study of Italian opera in this country. Masiello came to the Metropolitan Opera as a rehearsal pianist in 1959. She quickly established herself as the premiere coach of the Italian repertoire and has been the head of that division of the Met's coaching staff since the early 1960s. The last several generations of Metropolitan Opera artists have had the style and correctness of their Italian singing greatly influenced by this exacting woman. In fact, Masiello's understanding and knowledge of Italian performance traditions has been imparted to other coaches who have, in turn, helped to pass along her devotion to matching the Italian language and the Italian operatic style in opera performances all over America.

Equally impressive within the French repertoire is the elegant Janine Reiss, who came from the Paris Opéra to the Metropolitan Opera in 1979. This trans-Atlantic commuter heads the French coaching staff at both opera houses; she has made a great impact with her understanding of her native French language, its use in singing, and the combination of the two in training opera singers.

The most outstanding characteristic of American coaches has been their ability to assimilate many national styles and to find a way to make them comprehensible in the American studio. The most visible example of the American opera coach who is highly respected in many styles is Joan Dornemann. Dornemann, presently coach and head prompter at the Metropolitan Opera, was the first American coach—man or woman—to achieve high visibility without ascending to the podium.

In the late 1970s as Dornemann's reputation was advancing, so was that of conductor Judith Somogi. Aided by the adventurous outlook of the New

York City Opera, Somogi made a very successful transition to the podium, becoming the first American woman of note to do so.

The transition from coach to conductor is rarely an easy one. For a reason that has never made much sense to me, debuting conductors are often given "light" material to begin with—in Ms. Somogi's case, Gilbert and Sullivan. There seems to be a feeling, however erroneous in fact, that the light repertoire is easier to deal with. Somogi was able to handle this difficult repertoire, however, and subsequently has used her skills in a wide variety of operas. She has conducted with great success in such diverse locations as the Pittsburgh Opera and the Frankfurt Opera (for which she was named principal conductor for the 1982-1983 season); she is now established as an international artist, a fine example of the coach-to-conductor progression system established in Italy two hundred years ago.

In contrast to Judith Somogi's natural rise through the operatic ranks, the careers of Eve Queler and Sarah Caldwell exemplify diverse progressions, as different from each other's as they are from Judith Somogi's.

Eve Queler is a dynamic artist who in many respects has been a real trailblazer. Her career started on a fairly normal path. She became a rehearsal pianist at the New York City Opera in 1957, the same year that Julius Rudel took charge of that organization. During her first season with City Opera, she encountered a problem peculiar to women—she had to manage a brand-new baby and a brand-new career at the same time. Trying to learn repertoire, deal with motherhood, and get enough rest to survive both was a trying combination. Like many other women, she found the conflicting demands on her time took their toll and she was not reengaged for the next opera season.

In retrospect, having to leave the City Opera was but the beginning of a long-range ascent that would culminate in the founding of the Opera Orchestra of New York. In the meantime, however, it meant six years of coaching and studio work, which eventually resulted in the founding of the New York Opera Workshop. Without the funding available to larger organizations, opera workshops have to offer something special to survive and flourish—in this case, the presentation of obscure works. Queler's workshop started to attract excellent quality singers, and fine artists always attract their peers. Ultimately, the workshop grew into the Opera Orchestra of New York—a showcase for rarely-performed operatic works of international renown. This organization does almost exclusively concert presentations of opera (no staging, sets, costumes or makeup) with casts of first-rate singers.

Despite the tremendous accomplishment of having founded, artistically developed, and conducted this orchestra, Eve Queler still chafes at certain limitations in not being able to capitalize on these achievements and expand her career. In a 1978 interview in *Opera News* she stated: "Some critics are offended because I'm a conductor and a woman; I can see it in the writing. They are reviewing me as a producer but not as a conductor, and I feel that good, bad or otherwise, my artistic work should be evaluated."[1]

There is a wide gap in philosophy, approach, and artistic technique between the erudite and exacting Ms. Queler and the free-wheeling, experimental, and sometimes bizarre Sarah Caldwell of the Opera Company of Boston.

These two women, both visible, important people in American opera, are artistic directors of their respective organizations. And the Opera Orchestra of New York and the Opera Company of Boston well reflect their leaders' very different perspectives on opera theater.

Sarah Caldwell has enjoyed notoriety even outside the opera world by being outrageous. In personality as well as in physical appearance, she presents an eccentric figure to the public.

Unlike Eve Queler or Judith Somogi, Sarah Caldwell did not follow the traditional keyboard-to-podium progression. She was a symphonic player, a violist and violinist, who was drawn into opera via the creative combinations it offers. Unlike either Somogi or Queler, Caldwell established her reputation by taking on the enormous task of being both stage director and conductor of almost all of her productions—despite the fact that it is often the differences between the director and the conductor, as well as their points of agreement, that create dynamism in the opera theater. Taking on this dual role, especially after a few major successes, had the effect of catapulting Caldwell to national prominence.

That Sarah Caldwell has become the prominent figure that she is, is due to a combination of factors worthy of mention. Obviously, her great basic skills and talent exist and have been cultivated and developed over the years. Equally obviously, the media have drawn attention to the phenomenon of an antiglamourous woman in the cultural limelight. Caldwell continually refused to modify her appearance to accommodate her increasing media exposure although she was aware of the impact it had on her colleagues. The end result was surprising, to say the least: this antiheroine became a focal point of American women conductors. It is fair to say that Caldwell's notoriety stems largely from the combination of talent and skills combined with an unconventional female public figure whose appearance says, "Take me as I am."

Why dwell on appearance, on publicity, on marketability? Because these are very real factors used to distinguish among the many talented and capable conductors now vying for the chance to establish themselves in the opera forum. Achieving distinct individual recognition is difficult in a field where everyone has gone through a fairly typical training regimen. In a sense, a skilled woman may stand out in this field merely because she is a woman. On the other hand, the idea of having two women conductors in one opera season is a difficult one for most opera companies to accept.

The opera world is still a very conservative one; this is very readily noted in the selection of repertoire and the hiring of artists—every company wants the big name artist who is a known performing entity and a proven ticket-seller. Conductors (except in rare circumstances) don't contribute to ticket sales, so most companies tend to hire and rehire the capable and dependable conductors who have worked for them in the past. This naturally creates difficulties for the many young women who are trying to establish careers in conducting.

My own position as music director of a major opera company, the Connecticut Opera, is a rarity for a woman. The Connecticut Opera is a growing company, gaining in national recognition and stature. In 1981 Connecticut Opera engaged significant international attention with its spectacular production of *Aida* in the Hartford Civic Center; this was followed, in October 1982, by *Turandot,* also mounted as a spectacle opera. By marketing operas in festival style and appealing to the general public in addition to traditional opera-goers, Connecticut Opera boosted its attendance figures and international profile greatly. The company is also up-to-date in fostering the development of American artists, which is one of the reasons that I have been able to achieve my present position as music director. In today's competitive market, the opportunity to conduct a fine orchestra (members of the Hartford Symphony) under the general directorship of an able and shrewd producer (George Osborne) is a welcome challenge.

In my personal experience, orchestral players as well as singers have treated me much as they have treated other *maestri*—first with caution and then with respect. The only difference I have encountered because I am a woman is a certain initial skepticism on the part of older artists. I feel that my musical preparedness and self-confidence have erased all doubts as far as I am concerned, thus helping to reduce problems for future women conductors.

There are alternate routes to a conducting career in opera in addition to the basic European path. The university/conservatory, usually at the graduate level, is a good place to acquire conducting skills and coaching techniques. The workshop forum existing at several institutions provides opportunities in which learning (operatic repertoire) and teaching (via conducting) can happen simultaneously. Several universities/conservatories with outstanding opera departments are presently training superb opera talents of all kinds—singers, conductors, and technical and artistic personnel. Indiana University, the Juilliard School (American Opera Center), and the American Vocal Academy (Philadelphia) are three of the best.

In trying to establish a conducting career, a degree program is a helpful base. But academic credits only contribute up to a point to getting work in professional opera houses. As in all the performing arts, university training is considered merely an adjunct to concrete performing experience in a professional setting.

It is often the contacts that are established through nonconducting work in professional companies that really provide the opportunities that can eventually lead to conducting engagements in professional companies. A good example of this is the following set of personal experiences.

In 1970 in Vienna, Virginia, the Wolf Trap National Park for the Performing Arts had its first season. I was the only coach and pianist on the staff. (I earned that position by playing through much of the standard repertoire during open auditions for the resident company of singers, playing four days in a row, eleven hours each day.) As the pianist/coach for Wolf Trap, I did all the musical preparation for the major performances as well as playing all recitals sung by members of the resident ensemble. From that position, with a few words of personal recommendation by Joseph Leavitt (then general director of Wolf Trap as well as a percussionist with the National Symphony), I became the principal coach and pianist for the Washington Opera.

During my seasons with the Washington Opera, I had occasion to coach the opera *Mahagonny* by Kurt Weill. The season following its presentation in Washington, the Opera Company of Boston scheduled that opera. As Sarah Caldwell had trouble finding local coaches to prepare the opera, I commuted every other day back and forth between Boston and Washington for several weeks to help prepare the work. Having successfully coached *Mahagonny* and also having played the pit piano part, I was reengaged by the Opera Company of Boston to coach the first presentation of Verdi's *Don Carlos* in French. (My duties here included transcribing original manuscript parts into workable orchestral parts, as there are many differences between the *urtext* version and the commonly used Italian editions.)

From Boston came contacts and recommendations that led to a teaching position at the Hartt School of Music of the University of Hartford. During my teaching career there, I became the chorus mistress of the Connecticut Opera in 1973. In 1976 I became the music director of the touring branch of the Connecticut Opera (now called "Opera Express") and conducted a wide variety of operas.

In 1981 I debuted with the larger grand opera company, conducting *Porgy and Bess.* Later the same year I was appointed music administrator of the overall Connecticut Opera Association and in 1982 was given the title of music director.

An interesting adjunct to my personal history of interconnecting recommendations and performance opportunities is that my first mentor in professional conducting, Maestro Anton Guadagno (currently principal conductor of Italian repertoire at the Vienna Staatsoper, and with whom I worked at Wolf Trap in 1971), has been a colleague in several productions with Connecticut Opera and continues to be both an inspiration for me and a refiner of my skills. From him, more than any other maestro, I have learned the skills of being both a leader and a colleague to singers and of developing a creative dialogue with stage directors.

It is vital to realize that, in the demanding world of the opera conductor, there is simply no substitute for experience; one must know how to learn from and contribute to a total performance experience in which established singers are relying on the direction that comes from the podium. Seasoning and expertise really develop through learning how to cope with last-minute cast changes and varying temperaments (as well as varying tempi!) and through taking charge of the mix of musical and personal considerations that factor into any production.

There is no magic formula for getting a chance to conduct opera. Personal considerations will always influence who gets certain opportunities, but this is true of the entire operatic selection process—for singers, directors, and conductors. Tenacity is a distinctly helpful characteristic to have. So is being on the spot; regularly-scheduled conductors will cancel from time to time, and the glorious last-minute substitute may flourish.

For women, the podium is more attainable than ever before. The more genuinely talented women conductors there are that can handle the challenge, the more acceptable it will become to an increasing number of opera houses to hire women. This is already happening now in America faster than anywhere else. I see no reason at all why the word "maestra" shouldn't soon become a familiar one in opera houses across America.

NOTE

1. Eve Queler, quoted in Thomas P. Lanier, "Adamant Eve," *Opera News* 42, no. 20 (April 8, 1978), p. 59.

13

Women Music Critics in the United States

BARBARA JEPSON

In 1853 a reviewer of the *Gazette Musicale de Paris* characterized Verdi's *Rigoletto* as lacking in melody and unlikely to remain in the repertoire.[1] History tells us that the long-term impact of such critical bloopers is minimal. In the short term, however, music critics—particularly those with major daily newspapers—exercise considerable influence in their respective musical communities and in the musical world at large. A critic's position on vital musical issues of the day can help shape public taste, influence programming, and modify performance practices. Favorable reviews can aid young artists in obtaining concert management and assist composers or institutions in obtaining funding. Reviews indirectly affect audiences as well. According to a 1980 study of classical music audiences and promoters by Professor William J. Baumol of New York University and Princeton, concertgoers said that advertising brochures quoting reviews played an important part in their attendance decisions.[2] Finally, preconcert publicity in the form of profiles or interviews—a standard part of the newspaper critic's job today—can help fill halls that might otherwise remain half empty.

How much of this power is wielded by women? Critics, like conductors, have traditionally been viewed as authority figures, and newspaper journalism has been a male preserve until recently. To what extent have American women been employed as music critics in the past, and to what extent are they active as music critics at present? What kinds of positions do today's female music critics hold, and how do they view their chances for advancement within their profession? How do they get along with colleagues and superiors? Do they feel any special responsibility to cover and/or promote the efforts of women composers and conductors in the way that some critics champion new music? These are some of the questions this chapter will attempt to answer.

In order to assess women's participation in music criticism, it is necessary to understand the nature of the field itself. Composer Virgil Thomson, often called the dean of American music critics, defined the critic's main responsibility as "explaining the creative or executant artist to the public."[3] Such "explanations," in the form of concert reviews, record reviews, and critical essays, appear in numerous publications ranging from daily, weekly, and monthly newspapers to mass media magazines, specialized music periodicals, and scholarly journals. Criticism may also be included in record liner notes, program guides, and books.

In the course of his or her career, the typical critic may contribute to a majority of these outlets. Those who primarily author critical books and scholarly essays, however, have been excluded from this article, not because they lack importance but because such individuals often have a teaching job or other occupation as their main source of income. Rather, this study focuses on critics holding positions with major daily newspapers in the United States, since these publications generally have the largest readerships and the most influence and are usually located in cities with the greatest amount of musical activity. To a lesser extent, leading national and specialized magazines regularly containing classical music criticism (for example, the *New Yorker, High Fidelity*) are also considered.

WOMEN MUSIC CRITICS OF THE PAST

Most reference books date the beginnings of serious music criticism in the United States to the establishment of *Dwight's Journal of Music* in 1852. Founded by John Sullivan Dwight, the Boston-based publication was an important factor in shaping musical opinion until discontinued in 1881.[4] Newspaper music coverage around this time typically consisted of flowery reviews ("We almost thought we could see those exquisite notes take wings like angels, and float aloft"[5]), short concert announcements, and articles advocating various improvements in the nation's fledgling cultural life (less spitting of tobacco in the concert halls) and proficiency in music as a fitting social accomplishment for women.[6]

It is difficult to ascertain how many women were music critics prior to 1900 because reviews were often unsigned or initialed before that date. However, a reviewer who signed herself "Betsy B." wrote for the San Francisco *Argonaut* beginning in 1883; one of her first assignments was to cover a symphony concert conducted by the legendary Theodore Thomas, then touring with his own orchestra.[7] In 1900 the same paper's critic was listed as Rose Soley.[8] Undoubtedly, it was sheer coincidence that the *Argonaut* had two female critics within a relatively short space of time, yet it is fascinating to note how often this pattern recurs. Once a paper has hired a woman, it is more likely to do so again.

The most visible nineteenth-century woman critic appears to have been May Garrettson Evans (1866-1947), music critic for the *Baltimore Sun* from

1888 to 1895. Evans first studied music with her mother, a musician and descendant of "an old Colonial family."[9] In 1889 she received a certificate from the Peabody Conservatory of Music, where she played violin in the Peabody Symphony Orchestra. An obituary on Evans offers the following perspective on her entrance into music journalism:

While a student at the Peabody she began assisting her brother . . . then on the staff of a Baltimore newspaper, reporting on musical events for him. . . . This experience gave her courage to apply for a job on *The Sun*. [sic] Her adventure as the first woman reporter on a newspaper in Baltimore created quite a commotion in that mid-Victorian period, when it was almost unheard of for a young woman to be on the street alone after dark, in streetcars or in theaters.[10]

In 1894 May Garrettson Evans and a sister, Marion Dorsey Evans, opened a music school for talented children; one year later, she left the *Sun* to devote more time to her new endeavor. In 1898 the school became the Peabody Preparatory Department; by the time Evans retired as its director in 1930, the division had grown from 300 to over 3,200 students.

Another woman subsequently associated with the *Baltimore Sun* was Henrietta Straus (1888-1931), a music correspondent for the *Sunday Sun* during the 1920s, a New York-based national publication. She held the job from approximately 1920 to 1926.[11] Two items in the *Sun* describe Straus as "among the foremost music critics of New York" and "widely known for her reviews which combined an unusual critical judgment with a sparkling literary style."[12] In the absence of additional information—she is not included in standard biographies or music criticism anthologies—it is difficult to evaluate the validity of those statements. However, a copy of a lengthy article Straus wrote for the *Sunday Sun* in 1924 was obtained. It proved to be a lively, provocative discussion of the European bias of many musical institutions here and abroad and its impact on American conductors and composers. Her most controversial article was said to be an attack on the Metropolitan Opera for "stifling composers and artists" that appeared in the *Nation*; though "hotly protested" by Met officials, they declined an offer to disprove the charges.[13] Unfortunately, Straus died at forty-three, three years after "a nervous collapse from which she never fully recovered."[14]

One of the prominent male reviewers around this time was Henry T. Finck, music critic of the *New York Post* from 1881 to 1924. An amusing aside to Finck's career is revealed in his memoirs, where he discusses the contributions of his wife, Abbie Cushman Finck, to his reviews. He credits her with identifying many obscure piano pieces played as encores at recitals and "writing so cleverly in my style that few could detect the author."[15] When reviewing new operas, the couple often divided the task, Finck writing about the music, his wife tackling the scenery and costumes. Occasionally she wrote the entire review. In fact, when Finck was sick with bronchopneumonia, Abbie covered the Chicago Opera Company, the Metropolitan, and other concerts, doing it "so well that people said: Why no! Finck is not sick—I see his articles in the *Post* everyday."[16]

West Coast newspapers continued to hire women as music critics during the first half of the twentieth century. Isabel Morse Jones (1891-1951), a violinist who was a member of the Los Angeles Women's Symphony and various chamber ensembles, became music editor and critic for the *Los Angeles Times* in 1925. She had previously worked briefly for the *Fresno Bee* and *Los Angeles Daily News.* After twenty-two years with the *Times*, she retired to found the Music Academy of the West, which sponsored lecture recitals and a variety of music appreciation courses for the general public. Jones also served as correspondent for *Musical America* from 1940 to 1947. She was known as an early supporter of the Hollywood Bowl and apparently served as its press representative for many years.

An Anthology of Music Criticism, part of a Work-Project Administration sponsored study on the history of music in San Francisco, lists ten women among forty reviewers working as music critics during 1906 to 1940. Among these are Blanche Partington, music critic with the *Call* (1906 to 1940 or later), Ada Hanifan, with the *Examiner* (1928 to 1940 or later), and Margery Markres Fisher (1895-?), music critic of the *News.* The latter founded the Pacific Ladies String Quartet, which concertized throughout northern California, and invented a shoulder pad and chin rest for violinists.[18] Fisher began her journalism career as correspondent for *Musical America* in 1915 and served as music and drama critic for the Christian Science Monitor from 1920 to 1929. She became music critic for the *News* in 1929 and still held that position in 1951.

Another woman who began her career during the 1920s was Claudia Cassidy, one of the most influential critics of her generation. Cassidy, who holds an A.B. in journalism from the University of Illinois, was arts critic for the *Chicago Journal of Commerce* from 1925 to 1941. After a one-year stint with the *Chicago Sun,* she became music and drama critic for the *Chicago Tribune.* Her column, "On the Aisle," appeared regularly in the *Tribune* throughout her tenure. A selection of columns written during summer travels to European music festivals was published in 1954 as *Europe on the Aisle.* Although Cassidy, now in her eighties, retired in 1965 from the *Tribune,* she remains active. Until recently she hosted a half-hour weekly radio show, "Critic's Choice," on WFMT, Chicago's leading classical music station, and she is critic-at-large for *Chicago Magazine.*

Cassidy was known as a generalist, in the best sense of the word, who enjoyed the cross currents of covering the various arts.[19] She had a reputation for high standards, strong opinions, and a caustic wit, the latter of which earned her the nickname "poison pen Cassidy." During her heyday, she was accused of dealing a deathblow to the roadshows and of railroading Rafael Kubelik, conductor of the Chicago Symphony from 1950 to 1953, out of town. She also had an eye for promising young talent and was among the first to recognize Tennessee Williams and George Balanchine.

Tom Willis, who began working for Cassidy at the *Tribune* in 1957 and succeeded her when she left, holds her in high regard. "Claudia Cassidy is probably the most skillful professional I've ever worked for," says Willis, now concert manager and associate professor of music at Northwestern University. "She had a virtuosity as a journalist that rivaled Harold Schonberg's."

Numerous women have attributed the relatively high number of females hired as music critics in Chicago since Cassidy's retirement to her influence and have acknowledge her importance as a role model. Outside of Chicago circles, however, she is less well known, and some women feel that her talent and position as a major chronicler of the American cultural scene for forty years is less widely recognized than it should be. "If Claudia had been a man," says one critic, "there would be theaters (like the Brooks Atkinson) and parks (like Boston's Elliott Norton Park) named after her. Why isn't she in the Theater Hall of Fame?"

The career of Harriet Johnson, music critic of the *New York Post* for the last forty years, forms a link between women critics of the past and present. In 1943 Johnson became the second woman hired as head critic by the *Post*; the first, Olga Samaroff (1926 to 1927), quit in frustration over the editor's rejection of her plan for an expanded music section. Although best known as a critic, Johnson received a fellowship in composition from the Juilliard School following graduation from the University of Minnesota. She has continued to compose sporadically and is the author of vocal and instrumental works, including *Pet of the Met,* a work for soprano, baritone, and orchestra most recently performed by the Chicago Symphony at a 1981 children's concert.

Johnson's reviews and articles are characterized by a lively, accessible style, and it was the ability to make a musical event come alive for the reader that helped land her the *Post* job in the first place. "When I went for my interview," Johnson recalls, "Ted Thackrey, then editor and general manager of the paper, asked me how I would write music criticism that would be intelligible to both the concertgoer and the person reading the comics." Johnson detailed her experiences as a traveling lecturer and as artistic director of the Layman's Music Courses at Town Hall from 1939 to 1942. What was supposed to have been a short interview turned into a four-hour discussion, and when it was over, she was hired.

WOMEN MUSIC CRITICS TODAY

During Harriet Johnson's forty-year tenure with the *Post*, there has been a tremendous expansion in the nation's musical life. Unfortunately, her vocation has not seen a similar expansion. The field of music criticism today

Figure 13.1 Harriet Johnson, head critic, *New York Post* (1943 to present) and a composer of vocal and instrumental works, notes that "women have played a greater role in music of the past than has been generally recognized." Photograph by Arty Pomerantz

is a competitive one with limited numbers of substantive job opportunities. Of sixteen magazines surveyed, seven use one classical music critic, one uses two, and the remainder rely on a stable of freelancers for record reviews. Newspapers, more likely to have larger staffs, are suffering from dwindling circulation, a trend that began in the 1960s and has recently forced the folding or merging of many large dailies. As of year end 1982, there were 1,712 daily newspapers in the United States, but insiders estimated the existence of only about fifty to sixty full-time positions for classical music critics; many of these combine classical music with dance or some other area of the arts.[20] In fact, the highly regarded Rockefeller Foundation Project for the Training of Music Critics, held at the University of Southern California from 1964 to 1973 under the aegis of the late Raymond Kendall, was disbanded because its graduates quickly glutted the market. "We didn't want to be in the position of training people for jobs that didn't exist," says Robert Marsh, head music critic for the *Chicago Sun-Times* and a member of the Rockefeller Project's Steering Committee. Smaller newspapers or those based in areas with less active music scenes often subsist with one full-time critic, who covers all the arts except film, or utilize stringers—nonstaffers paid by review at rates ranging from $5 to $75. By contrast, base salaries for full-time critics with big-city papers range from about $20,000 to $40,000 and are usually set by union contracts, although established critics can negotiate considerably higher amounts.[21] This makes competition intense for the best-paying, most desirable jobs, and, like principal players in leading symphony orchestras, critics who attain these coveted slots often hold them until retirement.

The real scarcity of jobs should not, however, prevent us from comparing the relative positions of males and females within the music criticism profession today. Each year openings occur as critics move up the career ladder, retire, die, or leave the field. How do women fare in this game of musical chairs?

"The field of music criticism is male-dominated but open to women," says Marilyn Tucker, one of three full-time music and dance critics for the *San Francisco Chronicle*. A majority of those interviewed—males and females—agreed with this overall assessment. Part of that dominance reflects a numerical advantage. No definitive statistics are available, but judging from sources including membership statistics provided by the Music Critics Association (MCA), an organization founded in 1957 to promote higher standards of music criticism, it would appear that women make up about 32 percent of the profession as of April, 1983.[22] This proportion seemingly reflects the lower number of women seeking employment as music critics, since none of the women contacted reported any difficulties whatsoever breaking into the field via typical entry-level positions.

"I came up through the ranks as a stringer," says twenty-eight-year-old Roxane Orgill, who became head music critic of the *Milwaukee Journal* in

Figure 13.2 Marilyn Tucker, one of three full-time music and dance critics on the *San Francisco Chronicle* (1967 to present), is a trained organist and pianist who used to sing in the Oakland Symphony Chorus.

Figure 13.3 Roxane Orgill, music critic of the Bergen, N.J., *Record*, has more than twelve years training as a violinist and a master's degree in music theory from the University of London.

1980 after working part-time for that paper for two years. *High Fidelity* reviewer Karen Monson's career displays a similar progression: after stringing for the *Boston Globe* and the *Los Angeles Times*, she became music critic of the *Los Angeles Herald-Examiner* in 1969. Four years later, she left to become head music critic of the *Chicago Daily News*, a postion she held until that paper's demise in 1978. One young critic, Linda Charlton, didn't even seek her current slot as stringer for the *Miami Herald*. Unknown to Charlton, three individuals recommended her to head critic James Roos when an opening became available; each had admired her reviews for the University of Miami newspaper.

Both the Rockefeller Foundation training project mentioned above and various educational seminars sponsored by the MCA have aided aspiring critics in honing their skills and advancing their careers. Women have been readily appointed as "fellows" to both: eleven of the thirty-seven (or 30 percent) Rockefeller project graduates were women, and former *Boston Globe* critic Michael Steinberg, who has taught many MCA Institutes over the last decade, estimates that about one-third of his students were women.[23]

However, when the quantity and type of positions women music critics hold are examined relative to their proportion, a pattern of underrepresen-

Table 13.1
Male and Female Classical Music Critics
on Various Professional Levels as of 4/83

	Number of Males	Percentage of Males	Number of Females	Percentage of Females	Male/Female Ratio
M.C.A. members, U.S. only	165 of 242	68	77 of 242	32	2.1:1
M.C.A. members working for top 100 U.S. dailies, as staff or stringers[a]	c.38[b]	67	c.19	33	2.0:1
Head critics, top 91 U.S. dailies[c]	76	84	15	16	5.1:1
Full-time critics, top 20 dailies[d]	24	86	4	14	6.0:1
Full-time critics, most prestigious dailies[e]	9	100	0	0	9.0:0

[a]*Editor & Publisher International Yearbook*, "The 100 Top Daily Newspapers in the U.S. According to Circulation, Sept. 30, 1981" (New York, Editor & Publisher, 1982), p. xiv.

[b]This figure is somewhat misleading. One year ago, 58 males on these top 100 papers belonged to M.C.A.; the decrease may simply reflect the number who have not yet paid their 1983 M.C.A. membership dues. By comparison, there were 20 female M.C.A. members on these top 100 papers a year ago.

[c]*'82 Ayer Directory of Publications*, "List of editors of the most popular features appearing in daily newspapers with 100,000 or more circulation" (Bala Cyn Wyd, Pa., IMS Press, 1982). Only the top 91 U.S. dailies were used, and six of them did not list music departments. (Remaining papers listed were Canadian or Puerto Rican.)

[d]Telephone survey, April, 1983, by the author.

[e]*New York Times, Washington Post, Los Angeles Times* and *Chicago Tribune*.

tation occurs, with the lowest percentage of women found at the highest levels of the profession (see table 13.1). The most dramatic difference is seen when the percentage of women in the field, about one-third, is contrasted to the total absence of any full-time female classical music critics on the four dailies generally considered most prestigious—the *New York Times, Washington Post, Los Angeles Times* and *Chicago Tribune* (as of April 1983 none of the nine positions on these papers was held by a woman). Even when head critics of the top 100 dailies ranked by circulation are surveyed, women hold only 16 percent of those positions.

A perusal of important national, regional, or specialized magazines yields similar results. Two out of nine positions, or about 22 percent of eight general-interest publications regularly running classical music reviews, has a female music critic (see table 13.2). Specialized music magazines customarily use a stable of record reviewers. Here the percentages of women are even lower, ranging from none (*Stereo Review, Ovation,*

Table 13.2
Representation of Women on Leading Magazines
Containing Classical Music Criticism as of 4/83

General Interest Publications	Critic(s)	Percentage of Women
California Magazine	Alan Rich	
Commentary	Samuel Lipman	
Nation	David Hamilton	
New York	Peter G. Davis	
New Yorker	Andrew Porter	
Newsweek	Annalyn Swan	
Saturday Review	Linda Sanders	
	Gregory Sandow	
Time	Michael Walsh	
Summary	2 out of 9 reviewers	22

Specialized Publications	Women among Total Reviewers	Percentage of Women
American Record Guide	1 out of 41	2
Fanfare	2 out of 33	6
High Fidelity	2 out of 24	8
Keynote (WNCN)	0 out of 8	0
Musical America	6 out of 35a	17
Stereo Review	0 out of 5	0

aThis figure is based on the number of correspondents contributing two or more concert reviews during 1981, plus regular new music critic Joan La Barbara.

Keynote) to about 8 percent (*High Fidelity*)—with one intriguing exception: *Musical America*. The latter is the only specialized magazine with a female editor, and about 17 percent of its thirty-five frequent correspondents are women.

It would be easy to conclude from the above that sexism is rampant in music criticism and that the majority of women, mirroring patterns documented in other professions, are stuck in lower-paying, less influential jobs as a result. In reality, the answer is more complex. Reviewers traditionally have fallen into two groups: those who pursue criticism as a part-time avocation, and those who do so as a full-time career. Efforts to determine the approximate ratio of males to females applying for jobs on both levels proved frustrating and met with a good deal of defensiveness on the part of male editors and critics. However, certain patterns were revealed.

Women appear to be less interested or less aggressive in pursuing work as freelance record reviewers for specialized magazines. (Editor Joel Flegler of *Fanfare* and Assistant Editor Jenny Elliott of *American Record Guide* maintained that at least 90 percent of queries received were from men.) In the newspaper arena, women seem to be seeking jobs as stringers in greater numbers than they are seeking positions as full-timers or head critics. Estimates for women applying as stringers ranged from about 20 percent of all candidates (Martin Bernheimer, *Los Angeles Times*) to 50 percent—substantially above their representation in the field (Robert Marsh, *Chicago Sun-Times*).[24] Estimates for those seeking full-time or head critic slots were considerably lower. Thus, the underrepresentation of women on the higher levels of the profession may partly mean that fewer women are seeking those jobs.

Women music critics apparently fall into three groups at present: (1) ambitious, young women who have recently entered the field but are not yet sufficiently experienced to go after major full-time positions; (2) family or traditionally oriented women who prefer either part-time employment or full-time employment in cities with less musical activity than the hectic pace and grueling, evening/weekend hours of full-time positions on big-city dailies; and (3) women who entered the field a decade or more ago and have already attained full-time or head-critic slots on the top one hundred dailies. In general, the latter are more career-oriented than the family-oriented group and are more willing to move to attain their goals. But even some of these full-timers ruled out relocation because it might interfere with their husbands' careers.

John Rockwell cited the latter factor as one reason why the *New York Times*, which has never had a female music critic, did not hire any for the three openings occurring on its classical music staff between 1980 and 1981. In a recent interview with the author, Rockwell noted that at the time these particular slots opened up, none of the women who made themselves known were as good as we would ideally have wanted. There *are* a number of good women critics, but many of them are unwilling to move to New York City, either because they don't wish to leave a job as head critic for a lesser position on our staff, or, as in the case of one woman who made a pleasing impression on a personal and intellectual level, because they don't want to uproot their husbands and children.

Several experienced women critics who *were* willing to relocate, however, suggested that they would have applied more openly for the *New York Times* positions, but insiders denied that a full-timer would be hired to replace Donal Henahan once he moved into Harold Schonberg's job as head critic. This misconception highlights another possible factor in the lower number of women applying for important full-time slots: the nebulous manner in which such openings are filled in the first place. Unlike symphony orchestras, which are required by union regulations to hold auditions for openings, the best jobs for music critics are rarely advertised. Rather, they are filled by a combination of word-of-mouth recommendation and happenstance. Because classical music is such a specialized discipline, editors (who actually do the hiring) understandably rely on the advice of critics they respect when hiring replacements or additional staff.

Aspiring young critics, or those with plenty of maneuvering room left on the career ladder, typically send in clips, resumés, and letters expressing interest in upcoming openings; if possible, they ask an established colleague to recommend them. However, anyone already holding a major slot on a large paper for a decade or longer is likely to follow a more circuitous route of indicating receptivity to a job change. "It would be demeaning for someone in my position to send in clips," explained one male twenty-year veteran. "What I would do is find out, first via the grapevine and second by telephoning a colleague on the paper, the kind of person the paper is looking for—a young hotshot, an established name—and who else might be a candidate. If the fit sounded right, then I'd discreetly express interest in the job." Similarly, the head critic might sit down with the appropriate editor or other staff members and run through names of those whose work they admire with a view toward determing who might be available and appropriate for the job. Needless to say, contacts and visibility become extremely important in such an environment. With men holding the majority of senior positions in the field, an informal "old-boy network" exists, and most women critics interviewed perceive this network as the most formidable obstacle to their success.

"I don't believe women are discriminated against on the typical daily newspaper," says Wilma Salisbury, a full-time music and dance critic with the *Cleveland Plain Dealer*. "But on the most powerful papers, there seems to be an assumption that music critics are automatically male—someone who's tough, who can take a lot of criticism and dish it out." Marilyn

Tucker of the *San Francisco Chronicle* echoes this sentiment. "I'm sure the *New York Times* still thinks of itself as a private male club," she says. Joanne Hoover, director of a music school in the Washington, D.C., area and a stringer for the *Washington Post* since 1977, noted the absence of women critics on that paper's staff in any arts area. "It's hard to sort out how much of that situation reflects those seeking the job itself and how much it reflects men having a tendency to recommend other men, and bring them in when positions open up."

Obviously, tapping into that old-boy network is a must for any career-minded woman. "This is a grapevine business," says Karen Monson.

Figure 13.4 Karen Monson, music critic. Monson was head critic of the *Chicago Daily News* from 1973 to its demise in 1978 and won the Deems Taylor award for criticism in 1977. Her biography of Alma Mahler was published in 1983 by Houghton Mifflin. Photograph by Robert M. Lightfoot III

"Everyone who is serious about his or her job makes sure he knows everyone else." Attending important premieres in other cities and MCA meetings is one way to meet influential colleagues—provided your newspaper is willing to foot the bill. (Ellen Pfeifer, film and music critic for the *Boston Herald American,* points out that women are at a disadvantage here, since they tend to work for less prosperous papers.) Latching onto an established critic who shares your enthusiasms is another strategy. "If you really love opera," explains Karen Monson, "get to know a critic who specializes in opera, rather than someone whose passion is piano performance."

It is interesting to note that Monson and many of today's best-known women critics—Wilma Salisbury, Ellen Pfeifer, Nancy Malitz, Linda Winer (a former music and dance critic for the *Chicago Tribune* who is now dance critic of *USA Today*), and others had male mentors during the early stages of their careers and/or were graduates of the above-mentioned Rockefeller Foundation training project. The foundation arranged one-year internships at major newspapers throughout the country for its graduates, thus providing an entree and an opportunity to display their skills that many women might not otherwise have had. Similarly, composer Joan La Barbara was recommended to succeed Tom Johnson as new music critic of *Musical America* by John Rockwell.

In 1981, McMaster University in Ontario, Canada, introduced a master of arts program in music criticism, and the Peabody Conservatory in Baltimore is now planning a similar program. Both may ultimately serve as a springboard for young critics. In the meantime, many critics feel that a conservatory or musicological degree is the best preparation for the job, but whatever their background, newcomers are advised to start reviewing as soon as possible, if only for a college or local newspaper. Roxane Orgill of the Bergen, N.J., *Record* followed that approach, and by the time she graduated, she had a sufficient number of clips to be appointed to an MCA Institute. While most critics start as stringers, *Washington Post* freelancer Joanne Hoover suggested that women might do better to aim for a full-time position with a major newspaper in a smaller city and get into the circle in order to move up, rather than stringing for a local paper outside a major metropolitan area. "So many people in the field operate on a freelance basis," she explains. "It's better never to allow yourself to be defined in those terms."

Of course, landing that important job is just the beginning. Critics must cope with long hours, deadline pressures, musically illiterate editors, and nasty letters or phone calls from irate musicians, composers, and heads of local institutions, all of whom are convinced that the critic is a musical moron. They also must integrate whatever personal life they have into the oddball hours the job requires. Although some male critics successfully combine major careers with marriage and family, the profession has always included a large number of single men. Women, who still bear the primary

Figure 13.5 Donna Perlmutter, head critic of the *Los Angeles Herald Examiner* since 1975 and currently the Los Angeles and San Diego correspondent for *Opera News*, has a B.A. in music and English from Penn State University and an M.A. in psychology and education from Yeshiva University. She discovered music criticism via a course at UCLA and found it "so draining, frustrating, and challenging—so satisfying to a basic masochist like myself." Photograph by Alan Hipwell

responsibility for child-care in most relationships, are divided over the issue of combining motherhood with a full-time career in criticism.

Roxane Orgill, Karen Monson, and Wynne Delacoma, a dance and music critic for the *Chicago Sun-Times*, were among those who felt that the demands of the job make it difficult to be a responsible parent. Others, like Melinda Bargreen, head critic of the *Seattle Times,* and Ellen Pfeifer of the *Boston Herald American,* viewed the unorthodox hours as a plus. "Juggling careers and babies can be very difficult for women who work nine-to-five hours," says Bargreen. "But since reviewing takes place at night, I can leave my children with their father, and still spend some time with them in the afternoon." Obviously, the answers reflect personal preferences as well as differing job requirements in particular cities.

How do women get along with colleagues and editors? None of the women contacted reported any difficulties in working with male critics on their own newspapers or any inequities in the ratio of reviews to features assigned to critics on the same job level. (It has always been the head critic's

Figure 13.6 Betty Dietz Krebs, head critic for the *Dayton Daily News,* began writing for that paper while in high school. She also covers the visual arts, as well as major musical events in Cincinnati, and is active in the Music Critics Association.

prerogative to select the most desirable concerts to review.) However, Melinda Bargreen noted a disparity in the way readers responded to negative criticism of performers or composers. "Many a male colleague has made a reputation for himself by indulging in catty witticisms," she observes, "but when I use a little sarcasm, I get letters calling me 'bitchy.'" Relationships with colleagues on other papers were variously categorized as "friendly" and "normally competitive." The MCA was frequently characterized as a "male club," tolerant of but somewhat patronizing to its female members. One participant at a recent MCA Institute recalled "a low point" during a seminar when a student asked the male instructors if any women had ever been well-known music critics. "There was an embarrassed silence," she says, "and then someone asked, 'What about that crazy lady in Chicago—Claudia Cassidy?' And they all laughed. Little by little, they managed to come up with Karen Monson and Betty Dietz Krebs, head critic of the *Dayton Daily News,* the latter of whom they classified as a 'housewife type.'"

Krebs, unaware of that description when interviewed, characterized herself as "the most visible woman in the MCA and their favorite token on its board and committees. There's very much a good-old-boy atmosphere," she explains, "particularly on the nominating committee, which is made up of critics from the most influential papers. [MCA has had one female president in its twenty-six-year existence, but women other than Krebs have served on its board, committees and seminars.] In fact, when I think of the men who have been leading factors in MCA, such as Virgil Thomson, most of them have been strong male chauvinists—always very cordial, but they don't seem to recognize that women can be good critics."

Numerous sources have verified that Thomson, who retired as head critic of the New York *Herald Tribune* in 1954, had some old-fashioned ideas about women. *Chicago Sun-Times* critic Robert Marsh and two other sources recalled Thomson making a statement, during an MCA Institute held at Ravinia, Illinois, in the summer of 1973, to the effect that women could never be first-rate critics because their personal feelings and loyalties would interfere with their professional obligations. "I was shocked," says Marsh, whose former assistant, Nancy Malitz, is now national music critic for *USA Today.* "It's true that there are always a few critics who have those kinds of conflicts, but obviously the problem is not limited to women."

At least one editor seemed to share Thomson's view when it came to the subject of covering music by women composers. "We don't have a lot of contemporary music here in Cleveland," observes Wilma Salisbury of the *Plain Dealer.* "When Elaine Barkin's opera was to be premiered, I did a profile of her prior to the concert. There was a big scene with the editor, who accused me of interviewing her because she is a woman. I said, 'No, I'm interviewing a composer who is having an opera premiered here!'"

Many women critics admitted, however, to going out of their way to give preconcert publicity, in the form of a photo, profile, or interview, to women composers and conductors. The reasons cited were that such individuals are still a rarity in their communities, and they believed these women have been discriminated against in the past. (Interestingly, a majority of these women also expressed a commitment to contemporary music, to the extent that they tried to cover it whenever possible even though their editors preferred having them cover events that draw bigger audiences.)

However, even the most ardent feminists rebelled at the notion of giving less-than-honest reviews to music by women, in an attempt to be supportive. "I don't feel a special responsibility to *anyone*," insists Melinda Bargreen. "It's demeaning to women and self-defeating in the long run."

"We did have an instance," recalls Wilma Salisbury, "where I had done a feature on an upcoming concert of music by women composers of the past. The concert organizers expressed surprise when I wrote a negative review, but the music was second-rate in my opinion, and I said so."

Most women critics contacted expressed objections to such all-female events in the first place, unless they occurred in the context of scholarly conferences where new research was presented. "I object to all-anything," says Karen Monson, in a typical statement. Rather, they prefer to see women's music included on contemporary music programs or those featuring works of a particular genre, such as string quartets. (Of course, so would women composers.)

In fact, an informal sampling of women composers in the New York City and Los Angeles areas disclosed similar sentiments. Composer Beth Anderson, former critic and editor of *Ear,* a contemporary music magazine, observes that all-women events often prove counterproductive. "On the West Coast," she says, "such events are covered because they're by women; in New York City, they're *ignored* because they're by women." Composer/critic Joan La Barbara spoke for many women composers when she said the following: "I think it was necessary to do concerts of music exclusively by women initially, if only to make a statement, to increase awareness of our existence. The time has come, though, to integrate women's works into the mainstream of our musical life."

As for the "special treatment" issue, most women composers neither want nor need it. "None of us is in the fragile ego department," says composer Ellen Taaffe Zwilich, "or we wouldn't be in this field. If a piece doesn't measure up to a critic's standards, he or she should say so."

In fact, the whole touchy question of whether it is better to assign a female reviewer to cover women's music because she will supposedly have more credibility than a male would be diffused by having greater numbers of women critics on the most influential papers. Perhaps the biggest remaining obstacle to that happening lies in the nature of the job itself and in the complex sociological factors that have tended to limit and denigrate women's contributions to the musical world in the past.

Critics are widely perceived as trend setters, opinion molders, authority figures. Strong convictions and strong egos—qualities that fly in the face of traditional female conditioning—seem to be prerequisites for the job. If one examines the critical profession as a whole, until recently it has been male-dominated in all disciplines, with one exception: dance. Here, women outnumber men in holding and seeking jobs as critics. "Whenever there is an opening for a dance critic," observes Martin Bernheimer, head critic of the *Los Angeles Times,* "women candidates come out in hordes." Furthermore, women dance critics, such as Arlene Croce, Anna Kisselgoff, Deborah Jowitt, and Marcia Siegal are among the most respected and influential in their field. Linda Winer, dance critic of the *New York Daily News,* offered one possible explanation for this phenomenon. "The whole modern dance movement in America was founded by women, whereas women composers have not yet become trend setters in their particular discipline."

By contrast, American musical life has been dominated until recently by scores of talented European musicians, musicologists, and composers who fled their native lands during the first half of this century. Many left Germany to escape Nazi persecution and brought to our shores, along with their skills, old-world attitudes toward women's "proper place" in society. (While that country obviously has no monopoly on male chauvinism, women in West Germany are still greatly under-represented in professional symphony orchestras.) It is interesting that the influx of female musicians into American symphony orchestras, the increase in American women pursuing careers in composition, and the begrudging, if limited, acceptance of women as orchestral conductors during the last decade has coincided not only with the women's movement, but with the growing prominence of American musicians of either sex in our nation's musical life. Perhaps as more women assume leadership positions in the musical world, there will be a parallel rise in the number of influential female critics. Ultimately, however, what is needed are more critics of either gender who are aware of women's contributions to our musical life in the past and receptive to reviewing their creative efforts in the present.

NOTES

1. Nicolas Slonimsky, *Lexicon of Musical Invective: Critical Assaults on Composers Since Beethoven's Time,* 2d. ed. (Seattle and London: University of Washington Press, 1965), p. 218.

2. "Music Critics' Influence Studied," *New York Times,* June 2, 1980.

3. Virgil Thomson, *Music Reviewed 1940-1954* (New York: Vintage Books, 1967), p. 397.

4. Arthur Jacobs, "Musical Criticism," *The International Cyclopedia of Music and Musicians,* 10th ed. (New York: Dodd Mead, 1975), p. 493.

5. Cornel A. Lengyel, ed., *An Anthology of Music Criticism,* History of Music

in San Francisco, Vol. 7 (Northern California Writer's Program, Work Project Administration, 1942), p. 1.

6. Ibid., p. 3.

7. Ibid., p. 172.

8. Ibid., p. 214.

9. "Her Retirement Means No Idleness," *Baltimore Sun,* evening edition, September 29, 1934. My thanks to Clement G. Vitek, chief librarian of the *Sun,* for his assistance in obtaining material on women music critics with that newspaper.

10. Obituary, "Miss Evans, 80, Peabody Music Pioneer, Dies," *Baltimore Sun,* morning edition, January 13, 1947.

11. These approximate dates were provided by the *Nation;* it is possible Straus worked there for a longer period, but records are spotty.

12. Obituary, "Miss Henrietta Straus, Music Critic, Dies in New York," *Baltimore Sun,* May 12, 1931.

13. Henrietta Straus, "Baltimore Symphony—Of, By and For the People," *Baltimore Sunday Sun,* February 10, 1924. An editorial blurb prefacing the article provides information on the controversial *Nation* article.

14. Obituary, Straus, *Baltimore Sun,* May 12, 1931.

15. Henry T. Finck, *My Adventures in the Golden Age of Music* (New York and London: Funk and Wagnalls, 1926), pp. 272, 282.

16. Finck, *Golden Age,* p. 273.

17. Obituary, "Isabel Morse Jones," *Musical America,* October 1951, p. 22.

18. Lengyel, *Anthology of Music Criticism,* p. 465.

19. Claudia Cassidy, "Cross Currents," *Chicago Magazine,* March 1982, p. 129.

20. '82 *Ayers Directory of Publications,* "Total U.S. Dailies," (Bala Cyn Wyd, Pa.: Ayers Press, 1981), p. viii.

21. David Eisen, Research and Information Director, The Newspaper Guild (AFL-CIO, Canadian Labor Council), Washington office, and other sources in the criticism profession.

22. This estimate is based on a combination of sources. Thirty-two percent of MCA's membership as of April, 1983, is female; 30 percent of the Rockefeller Foundation Training Project graduates were female, and estimates by professionals in the field yielded similar percentages.

23. Statistics supplied by Robert Marsh, *Chicago Sun-Times,* a member of the Rockefeller Project's Steering Committee.

24. According to Robert Marsh, even before his former assistant, stringer Valerie Scher, was hired as full-time dance critic for the *Philadelphia Inquirer,* he received a dozen queries from aspiring critics; exactly half of these were women, in line with his previous experience.

14

Creating a College Curriculum for the Study of Women in Music

CAROL NEULS-BATES

The inquiry about the role of women in Western art music has recently come of age. Motivated by a keen desire to reclaim women's past, researchers have rediscovered works by numerous female composers and meanwhile have begun the lengthy process of documenting all phases of women's activities as musicians. That the discipline of women's studies has been slower to develop in the field of music than elsewhere is certainly true, mainly because of the necessary, time-consuming tasks involved in obtaining performances of composers' works—as opposed to reprinting books or collecting paintings for an exhibition. Nonetheless, since the late 1970s, the number of live performances and recordings has been increasing steadily. Other research has produced a small but solid canon of bibliographies, dissertations, books, articles, and reprints of scores.

In short, at the present time there are quite sufficient materials to implement courses about women in music at the undergraduate level, and at a number of institutions such courses have been offered with good success. This chapter has been prepared to encourage the development of many more "women in music" courses. In an effort to break the "reinventing the wheel syndrome," it will outline a detailed curriculum of topics grouped by historical period and then present a selected bibliography and discography.[1] To begin, however, some general comments about the nature of women's experience and methodology in teaching seem in order.

HISTORICAL OVERVIEW AND APPROACH*

Although this statement may be obvious to many readers, I should emphasize at the outset that while women have indeed always made music,

*This section has been adapted from pages xi to xv from *Women in Music* by Carol Neuls-Bates. Copyright © 1982 by Carol Neuls-Bates. Reprinted by permission of Harper & Row, Publishers, Inc.

they have been subject to limitations and prescriptions. Historically they have been encouraged as amateurs but not as professionals. Thus, prior to the rise of conservatories in Europe and the United States in the late eighteenth and nineteenth centuries, professional women musicians stemmed from very few backgrounds only: the convent, the aristocracy, and those families of musicians who nurtured their daughters' talents as well as their sons'. Therefore, a well-advised approach to teaching about women in music is one which takes proper cognizance of all special circumstances whereby women have been able to obtain encouragement and training for a professional career.

Second, an approach to teaching about women musicians of the past should address the limitations society prescribed regarding appropriate activity for females. As singers, women were excluded from the church beginning in the fourth century, and while, to compensate somewhat, they could and did make music in their separate convents, these institutions hardly offered a scope of activities comparable to those available to male musicians in the church at large. Subsequently, when late in the sixteenth century women established themselves as professional singers in the secular mainstream and thereby created a general demand for their high sound, the Catholic Church—in the throes of the Counter Reformation—advanced the castrato.[2]

Castrati, of course, went on to triumph in the new baroque genre of *opera seria*, in which female sopranos were also widely acclaimed. But since women were banned from the stage in parts of Italy and also north of the Alps, castrati sang women's roles too, both in *opera seria* and comic opera.[3] Therefore only with the decline of the castrati late in the eighteenth century did women achieve their rightful place in all opera. Concurrently they were accepted as solo artists in the expanding concert life of the time, but not until the nineteenth century could they generally participate in choruses and church choirs.

As instrumentalists women in the past faced restrictions because of the sexual stereotyping of instruments that began during the Renaissance with the rise of instrumental music. Women were expected to cultivate "feminine" instruments—instruments requiring no alteration in facial expression or physical demeanor. Accordingly, keyboard instruments such as the harpsichord and the piano were deemed especially desirable, all the more because they could be played at home. Other "feminine" instruments included the viol and the lute in the Renaissance and baroque, and the harp and the guitar in the classic and romantic periods. Not all women observed these prescriptions, to be sure, and in unique circumstances such as the famed Venetian conservatories for women in the seventeenth and eighteenth centuries, women played a great variety of instruments. But for women in general, the psychological pressure to conform was considerable. Only with the second half of the nineteenth century did the choice of instrument among women widen significantly, and even today the effects of sexual stereotyping linger.

Like singers, women instrumentalists also experienced limitations in professional opportunities. While they were active among the minstrels in the High and Late Middle Ages and in medieval and Renaissance convents, elsewhere in the church, at courts, or in theater orchestras in the baroque era, employment was not open to them. As concert artists, women keyboard players and violinists found acceptance in the eighteenth century, thereby gaining recognition of female instrumental prowess. Nevertheless, orchestras and other ensembles remained closed, all-male affairs. Later the all-female orchestras and chamber ensembles of the late nineteenth and twentieth centuries proved positive ways in which women players and conductors reacted to their exclusion and found experience and employment by advancing their own institutions.

Turning now to the history of women in composition, it must be remembered that until the nineteenth century the roles of composer and performer were totally intertwined and that therefore the restrictions placed upon women as singers and instrumentalists directly influenced their potential as composers. Women accordingly came to composition through the convent in the Middle Ages and the Renaissance, as secular singers beginning in the second half of the sixteenth century, and as keyboard players and violinists in the seventeenth and eighteenth centuries, respectively. They did compose large works, but not in the same proportion as men—because they did not hold the prestigious positions that offered optimum opportunities for performance as well as crucial on-the-job training. Women were not *maestri di capella* at courts and churches; they did not head opera companies and orchestras. Furthermore, they faced still another barrier in the age-old association of musical creativity with masculinity.

With the proliferation of conservatories in the nineteenth century, the number of women who were able to train for professional careers as musicians increased dramatically, even though initially these women were accepted as students in performance only, not composition. Indeed, it was not until the end of the century, through the efforts of many a pioneer, that theory and composition classes at most institutions were open to females. And as more and more women aspired to careers as composers in the turn of the century period, the so-called "woman composer question" raged.

The "woman composer question" remains with us still—if in a refined state—and aspects of the question apply to performers, educators, and other women in music as well. In concluding this very brief overview of women's experience in the past, I would contend that it is essential that we use history to demonstrate to ourselves and our students the inequities faced by women in music in order that the significance of their achievements in the face of overwhelming odds may be clearly appreciated.

TOPICS FOR THE CURRICULUM

In a certain sense, the topics grouped below by historical period reflect the incomplete state of the art in documenting women's history in Western art music. Significant layers and episodes have been uncovered, but much more research remains to be done before a comprehensive text-book survey can be attempted.[4] Lacking such a survey but wanting to provide my students with reading material, in 1980 I began to compile an anthology of source readings that has since been completed and published in paperback and hardcover by Harper and Row.[5] This collection of selected correspondence, diary entries, autobiographical writings, court records, and other first-hand accounts hardly pretends to trace the entire history of women in music, but it does outline parts of it and charts women's progress. Even when one or more textbook surveys are available, I trust the anthology will remain valuable for the vividness of its personalities. Some of the topics listed below are subjects in the anthology; many more are not.

In the case of the nineteenth and twentieth centuries, where possible topics are more plentiful than earlier periods, some topics could serve as subjects for student projects. I personally have found students extremely eager to do research in this relatively untrodden field. Student and faculty performances of unrecorded works will further enhance the adventure of the course. A "class interview" with a composer currently active on the faculty or elsewhere in the community can provide a fine session or two—especially if she shares tapes of performances of her works and discusses her ideas about music. Alternately, in many states, live performances partially funded through the Meet the Composer Program might be an attractive option. Finally, I should note that at a number of liberal arts institutions courses have been offered which combine the study of women's involvement in both music and art. Many more students have shown an interest in the combined approach than for a course about music alone, and, in regard to the creative experiences of women, there are many parallels between the two fields.

CURRICULUM OUTLINE

Introduction: The "Woman Composer Question," Then and Now

Suggested Reading

Carol Neuls-Bates, *Women in Music: An Anthology of Source Readings from the Middle Ages to the Present,* readings nos. 34-38, nos. 46-47, no. 50.

Complete bibliographic information for the readings suggested in this outline is given in the bibliography section.

Judith Tick, "Why Have There Been No Great Women Composers?"

Judith Rosen and Grace Rubin-Rabson, "Why Haven't Women Become Great Composers?"

Linda Nochlin, "Why Are There No Great Women Artists?"

Middle Ages

Knowledge of women's activity in this period centers on the twelfth through the fourteenth centuries and includes the following subjects:

Women as musicians in convents

Hildegard of Bingen, abbess and composer

The women troubadours

Women musicians among the minstrels

Women as amateur music makers, as depicted in literary sources

Renaissance

Two articles—"Sanctity and Power: The Dual Pursuit of Medieval Women" by JoAnn McNamara and Suzanne F. Wemple, and "Did Women Have a Renaissance?" by Joan Kelly-Gadol—provide background for considering the different status of women in the two periods. Turning then specifically to music, the following topics might be pursued:

The Renaissance lady as amateur musician

The Renaissance lady as patron, for example, Isabella D'Este and Anne de Bretagne

The rise of women as professional singers at Italian courts late in the sixteenth century

Women as composers and performers in Italian convents, beginning late in the sixteenth century, for example, Raffaella Aleotti and Vittoria Aleotti

Baroque

A survey of Baroque era might include:

Francesca Caccini and Barbara Strozzi, singer-composers

Isabella Leonarda, composer and woman religious

Elisabeth-Claude Jacquet de La Guerre, harpsichordist and composer

The Venetian conservatories for women

Faustina Bordoni and Francesca Cuzzoni, prima donnas in Händel's England

Classic

In the Classic period, these topics can be considered:

Maddalena Lombardini-Sirmen and Regina Strinasacchi, two "graduates" of the Venetian conservatories

Composers Anna Amalia, Duchess of Saxe-Weimar, Julie Candeille, Marianne von Martinez, Maria Theresia von Paradis, and Corona Schröter

Music as an accomplishment for the lady amateur

Beethoven's piano sonatas and their connections with contemporary women pianists

1820-1920—Composers

Beginning with the Romantic period, there are many composers to consider. Here, listed alphabetically by country, are primarily those composers whose works are currently available on disc. Please consult the discography for details of each recording.

England: Ethel Smyth

France: Lili Boulanger, Cécile Chaminade, and Louise Farrenc

Germany: Fanny Mendelssohn Hensel, Josephine Lang, Louise Reichardt, and Clara Schumann

Norway: Agathe Backer-Grøndahl

Poland: Maria Szymanowska

United States: Amy Marcy Cheney Beach

1820-1920—Other Topics

Women composers of vernacular music in the United States, including ragtime

Terminating the question about respectability for women as singers

American musicians studying abroad, for example, Amy Fay and Lillian Nordica

The emergence of black performers in the United States after the Civil War

Women as orchestral musicians and conductors in all-female groups

Women as music teachers

Women as patrons in the club movement

1920-1982—Composers

Here the emphasis is on (1) American composers, because of the availability of recordings, and (2) women active to about 1950, since readers will presumably be familiar with contemporary composers.

England: Rebecca Clarke and Ethel Leginska

France: Germaine Tailleferre

Poland: Grażyna Bacewicz

United States: Marion Bauer, Ruth Crawford-Seeger, Mabel Daniels, Elizabeth Gyring, Mary Howe, and Julia Perry

1920-1982—Other Topics

Black women in classical composition, for example, Florence Price, Margaret Bonds, and Julia Perry

Women in jazz, including Mary Lou Williams

Women conductors, including Ethel Leginska and Antonia Brico

Strides made by women as orchestral musicians

Women's music in the labor movement

Marian Anderson and the recent progress by black women singers

Nadia Boulanger as teacher, creator, inspirer

Individual women as patrons, for example, the contribution of Elizabeth Sprague Coolidge

NOTES

1. The session "Teaching the History of Women in Music on the College Level" at the congress on women in music at New York University in March 1981 was offered very much in the same spirit. See Nancy Reich's brief "Report from the First National Congress on Women in Music," *College Music Symposium* 22, no. 1 (Spring 1982): 120-24.

2. Owen Jander, "Singing," *The New Grove Dictionary of Music and Musicians,* ed. Stanley Sadie (London: Macmillan, 1980), vol. 17, pp. 341-42.

3. Thomas Walker, "Castrato," *The New Grove Dictionary of Music and Musicians,* vol. 3, pp. 875-76. The castrato was not accepted in France, and women as solo singers were prized.

4. A series of crucial steps in this direction are taken in the volume of essays edited by Jane Bowers and Judith Tick entitled *Women Making Music: Studies in the History of Women in Music from the Middle Ages to the Present* (Berkeley, Calif.: University of California Press, 1983).

5. *Women in Music: An Anthology of Source Readings from the Middle Ages to the Present* (New York: Harper and Row, 1982).

SELECTED BIBLIOGRAPHY AND DISCOGRAPHY

This selected bibliography lists recently published reference works, general studies and general histories, and finally writings about individual women. The emphasis is on women as composers, and in the third section the concentration has purposefully been on European women, since the literature on Americans has been covered in several recent bibliographies that are listed in the reference section.

Readers will also want to consult articles about individuals in *The New Grove Dictionary of Music and Musicians,* edited by Stanley Sadie (London: Macmillan, 1980) and, when appropriate, *Notable American Women, 1607-1950,* edited by Edward T. James, Janet Wilson James, and Paul S. Boyer (Cambridge, Mass.: Harvard University Press, 1971). The latter has a supplement entitled *The Modern Period,* edited by Barbara Sicherman and Carol Hurd Green (1980).

Regarding scores, extensive coverage of works by American women is provided in *Women in American Music: A Bibliography of Music and Literature,* which I compiled with Adrienne Fried Block. No comparable resource exists to date for compositions by European women. Da Capo Press is publishing a series of reprints of scores—many with new introductions—that at the time of this writing includes works by Agathe Backer-Grøndahl, Amy Beach, Cécile Chaminade, Rebecca Clarke, Louise Farrenc, Fanny Mendelssohn Hensel, Josephine Lang, Mary Carr Moore, Louise Reichardt, and Clara Schumann. From Broude Brothers there is a series entitled "Nine Centuries of Music by Women," edited by Carolyn Raney, C. Ann Clement, and Stewart Carter. To date the series contains choral works by Raffaella Aleotti, Vittoria Aleotti, Francesca Caccini, Elisabeth-Claude Jacquet de La Guerre, Isabella Leonarda, Louise Reichardt, and Barbara Strozzi. Finally, readers shoud be aware that the 1977 edition of *The Norton Scores: An Anthology for Listening,* edited by Roger Kamien, includes the slow movement of Ruth Crawford Seeger's Quartet (1931). The selected discography lists recordings of works of women composers from the past that were available commercially in June 1982.

Bibliographies and Other Reference Works

"Available Recordings of Works by Women Composers," *High Fidelity/Musical America* 23, no. 2 (February 1973): 53.

Block, Adrienne, and Carol Neuls-Bates, comps. *Women in American Music: A Bibliography of Music and Literature.* Westport, Conn.: Greenwood Press, 1979.

Bowers, Jane. "Teaching About the History of Women in Western Music," *Women's Studies Newsletter* 5, no. 3 (Summer 1977): 11-15. Includes discography.

Cohen, Aaron I. *The International Encyclopedia of Women Composers.* New York: R.R. Bowker, 1981.

Hixon, Don. L., and Don Hennessee, comps. *Women in Music: A Biobibliography.* Metuchen, N.J.: Scarecrow Press, 1975.

Mitchell, Charles, comp. *Discography of Works by Women Composers.* Paterson, N.J.: Paterson Free Public Library, 1975.

Pool, Jeannie G. *Women in Music History: A Research Guide.* Ansonia Station, P.O. 436, New York: Author, 1977. Includes discography.

Skowroneki, JoAnn. *Women in American Music: A Bibliography.* Metuchen, N.J.: Scarecrow Press, 1970.

Smith, Julia, comp. *Directory of American Women Composers.* Chicago: National Federation of Music Clubs, 1970.

Stern, Susan. *Women Composers: A Handbook.* Metuchen, N.J.: Scarecrow Press, 1978.

Stewart-Green, Miriam. *Women Composers: A Checklist of Works for the Solo Voice.* Boston: G. K. Hall, 1980.

Williams, Ora. *American Black Women in the Arts and Social Sciences: A Bibliographic Survey.* Rev. ed.; Metuchen, N.J.: Scarecrow Press, 1978.

Women and Folk Song, A Select Bibliography. Washington, D.C.: Archive of Folk Song, Library of Congress, 1978.

Zaimont, Judith Lang, and Karen Famera, comps. and eds. *Contemporary Concert Music by Women: A Directory of the Composers and Their Works.* Westport, Conn.: Greenwood Press, 1981.

General Studies and General Histories

Ammer, Christine. *Unsung: A History of Women in American Music.* Westport, Conn.: Greenwood Press, 1981.

Arnold, Dennis. "Instruments and Instrumental Teaching in the Early Italian Conservatories," *Galpin Society Journal* 18 (1965): 72-81.

————. "Orphans and Ladies: The Venetian Conservatories (1680-1790)," *Proceedings of the Royal Musical Association* 89 (1962-63): 31-48.

Bagnall, Anne D. "Musical Practices in Medieval English Nunneries," Ph.D. diss., Columbia University, 1975.

Borroff, Edith. "Women Composers: Reminiscence and History," *College Music Symposium* 15 (Spring 1975): 26-33.

Bowers, Jane, and Judith Tick, eds. *Women Making Music: Studies in the History of Women in Music from the Middle Ages to the Present.* Berkeley, Calif.: University of California Press, 1983.

Daughtry, Willa E. "A Study of the Negro's Contribution to Nineteenth Century American Concert and Theatrical Life," Ph.D. diss., Syracuse University, 1968.

Driggs, Frank. *Women in Jazz: A Survey.* New York: Stash Records, 1977.

Drinker, Sophie Lewis. *Music and Women: The Story of Women in Their Relation to Music.* Washington, D.C.: Zenger Publications, 1975. A reprint of the 1948 edition.

Elkins-Marlow, Laurine. "Have Women in This Country Written for Full Orchestra?," *Symphony News* 27, no. 2 (April 1976): 15-19.

Elson, Arthur. *Woman's Work in Music.* Portland, Me.: Longwood Press, 1974. A reprint of the 1903 edition.

Elson, Louis Charles. *Woman in Music.* New York: Gordon Press, 1976. A reprint of the 1918 edition.

Heriot, Angus. *The Castrati in Opera.* London: Calder and Royars, 1975. A reprint of the 1956 edition.

Jackson, Irene V. "Black Women and the Afro-American Song Tradition," *Sing-Out!* 25, no. 2 (July-August 1976): 10-13.

Kelly-Gadol, Joan. "Did Women Have a Renaissance?" In *Becoming Visible: Women in European History,* ed. Renate Bridenthal and Claudia Koonz. Boston: Houghton Mifflin, 1979, pp. 137-64.

Le Page, Jane Weiner. *Women Composers, Conductors, and Musicians of the Twentieth Century.* Metuchen, N.J.: Scarecrow Press, 1980.

Lerner, Gerda. "Placing Women in History: Definitions and Challenges," *Feminist Studies* 3, nos. 1-2 (Fall 1975): 5-14.

Loesser, Arthur. *Men, Women, and Pianos: A Social History.* New York: Simon and Schuster, 1954.

McNamara, JoAnn, and Suzanne F. Wemple. "Sanctity and Power: The Dual Pursuit of Medieval Women." In *Becoming Visible: Women in European History,* ed. Renate Bridenthal and Claudia Koonz. Boston: Houghton Mifflin, 1979, pp. 90-118.

Neuls-Bates, Carol. "Sources and Resources for Women's Studies in American Music: A Report," *Notes: The Quarterly Journal of the Music Library Association* 35, no. 2 (December 1978): 269-83.

_____, ed. *The Status of Women in College Music: Preliminary Studies.* Binghamton, New York: College Music Society, 1976.

_____. *Women in Music: An Anthology of Source Readings from the Middle Ages to the Present.* New York: Harper and Row, 1982.

Newcomb, Anthony. *The Madrigal at Ferrara, 1579-1597.* 2 vols. Princeton, N.J.: Princeton University Press, 1979.

Nochlin, Linda. "Why Are There No Great Women Artists?" In *Women in Sexist Society,* ed. Vivian Gornick and Barbara K. Moran. New York: Basic Books, 1971, pp. 480-510.

Oliveros, Pauline. "And Don't Call Them 'Lady' Composers," *New York Times,* September 13, 1970, Section 2, pp. 23, 20. Includes discography.

Pool, Jeannie G. "America's Women Composers," *Music Educators Journal* 65, no. 5 (January 1979): 28-41. This issue includes four other articles about the activity of women.

Power, Eileen. *Medieval Women.* Edited by M. M. Postan. Cambridge, England: Cambridge University Press, 1975.

Quasten, Johannes. "The Liturgical Singing of Women in Christian Antiquity," *Catholic Historical Review* 27, no. 2 (July 1941): 149-65.

"Report of the Nineteenth Annual Meeting. Joint Sessions CMS-AMS II. Women's Studies in Music," *College Music Symposium* 17, no. 1 (Spring 1977): 180-91. Edited by Henry Woodward.

"Report of the Twentieth Annual Meeting. CMS Interest Group Session on Women's Studies," *College Music Symposium* 18, no. 1 (Spring 1978): 219-22. Edited by Barbara English Maris.

"Report of the Twenty-First Annual Meeting, CMS Proceedings. Women's Studies: Organizing Courses about Women in Music," *College Music Symposium* 19, no. 1 (Spring 1979): 268-71. Edited by Barbara English Maris.

Rieger, Eva. *Frau und Musik.* Frankfurt am Main: Fischer Taschenbuch Verlag, 1980.

Riley, Joanne M. "The Influence of Women on Secular Vocal Music in Sixteenth Century Italy." Master's thesis, Wesleyan University, 1980.

Rosen, Judith, and Grace Rubin-Rabson, "Why Haven't Women Become Great Composers?" *High Fidelity/Musical America* 23, no. 2 (February 1973): 46-52. Includes discography.

Rossi, Alice S. "Introduction: Social Roots of the Women's Movement in America." In *The Feminist Papers,* ed. Alice S. Rossi. New York: Bantam Books, 1974, pp. 241-81.

Roxseth, Yvonne. "Les femmes musiciennes du XIIᵉ au XIVᵉ siècle," *Romania* 61 (1935): 464-80.

Shapiro, Marianne. "The Provençal Trobaritz and the Limits of Courtly Love," *Signs* 3, no. 3 (Spring 1978): 560-71.

Tick, Judith. "Towards a History of American Women Composers Before 1870," Ph.D. diss., City University of New York, 1979.

_____. "Why Have There Been No Great Women Composers?," *International Musician* 79, no. 1 (July 1975): 6, 22.

_____. "Women as Professional Musicians in the United States, 1870-1900," *Yearbook for International Music Research* 9 (1975): 95-133.

Van de Vate, Nancy. "The American Woman Composer: Some Sour Notes," *High Fidelity/Musical America* 25, no. 6 (June 1975): 18-20. Includes discography. This issue contains four other articles on women.

"Women in Music," *Heresies* 3, no. 2 (Summer 1980). An entire "women's issue."

"Women of Music," *Music Journal* [New York] 30, no. 1 (January 1972): 9-24, 55, 58-59.

Wood, Elizabeth. "Review Essay: Women in Music," *Signs* 6, no. 2 (Winter 1980): 283-97.

Books, Articles, and Dissertations by and about Individual Women

Barth, Prudentia, et al. *Hildegard von Bingen: Lieder.* Salzburg: Otto Mueller, 1959.

Bates, Carol Henry. "The Instrumental Music of Elisabeth-Claude Jacquet de La Guerre." Ph.D. diss., University of Indiana, 1975.

Bedford, William Charles. "Elizabeth Sprague Coolidge, the Education of a Patron of Chamber Music: The Early Years." Ph.D. diss., University of Missouri, 1964.

Bogin, Meg. *The Women Troubadors.* New York: W. W. Norton, 1980. A reprint of the 1976 edition.

Bonime, Stephen. "Anne de Bretagne (1477-1514) and Music." Ph.D. diss., Bryn Mawr College, 1975.

Borroff, Edith. *An Introduction to Elisabeth-Claude Jacquet de La Guerre.* Brooklyn, New York: Institute of Medieval Music, 1966.

Bradshaw, Susan. "The Music of Elisabeth Lutyens," *Musical Times* 112 (July 1971):653-56.

Carter, Stewart. "The Music of Isabella Leonarda (1620-1704)." Ph.D. diss., Stanford University, 1982.

Chauvin, Marie-José. "Entretien avec Betsy Jolas," *Le Courier Musical de France* 27 (1969): 163-72.

Citron, Marcia J. "Corona Schröter: Singer, Composer, Actress," *Music and Letters* 61, no. 1 (January 1980): 15-27.

_____. "The Lieder of Fanny Mendelssohn Hensel," *Musical Quarterly* LXIX, no. 4 (October 1983).

Dale, Kathleen. "Ethel Smyth's Prentice Works," *Music and Letters* 30, 4 (October 1949): 329-36.

Du Moulin-Eckart, Richard M. F. *Cosima Wagner.* Trans. Catherine Alison Phillips, with an introduction by Ernest Newman. New York: Alfred A. Knopf, 1930.

Elkins-Marlow, Laurine. "Gena Branscombe, American Composer." Ph.D. diss., University of Texas at Austin, 1981.

Ellman, Barat. "Raising the Curtain on All-Women Orchestras." Unpublished paper; Northampton, Mass.: Smith College, Center for Research on Women and Social Change, 1982. A study of the Boston Fadette Lady Orchestra.

Friedland, Bea. *Louise Farrenc, 1804-75: Composer, Performer, Scholar.* Ann Arbor, Mich.: UMI Research Press, 1981.

_____. "Louise Farrenc (1804-75): Composer, Performer, Scholar," *Musical Quarterly* 60, no. 2 (April 1974): 357-74.

Gaume, Mary Mathilda. "Ruth Crawford-Seeger: Her Life and Work." Ph.D. diss., Indiana University, 1973.

Gies, Frances, and Joseph Gies. "An Abbess: Hildegard of Bingen." In *Women in the Middle Ages.* New York: Barnes and Noble, 1980, pp. 63-96.

Grant, Barbara L. "An Interview with the Sybil of the Rhine: Hildegard von Bingen (1098-1179)," *Heresies* 3, no. 2 (1980); 6-10.

_____. "Five Liturgical Songs by Hildegard von Bingen (1098-1179)," *Signs* 5, no. 3 (Spring 1980): 557-67.

Handy, D. Antoinette. "Conversation with Mary Lou Williams. First Lady of the Jazz Keyboard," *Black Perspective in Music* (Fall 1980): 194-214.

Henderson, Robert. "Elisabeth Lutyens," *Musical Times* 104 (August 1963): 51-55.

Hensel, Sebastian. *The Mendelssohn Family (1792-1847).* Trans. Carl Klingemann. 2 vols. New York: Harper Brothers, 1881.

Howe, Ann Whitworth. "Lily Strickland: Her Contribution to American Music in the Early Twentieth Century." Ph.D. diss., Catholic University of America, 1969.

Jackson, Barbara Garvey. "Florence Price (1888-1953)," *Black Perspective in Music* 5, no. 1 (Spring 1977): 30-43.

Jepson, Barbara. "American Women in Conducting," *Feminist Art Journal* 4, no. 4 (Winter 1975-76): 13-18, 45.

_____. "Looking Back: An Interview with Doriot Anthony Dwyer," *Feminist Art Journal* 5, no. 3 (Fall 1976): 21-24.

_____. "Ruth Crawford-Seeger. A Study in Mixed Accents," *Heresies* 3, no. 2 (Summer 1980): 38, 40-43.

Kagen, Susan. "Camilla Urso: A Nineteenth-Century Violinist's Viewpoint," *Signs* 2, no. 3 (Spring 1977): 727-34.

Kerr, Jessica. "Mary Harvey—The Lady Dering," *Music and Letters* 25, no. 1 (January 1944): 23-33.

Kupferberg, Herbert. *The Mendelssohns. Three Generations of Genius.* New York: Scribner's, 1972.

Lerner, Ellen. "Music of Selected Contemporary American Women Composers: A Stylistic Analysis." Master's thesis, University of Massachusetts at Amherst, 1976.

Litzmann, Berthold. *Clara Schumann: An Artist's Life Based on Material Found in Diaries and Letters.* Trans. Grace E. Hadow. 2 vols. London: Macmillan, 1913.

Lutyens, Elisabeth. *A Goldfish Bowl.* London: Cassell, 1972.

Mahler, Alma. *And the Bridge Is Love.* New York: Harcourt, Brace, Jovanovich, 1958.

Merrill, Lindsey. "Mrs. H.H.A. Beach [Amy Marcy Beach]: Her Life and Works." Ph.D. diss., University of Rochester, 1963.

Mitgang, Laura. "One of 'Les Six' Is Still at Work: Tailleferre at 90." *New York Times,* May 23, 1982, Section 2, pp. 25, 28.

Myers, Roland. "Augusta Holmès: A Meteoric Career," *Musical Quarterly* 53, no. 3 (July 1967): 32-35.

Neuls-Bates, Carol. "Five Women Composers, 1587-1875," *Feminist Art Journal* 5, no. 2 (Summer 1976): 32-35.

Pougin, Arthur. "Une charmeuse: Julie Candeille," *Le Menestrel* 49 (1883): 356, 365-66, 372-73, 380-81, 388-89, 403-5, 413-14.

Raney, Carolyn. "Francesca Caccini, Musician to the Medici, and her *Primo libro*." Ph.D. diss., New York University, 1971.

_____. "Francesca Caccini's *Primo libro*," *Music and Letters* 48, no. 4 (October 1967): 350-57.

_____. "Vocal Style in the Works of Francesca Caccini," *Bulletin of the National Association of Teachers of Singing* 23, no. 3 (February 1966): 26-29.

Reich, Nancy B. "Louise Reichardt," *Ars Musica, Ars Scientia: Festschrift Heinrich Hueschen.* Köln: Gitarre & Laute Verlag, 1980, pp. 369-77.

Rosand, Ellen. "Barbara Strozzi, *virtuosissima cantatrice:* The Composer's Voice," *Journal of the American Musicological Society* 31, no. 2 (Summer 1978): 241-81.

Rosenberg, Dena, and Bernard Rosenberg. *The Music Makers.* New York: Columbia University Press, 1979. Includes interviews with Margaret Hillis, conductor; Eileen Farrell and Dorothy Maynor, singers; and Natalie Limonick, operatic coach and music educator.

Rosenstiel, Leonie. *The Life and Works of Lili Boulanger.* Rutherford, N.J.: Farleigh Dickinson University Press, 1978.

_____. *Nadia Boulanger: A Life in Music.* New York: W. W. Norton, 1982.

Roxseth, Yvonne. "Antonia Bembo, Composer to Louis XIV," *Musical Quarterly* 23, no. 2 (April 1937): 147-69.

St. John, Christopher. *Ethel Smyth. A Biography.* With additional chapters by V. Sackville-West and Kathleen Dale. London: Longmans, Green, 1959.

Scott, Marian. "Maddelena Lombardini, Madame Syrman," *Music and Letters* 14, no. 2 (April 1933): 149-63.

Silbert, Doris. "Francesca Caccini, called 'La cecchina'," *Musical Quarterly* 32, no. 1 (January 1946): 50-62.

Smyth, Ethel. *A Final Burning of Boats.* London: Longmans, Green, 1928.

———. *As Time Went On.* London: Longmans, Green, 1936.

———. *Female Pipings in Eden.* London: Peter Davies, 1933.

———. *Impressions That Remained.* New York: Alfred Knopf, 1946.

———. *Streaks of Life.* New York: Alfred A. Knopf, 1922.

———. *What Happened Next.* London: Longmans, Green, 1940.

Sollins, Susan. "Interview with Betsy Jolas," *Feminist Art Journal* 2, no. 3 (Fall 1973): 16-17, 22.

Stookes, Sacha. "Some Eighteenth-Century Women Violinists," *Monthly Musical Record* 84, no. 1 (January 1954): 14-17.

Tuthill, Burnette. "Mrs. H.H.A. Beach [Amy Marcy Beach]," *Musical Quarterly* 26, no. 3 (July 1940): 297-306.

Ullrich, Hermann. "Maria Theresia Paradis (1759-1824) als Musikpädagogin," *Musikerziehung*, 14, no. 1 (September 1960): 9-15.

———. "Maria Theresia Paradis and Mozart." *Music and Letters* 27, no. 4 (October 1946): 224-33.

Wagner, Cosima. *Cosima Wagner's Diaries.* Ed. Martin Gregor-Dillon and Dietrich Mack. Trans. Geoffrey Skelton 2 vols. New York: Harcourt, Brace, Jovanovich, 1978, 1980.

Werner, Jack. "Felix and Fanny Mendelssohn," *Music and Letters* 37, no. 4 (October 1947): 303-37.

Wright, Josephine, and Eileen Southern. "Sissieretta Jones, 1868-1933," *Black Perspective in Music* 4, no. 2 (July 1976): 191-201.

Discography—Collections

The Ragtime Women. Morath, Morath Ragtime Quintet. Contains rags by the following composers: May Aufderheide, Charlotte Blake, K. Craig, Louise V. Gustin, Julia Lee Niebergall, Muriel Pollock, Adeline Shepherd, M. Tilton, and G. Yelvington. Vanguard VSD 79402.

Woman's Work: Works by Famous Women Composers. Bramson, Johns, May, Vieuxtemps String Quartet, Rundle, Cable, Thomas. Includes songs and other vocal selections, piano works, and chamber music by the following composers: Anna Amalia, Duchess of Saxe-Weimar; Anna Amalia, Princess of Prussia; Eldrida André, Lili Boulanger, Ingebord von Bronsart, Francesca Caccini, Cécile Chaminade, Louise Farrenc, Louise Héritte-Viardot, Elisabeth-Claude Jacquet de La Guerre, Josephine Lang, Maria Malibran, Fanny Mendelssohn Hensel, Maria Theresia von Paradis, Poldowski [Irene Wieniawska Paul], Clara Schumann, Germaine Tailleferre, and Pauline Viardot-Garcia. Gemini Hall 1010.

Women In Jazz. I: All Women Groups; II: Pianists; III: Swing Time to Modern. (Each of these volumes contains several recordings, making a complete list of works, composers, performers, and arrangers beyond the scope of this chapter.) Stash ST 111-113.

Discography—Individual Composers and Works

Anna Amalia, Duchess of Saxe-Weimar (1739-1807). *Concerto for 12 Instruments and cembalo obbligato; Divertimento for Piano and Strings.* Marciano, Rapf, Vienna Chamber Orchestra. Turnabout TV 34754.

Bacewicz, Grażyna (1913-1969). *Piano Sonata no. 2.* Fierro. Avant Records 1012.

Backer-Grøndahl, Agathe (1847-1907). Piano Music: *Serenade* in F Major, op. 15, no. 1; *Au bal* in D-flat Major, op. 15, no. 2; *Humoreske* in G Minor, op. 15, no. 3; *Etude de Concert* in A Minor, op. 57, no. 1; *4 Skizzer,* op. 19; *Etudes de Concerts,* op. 11, no. 1 in B-flat Minor, no. 2 in D-flat Major, no. 6 in A Major. Pines. Genesis GS 1024.

Bauer, Marion (1887-1955). *From the New Hampshire Woods,* op. 12, nos. 1-3; *Turbulence,* op. 17, no. 2 for piano. Eskin. Northeastern 204.

Suite, for string orchestra (1955); *Prelude and Fugue* (1948). Adler, Vienna Orchestra. CRI 101 SRD.

Beach, Amy Marcy (1867-1944). *Concerto in C-sharp Minor,* for piano and orchestra, op. 45. Boehm, Landau, Westphalian Symphony Orchestra. Turnabout QTV-S 34665.

Piano Music: *Ballad,* op. 6; *Valse-Caprice,* op. 4; *Trois Morceaux Caractéristiques,* op. 28; *Nocturne,* op. 107; *Prelude and Fugue,* op. 81; *Hermit Thrush at Eve,* op. 92, no. 1; *Hermit Thrush at Morn,* op. 92, no. 2; *Five Improvisations,* op. 148. Eskin. Genesis GS 1054.

Piano Music: *By the Still Waters,* op. 114; *A Humming Bird; From Grandmother's Garden,* op. 97, nos. 1-5. Eskin. Northeastern 204.

String Quartet, op. 89. Crescent Quartet. Leonarda LPI 111.

Piano Quintet in F-sharp Minor, op. 67. Kooper, Rogers, Maximoff, Sherry, Boehm. Turnabout TV-S 34556.

Piano Trio, op. 150. Macalester Trio. 3 Vox SVBX-5112.

Sonata in A Minor for violin and piano, op. 20. Silverstein, Kalish. New World Records 268.

Theme and Variations, for flute and string quartet. Gold, Alard Quartet. Leonarda LPI 105.

Three Browning Songs, op. 44. Heafner, Neill. CRI 462 SD.

Woodwind Quintet: Pastorale. Lawrence, Arrowsmith, Neidich, Vrotney, Tillotson. Musical Heritage Society 3578.

Boulanger, Lili (1893-1918). *Clairières dans le ciel,* for voice (1914). Leonarda LPI 118.

Cortège, for piano. Fierro. Avant Records 1012.

Faust et Hélène (1913); *Pour les funérailles d'un soldat.* Dourian, Mallabrera, Carey, Markevitch, Monte Carlo National Opera Orchestra and Chorus. Varèse/Sarabande 81095.

Nocturne; Cortège, for violin and piano. Roche, Freed. 3 Vox SVBX-5112.

Nocturne; D'un matin de printemps, for flute and piano. Hoover, Eskin. Leonarda LPI 104.

Chaminade, Cécile (1857-1944). *Concerto,* for flute and orchestra, op. 107 Galway, Dutoit, Royal Philharmonic Orchestra. RCA ARL 1-3777. Pellerite, Ebbs, Indiana University Wind Ensemble. Coronet S-1724.

Concertstück, for piano and orchestra. Johnson, Freeman, Royal Philharmonic Orchestra. DBX 2005. Marciano, Rapf, Vienna Chamber Orchestra. Turnabout TV 34754.

Piano music: *Sonata in C Minor,* op. 21; *Serenade,* op. 29; *La Lisonjera; Gavotte,* op. 9, no. 2; *Pierretté,* op. 41; *Valse caprice,* op. 33. Pines. Genesis GS 1024.

Piano Sonata in C Minor, op. 21. Fierro. Pelican 2017.

Piano Trio no. 1 in G Minor, op. 11. Macalester Trio. 3 Vox-SVBX 5112.

Clarke, Rebecca (1886-1979). *Piano Trio.* Ornstein, Kreger, Eskin. Leonarda LPI 103.

Countess of Dia (b. ca. 1140). *A chantar m'er de so qu'ieo non volria.* Telefunken 95673.

Crawford-Seeger, Ruth (1901-53). *Diaphonic Suite no. 1,* for oboe solo. Ostryniec. CRI 423 SD.

Piano Study in Mixed Accents; Nine Preludes, for piano. Bloch. CRI 247 SD.

Preludes, for piano, nos. 6-9; *Piano Study in Mixed Accents.* Eskin. Northeastern 204.

String Quartet (1931). Composers Quartet. Nonesuch 71280. Fine Arts Quartet. Gasparo 205.

Suite, for wind quintet (1952); Lark Quintet. CRI 249 SD.

Three Songs after Carl Sandburg (1933). Morgan, Dunkel, Speculum Musicae. New World NW 285.

Two Movements for Chamber Orchestra (1926). Pittman, Boston Musica Viva. Delos 25405.

Daniels, Mabel (1878-1971). *Deep Forest* (1931). Strickland, Imperial Philharmonic. Orchestra, Tokyo. CRI 145 SRD.

Three Observations, for woodwinds (1943). Roseman, Rabbay, McCord. Desto 7117.

Farrenc, Louise (1804-1875). *Nonetto,* for 9 instruments: flute, oboe, clarinet, bassoon, horn, violin, viola, cello, double bass. Bronx Arts Ensemble. Leonarda LPI 110.

Trio in E Minor, for flute, cello, and piano, op. 45. Hoover, Brey, Weintraub. Leonarda LPI 104.

Grimani, Maria Margherita (fl. 1715-18). *Simphonie.* Gardner, New England Women's Symphony Orchestra. Galaxia 004.

Gyring, Elizabeth (1886-1970). *Piano sonata no. 2.* Andrews. CRI 252 SD.

Hildegard of Bingen (1098-1179). *Kyrie.* Groh, women's voices of the Schola Cantorum. University of Arkansas at Fayetteville. Leonarda LPI 115.

Howe, Mary (1882-1964). *Castellana,* for two pianos and orchestra. Dougherty, Ruzicka, Strickland, Vienna Orchestra. CRI 124.

Spring Pastoral. Strickland, Imperial Philharmonic Orchestra, Tokyo. CRI 145 SRD.

Stars; Sand. Strickland, Vienna Orchestra. CRI 103 SRD.

La Guerre, Elisabeth-Claude Jacquet de (1664-1729). *Suite in D Minor,* for keyboard. Fierro. Avant Records 1012.

Two Cantatas: Samson and *Le sommeil d'Ulisse.* Ostendorf, Somary, Bronx Arts Ensemble Chamber Orchestra. Leonarda LPI 109.

Lang, Josephine (1815-1890). Songs: "Wie, wenn die Sonn' aufgeht"; "Der Winter"; "Frühzeitiger Frühling"; "Wie glänzt so hell dein Auge";

"O sehnest du dich so nach mir." K. Ciesinki, Ostendorf, Palmer. Leonarda LPI 107.

Leginska, Ethel (1886-1970). *Three Victorian Portraits,* for piano. Dowis. Orion 75188.

Leonarda, Isabella (1620-1704). *Missa prima,* op. 18. Groh, Schola Cantorum, University of Arkansas at Fayetteville. Leonarda LPI 115.

Mahler, Alma (1879-1964). Songs: "Licht in der Nacht," "Waldseligkeit," "Ansturm," "Ernstelied." Leonarda LPI 118.

Martinez, Marianne von (1744-1812). *Sonata in A Major* for keyboard. Fierro. Pelican 2017.

Mary. (The only identification is the first name, which was a common practice of amateur women composers of the late eighteenth and early nineteenth centuries.)
Rosebud Quickstep. VOX SVRV 5302.

Mendelssohn Hensel, Fanny (1805-1847). Songs, op. 1: "Schwanlied"; "Wanderlied"; "Warum sind denn die Rosen so blass"; "Mayenlied"; "Morgenständchen"; "Gondolied". Hirst, Yuspeh. Leonarda LPI 112.

Songs. "Die Nonne"; "Im Herbste"; "Du bist die Ruhe"; "Vorwurf"; "Nachtwanderer"; "Rosenkranz". K. Ciesinski, Ostendorf, Palmer. Leonarda LPI 107.

Piano Trio in D Minor, op. 11. Macalester Trio. 3 VOX SVBX-5112. Camerata Canada. Crystal 642.

Parkhurst, Susan (1836-1918). "Father's a Drunkard and Mother Is Dead." Rivers, Cincinnati University Singers. New World Records 267.

Perry, Julia (1927-1979). *Homunculus, C. F.,* for 10 percussionists, Manhattan Percussion Ensemble. CRI 252 SD.

Stabat Mater. Asakura, Strickland, Japan Philharmonic Orchestra. CRI 133 SD.

Short Piece, for orchestra. Strickland, Imperial Philharmonic Orchestra, Tokyo. CRI 145 SRD.

Reichardt, Louise (1779-1826). Songs: "Giusto amor"; "Notturno"; "Vanne felice rio"; "Die Blume der Blumen"; "Hier liegt ein Spielmann begraben"; "Betteley der Vögel"; "Bergmannslied"; "Heimweh"; "Duettino." K. Ciesinski, Ostendorf, Palmer. Leonarda LPI 107.

Schumann, Clara (1819-1896). Piano music: *Prelude and Fugue,* op. 16; *Piece Fugitive,* op. 15, no. 1; *Impromptu; Scherzo* in C Minor, op. 14. Fierro. Pelican 2017.

Piano music: *Variations on a Theme of Robert Schumann,* op. 20; *Two Romances,* op. 21, *Mazurka* in G Major, op. 6. Sykes. Orion 75182.

Marciano (Variations only) Turnabout 34685.

Piano Trio in G Minor, op. 17. Beaux Arts Trio. 2 Phillips 6700 051. Macalester Trio. 3 Vox SVBX-5112.

Songs: "Warum willst du And're fragen"; "Er ist gekommen in Sturm und Regen"; "Liebst du um Schönheit"; "Ich stand in dunkelen Träumen"; "Was weinst du, Blümlein"; "Die stille Lotosblume"; "Das ist ein Tag, der klingen mag". K. Ciesinski, Ostendorf, Palmer. Leonarda LPI 107.

Szymanowska, Maria (1789-1831). Piano music: *Etudes* in F, C, and E Major: *Nocturne* in B-flat Major. Fierro. Avant Records 1012.

Tailleferre, Germaine (1892-1983). *Ballade*, for piano and orchestra. Marciano, Rapf, Vienna Chamber Orchestra. Turnabout TV 34754.

Concertino for harp and orchestra (1927). Gardner, New England Women's Symphony Orchestra. Galaxia 004.

Six chansons françaises. Bogard. Cambridge 2777.

Pastorale, for flute and piano. Hoover, Eskin. Leonarda LPI 104.

Viardot-Garcia, Pauline (1821-1910). Songs: "Des Nachts"; "Das Vöglein"; "Die Beschwörung". K. Ciesinski, Ostendorf, Palmer. Leonarda LPI 107.

15

Women Composers' Songs: An International Selective List, 1098-1980

MIRIAM STEWART-GREEN

INTRODUCTION

The select listing of 414 songs by women that follows is structured as a guide to aid in developing repertoire. It is designed *by* a singer *for* singers and consists largely of songs that are unfamiliar.

The singer's selection of vocal repertoire is a very personal matter. It depends not only on the specific voice that will perform the music and the type of recital being planned, but also on the character of the anticipated audience. This list, therefore, encompasses these considerations. Since I have been a singer for fifty years and have taught voice and repertoire at the Universities of Illinois and Kansas for the past thirty years, I have become aware of the variety and extent of the vocal repertoire overall as well as of audience responses. As a recitalist, I have sung in Mexico and have given European recitals; my performing perspective was enhanced through further experience in opera and oratorio. Actually, it was from my particular interest in subject-oriented recitals in combination with some revealing historical facts that my fourteen-year research on women composers began. The music that I found was so intriguing, and much of it was of sufficiently high quality, that I wished to share it with others. Lecture-recitals, on which I sang eighteen songs by women, were given in this country from coast to coast. The main interest of audiences attending these recitals was different from that which I had experienced with other formats. Always there was an amazement that women had created so much of significance.

The development of a sizable personal library of scores of songs by women (approximately two thousand) created a natural direction for my research to take. Since I was a performer, obtaining scores was my top priority; a nagging curiosity as to the actual sound of the music urged the research on as rapidly as possible. The musical quality found in the scores motivated me relentlessly for fourteen years.

A sequence of publications and projects developed out of my curiosity about this subject. A requested article, "Women: From Silence to Song," appeared in the *American Music Teacher,* October 1974, and was subsequently published by two other journals. Appearances as a lecture-recitalist from coast to coast followed. The National Headquarters for Women's Year in Washington, D.C., then requested an article from me on American women composers entitled "Consider These Creators," which was published in the January 1976 issue of *American Music Teachers Journal.* These publications and performances made it possible for me to appraise the continuing escalation of interest in music written by women.

To avoid overlap in research, the specific area of my work needed to be "staked out." This was accomplished by having information concerning my work circulate through the College Music Society. I consider this a matter of considerable importance, for it was a great help to me and could be to others engaged in other aspects of musical research.

My first published book is the bibliography titled *Women Composers: A Checklist of Works for Solo Voice,* which was published by G. K. Hall of Boston in December 1980. Three thousand seven hundred and forty-six (3,746) composers are listed, and many song titles, with sources for obtaining performance materials, are included. Separate listings are given in this volume to operas, oratorios, cycles, music for voice with instruments, and dramatic scenes.

Performing editions of songs dating from about A.D. 1130 to the present are soon to be available in the four-volume anthology *Art Songs by Women: Across Time.* Each volume will be approximately 125 pages long—two volumes for medium-low and two for medium-high voices. Songs in foreign languages will have singable English translations. (In anticipation of their publication, these collections are included in the select listing as a source, where appropriate.)

All singers have a desire to select for themselves the most distinctive and ingratiating repertoire possible. Since many particularly interesting compositions had surfaced during my research, I determined to select those which I thought to be of greatest interest. These are the 414 songs listed here.

While an examination of this list may stimulate curiosity, it may also activate reflective thought involving the discrimination that women composers have faced through the ages. The reader has surely pondered: When was it that it first occurred to me to ask myself if there were women composers who might have written music of significance? Or, when could they have lived? Or even, if their music had merit, why haven't we heard of it? In recalling the text you used in music history, do you recall any women composers mentioned by the author? Even now, with many available new

Figure 15.1 Miriam Stewart-Green. Watercolor portrait by Robert Berkeley Green

scores and recordings of music by women, conscientious concern for this music is rare. Our culture has inadvertently acclimated us subconsciously to a background of prejudice. Even those women who desire to be most supportive of women composers and their works by performing and researching the music, may well experience numerous bouts with their own consciences versus their educated interest. It is so human to settle for the tried and true. Without doubt still other questions concerning the recognition of women composers must have certainly arisen. Some women composers themselves have done some questioning, and a few of them have established strong personal convictions—both pro and con—concerning the relationship between their gender and their music.

During the period of my research, various women composers have been discovered who resent being grouped under the heading "women composers." Such identification has carried a negative stigma in past years, and certainly the fact that an individual is a woman does not give her music immediate stature. Those who respond negatively to such a grouping wish to establish their reputations solely on the quality of their own music and that *alone*. Elisabeth Lutyens and Kakuko Kanai are among these women. Needless to say, this reaction is the ideal and, when this desire is expressed, it should be honored. Due to music history's oversight, however, the majority of women composers find it important to make it clear to the present generation that women have indeed composed music of excellence. Until women are recognized in history, the public must be alerted to their works.

The following selective list provides ready access to songs across ten centuries and from twenty-five nations. The excellence of the lieder of Fanny Mendelssohn Hensel, Pauline Viardot-Garcia, Clara Schumann, and many others speaks eloquently for women composers of their period. There is a wealth of song literature in the French and Italian schools. Among the French composers particularly worthy of notice are Marguerite Canal, Irene Wieniawska Poldowski, the Boulanger sisters and Germaine Tailleferre. The Italian composers include Ada Jesi, Barbara Guiranna, Giulia Recli, and Emilia Gubitosi. Thea Musgrave is a real leader among composers of the United Kingdom, along with Elizabeth Maconchy and her daughter Nicola LeFanu, Peggy Glanville-Hicks, Madeline Dring, Priaulx Rainier, Jean Coulthard, and Barbara Pentland—each making musical statements of quality. These composers and many others are making contributions throughout the world. Special mention must also be made of one of the leading Hungarian composers, Erzsébet Szönyi.

Significant works by the Americans Margaret Bonds, Esther Ballou, Ludmila Ulehla, Judith Zaimont, Gloria Coates, Miriam Gideon, Emma Lou Diemer, Roslyn Brogue, and Julia Perry are among those adding further distinction to the total sum of works by women. Each composer will be found to speak eloquently of her world using her individual musical language.

RESEARCH PROCESS

When I started my research, library listings of works by women composers were nonexistent. The Library of Congress told me that their formulating a specialized listing of women's works would be "unconstitutional"; however, the Free Library of Philadelphia wrote to thank me for the assistance I gave them in starting their listing of works by women composers. During this period also, one publisher, whom I contacted asking for the names of the women composers whose works were among its publications, wrote saying that to divulge this information would be "irrelevant, unethical, and in all cases illegal." Other publishers were helpful. The general scene has now adjusted somewhat: many libraries nationwide have listings of works by women, and this trend continues to grow.

The first research approach I used was to read through all available music encyclopedias, dictionaries, and references line by line for all bits of information concerning location of scores and data on women composers. (I soon discovered that women are too rarely honored with an entry of their own.) Laborious as this seems, it was the only process that could be used to find information on women and their works. Occasionally, near the end of a man's entry, mention would be made of a wife, daughter, or female family member who composed. Every lead was pursued, and through the exploration of these clues some rewarding information was revealed.

Second, the file cards for scores in many libraries were gone through card by card. Sibley Library in Rochester, New York, was thoroughly scanned, and the Library of Congress, New York Public Library, Österreichische Nationalbibliothek in Vienna, and Bayerische Staatsbibliothek in Munich were among those in which much work was done. (The libraries from which scores were obtained are included on the selected listing, as are the publishers.)

The third step consisted of corresponding with the living composers. An enormous portfolio of correspondence with women composers developed, including letters from composers from the most distant corners of the earth. Correspondence with American composers has been—and continues to be—considerable, for there are a great number of them in this country. Some of these composers shared their music with me, providing a first-hand acquaintance with their works. In addition, I purchased at least three-hundred songs from composers and publishers directly. Publishing houses no longer allow perusal privileges, necessitating "blind purchasing": a practice that swells one's personal library with numerous scores that may be of low quality. On occasion, when scores were not available at retail stores, I queried the publisher directly and discovered that, although a particular work was currently under the publisher's copyright, in fact the publisher had retained no copy of that song even for its personal archives. Such a situation necessitated locating a family member of the composer and requesting his or her assistance—a process that has proven to be surprisingly successful.

Early in the research process, obtaining manuscripts and scores from the many national and international libraries depended on knowing not only the name of the composer, but also the location of the specific scores. The gathering of scores from libraries was the fourth step, and this continues to this day. Usually each song by a woman was not in a collection—rather it appears as a single number. It therefore has been reassuring to find complete volumes of collected songs by composers such as Fanny Mendelssohn Hensel, Ingeborg von Bronsart, Alma Mahler, and Marguerite Canal, indicating the acceptance of their music. Many library scores were also in manuscript, some of which required experts to decipher the outmoded script used for the text. There was also an amazing quantity of uncatalogued music discovered unexpectedly in boxes in several libraries. Some real jewels were found in this way, and other still may be awaiting discovery.

When scores had been gathered and the information concerning the women composers and their works compiled, music from seventy-two countries was represented. The earliest score in my library dates from about A.D. 835 and is by the Byzantine composer Kasia (Cassia). There is also documentation that there was a music school for women in Greece in 600 B.C., so there is considerable history with which to become acquainted. On the select list, the earliest song is by St. Hildegard von Bingen (1098-1179). Her manuscripts consist of neumes placed on four-line staves, which necessitated transcriptions for today's artists. Additional technical preparation was needed for many of the other works. Reductions of orchestral works needed to be made for keyboard, particularly for arias that were from larger works. Similarly, other music from the fifteenth to the nineteenth century, which was available only with melody and figured bass, required realization for keyboard in the appropriate style for each period.

So it was that the creation of transcriptions, realizations, and reductions became the fifth step in this work, and for this I engaged music historians of compositional talent, so that authentic and appropriate realizations could be made available. This process allows twentieth-century musicians to perform works that they might otherwise not be able to read. By this means, also, I was able to consider music from all historical periods.

Perusal of the scores and the process of selection comprised the sixth step. Approximately 4,000 scores were perused, and of these, I sang through nearly 2,000 with an accompanist in order to prepare the 414-song list. There remain many fine and worthy scores that could not be included. Effort was made to choose music of fine quality, represent a broad spectrum of styles, and encompass works from many countries and periods.

PROGRAMMING SUGGESTIONS

It is encouraging to note that today young singers are increasingly apt to pose searching questions concerning women composers; they and their teachers are also much more alert to the need to increase their repertoire in keeping with this growing awareness. Passing their new knowledge along to the audience may be enhanced by using inventive and unique techniques in program building.

Before presenting a few innovative recital format ideas, a word about the concerns that are ever-present in program building. At all times, the three most important points to keep in mind in program building are the musical quality of the songs chosen, the sensitive musical presentation given to them, and the hall in which the concert is to take place. All songs selected for performance should be complementary to the individual voice and based on an emotional mood with which the singer can identify.

Songs by women have proved to be new to both me and my listeners. We are all aware that a new song on a program is seldom heralded previous to its being heard, and audiences often need to have some special interest before making the effort to attend a recital. This brings to mind a unique audience I had when singing a concert in the castle at Montabaur on the Main River in Germany. The public schools there strongly reenforced musical performances, and my recital was no exception. Adults and young people attended. The program selections were known in advance, and I was told that the poetry from which the songs had developed had been studied by the young people, as had the music. It was a superbly responsive audience. Often I noticed my lyrics were being mouthed by members of the audience. This gave the total musical experience a unique vitality. Under these circumstances, performances are particularly fulfilling for the performer as well as for the listener.

A listener can benefit from hearing unfamiliar music several times, and some knowledge of the composer and the historical period from which it comes also makes the music more enjoyable. A plan for a preview of this unfamiliar music might well be considered. Such a "recital prelude" to this literature would doubtless be welcomed by music and study groups. The inclusion of some meaningful, brief information concerning the personality who created the music could add to the human-interest dimension. Without question, these songs, when well sung, increase interest in the music and creative gifts of women.

Many audiences respond favorably on first hearing unfamiliar music when it is programmed in combination with other works that they know. By gathering information in advance concerning the taste of an audience, program choices may be more artfully made, providing an advantage for the singer and for the music's reception. An innovative and highly successful recital program that might be considered when introducing unfamiliar works could utilize a format in which songs to one poem are presented in pairs—one set by a woman, the other by a man. This is an arrangement that stimulates the audience to consider its personal preferences. (See Miriam Stewart-Green, "POEM: F_1 + M_1 + $SONGS_2$," in *National Association of Teachers of Singing Bulletin, February 1976.*)

It is possible that a program could be particularly forceful if two singers, a man and a woman, performed. The decision as to whether the man would sing songs by men and the woman those by women, or vice-versa, would need to be made. Songs based on similar subject matter or with similar titles could be another possibility. Whether it would prove of interest to hear both singers sing together would primarily depend on the perceptible differences of interpretation and vocal timbre.

Lecture-recitals are another possibility. As a result of first-hand experience in giving this sort of presentation throughout the United States, I found that the occasional inclusion of historical highlights aided audiences in placing the music in context and thus increased their appreciation. Program notes might be a satisfactory alternative to this suggestion, should the singer prefer not to speak.

There is another plan that could stimulate audience interest in the lecture-recital. This is based on the reenforcing support of having a man on a program of songs by women, performed by a woman. The structure of the program might consist of works by four or five composers. Each group of songs could be made up of examples of one composer's style, with varied moods included. Before the performance of each group of songs, the biographical background of the composer could be read by the man. By relating facts about her life to generally known historical data concerning the humanities and the political scene, each composer is placed in perspective.

An intriguing additional possibility might be that of a man performing an entire recital of music by women. Most women have sung a majority of songs by men throughout their singing experiences, and it is only proper to turn the tables on occasion. Songs suitable for male singers are individually noted on the select list.

Most programs utilize a chronological format. For many this has become rather dull. Visual demands have been increasing greatly, and these can be met, even on the recital stage. Most audiences are receptive to tastefully presented innovations. For example, through using a few significant items of apparel over a one-color, simple dark dress, a limited transformation in atmosphere and time can be accomplished. Even more subtle mood changes might be created through lighting. Candles, lamps, and single or multicolored spots are among the possibilities. The lighting styles also depend on the periods in which the music was conceived. Through complying with this criteria, artful decisions can be made.

Although all the possible songs for the following program ideas are not

included in the selective song list, there is sufficient material for a program
of songs by the wives of well known composers in combination with works
of their husbands. Consider songs by these composers: Isabella Colbran,
Rossini's wife; Clara Schumann, Schumann's wife; Alma Mahler, Mahler's
wife; and Elsa Sangiocomo-Respighi, Respighi's wife. Another possibility
might be a family recital format of fathers and daughters: Francesca and
Giulio Caccini; Lucile and André Grétry; Margaret Ruthven Lang and her
father, Benjamin Lang; Irene Wieniawska Poldowski and Henryk
Wieniawski.

Another family format might include such family members as the
Boulanger sisters; Elizabeth Maconchy and daughter, Nicola LaFanu;
Fanny Mendelssohn Hensel and brother Felix Mendelssohn; Luise
Reichardt with either her mother or father; and Julia Weissberg with her
father-in-law and mentor, Rimsky-Korsakov.

If ample research was done, the songs of students and their teachers could
also be combined in a revealing recital. The possibilities for intriguing
programming are numerous.

PRACTICAL CONSIDERATIONS

A word about obtaining copies of songs from libraries. When a song on
the select list is desired and there is the indication that it is in a specific
library, write to that library and make your request as complete as is
possible, giving full title (in two languages, if applicable), composer's full
name, and key desired. If it is in a collection or cycle, include that
information. Ask for no more than five to ten scores at one time. State
clearly the type of reproduction desired; microfilm is the least costly. Allow
from three to six months for processing. Depleted staffs in various libraries
make it impossible to honor duplication requests, as is the case at the New
York Public Library. Should the desired score be copyrighted between 1907
and the present, requests for duplication must be accompanied by letters
from the original publisher, current publisher, or individual presently
holding the copyright. Note that these permissions are a matter of form for
most publishers. When writing to request that a publisher send an original
copy of a song, request permission to have a copy duplicated, should the
original music not be available. Such preparation is time-consuming, but
well worth the effort.

Each process in the development of such a project demands much of the
researcher. In this case, I did most of the work. The commonly held notion
that work such as this is funded, either publicly or by a foundation, is not
always so. My work has had three relatively small grants from the
University of Kansas, for which I am grateful. However, personal funds
used far surpassed those of the grants. This research is, therefore, the
university's and my gift to posterity. I mention this primarily because I

believe that the motivation of the investigator in research of this kind must be the prime factor. In viewing the future, it well may be that if such research is accomplished, it will be because of personal dedication to the subject and because of one individual's insatiable "need to know."

SELECTIVE SONG LIST

Composer	Title[a]	Character of Song	Availability[b]	Range[c]	Performance Suitability[d]
Abrams, Harriet (Br).[e] (c1760-1825)	Friend of My Soul, when Far Away (composer)	Charm. Early flavor of Handel via rhythm. Substantial—3 verses. Piano or harp acc.[f]	CHA	$-C/F_2$	B
Alsop, Mrs. Frances (Br.) (?-1821)	The Poor Hindoo (Mrs. Opie)	Colonial Am. charm. Excels as a ballade of this period; 2 stanzas.	GW/	$-C/C_2$	B

[a]The parenthetical information following each title notes the overall song cycle from which it comes and the author of the original text.

[b]An explanation of the Publisher/Library abbreviations follows this list.

[c]Range is expressed from low to high. $-C$ = middle C. If a note is below middle C, a line will appear above the letter. (For example, the C below middle C is $\overline{C}$.) If a note is above middle C, numerals will indicate the distance above middle C, with subscript 1 used to refer to all notes in the first octave above middle C. (For example, the first A above middle C is A_1, the C one octave above middle C is C_1, and the A above that is A_2.) Accidentals are expressed as plus or minus signs following the name of the pitch. (For example, $E-$ is E-flat; $F+$ is F-sharp.)

[d]W = woman; M = man; B = both.

[e]An explanation of the abbreviated countries of origin follows this list.

[f]Tessitura will be abbreviated "tess." throughout the list. Accompaniment will be abbreviated "acc." throughout the list.

[g]Unpublished works which are available from the composer are indicated by "Comp." in the Availability column. To contact these composers, refer to the Addresses of Composers list at the end of this chapter.

[h]MS refers to an unpublished manuscript that is available at the indicated library.

Composer	Title[a]	Character of Song	Availability[b]	Range[c]	Performance Suitability[d]
Alter, Martha (AM) (1924-1976)	The Forgiveness #21 (no. 5 from Prayers of Kierkegaard)	With passion. A strong yet brief plan for forgiveness; meaningful.	Comp.[g]	$-C/F+_2$	B
Anna Amalia Von (G.) Weimar (1739-1807)	Ein Veilchen (Goethe) (no. 8 from Erwin und Elmire—singspiel; in coll.: Art Songs by Women: Across Time)	Text's first setting. Charming undulating melodic and strophic song. Light in texture. Composed 10 years before Schubert's.	SIE	$F+_1/G_2$	B
Anna Amalia Von Weimar	Erwin's Aria/Zweiter Aufzug (from Erwin und Elmire) (Goethe)	Lento. Two stanzas with some variation. An easy pleasantness. High tess.[f]	SIE	E_1/G_2	M
Archer, Violet (Can.) (1913-)	Flying Geese (no. 3 from cycle Under the Sun) (Bounnot)	Descriptive text. Music of vast expanse. Focuses on birds's flight. Musically satisfying. (3 min.)	CMC	$-C+/B_2$	B
Archer, Violet	Miserere et Jubilate (#II from 3 Biblical Songs)	Opening recit. Enthusiastic exultation. Healing takes place. Rather long, reaffirmation of joy.	CMC	$D_1/G+_2$	B
Archer, Violet	Train at Night (no. 1 from cycle Under the Sun) (Bounnot)	Excellent harmonic colors and textures. Train whistles, etc. Fascinating.	CMC	$-C/F_2$	B

Composer	Title	Description	Source	Range	
Assandra, Caterina (It.) (c1550-c1622)	Jubilate Deo (in collection Art Songs by Women: Across Time)	Homophonic structure. Ornamental phrases compose themes. Imaginative for early 1600s.	MS in author's library[h]	$-C/F_2$	B
Aubigny Von Engel-Brunner, Miss Nina d' (G.) (1777-?)	Weep No More (composer)	Charm. Holds promising potential. Tasteful and honest. Grateful vocal line.	VOL	$\overline{G}/G_2$	B
Bach, Maria (Au.) (1896-)	Maria auf dem Berge (from 6 Marien Lieder) (traditional)	Simple means of peaceful expression in late romantic style. Tenderness toward Joseph & forthcoming son essence. Individual idiom.	AT	D_1/G_2	W
Bach, Maria	Joseph (from 6 Marien Lieder) (traditional)	Old German Texts. The dedication and loving consideration of Joseph radiates as the lyrics of the traditional song "Joseph oh dear Joseph mine" are incorporated. The harmonic insight provides individual charm.	AT	D_1/G_2	W
Bachmann, Charlotte Karoline Wilhelmine (G.) 1757-1817	Mädchen, wenn dein Lächeln winket (composer)	Flirtation. Expressed with gentle touch. Interesting	in UMG	$-C+/F_2$	M

Composer	Title[a]	Character of Song	Availability[b]	Range[c]	Performance Suitability[d]
	(in coll.: Art Songs by Women: Across Time)	twist in final phrase. Two verses.			
Backer-Grøndahl, Agathe (Nor.) (1847-1907)	Now Sleeps the Wave (in collections Scandinavian Composers, I) (Topelius)	Sea moods tumultuous. Man hears and responds to God's message. Strong reinforcing—3 pgs.	DIT	D_1/F_2	B
Backer-Grøndahl, Agathe	Spinnen, lass uns spinnen (Op. 50/4, from cycle: Sommer) (Jynje)	Animated expansion of constant activity. Melodic exuberance. The acc. continues spinning motif. Vocally grateful.	NRS	E_1/A_2	W
Badarzewska-Baranowska, Thekla (Pol.) (1834-1861)	The Maiden's Prayer (John S. Adams)	Melodic flow, pleasant. Early in style. Lead way for ballads of late 1800's.	B&B	$-C+/F+_2$	B
Ballou, Esther Williamson (Am.) (1915-1975)	The Christening (from Five Songs) (Peck)	Consonant harmonies may be found surrounded by gentle dissonances radiating the uncertainty of the 1835 Kentucky text. Carried within an Atonal scheme, this is particularly appealing. Moving.	ACA	$-C/G_2$	B

Ballou, Esther Williamson	Wild Geese (from Five Songs; in coll.: Art Songs by Women: Across Time) (Elizabeth Peck)	Captures the challenging excitement of these birds. Musical timings allow for the dimension of listening to outbursts of pleading and all combine in an integrated whole of surging emotion. Atonal and tonal. For dramatic high voice.	ACA	E_1/B_2	B
Barkin, Elaine (Am.) (1932-)	Strings in the Air (from Chamber Music) (J. Joyce)	Fresh, delightful settings with an individual idiom.	Comp.	$-C/A_2$	B
Barraine, Elsa (Fr.) (1910-)	La Lumière (composer)	Stunning and slow as it moves. Atmosphere permeates. Impressionistic. Chromaticisms tasteful.	EN	D_{+_1}/G_2	B
Bauer, Marion (Am.) (1887-1955)	The Red Man's Requiem (Emilie Frances Bauer)	Mysterious. A real tribute to Indian chief. An openness in structure with a drum beat background.	SUM	$\bar{A}/F_{+_2}$	B
Beach, Mrs. H.H.A. (Am.) (Amy Cheney) (1867-1944)	Benedictus (from Mass in E − ; in coll.: Art Songs by Women: Across Time) (Biblical-traditional)	Commanding aria and an excellent vehicle stylistically and vocally.	SUM	$\bar{G}/D_{-_2}$	M

Composer	Title[a]	Character of Song	Availability[b]	Range[c]	Performance Suitability[d]
Beach, Mrs. H.H.A.	Chanson d'amour (Victor Hugo)	Fr. text from Am. perspective. Warm, outgoing. Very vocal, dramatic.	SUM	$E-_1/B-_2$	B
Beach, Mrs. H.H.A.	Et incarnatus (from Mass in E−; in coll.: Art Songs by Women: Across Time) (Biblical)	Soprano solo. Stylistically substantial. Traditional approach. Holds individuality. Fine vocal vehicle.	SUM in MKC	$D_1/A-_2$	W
Beach, Mrs. H.H.A.	Gratias Agimus (from Mass in E−) (Biblical)	Alto solo; lento. Modulations of interest which mesmerize. An aria of substance. Excellent for voice.	SUM in MKC	E/F_2	W
Beach, Mrs. H.H.A.	Ich sagte nicht (Eduard Wissmann)	Very good, heartfelt music. Sincerity. Lieder style.	SUM	D/F_2	B
Beach, Mrs. H.H.A.	My Love Is Like a Red Red Rose (Burns) (no. 13 from Song Album)	Allegretto expressive. Develops effectively with key changes. Tantalizing unexpected melodic turns. Not strophic. High tess.	SUM	$D-_1/A-_2$	B

Composer	Title	Comments	Source	Range	Voice
Beach, Mrs. H.H.A.	Night Song at Amalfi (in coll.: Art Songs by Women: Across Time) (Teasdale)	Barcarole. Substantial. Extended melodic intervals. Grateful. Requires strong upper mid-voice.	GS in MKC	$D_1/G+_2$	B
Beach, Mrs. H.H.A.	O Mistress Mine (in coll.: Art Songs by Women: Across Time) (Shakespeare)	Allegretto grazioso. Sprightly, mischievous. Lilting melodic line.	SUM in MKC	$F+_1/A_2$	M
Beach, Mrs. H.H.A.	Dark Is the Night (William Ernest Henley)	Allows for vocal beauty. Spacing of phrases and text reinforces harmonic patterns and colors.	SUM	E_1/B_2	B
Beatritz de Dia, Countess (Fr.) (c1160-1212 or 1214)	A chantar m'er so qu'en no volria (in coll.: Der Musikalische Nachlass der Troubadours) (composer)	Composed "winileodos." Passion poetry. Poem's intricate—uncomplicated music.	DAL	$-C/C_1$	W
Bembo, Antonia (It.-Fr.) (1643-1715)	Mormorate (from opera L'Ercole Amante; in coll.: Art Songs for Women: Across Time)	Dynamic and demanding. Melodic line with rhythmic interest. Long phrases. Strong. Outstanding for period.	in BN	$E_1/A-_2$	W
Blanche de Castile (Fr.) (1188-1252)	A l'entrada del tens clar (composer)	Opening repeats with imaginative and interesting developments.	DAL	$\bar{B}/D_2$	B

Composer	Title[a]	Character of Song	Availability[b]	Range[c]	Performance Suitability[d]
Blomfield-Holt, Patricia (Can.) (1910-)	Quiet (composer)	Good vocal vehicle. Requires sensitivity to express its particular charm. Not difficult.	HARF	$E_1/F+_2$	B
Bolz, Harriett (Am.) (1912-)	Winds of the Waters (from Winds) (Goethe/E.R. Martin)	Strong declamation combined with a sustained midsection. Closes strongly. Very active acc. surge.	Comp.	$\overline{B}/G_2$	B
Bonds, Margaret (Am.) (1913-1972)	Dream Variation (from Three Dream Portraits) (Langston Hughes)	Forward easy movement. Dance facility integrates melody and harmonies with rhythm. Tender Southern charm.	RIC	$\overline{B}/G-_2$	B
Borroff, Edith (Am.) (1925-)	From a Daughter to a Mother (Marie Borroff)	Holds unusual interest. Traditional harmonies take on new quality here. Chromaticism.	Comp.	D_1/E_2	W
Borroff, Edith	"The Winter It Is Past" (Burns)	Charm in its near folk-flavor. Tantalizing. Flows. In A minor.	Comp.	E_1/E_2	B
Bosmans, Henrietta (Du.) (1895-1952)	La Comtesse Esmérée (Jean Moréas)	Narrative. Strength throughout exemplified	DON	$-C/G+_2$	B

Bosmans, Henrietta		by lover's determination to marry king's daughter. Intriguing.		
	Les Médisants (from Melodies, #10) (M. Desaugiers)	Allegro. Gossipers—very clever, bright. Considerable charm. Rapid motion—wordy.	PTR	E_1/F_2	B
Boulanger, Lili (Fr.) (1893-1918)	Dans l'immense tristesse (Galeron de Calone)	Anticipating eternal sleep—with resignation and trust, as an elegy—with stark, overcast atmosphere. A permeating essence of wisdom in this late work.	RCFR	$\overline{B}/C_1$	B
Boulanger, Lili	Les lilas qui avaient fleuri (in coll.: Clairières dans le ciel) (Francis Jammes)	A knowing yet saddened realization is the culmination of this sensitive impressionistic song, built as though viewed from above.	DUR	$-C/A-_2$	B
Boulanger, Lili	Nous nous aimerons tant (from coll.: Clairières dans le ciel; in coll.: Art Songs by Women: Across Time) (Francis Jammes)	Lento. Harmonic subtleties and understatements. Earnest and loving in the constancy expressed. Exquisite control a must.	DUR	$\overline{A}/D_2$	B

Composer	Title[a]	Character of Song	Availability[b]	Range[c]	Performance Suitability[d]
Boulanger, Lili	Un poète disait (from coll.: Clairières dans le ciel) (Francis Jammes)	Ecstatic with poetic thought, breathlessly overflowing. Suspension felt in tonal colors. Rather high tess.	DUR	E_1/A_2	B
Boulanger, Lili	Le Retour (Delaquys)	Optimistic commentary on Ulysses composed one year before she won the Prix de Rome. Vital and positive.	RCFR in ROCH	$\overline{B}+/D+_2$	B
Boulanger, Nadia (Fr.) (1887-1979)	Chanson (Delaquys) (in coll.: Art Songs by Women: Across Time)	Buoyant and gay. Two stanzas. Delightful melody.	HAM	E_1/G_2	B
Boulanger, Nadia	Larme Solitaire (Delines)	With resignation, this song of dynamic demands proceeds in a nearly Germanic style. Begins with understatement, develops to unexpected ending.	HAM	$E-/A-_2$	B
Boulanger, Nadia	Prière (Bataille)	Very high tess. A voice which spins and floats and is of flute-like quality is ideal. Rich harmonic	HAM	E_1/A_2	B

foundation. Free melodic form. Comprehension of the meaningful essence of the text seems to assume a superimposed position by means of the structure.

Boulanger, Nadia	Soleils couchants (in coll.: Art Songs by Women: Across Time) (Verlaine)	Rocking rhythm. Delicate. Light acc. Vocally grateful. Pensive, melancholy. Charm.	HAM	$-\text{C}/\text{G}_{-2}$	B
Boulanger, Nadia	Versailles (Samain)	Insistent rhythm. Includes gentle harmonic gradations of color. Song bridges into impressionism.	HAM	D_1/G_2	B
Branscombe, Gena (Am.) (1881-1977)	Old Woman Rain (in coll.: Contemporary American Songs) (Louise Driscoll)	Tasteful acc. Melody and text mesh. Slosh of water in shoes indicated. Good program song. Midrange tess.	SUM	E_1/G_2	B
Branscombe, Gena	With Rue My Heart Is Laden (in coll.: Art Songs by Women: Across Time) (A.E. Housman)	Fine for voice. Effectively structured with limited means. Brief.	GS	$\overline{3}-/\text{C}_1$	B
Bringuer, Estela (Ar.) (1931-)	Ecos de Tupac (composer)	Strophic-tonal. Rhythmic patterns of prime importance. Individual flavor of whimsy, surprise. Particularly winsome.	RICS	E_1/A_2	B

Composer	Title[a]	Character of Song	Availability[b]	Range[c]	Performance Suitability[d]
Bringuer, Estela	Sueño de Luna (composer)	A somewhat carefree melody with long positive upward leaps. Furtive melody and rhythmic style. Not difficult. High tess.	RICS	$E_1/A-_2$	B
Britain, Radie (Am.) (1903-)	Overtones (Wm. Alexander Percy)	Delightful. Mid-range. Flute acc. interweaves with voice.	Comp.	$E_1/E-_2$	B
Britain, Radie	The Earth Does Not Wish for Beauty (Lester Luther)	Recit. in style. Powerful, careful interpretation needed. Vacillates between singing and speech. Tempo varies. Commanding.	Comp.	$\bar{B}/E_2$	B
Brogue, Roslyn (Am.) (1919-1981)	Ayre: Fain Would I Change That Note (Hume) (from Four Elegies)	Real substance. Sensitive to text's flavor within individual contemporary idiom. Terse, penetrating. Excellect opener for a group.	Comp.	$-C/A-_2$	B
Brogue, Roslyn	As By Water (Merwin) (from Four Elegies)	Minimal means. Poignantly effective. Honest forward thrust. Depicts emotional emptiness.	Comp.	$-C/F+_2$	B

continued

Composer	Title	Comments	Publisher	Range	Voice
		Verbal essence mirrored in music. Contemporary approach.			
Brogue, Roslyn	Ode (Whitman) (from: Song of Exploration)	Sparse. Very powerful—as if one soul is searching out its eternity in endless space.	Comp.	$-C+/G-_2$	B
Brogue, Roslyn	Pastorale (Slobodkin) (no. 3 from Five Songs of Courtly Love)	Interesting rural chant. Especially colorful intervals. Imaginative.	Comp.	$-C+/G_2$	W
Brogue, Roslyn	Serenade (Slobodkin) (no. 4 from Five Songs of Courtly Love)	Vocally good vehicle. Verges on the atonal. Thoughtful. Appreciative charm.	Comp.	$-C+/G+_2$	B
Brogue, Roslyn	A Valediction: Of Weeping (Donne)	Substantial in depth, duration, concept and harmonic understatement. Emotionally urgent. Demanding musically.	Comp.	$-C+/B-_2$	B
Bronsart, Ingeborg (G.) (1840-1913)	Heidenröslein (Goethe) (Op. 25; no. 2 from Drei Lieder)	Personalized idiom delightfully applied to strophic form comparing favorably with other settings of this Goethe poem.	BH in BAY	E_4/F_2	B
Bronsart, Ingeborg	Ich stand in dunkeln Träumen (Heine) (Op. 25; no. 3 from Drei Lieder)	Ultimate despair mingled with substantial musical style. Demands particular interpretive care in the lieder tradition.	BH in BAY	$-C/F_2$	B

Composer	Title[a]	Character of Song	Availability[b]	Range[c]	Performance Suitability[d]
Butler, Lois (Am.) (1912-)	Sellers of Markers (Composer)	Vital rhythmic insistence in button counting style. Interesting, brief. Pace-changer.	CK	E_1/D_2	B
Caccini, Francesca (It.) (1587-c1630)	Aria Sopran la Romanesca (from Primo Libro, "Nube gentil") (composer)	Substantial quality. Brief melodic statement. Good.	in USC	G_1/D_2	B
Caccini, Francesca	Alcina's aria: Deh se non hai pieta (from La Liberazione di Ruggiero dall Isola d'Alcina—opera) (Saracinelli)	Expansive verve. Tautness required. Insistent plea.	in KUM	E_1/E_2	W
Caccini, Francesca	Melissa's aria: Cosi, perfida Alcina (from La Liberazione di Ruggiero dall Isola d'Alcina) (Saracinelli)	Intense interpretation necessary. Limited range and emotional content. Restrained aria.	in KUM	$-C/A_1$	W
Caccini, Francesca	Nunzia's aria: Non so qual sia maggiore (from La Liberazione di Ruggiero dall Isola d'Alcina) (Saracinelli)	In formula-like form. Rhythmic interest with dramatic intensity. Texture variation. Frequent trills.	in KUM	F_1/D_2	W

Caccini, Francesca	Pastore's aria: Per la piu vaga (from La Liberazione di Ruggiero dall Isola d'Alcina) (Saracinelli)	Very expressive. Variations of rhythmic motion. Good dynamic contrasts and melodic interest.	in KUM	G_1/F_2	M
Caccini, Francesca	Sirena's aria: Chi desia di vago (from La Liberazione di Ruggiero dall Isola d'Alcina) (Saracinelli)	Much movement. Runs of some complexity with trills, all in style of period.	in KUM	D_1/F_2	W
Caldwell, Mary (Am.) (1909-)	In the Bleak Midwinter (Christmas) (Christina Rossetti)	Delightful bleakness in a minor key. Poignant.	PRE	D_1/E_2	B
Canal, Marguerite (Fr.) (1890-1978)	Bien loin d'ici (from cycle Sept Poème de Chas. Baudelaire)	Particular rhythmic interest. Quick notes, tart phrases, lend to fine balance. Winsome. Midrange.	LEM	E/E_2	B
Canal, Marguerite	J'ai rêvé d'un jardin primitif (Samain) (from cycle Au Jardin de Infante; in coll.: Art Songs by Women: Across Time)	Elegant. Depth in impressionistic style. True command of medium. Awe-inspiring scenes depicted.	JAM	$\overline{D}/G_1$	B
Canal, Marguerite	Narcisses (trad. Chinese) (from cycle La Flute de Jade)	Harmonies/rhythms plus understatements utilize musical colors. Whole cycle is stunning.	JAM	$\overline{E}-/G-_1$	B

Composer	Title[a]	Character of Song	Availability[b]	Range[c]	Performance Suitability[d]
Canal, Marguerite	Recuellement (from cycle Sept Poèmes de Chas. Baudelaire)	Alert rhythmic motion. Paces change. Opens lento. Distinct charm.	LEM	$E-_1/F_2$	B
Chaminade, Cécile (Fr.) (1857-1944)	Si J'étais Jardinier (Were I a Gardener) (R. Miles)	Fresh. Buoyant light song. Traditional harmonies.	GS	$E-/A-_2$	W
Chaminade, Cécile	Vous souvient-il (Marguerite Dreyfus)	Appealing melodic statement in two stanzas. Text effective when understated.	HAM	G_1/F_2	W
Clarke, Rebecca (Br.) (1886-1979)	Shy One (Yeats) (in coll.: Art Songs by Women: Across Time)	Hushed lyric line. All parts of music adjust to text.	WIN	$-C/A-_2$	M
Clarke, Rebecca	The Cherry-Blossom Wand (Anne Wickham) (in coll.: Art Songs by Women: Across Time)	Spring-like essence Melodic line sparsely reinforced by delicate accompaniment. Exudes delight in beauty.	OX	$-C+/G_2$	W
Coates, Gloria (Am.) (1938-)	They Dropped Like Flakes (Dickinson) (no. 5 from Emily Dickinson Songs)	Full chordal structure thoughtfully marks every beat with solemnity. Words with descriptive	AMC	D_1/A_2	B

meaningfulness deliber-
ately stretch over several
notes, adding intensity
and emotional depth.
Sensitive strength.

Name	Title	Description	Location	Range	
Colbran, Isabelle (Sp.) (1785-1845)	Vanne al mio sene (from: Petits Airs Italiens) (composer)	Largo. Effective. Period compositional patterns used. Gracious.	in NYP	$D+_1/A_2$	W
Colbran, Isabelle	Voi siete (composer) (from Petits Airs Italiens; in coll.: Art Songs by Women: Across Time)	Pretentious development melodically. Aids vocal display. (Figuration limited in intricacy.)	in NYP	$E-_1/A_2$	W
Coolidge, Elizabeth Sprague (Am.) (1864-1953)	Laughing Song (Blake)	Simple spaced naivete. Text carries melodic line. Simple accompaniment.	MS in LoC	$D_1/F+_2$	B
Corbin, Germaine (Fr.) (c 20th cent.)	Chanson Roumaine (no. 2 from Six Melodies) (Vacaresco)	Interesting. Dynamic key changes, pace and emo- tion. Impressionistic.	GRU in ROCH	$\overline{B}/A_2$	B
Corbin, Germaine	Nuit d'Été (no. 6 from Six Melodies) (Helene Vacaresco)	Unfolds colorful harmo- nies which move artfully. Sensitive interpreter needed.	GRU	$-C+/A_2$	B
Coulthard, Jean (Can.) (1908-)	Ecstasy (D. C. Scott)	Music of ascension. High tess. Demands good musi- cian. Rewarding vehicle with effective final climax.	MS in CMC	$F_1/G-_2$	W

Composer	Title[a]	Character of Song	Availability[b]	Range[c]	Performance Suitability[d]
Coulthard, Jean	Frolic (A.E.) (no. 2 from Five Irish Poems for Maureen)	Delightful. Fancy of children. Enveloped in a harmonic lightness, glowing atmosphere. Acc. reinforces.	MS in CMC	$\overline{A}/F+_2$	B
Coulthard, Jean	Rain Has Fallen (Joyce)	So right! Sincere mixture of musical and vocal. Highly satisfying and honest.	MS in CMC	F_1/G_2	B
Coulthard, Jean	Song for Fine Weather (C. Skinner)	Dramatic and modern, use of Indian flavor—emphasized in accompaniment	MS in CMC	E_1/A_2	B
Coulthard, Jean	Strings in the Earth & Air (Joyce) (from Three Songs)	Environmental and tenuous, near breathlessness. A sense of one's inner self. Phrases spaced with lifts. Very winning.	MS in CMC	$E-_1/F+_2$	B
Crews, Lucile (Am.) (1888-)	I Shall Not Care (Teasdale)	Slow, strange text. Two stanzas. Ballad with pathos. Sentimental. Interesting.	FL in ROCH	$\overline{B}/D_2$	W
Daniels, Mabel Wheeler (Am.) (1878-1971)	The Desolate City (Op. 21) (Blunt)	Authoritative dramatic scene. Varied moods. Well written. Challenging.	SUM	$-C/F+_2$	M

Composer	Title	Comments	Pub.	Range	
Daniels, Mabel Wheeler	When Shepherds Come Wooing (composer) (in coll.: Art Songs by Women: Across Time)	Lighthearted. Bright. Pleasant.	SUM	D_1/B_2	B
Davis, Katherine K. (Am.) (1892-1980)	I Have a Fawn (Thos. Moore)	Alluring. Quiet appreciation of nature while melody bespeaks its mystery.	GAL	D_1/E_2	B
Davis, Katherine K.	Nancy Hanks (Rosemary Benet)	Substantial folk setting of four stanzas with varying acc. Dramatic impact.	GAL	D_1/G_2	B
Deering, Lady (Br.) (1629-1704)	A False Designe to Be Cruel (Richard Deering) (in Book I—Henry Lawes: Treasury of Musick and Ayres & Dialogues, 1657; in coll.: Art Songs by Women: Across Time)	Four stanzas. (In three 5-measure phrases.) Unique structure. Minor key alerts caution. Fine vocal vehicle.	PLA	E_1/F_2	B
Demarquez, Suzanne (Fr.) (1899-1965)	L'Insecte d'Or (Belvianes)	Delicious impressionistic insect portrait ("a-tempo" a must).	ESC in LoC	$D_1/F+_2$	B
Diemer, Emma Lou (Am.) (1927-)	How Instant Joy (Warren) (no. 9 from A Miscellany of Love Songs)	Spirited. Exuberant. Text shocks. High tess. Ease in F_2's and wide leaps needed.	SMP	E_1/A_2	B

Composer	Title[a]	Character of Song	Availability[b]	Range[c]	Performance Suitability[d]
Diemer, Emma Lou	To the Great Self (Hindu) (no. 2 from Three Mystic Songs)	Interesting text. Musically substantial. Difficult intervalically. Far spaced acc.	SMP	$-C+/G_2$	W
Dring, Madeleine (Br.-Am.) (1923-1977)	Blow, Blow, Thou Winter Wind (no. 3 from Three Shakespeare Songs)	Vivo con brio. Insistent rhythmic pattern. Crisp close. Fresh approach to text in contemporary idiom.	LENG	$D-_1/F_2$	B
Dring, Madeleine	Come Away Death (no. 2 from Three Shakespeare Songs)	Hushed. Special mood quality achieved in setting.	LENG	D_1/E_2	B
Dvorkin, Judith (Am.) (1930-)	Song of the Flowers (composer)	Delightful freshness of music interwoven with lyric. Effective musical means.	Comp.	$F_1/G+_2$	W
Dychko, Lesia Vasil'evna (Rus.) (1934-)	Memory (no. 2 from Collected Songs) (Parlychko)	Effective ascending phrases build dynamic interest. Low tess. in mid-section. Late romantic; substantial as song and in length.	MY-K	$\overline{A}/A_2$	B

Composer	Title	Description	Source	Range	W/B
Edwards, Clara (Am.) (1887-1974)	The Little Shepherd's Song (13th century)	Pleasant, youthful text. Setting flows with graciousness.	BMS	D_1/G_{-2}	W
Eggleston, Anne (Can.) (1934-)	Daybreak at Deepwood (no. 1 from Songs from Deepwood) (Bourinot)	The final burst of light is in marked contrast with the gentle opening statements. Harmonic tonalities give color contrasts. Substantial range.	MS in CMC	$-C+/A_2$	B
Eggleston, Anne	To the Lute Player (Lampman)	Ingratiating. Seeking for life's mysteries. Harmony and melody reinforce mood. Good vehicle for voice.	MS in CMC	$D_1/F+_2$	B
Escot, Pozzi (Pe.-Am.) (1931-)	A Man Saw a Ball of Gold (Stephan Crane) (from Songs of Wisdom)	Independent vocal line. Atonal. Excellent inter-valic ability needed. Naive charm. Fine compositionally.	Comp.	D_1/A_2	B
Evanti, Lillian (Am.) (?-1920)	23rd Psalm (biblical)	Good vocal vehicle. Dramatic. Traditional harmonic structure.	HA	D_1/A_{-2}	B
Flood, Dora Flick (Am.) (c1895-)	The Windows of Sainte Chapelle (Mabel MacDonald Carver)	Substantial concept. Colors evident from text and music. Requires good interpretation.	RINY	E_1/G_2	B

Composer	Title[a]	Availability[b]	Character of Song	Range[c]	Performance Suitability[d]
Fontyn, Jacqueline (Be.) (1930-)	Dedens mon livre de pensie (from Deux Rondels de Chas. d'Orleans)	CBD	Vocal line independent. Mysticism and flights of thought well stated musically. Eloquent.	$-C/F+_2$	W
Gambarini, Elisabetta de (It.-Br.) (c1731- ?)	Behold & Listen (composer)	in ROCH	Andante. Rather dramatic scene. Simply stated. Pleasant.	$-C+/E_2$	B
Gerstman, Blanche (Du.-Uof.) (1910-1973)	How Sweet the Moonlight Sleeps Upon This Bank (Shakespeare)	MS	Markedly sensitive phrases. Perfect wedding of lyric and music. Very tasteful. Harmonic beauty.	$D_1/F+_2$	B
Gerstman, Blanche	The Donkey (Chesterton)	Comp.	The "bray" of the donkey is in acc. Alert. Interesting harmonic progressions. Surge of inner strength.	D_2/G_2	B
Gideon, Miriam (Am.) (1906-)	Farewell Tablet to Agathocles (Florence Wilkinson) (from Songs of Voyage)	ACA	High tess. Independent sensitive vocal line. Determined dissonances. Requires excellent diction and musicianship. Powerful.	E_1/A_2	B

Composer	Title	Description	Publisher	Range	Difficulty
Gideon, Miriam	The Bells (Wm. Jones) (in coll.: Art Songs by Women: Across Time)	An impressive and poignant statement on Abraham Lincoln. Setting gives marked stature to text. Brief.	ACA	$\overline{A}/B_1$	B
Gideon, Miriam	Little Ivory Figures Pulled With Strings (Amy Lowell)	Aleatory music—spoken pitch line as indicated except where phrases mirror oriental inflection. Fascinates listeners. Guitar or piano.	ACA	$\overline{B}-/E-$	B
Giuranna, Barbara (It.) (1902-)	Augurio (Greetings) (Popular)	Text is in traditional Greek. Intriguing Grecian melodic quality. Rather high tess. Description and whimsy. Well written.	RICO	G_1/G_2	B
Giuranna, Barbara	Stornello	Text is in popular Toscan in jovial minor. This Toscanish rhythmic dance weaves a carefree mood, partially through finishing flourishes. Largely lying in midrange, its rhythmic expressiveness gains significant importance.	RICO	D_1/G_2	B
Glanville-Hicks, Peggy (Aus.-Am.) (1912-)	Frolic (Geo. Russel) (in coll.: Art Songs by Women: Across Time)	Fresh newness. Buoyant. Delightful melody. Acc. adds sparkle.	LYR	$E_1/A-_2$	B

Composer	Title[a]	Character of Song	Availability[b]	Range[c]	Performance Suitability[d]
Glanville-Hicks, Peggy	Nanda's aria: Lovesick (from opera Transposed Heads) (Thos. Mann)	Ballad with two verses which closes with 14 bars of "sprechstimme." Very original and different.	AMP	$\bar{B}$/A_2	M
Glanville-Hicks, Peggy	Come Sleep (Fletcher) (in coll.: Art Songs by Women: Across Time)	Maintains a hushed suspension throughout. Closely woven melodic line allows sleep to "spin off." Totally satisfying acc.	LYR	E_1/E_2	B
Gould, Elizabeth (Am.) (1904-)	Charm of Dea(th) Fear (from cycle Fraileries) (Sonja Friend)	Minimal means. Advanced harmonically. Unusual lyrics—thought provoking. Defiance. Forceful, pressure on single words.	MS in AMC	$F+_1$/$G+_2$	B
Gould, Elizabeth	Notes for a Southern Road Map (Phyllis McGinley) (from cycle Personal and Private)	Voice and flute. Humorous contemporary musical language. References to Southern tunes and cookery. Jogging rhythmic play teases. Excellent diction a must.	MS in AMC	E_1/$B-_2$	W

Composer	Title	Description	Location	Range	Voice
Grétry, Lucile (Angelique Dorothée Lucie) (Fr.) (1770-1791)	Que ce Chapeau (from opera, Le Mariage d'Antonio; in coll.: Art Songs by Women) (composer)	Youthful aria from the opening scene in her first opera. Provides delightful means for the light lyric soprano. Wordy.	in LoC	E_1/B_2	W
Grever, Maria (Mx.) (1894-1951)	Mulita (Raymond Leveen)	Humorous lyrics. Simple. Folk melody with suitable harmonization. Good relief from heavier thoughts. Of Muriel, the Mule. Clever.	REM	$E-_1/E-_2$	M
Gubitosi, Emilia (It.) (1887-1972)	Dialogo di Marionette (no. 2 from Tres Liriche) (Corazzini)	Characters introduced via jerky action. Middle section sustained. Delightful.	CUC	$\overline{B}+/F+_2$	B
Gubitosi, Emilia	Disperata (G. Carducci) (no. 2 from Due Liriche)	Vivo. Galloping action in acc. Develops into dynamically powerful declamation of sonorous outpouring.	CUC	$-C-/F_2$	B
Gubitosi, Emilia	Le Illusioni (Corazzini) (no. 1 from Tres Liriche)	Conviction via repeated pitches. Chromaticism and scale pitches effectively balanced in acc. Confined dynamic emotion controls vocal line.	CUC	$-C/F+_2$	B

Composer	Title[a]	Character of Song	Availability[b]	Range[c]	Performance Suitability[d]
Gubitosi, Emilia	L'Ultimo Sogno (Corazzini) (from Tres Liriche)	Requires dramatic voice which can sustain long passages with minimal acc. Develops dynamic surge, closes in dream reverie, low in range. Structural strength.	CUC	$\bar{B}/G+_2$	B
Guilbert, Yvette (Fr.) (1867-1944)	Madame Arthur (10 Chansons de Paul de Kock)	Allows for personality to show forth. Social humor. Musically not difficult.	HEU	$\bar{B}-/C_1$	B
Hall, Pauline (Nor.) (1890-1969)	Tagelied (Trad.) (from Drei Lieder)	Tantilizing allegretto song based on old Dutch folk songs.	NRS	$D-_1/G-_2$	B
Hall, Pauline	Winterabend (Mombert)	Blanketed winter mood of interest. Quasi recitative. Individual idiom.	NRS	$\bar{B}/F-_2$	B
Hansen, Kate (Am.) (1879-1968)	When I Am Glad	Charm. Musically direct. Simple exuberance. Brief.	MS in SLK	$-C+/D_2$	B
Hensel, Fanny Mendelssohn (G.) (1805-1847)	Bergeslust (Eichendorff) (Op. 10)	Significant. Alerts an awareness through numerous octave leaps upward. Joyous lightheartedness.	BH in LoC	E_1/A_2	B

Composer	Title	Description	Availability	Range/Code	Level
Hensel, Fanny Mendelssohn	Bitte (Lenau) (Op. 7)	Larghetto. Modulations in harmonic flow hold taut interest interpretively. Brief song of depth. Effective. Thoughtful.	BO in LoC	$E_1/F-_2$	B
Hensel, Fanny Mendelssohn	Dein ist mein Herz (Lenau) (Op. 7; in coll.: Art Songs by Women: Across Time)	Strong audience appeal throughout with stirring end. Starts on $E+_2$ and descends. Effective flourishes provide fine voice vehicle. Ends on fourth of minor key with resolution in acc. In 7 sharps.	BO in LoC	$E+_1/G+_2$	B
Hensel, Fanny Mendelssohn	Du bist die Ruh (Rückert) (Op. 7; in coll.: Art Songs by Women: Across Time)	Appreciative and loving essence. Ingratiating musically with melody and acc. reinforcing each other. Same text as Schubert's.	BO in Loc	$\supset+_1/F+_2$	M
Hensel, Fanny Mendelssohn	Frühling (Eichendorff) (Op. 7; in coll.: Art Songs by Women: Across Time) ("uber Garten durch die Lüfte")	Awakening and unfolding of spring graciously revealed. Buoyant, fresh. In 6 sharps.	BO in LoC	$F+_1/A+_2$	B
Hensel, Fanny Mendelssohn	Gondelied (composer) (Op. 1, from Sechs Lieder)	Linkage of chordal forms provides an attitude of open arms, with harmony providing added allure. High tess. Two stanzas.	BO in ROCH	D_1/A_2	B

Composer	Title[a]	Character of Song	Availability[b]	Range[c]	Performance Suitability[d]
Hensel, Fanny Mendelssohn	Im Herbste (Geibel) (Op. 10)	Somewhat H. Wolf-idiom. Thoughtful consideration of a disappointment in love. Expertly composed.	BH in LoC	$E-_1/G_2$	W
Hensel, Fanny Mendelssohn	Die Mainacht (Hölty) (Op. 7; in coll.: Art Songs by Women: Across Time)	Interesting expansive melodic line with gracious quality. Two stanzas. Elongated melodic leaps. (Same text used by Brahms.)	BH in NYP	$\overline{B}-/G_2$	B
Hensel, Fanny Mendelssohn	Nachtwanderer (Eichendorff) (Op. 7; in coll.: Art Songs by Women: Across Time)	Creates a nocturnal mysticism coupled with nostalgia. Grateful vocal idiom. Substantial.	BO in LoC	$-C/F_2$	B
Hensel, Fanny Mendelssohn	Schwanenlied (Heine) (Op. 1, from: Sechs Lieder; in coll.: Art Songs by Women: Across Time)	Pleasing motion in a plaintive minor. Well attuned to the singer. Gracious vocalism. Dynamic interest.	BO in ROCH	D_1/G_2	B
Hensel, Fanny Mendelssohn	Vorwurf (Lenau) (in coll.: Art Songs by Women: Across Time)	Prophetic quality. Anticipating H. Wolf's style. Begins starkly. Musically and dynamically strong.	BH in LoC	$-C+/G+_2$	B

Composer	Title	Description	Source	Range	Voice
Herbert, Muriel	The Lake Isle of Innisfree (Yeats)	Watery accompaniment. Rhythmic and harmonic propulsion. Consonant throughout. Radiates easy motion.	ELK	D_1/E_2	B
Hier, Ethel Glenn (Am.) (1899-1971)	The Gulls (Lenora Speyer)	Triplet Fs throughout sustain flight pattern, except for the midsection with different sort of vocal line. Closes with effective flight.	SMP	$E-_1/F_2$	B
Hildegard von Bingen, Saint (G.) (1098-1179)	Quia ergo femina from: Ordo Virtutum (in coll.: Art Songs by Women: Across Time) (composer)	Plain song as transcribed from 12th-century original. In Latin, unbarred. Buoyant and vocal timbre enhances song form. Considerable rhythmic and melodic motion.	in LAN	$-C/E_2$	M
Hill, Mabel Wood (Am.) (1870-1954)	Ebb Tide (Teasdale)	Lento. Creates a pleading for love's return. Desirous. In natural minor key. Tasteful.	GS in ROCH	$D-_1/A-_2$	B
Hill, Mabel Wood	Morgengebet (Eichendorff)	Gentle morning atmosphere in this well-written German/Am. lied.	FS	$-C/G_2$	B
Hill, Mabel Wood	Nancibel (from Vagabondia Songs) (text.: B.C.)	Brief. Wisp of lyrical Gypsy sealife. Mezzovoce. Ends in minor key.	SHP in MKC	$\overline{B}/E_2$	W

Composer	Title[a]	Character of Song	Availability[b]	Range[c]	Performance Suitability[d]
Hogben, Dorothy (Br.) (20th cent.)	The Shawl (L. Atkinson)	Opens and closes with recit.—other portions are like musically illumined speech. A social commentary. Good "change of pace" number. Substance.	OX	$-C/F+_2$	M
Hogsbro, Inga (Den.) (fl. 1934)	For Slide! (Too Late) (composer)	Modal. Rhythmic and time signature changes give song an alert angular quality. Individual idiom.	WH	$E_1/G+_2$	B
Holmès, Augusta (Fr.) (1847-1903)	Au Pays (The Warrior Returns) (composer)	A "Dear John" story. Heavy-footed march idiom of ragged dejected soldier. Social commentary.	CF	$-C/F_2$	B
Hortense (Queen of Holland) (Du.) (1783-1837)	Les Jeunes rêves d'Amour (Anon) (no. 2 from Album Artistique de la reine Hortense)	Allegro agitato. A pleasant chanson. Opening statement brings rapid focus to the music.	MEN in NYP	$D_1/E-_2$	B
Howe, Mary (Am.) (1882-1964)	The Bailey and the Bell (in coll.: English Songs, Vol. II) (15th cent)	Weighty procession precedes entrance of voice. Time allowed for musical reactions. Requires fine musician. Excellent.	GAL	D_1/A_2	B

Composer	Title	Notes	Source	Range	Cat.
Howe, Mary	Let Us Walk in the White Snow (Elinor Wylie)	Rhythmically complex. An "above earth" sensation. Very interesting.	CF in ROCH	D_1/G_2	B
Inness, Gertrude (Can.) (20th cent.)	The fair but Cruel Girle (Sir Glo. Etheridge)	Tasteful setting of British folk song—3 stanzas of "nymph that undoes me." Best for man. Charming.	HARF	E_1/E_{-2}	M
Isherwood, Cherry (Br.) (20th cent.)	Sleep (Sig. Sassoon)	Characterful depth of sensitive understanding. Interpretive skill needed. Harmony reinforces.	OX in ROCH	$\overline{B}-/E_2$	B
Jerea, Hilda (Rm.) (1916-)	Oamendi Plecînd ia Rozboi (Magda Isanos) (from cycle Lieduri pe vesuri)	Structural vitality. Strong melody and rhythm. Sincere emotional intensity. Stunning grip on text.	EMU in LoC	$\overline{A}-/F_1$	B
Jesi, Ada (It.) (1912-)	Via delle tre pulzelle (no. 2 from: Cino da Pistoia; text from A. Orvieto's "Rinascite")	Delightful. Marked "vivace," displays playful and vital rhythms with melodic surge. Also contains moments of retrospection; mischievous overtones add interest.	Comp.	$-C/F_2$	B
Jolas, Betsy (Fr.-Am.) (1926-)	Mon ami (composer)	Atmosphere created through atonal harmony. Enriching sequences devel-	HEU	$\overline{B}/F_2$	W

323

Composer	Title[a]	Character of Song	Availability[b]	Range[c]	Performance Suitability[d]
		op some "tonality." Reflects love amid dissonance. Elongated postlude. (Designated as suitable for "woman or child singer.")			
Kamien, Anna (Am.) (1912-)	Memories (Longfellow)	Varied time signatures and dissonances. Independent melodic flow. Philosophical and meditative. Closes with question. Individual quality.	LYA	D₁/G₂	B
Kanai, Kikuko (Ja.) (1911-)	Furusato (Anon) (from Songs of Okinawa)	Haunting theme. Oriental and Occidental influence. A gracious song.	ONG	B̄–/G₂	B
Kapralova, Vitezslava (Cz.) (1915-1940)	The Farewell Kerchief (V. Nezvala)	Interesting youthful and sprightly quality. An expression of individuality.	PRA	B̄/A₂	B
Kayden, Mildred (Am.) (20th cent.)	Psalm 121 (Bible)	An excellent setting. Undulating melody with some extended leaps. High tess. Finishes high. Substantial.	MER	D₁/A₂	B

Composer	Title	Comments	Source	Range	Voice
Kendrick, Virginia (Am.) (1910-)	Look Unto Me Saith the Lord (Isaiah) (in coll.: 11 Scriptural Songs of the 20th Century)	Strong statement. Hebraic quality. Standard liturgical harmonic structure.	CBP	$-\mathrm{C}/\mathrm{E}_2$	B
Kennedy-Fraser, Marjory (Sc.) (1857-1930)	The Whistle (C. Murray) (in coll.: Art Songs by Women: Across Time)	Charming Scottish flavor in this strophic song. Folk-like. Appropriately realized. Humor. Rolled Rs enhance text.	PAT	$\mathrm{D}_1/\mathrm{F}+_2$	B
Kettering, Eunice (Am.) (1906-)	Compensation (Teasdale) (in coll.: Contemporary American Songs)	Excellent harmonic interest. Effective; reveals an understanding of the voice. Brief.	SUM	$\mathrm{E}-_1/\mathrm{F}+_2$	B
Kettering, Eunice	The Gull (Robt. Hillyer)	Surging against stiff winds. High tess. Melody disjunct. Meter changes.	MS in UNM	$\mathrm{D}_1/\mathrm{B}-_2$	B
Kettering, Eunice	Longing (Anon)	Depressed—rejection. Thoughtful anxiety. Sustains convincing musical continuity.	MS in UNM	$\mathrm{D}_1/\mathrm{F}+_2$	W
Kettering, Eunice	Myriam (biblical) (no. 11 from cycle: Portraits from the Holy Scriptures; in coll.: Art Songs by Women: Across Time)	Hebraic modal quality. Rhythmic strength and motivation. With organ; or, in coll., with piano.	MS in UNM	$\overline{\mathrm{A}}-/\mathrm{A}_2$	B

Composer	Title[a]	Character of Song	Availability[b]	Range[c]	Performance Suitability[d]
Kettering, Eunice	Serenade (Robt. Hillyer)	Whimsy. Philosophical aspects at life's close. Sincere atmosphere. High tess.	MS in UNM	D_1/A_2	M
Klein, Ivy Frances (Br.) (1895-)	A Cyprian Woman (Anon)	A simple approach that yields a profound impact. Vocally gratifying.	GAL	$D+_1/F_2$	B
Koshetz, Nina (Rus.-Am.) (1894-1965)	Prayer (composer) (no. 2 from cycle: Wreath of Miniatures)	An inspirational idea in text and musical form—a concentrated totality. Very brief.	CF	$F_1/A^{-}{}_2$	B
Koshetz, Nina	Resignation (composer) (no. 1 from Wreath of Miniatures)	Wisp of desire and whimsy set musically. Due to brevity, two of these miniatures should be used together. High tess.	CF	D_1/G_2	B
Kuss, Margarita Ivanovna (Rus.) (1921-)	Vse Olyoobi, Olyoobi (composer)	Rhythmic surge. Bright. Very well written.	UK	$\bar{B}-/E_2$	B
La Guerre, Elisabeth Jacquet de (Fr.) (c1665-1729)	Juste ciele pardone à la rage (biblical) (from cantata Jephté; in coll.: Art Songs by Women: Across Time)	Recit. and aria. Vital rhythm and stately ayre for soprano. Strong statement. Fine vocal vehicle.	IMM	E_1/G_2	W

Composer	Title	Description	Source	Range	Voice
La Guerre, Elisabeth Jacquet de	Tempté, Trouble, Larme (from cantata Jephté; in coll.: Art Songs by Women: Across Time) (biblical)	Melody and rhythm grace central theme adding dignity and strength. The tragic moral issue of the father is here stated. Ideal for tenor. Dynamic dacapo aria.	in BN	E_1/G_2	M
Lang, Josephine (G.) (1815-1880)	An (Op. 25/1) (Müller) (from Vier Lieder; in coll.: Art Songs by Women: Across Time)	Conveys in 2/4 time a spirit of constancy, with relaxed strophic approach. (Schubert's Ungeduld uses the same text.)	SCHA in BAY	$-C+/F_2$	B
Lang, Josephine	Am Wasserfall (Anon) (in coll.: Art Songs by Women: Across Time)	Buoyancy and plunging of a waterfall. Vocally gratifying vehicle. Delightful.	MS in ÖN	$-C/G_2$	B
Lang, Josephine	Schmetterling (Heine) (in coll.: Lieder-Kranz, Heft III)	The $G\#_2$ in final phrase creates striking contrast to low tess. of earlier portion. Varieties of color changes add harmonic interest and description. Romantic style.	AI in BAY	$\bar{A}+/G+_2$	W
Lang, Josephine	Sie liebt mich (Goethe) (in coll.: Lieder-Kranz, Heft VII)	Exuberance and elation amid joyous disbelief are truthfully reflected in meaningful colors and textures in this buoyant expression.	AI in BAY	E_1/A_2	B

Composer	Title[a]	Character of Song	Availability[b]	Range[c]	Performance Suitability[d]
Lang, Margaret Ruthven (Am.) (1867-1972)	Chimes (Alice Meynell) (from: Two Songs; in coll.: Art Songs by Women: Across Time)	Spirit of bells is captured, spelling out their freedom. Musically gratifying.	SUM in ROCH	$E_1/G+_2$	B
Lang, Margaret Ruthven	Oriental Serenade (composer) (no. 1 from cycle: Three Songs of the East; in coll.: Art Songs by Women: Across Time)	Tasteful use of oriental idiom. Charming quality. Opens with vocalise.	SUM in ROCH	$-C/F+_2$	B
Lang, Margaret Ruthven	Snowflakes (John V. Cheney)	Delicate descent of snowflakes amid modulations. Understatement of acc. helpful. Vocally grateful.	SUM	D_1/G_2	B
Lang, Margaret Ruthven	Betrayed (L. W. Reese) (Op. 9/4)	Romanticism contrasts with dynamic declamation in lyric section. Strong melody. Excellent for spinto tenor.	APS	E_1/G_2	M
Lang, Margaret Ruthven	Song in the Songless (Geo. Meredith)	Interpretively gratifying through appropriate tonal colors which grace vital, flowing melody. Substantial.	APS	E_1/G_2	B

328

Composer	Title (Poet)	Description	Publisher	Range	Voice
Laufer, Beatrice (Am.) (1916-)	Soldier's Prayer (Australian Sgt. R.A.F. Hugh Brodie)	Extremely powerful humane poem with tasteful setting radiating inner strength of spirit. Free of dissonances and defiance. Moving.	AMP	$\overline{B}/F+_2$	M
LeFanu, Nicola (Br.) (1947-)	But Stars Remaining (C. Day Lewis)	Energetic involvement in emotional responses dominates. Surges. Wide leaps with ¼ tones—musicianship required. Unaccompanied—rather long. Uses individual idiom.	NOV	$\overline{A}-/A_2$	W
Leginska, Ethel (Br.) (c1886-1970)	At Dawn (Arthur Symons)	Advanced for this period. Substantial structure, controlled drama. Good.	GS	$-C/F_2$	M
Leginska, Ethel	Bird Voices of Spring (C. S. Whittern)	Descriptive acc. sets the scene. Grateful, with high tess. Ideal for light lyric voice.	GS in LoC	$-C/A_2$	W
Leginska, Ethel	The Frozen Heart (F. H. Martens)	Imaginative harmonies. Tone painting in acc. Atmosphere of bleakness which is convincing, reflecting an Eastern European perspective.	GS	$\overline{B}/E_2$	B

Composer	Title[a]	Character of Song	Availability[b]	Range[c]	Performance Suitability[d]
Leginska, Ethel	In a Garden (composer)	Strong. Positive thrust. Needs voice which can make strong statement. Brief. Direct. Imaginative structure.	AMP	E_1/G_2	B
Lehmann, Liza (Br.) (1862-1918)	At the Making of the Hay (S. M. Peck)	Allegretto grazioso. Pastorale. Simple, light, youthful.	UNS in KUM	E_1/A_2	W
Lehmann, Liza	Myself When Young (from In a Persian Garden) (Khayyam)	Flowing line. Pleasant strong melody. Substantial.	BOS	$\overline{E}_2/D_1$	M
Leleu, Jeanne (Fr.) (1898-1980)	Scene 1, from Beatrix (Gandrey-Rety)	Dante's scene, largely recit. form. Substance. Harmony of colors. Acc. reinforces periodically. Strong.	CHO	G_1/F_2	M
Levina, Zara (Rus.) (1905-1976)	Moe shlee (I Go) (from Muzykal'nye Karting) (M. Usakovskova)	A visualization of marching spirits around about all of us. Strong in surge, as though motivated by power beyond self. Excellent composition.	MY-L	$\overline{B}{-}/E{-}_1$	B

Composer	Title	Description	Publisher	Range	Diff.
Lewing, Adele (G.) (1866-1943)	Fair Rohtraut (trans. from Mörike)	Substantial in length and dynamic range. Patterned after German lieder. Individual musical language. Good!	DIT in MKC	E_1/A_2	M
Liddle, Clare (Sc.) (20th cent.)	Leave the Window Open (from: Impressions; text, Theodore Maynard)	Fresh buoyancy exuded through this delightful text, tastefully set with harmonic lightness.	Comp.	E_1/G_2	B
Lund-Skabo, Signe (Nor.) (1868-1950)	The Wanderer (J. S. Holt)	Forceful and declamatory, yet melodic. Anticipation of death. Harmonically decisive.	DIT	$-C/A_2$	M
Lutyens, Elisabeth (Br.) (1906-1983)	Epithalamion (Edm. Spenser)	Complex, disjunct difficult rhythmically. Vocal line independent. Can be used as organ solo, or organ and voice. Challenging.	OL	$-C/B_2$	B
Maconchy, Elizabeth (Br.) (1907-)	Have You Seen But a Bright Lily Grow? (Ben Jonson)	Beauty of lily seems "set apart" through the harmonic structure. Rather stark. Vocally satisfying.	OX	Ξ_1/F_2	B
Maconchy, Elizabeth	King Stephen (no. 3 from Shakespeare Songs)	Brief two pages. Gentle humor. Unusual intervals. Clever. Mischievous harmony.	CHA	$-C/G_2$	B

Composer	Title[a]	Character of Song	Availability[b]	Range[c]	Performance Suitability[d]
Maconchy, Elizabeth	The Sun Rising (from Three Donne Songs)	Undulating melodic line of dynamic impact. Very high tess. Dramatic thrust. Delightful perceptive text. Difficult.	Comp.	$-C/B_{-2}$	B
Maconchy, Elizabeth	The Wind and the Rain (no. 2 from Shakespeare Songs)	Allegro molto. Bright obtuse intervals of aggressive content. Closes with a flourish.	CHA	$\overline{B}/A_2$	B
Mahler, Alma (Au.) (1879-1964)	Ansturm (Dehmal) (from Vier Lieder)	Opening recit. eloquent. Light breaks through with appropriate spacing and harmonies. Striving for understanding is ultimate goal. Beautifully conceived musically.	UN	D_1/G_2	B
Mahler, Alma	Bei dir ist es Traut (Rilke) (no. 4 from Fünf Lieder; in coll.: Art Songs by Women: Across Time)	Hushed gentleness with simple vocal line. Exotic harmonies. Fine structure. Delightful.	UN	D_1/D_2	B
Mahler, Alma	Waldseligkeit (Dehmal) (from Vier Lieder; in coll.: Art Songs by	Moves between an awareness of trees in motion and a declaration of love.	UN	D_1/G_2	W

Composer	Title	Annotation			
	Women: Across Time)	Dense harmonies well chosen to eloquently express compelling emotions.			
Mahler, Alma	Laue Sommernacht (Falke) (from Fünf Lieder; in coll.: Art Songs by Women: Across Time)	Brief. Vitality within atmosphere of understatement. Chromatics and 9th leaps used. Of love. A passionate concept.	UN	$\overline{B}/F{+}_2$	B
Mahler, Alma	Licht in der Nacht (Bierbaum) (no. 1 from Vier Lieder; in coll.: Art Songs by Women: Across Time)	Explorative harmonic devices. Slow in pace, gentle in nature. Satisfying.	UN	$\overline{B}{-}/G_2$	B
Mahler, Alma	Die Stille Stadt (Dehmal) (no. 1 from Fünf Lieder; in coll.: Art Songs by Women: Across Time)	Surrealist atmosphere. Environmental haze achieved musically. Substance and charm.	UN	$\overline{B}/F_2$	B
Makarova, Nina V. (Rus.) (1908-1976)	Nochka-Nochenka (Belenckovo)	Strophic. Vibrant inner swelling of beneficial vibrations. Vocally gratifying.	SOV-M	$\overline{B}/F_2$	B
Makarova, Nina V.	Tay fklebach, zemlya (Shvedova)	Decided Russian flavor. Enhances voice. Contrapuntal acc. Easy flowing and interesting.	SOV-M	$\overline{E}{-}_1/G_2$	B

Composer	Title[a]	Character of Song	Availability[b]	Range[c]	Performance Suitability[d]
Makeba, Miriam (UoF.) (1932-)	Unhome (trad.) (Swazi folk song)	A sad but rhythmic, free-flowing ethnic narrative in Swazi. Very effective. (About a jilted bride.)	MKB	$\bar{A}/G_2$	W
Malibran, Maria (Fr.-Sp.) (1808-1836)	La Tarantelle (Betourné)	Decided charm. Has proper character when moving at a lively allegretto.	TROU in LoC	D_1/G_2	W
Mamlok, Ursula (G.-Am.) (1928-)	Daybreak (Longfellow)	As the melodic line meshes with harmony, gratifying points of reinforcement are created. Sings well. Vital whimsy. Good!	ACA	$\bar{B}/F_2$	B
Manning, Kathleen Lockhart (Am.) (1890-1951)	Shoes (composer)	Rapidly repeated pitches with wordy text propel voice through focused vowels. Alert, brief.	GS	$-C/D_2$	M
Manziarly, Marcelle de (Fr.) (1899-)	Berceuse (no. 5 from Six Chants) (composer)	Interesting. A drowsy atonal quality of impending sleep, as an enigma. Expressive harmonically.	SE	$-C/G-_2$	B

Composer	Title	Description	Source	Range	Voice
Manziarly, Marcelle de	La Grenouille qui veut faire aussi grosse que la Boeuf (The Frog Who Wishes to Be an Ox) (from Three Fables de la Fontaine)	Animé. The music emanates from a "croaking jig." Alert gaiety. Fine for pace change and humor.	AMP	E_1/A_2	B
Manziarly, Marcelle de	Le Cime (composer) (no. 6 from Six Chants)	Dynamic compelling thrust through rhythm, melody and harmony. Relentless acc. figure.	SE	$\bar{A}/E_2$	B
Mara (Gertrude Schmelling) (G.) (1749-1833)	Caro Gaffano mio (composer)	Ideal for display of high lyric coloratura's pyrotechnics. Substantial in length. By a famous coloratura. Impressive.	MS in LoC	E_1/D_3	W
Marcus, Adabelle (Am.) (1929-)	Stopping by Woods on a Snowy Evening (Frost)	Impressionistic. Vocal contours. Charm.	Comp.	E_1/G_2	B
Marcus, Adabelle	Here in This Spring (from Song Cycle; text, Dylan Thomas; in coll.: Art Songs by Women: Across Time)	Awe and wistfulness over nature's signs and signals. Rhythmic alertness establishes and maintains the climate for this song.	Comp.	$-C/E_2$	B
Maria Antonia (Walpurgis) (G.) (1724-1780)	Aria di Clori (in coll.: Art Songs by Women: Across Time) (composer)	Recit. and aria. Includes some limited coloratura passages, variations. Da capo aria. Pre-Mozart stylistically. Very vocal. Pleasant.	BH in ROCH	D_1/G_1	W

Composer	Title[a]	Character of Song	Availability[b]	Range[c]	Performance Suitability[d]
Mariani-Campolieti, Virginia (It.) (1864-?)	La cuisine de la poupée (composer)	Alert. Very simple. Wordy. Rapid motion. Traditional harmonies. Charming.	RIC	$\overline{B}/D+_2$	B
Marie Antoinette (Au.-Fr.) (1755-1793)	C'est mon ami (Florian) (in coll.: Art Songs by Women: Across Time)	A simple and modest strophic ayre (3). Pleasant.	DIT	$-C/E-_2$	W
Martinez, Isidora (Am.) (late 19th cent.)	Who Is Sylvia? (Shakespeare) (in coll.: Art Songs by Women: Across Time)	Interesting individual quality. High. Well written. Ornamentation tastefully included.	WS	$E_1/B-_2$	M
McLarry, Beverly (Am.) (c1945-)	The Queen of Hearts (from Recycled Nursery Rhymes I) (Traditional)	Perky, buoyant individual idiom. Delicious musical flavor in contemporary style with distinct personality.	Comp.	$E_1/G+_2$	W
McLaughlin, Marian (Am.) (1923-)	Lord of the Winds (in coll.: Art Songs by Women: Across Time) (Mary Elizabeth Coleridge)	A brief gem. Sensitive. Musical vitality.	Comp.	D_1/F_2	B
McLaughlin, Marian	To His Savior, A Child: A Present, By a Child (Robt. Herrick)	Excellent. Soundly structured. Modal quality arrived at via atonality.	GS	$\overline{B}/E_1$	B

Name	Title	Description	Source	Range	Voice
Meacham, Margaret (Am.) (1922-)	Le Papillon (Anon) (no. 1 from cycle: Three French Songs)	Exudes wistfulness and pity for the butterfly despite atonality. Plucked pianos and flutes add dimensions.	MS in AMC	$D-_1/G_2$	W
Medici de Orsina, Isabella (It.) (1542-1576)	Lieta vivo (composer)	Pleasant with rhythmic variation which adds zest to the melody. Acc. simple and tasteful. Early work.	WE	$E-_1/F_2$	B
Merriman, Margarita L. (Am.) (1927-)	Music I Heard With You (Aiken)	Flowing melodic line. Harmony varies between open and closed textures, emphasizing lyrical quality. Unexpected progressions veil dissonance.	Comp.	$-C/F+_2$	B
Moore, Mary Carr (Am.) (1873-1957)	Narcissa, Heed (tenor aria from opera Narcissa)	Strong statement of grandeur and beauty found in this country. Written well for vocal display. Deals with Nez Percé and Cherokee Indians.	in LoC	$D_1/B-_2$	M
Morgan, Dianne (Can.) (1929-)	Mystique (Mary L. Morgan)	Provocative text, highlighting the undue significance of names. A flowing, interesting composition.	MS in CMC	$D+_1/F+_2$	B

337

Composer	Title[a]	Character of Song	Availability[b]	Range[c]	Performance Suitability[d]
Morgan, Dianne	Walk Up the Mountain (Mary L. Morgan)	Expansive atmosphere. Sensitive innuendos dealing with philosophical delicacies of life. Individual charm.	MS in CMC	$E-_1/F_2$	B
Morrison, Julia (Am.) (20th cent.)	Love's Greeting on Your Day (composer)	Chatty. About acquaintance's ills. Somewhat extended. Closes with a kiss sound. Humor. Well conceived. Various moods —some spoken.	ACA	$\overline{G}/E_2$	W
Morrison, Julia	Newcomer's Lament (composer)	Produces an atmosphere rarely found in musical form. Minimal means. Compelling aura.	ACA	$\overline{G}/D_2$	B
Mracek, Ann (Am.) (1956-)	Red Bird (composer)	Different pitch sequences. Possesses interesting structure. Atonal.	MS in KUM	$\overline{A}+/F_2$	B
Müller-Hermann, Johanna (Au.) (1878-1941)	Abendstunde (from Acht Lieder, I, Op. 18) (Calé)	Brief, ingratiating and flowing in triple metre. Consonant. Exudes gratitude.	UN	$D-_1/F_2$	B

Composer	Title	Type	Range	Grade
Müller-Hermann, Johanna	Die stunde, da ich dich zuerst ersah (no. 2 from Acht Lieder, I, Op. 18) (Calé)	UN	D_1/A_2	B
	A few large intervalic leaps amid an array of colorful and meaningful modulations expressing stressful emotions. Late romantic. Demands interpretive insight.			
Müller-Hermann, Johanna	Von Sternen glitt ein stummer funke (no. 1 from Acht Lieder, I, Op. 18) (Calé)	UN	$\overline{B}/A_2$	B
	Many enharmonic changes. Descriptive and lyrical in Schoenbergian idiom. Ideal for dramatic tenor or soprano who sustains long phrases with vitality.			
Musgrave, Thea (Sc.) (1928-)	A Song for Christmas (attributed to William Dunbar)	CHR	$\overline{G}/A_2$	B
	Scottish text wondrously set for the spinto soprano or tenor of dynamic conviction. Sustained final A_2 needed plus ability to maintain high tess. Contrasting middle section utilizes lowest pitches of song. Exciting contemporary work of substantial length. Mature voice and interpreter a must.			
Musgrave, Thea	Willie Wabster (no. 3 from A Suite o Bairnsangs) (Maurice Lindsay)	CHR	E_1/E_2	B
	Markedly individualized song to narrative descriptive commentary. Artfully set.			

Composer	Title[a]	Character of Song	Availability[b]	Range[c]	Performance Suitability[d]
Musgrave, Thea	The Cherry Tree (The Green) (no. 5 from A Suite o Bairnsangs) (Maurice Lindsay)	Bright melody with a suggested drone bass acc. Rhythmic buoyancy. Upper middle tess. Effective for the voice.	CHR	F_1/G_2	B
Newlin, Dika (Am.) (1923-)	A Little Flower (Blake)	Spoken in last phrase. Atonal. Very different intervalically. Fine composition.	Comp.		B
Norton, the Honorable Mrs. (Am.) (19th cent.)	Absolom (biblical/comp.)	Ballade. Fairly long. A bit overdrawn dramatically. Expected harmonies. Melody strong. Illustrates the period. Period piece.	in FLP	$\overline{A}/D_2$	B
Nunlist, Juli (Am.) (1916-)	Oh, When I Was in Love With You (A.E. Housman) (in coll.: Contemporary Art Songs Album for Medium Voice)	Lively narrative for bass-baritone, of passing love. Holds interest. Effective closing song in a group.	GAL	C_1/D_2	M

		NOR	D_1/D_2	W
Orsina, Leonora (It.) (fl. 1560-)	Per pianto la mia carne (composer)	Earnest, brief. Song of sadness. Directly stated. Coloratura additions enhance. (First composer to have written out embellishments.) Three stanzas.		W
Osawa, Kazuko (Ja.) (1926-)	Kó-e (The Voice) (in coll.: Art Songs by Women: Across Time) (Toichiro Iwasa)	Text very different. Music imaginative and suits text well. Of telephone call from death. Rather long timings, silences—near awesome. Impressive.	ONG in ONG	$-C+/E-_2$	B
Osawa, Kazuko	Yu su ge bi to (Michizo Tatehara)	Impressionistic and delicate. Light flowing acc. Fine musicianship required.	MS in ONG	$\overline{B}/G_2$	B
Owen, Blythe (Am.) (1898-)	The Rain (Davies)	Descriptive accompaniment. Very pleasant. Positive mood. Sustained tones allow vocal timbre to register. Good ending on F_2.	ROC	E_1/F_2	B
Owen, Blythe	The Fountain (Teasdale)	Through continuous gentle motion of the fountain nature is drowsily observed. All is under-	Comp.	$\overline{A}+/F_2$	

341

Composer	Title[a]	Character of Song	Availability[b]	Range[c]	Performance Suitability[d]
		stated musically in range and dynamics. Fine change of pace number in med. range. Mesmerizing.			
Owen, Harriet Mary (Miss Browne) (Am.) (c1795-1858)	The Pilgrim Fathers (Mrs. Hemans)	Compelling, naive quality. Uncomplicated harmonically. Two stanzas and development. Strong. Of historical interest.	GW in LoC	$\overline{A}/F+_2$	B
Pachmutova, Alexandra (Rus.) (20th cent.)	How Young We Were (Dobrondrovoff)	In late romantic style. From intense minor with limited rhythmic impetus, it builds in mid-portion. Reflects understated emotion.	SOV-M	$\overline{A}/A_2$	B
Panetti, Joan (Am.) (20th cent.)	What Are Words (from cycle Three Songs) (Lydia Fakunding)	Striking effects achieved by inclusion of gliding sprechstimme, and extended wide leaps. Atonal.	NV	D_1/A_2	B

Name	Title	Annotation	Source	Range	Voice
Paradis, Maria Theresa von (Au.) (1759-1824)	Morgenlied eines armen Mannes (Hermes) (in coll.: Art Songs by Women: Across Time)	Fine example of Lieder strophic form. Poignant text of inner pathos. Well set.	GRA	G_1/G_2	M
Parra, Violeta (Ar.) (1917-1967)	La Carta (composer)	Rhythmic direction. Interesting individual charm and flavor.	LAG	D_1/A_2	B
Paull, Barberi (Am.) (1945-)	Where Shall We Go? (composer)	Despite obtuse intervals, it reveals honest contemporary commentary. Poetic dream guides the musical essence.	Comp.		M
Pentland, Barbara (Can.) (1912-)	Forest (Anne Marriott) (from Song Cycle, Untitled)	Majestic deep-rooted trees evident. Profound, awesome setting. All enveloped in dark green. Independent vocal line. Requires substantial vocal instrument.	MS in CMC	$-C+/A_2$	B
Pentland, Barbara	Tracks (Anne Marriott) (from Song Cycle, Untitled; in coll.: Art Songs by Women: Across Time)	Engine-effect with its forward surge, unrelenting. "Narrow iron bands." Allegro. Far-flung pitch positions. Needs strong voice.	MS in CMC	D_1/A_2	B

Composer	Title[a]	Character of Song	Availability[b]	Range[c]	Performance Suitability[d]
Perry, Julia (Am.) (1924-1979)	How Beautiful Are the Feet (Isaiah 52:7)	Simplified concept of text. Traditional voice leading. Melody indicates that the "feet" are "earthbound." Pleasant.	GAL	$E-_1/F_2$	B
Petersen, Marian (Am.) (1926-)	The Retreat (Henry Vaughn)	Contemporary idiom. Unaccompanied opening. Intervalic thinking imperative. 4 min. duration. Speech patterns. Has substance.	MS in MKC	$-C/F_2$	B
Philip, Elizabeth (Br.) (1827-1885)	Ninon (A. de Musset)	Brief recit. sections interspersed in aria. Bright predictable dance-like melody in 3/8, despite a somewhat serious text (in French).	in LoC	D_1/F_2	M
Pierce, Seneca (Am.) (1918-)	The Astronomer (David O'Niel)	Minimal means. Solitude described. Naive text of Navajo shepherd. Charm.	BOS	$\overline{B}/G+_2$	B
Piggott, Audrey (Can.) (1906-)	A Mind Content (Robt. Greene) (no. 3 from Six Elizabethan Songs; text, Robert Greene)	Atmosphere of calm radiates. Reminiscent of traditional British pace for emotions of reflective whimsy.	LL	$-C/E_2$	B

Pitcher, Gladys (Am.) (1890-)	Passacaglia (McBradd) (no. 3 from Long Wharf Songs)	Brief. Sensitive. Sparse impressions in space with reference to musical terms. Voice independent. Tritone structure. Requires good vocal control.	WM	$-C/E_2$	B
Plumstead, Mary (Br.) (1905-)	Sigh No More Ladies (Shakespeare)	Buoyant, direct melody with text which invites women to be philisophically "blithe and bonny." Traditional harmonies.	CUR, GS	$\overline{B}-/E-_2$	B
Poldowski (Lady Dean Paul; Irene Wieniawska) (Pol.-Br.) (1880-1932)	Brume (Verlaine) (in coll.: Art Songs by Women: Across Time)	Brief. Individuality. Delightful spirit. Gracious melodic line.	CHR in ROCH	D_1/F_2	B
Poldowski (Lady Dean Paul; Irene Wieniawska)	Crépuscule du Soir Mystique (Verlaine) (in coll.: Art Songs by Women: Across Time)	An entoned poem. Impressionistic melody takes second place to furies of temporal beauty. Mystery permeates.	CHR in ROCH	$F+_1/F+_2$	B
Poldowski (Lady Dean Paul; Irene Wieniawska)	Effet de Neige (Verlaine)	Atmosphere hushed—crisp snow's magic felt at opening and closing. Additional motion expressed between. Compelling attention.	CHR in ROCH	E_1/F_2	B

Composer	Title[a]	Character of Song	Availability[b]	Range[c]	Performance Suitability[d]
Poldowski (Lady Dean Paul; Irene Wieniawska)	Le Faune (Verlaine)	Surprise closing via hushed recit., preceded by laughter. Brief.	CHR in ROCH	E_1/A_2	B
Poldowski (Lady Dean Paul; Irene Wieniawska)	Mandoline (Verlaine)	Rapid repetitions reflective of mandolin playing in acc. Mesmerizing. Rhythmic insistence adds to individuality. Limited in range. Compelling quality.	CHR in UIN	$E_1/F+_2$	B
Poldowski (Lady Dean Paul; Irene Wieniawska)	Nocturne (text, Moreas)	Striking of the clock sets a sparkling bright pace. Acc. figures vary effectively. A good change of pace number.	CHR in ROCH	$-C+/G+_2$	B
Poldowski (Lady Dean Paul; Irene Wieniawska)	Pannyre aux talons d'or (Samain)	An extended narrative of an exotic and sensational dance by Pannyre. Opens with recit. Moves through emotional and visual aspects of the dance with an unexpected climactic final phrase. Very effective for an imaginative and mature singer.	CHR	D_1/A_2	B

Poldowski (Lady Dean Paul; Irene Wieniawska)	Spleen (Verlaine)	CHR in ROCH	D_1/F_2	B
Poldowski (Lady Dean Paul; Irene Wieniawska)	Sur L'Herbe (Verlaine)	CHR in ROCH	E_1/G_2	B
Poldowski (Lady Dean Paul; Irene Wieniawska)	Dansons la Gigue (Verlaine) (in coll.: Art Songs by Women: Across Time)	CHR in ROCH	D_1/G_2	B
Polignac, Armande de (Fr.) (1876-1962)	Chant d'Amour (from La Flute de Jade) (Chen-Teuo-Tsan)	HNN in LoC	D_1/G_2	B
Polignac, Armande de	Ngo Gay Ngy (Wou-Hau) (from La Flute de Jade)	HNN in LoC	$E_1/E-_2$	B
Popatenka, Tamara (Rus.) (1912-)	Ptitsi (Anon.)	SOV-M	E_1/A_2	B
Possaner, Erna Baronini (Au.) (19th cent.)	Der Eichwald (from Eleven Lieder)	MS in ÖN	$\bar{B}/G_2$	B

Descriptions (in order):
- Builds effectively at measured pace providing the voice with good vocal vehicle.
- Capricious. Moods commanding, then withdrawn. Great change of pace song. Includes some singing of syllables on appropriate pitches.
- Bright and vivacious. Wordy with quality of abandon.
- Impressionistic. Fine structure. Delicious for voice and exudes an elegant atmosphere.
- Enticing snatch of loneliness. Vocally attractive. Special charm.
- Rather traditional, yet fanciful. Imaginative.
- Imagery strong; gains added reinforcement through harmony. Vocally satisfying. In thoughtful minor key.

347

Composer	Title[a]	Character of Song	Availability[b]	Range[c]	Performance Suitability[d]
Poston, Elizabeth (Br.) (1905-)	The Stockdoves (Andrew Young)	Excellent. Expressive. Words assist in providing vocalism.	OX in ROCH	D_1/G_2	B
Poston, Elizabeth	Colin's Success (Boyce)	Clever. Winsome Old English text and bright. "Come-hither" in melody and rhythm. Traditional harmony.	CUR	D_1/G_2	W
Powers, Ada Weigel (Am.) (fl. 1927)	The Last Invocation (Whitman)	Recit. in style. Very strong. Impressive style. From "Leaves of Grass." Acc. largely chordal. Short. Limited range. Tender solemnity.	SL	$\overline{B}/D_2$	M
Pownall, Mary Ann (Wrighten) (Br.-Am.) (1751-1796)	Jemmy of the Glen (trad.)	An Early American song. Simple, direct. Uses the "Scottish snap" in its rhythm. Of historical significance.	JCB in EFM	D_1/G_2	W
Price, Florence B. (Am.) (1888-1953)	The Moon Bridge (Rolofson)	Bright, light allegro weaves a fairy webbed moon bridge disarmingly. Interesting song of contrast.	GAM in ROCH	E_1/G_2	W

Composer	Title	Description	Source	Range	
Price, Florence B.	Songs to a Dark Virgin (Langston Hughes)	Brief, emotional, impressionistic. Employs traditional harmonies and uses chromatics.	GS in DP-H	D_1/G_2	B
Price, Florence B.	Sympathy (P.L. Dunbar)	Powerful simplicity. Excellent for recital and a must for a Black music program.	MS in ROCH	$\overline{B}-/G_2$	B
Price, Florence B.	To My Little Son (Julia Davis)	An endearing text. Memorable. Compresses much into this eloquent brief song.	MS in ROCH	$-C/D+_2$	B
Price, Florence B.	Travel's End (Mary Hoisington)	Thoughtful. Well written. Worthwhile in substance. Limited range.	MS in ROCH	$\overline{G}+/C_1$	B
Prieto, Maria Teresa (Mx.) (?-1975)	Canzón da Noite Do Afiador (Letre de Augusto Casas)	Andante. High tess. Endless space within suspension. Thoughtful-conversational in phrasing.	EMM	$F_1+/G+_2$	B
Prieto, Maria Teresa	Oda (C.B. Prieto) (no. 1 from cycle Odas Celestas)	Curiously fascinating flavor. Repeated pitches and syncopations add to dramatic impact. Joyous quality.	EMM	$G+_1/A_2$	B
Prieto, Maria Teresa	Quien dijo acaso? (Vincente Aleixandre)	Andantino. Questioning. Jubilant finale. Startling harmonic interest.	EMM	E_1/A_2	B

Composer	Title[a]	Character of Song	Availability[b]	Range[c]	Performance Suitability[d]
Prieto, Maria Teresa	Sonatina (Sor Juana Ines de la Cruz)	In the Phrygian mode, 6/8. Light, easy motion. Folk-like. Interesting harmonically. Personality of it own. Lyrics of gifted poet.	EMM	E_1/F_2	B
Rainier, Priaulx (UoF.-Br.) (1903-)	A Dolphin (Anyte of Tegea) (from Three Greek Epigrams; in coll.: Art Songs by Women: Across Time)	Very brief. High tess. Compelling vitality throughout. Strong statement. Dramatic voice an advantage.	ST	F_1/A_2	B
Rainier, Priaulx	Nunc, le sonitu (from Cycle of Declamation; text from Devotions of John Donne)	Opens and closes with Latin. The body of this declamation is in English and all is unaccompanied. Extremely demanding in musicianship and diction. Stunning.	ST	D_1/A_2	B
Rawling, Barbara (Br.) (20th cent.)	The Old Tunes (Thos. Hardy)	Narration and commentary appealing, as in folksong style. Interesting choice of sonorities.	CUR	$D-_1/G-_2$	B

Composer	Title	Comments	Pub.	Range	B/W
Recli, Giulia (It.) (1890-1970)	Campanella (Liria Carme) (in coll.: Art Songs by Women: Across Time)	Delightful. Animated. Rhythm and pitches of bells mirrored in acc. Fine structure. High ending.	CUC	$-C+/C_2$	B
Recli, Giulia	La Barca (composer)	Liquid lyricism. Rhythmic interest. Charm. Admirable.	CUC	$-C/F_2$	W
Reichardt, Luise (G.) (1779-1826)	Canzone (Metastasio) (from Ausgemante Lieder; in coll.: Art Songs by Women: Across Time)	Enhances vocal timbre within surge of momentum. Lieder form—Italian text. Grateful vocally; satisfying melody.	DMV	E_1/A_2	W
Reichardt, Luise	Das Madchen am Ufer (Anon.)	Quite interesting in lieder style. Has flourishes within melody.	BK	$E-_1/A-_2$	B
Reichardt, Luise	Poesia (Metastasio) (from Ausgewante Lieder)	Allegro agitato. Melody enjoys structural developments. Pleasant.	DMV	$E_1/G-_2$	B
Richter, Marga (Am.) (1926-)	The Hermit (Li-Hai-ku) (no. 1 from Two Chinese Songs; in coll.: Art Songs by Women: Across Time)	Obtuse. Minimal means. Chant. Start opposition to traditional harmonies, so music matches the hermit's "heart of ice in a jade cup."	CF	$E_1/E-_2$	B

Composer	Title[a]	Character of Song	Availability[b]	Range[c]	Performance Suitability[d]
Richter, Marga	She at His Funeral (composer)	As a dirge. The emptiness of loneliness is magnified. Brief and bleak impact.	CF	$D_1/C+_1$	W
Richter, Marga	A Song of Ch'ang an (from Eight Songs to Chinese Poems) (Anon.)	Social commentary outlined musically. Stark, stressing the emptiness of man's moral concerns through the texture of music, taken at a vigorous pace.	Comp.	D_1/F_2	B
Ricketts, Lucy Woodworth (Am.) (20th cent.)	Prayer to Persephone (Millay)	Dramatic. Brief. Tonal. Harmonically thick.	SMP	$E-_1/G-_2$	B
Robertson, Donna Nagey (Am.) (1935-)	Psalm XXIII (Bible)	For flute and high voice. Intervalically and rhythmically difficult. Very contemporary. Sinuous.	Comp.	$-C/B-_2$	B
Rogers, Clara Kathleen (Br.-Am.) (1844-1931)	Apparitions (R. Browning)	Rhythms and undulating melody with balanced acc. create a song to enhance performance.	APS	E_1/G_2	B

Composer	Title	Comments	Source	Range	
Rogers, Clara Kathleen	Out of My Own Great Woe (Eliz. Barrett-Browning)	Woefulness in minor key. Uncertainty of love conveyed convincingly in rhythm and acc. Has some sophisticated harmony.	SUM	$-C/F_2$	M
Rogers, Clara Kathleen	Appearances (R. Browning)	Effective with harmonic interest. Large leaps/frequent modulations. Of special merit.	APS	$-C/A_2$	B
Rogers, Clara Kathleen	Sudden Light (D.G. Rossetti) (Op. 33/1)	Evasive illusion effectively handled. Secure ppp's for long phrases. Ideal closing song for sopranos or tenors.	APS	$D+_1/A_2$	B
Rogers, Elizabeth (Br.) (17th cent.)	Now the Spring Is Come (composer) (from coll.: La Chanson en Angleterre au Temps d'Elisabeth)	Very "olde" English—strophic. Balances between B+ and G− giving sense of the devious within directness.	OX	F_1/G_2	B
Rogers, Patsy (Am.) (1938-)	Recette et Chanson (Guillevic)	Quick-paced with musical dimension. Facility of diction is prime. Individual flavor of freshness in melody. Requires a facile accompanist.	Comp.	$\overline{A}-/A-_2$	B
Rozhavskaia, Iudif Grigoz'evna (Rus.) (1922-)	Nad Vadnim Proctorom Chictim (Anon.)	Vocally grateful. Descriptive. Buoyant rhythm.	SOV-K in LoC	D_1/E_2	B

Composer	Title[a]	Character of Song	Availability[b]	Range[c]	Performance Suitability[d]
Sadero, Geni (It.) (1886-1961)	Comu Quanno Tira Ventu (A Shepherd's Serenade) (composer)	A serenade to sleep (as a vocalise). Personal perspective. Quiet conclusion. Good F#$_2$ and upper tess. needed for opening section.	PP in KUM	D$_1$/G$_2$	B
Salter, Mary Turner (Am.) (1856-1938)	The Cry of Rachel (Lilette W. Reese)	Particularly dramatic contrasts and statement of musical substance from turn of the century. Effective for appropriate singer.	GS	– C/A$_2$	W
Salvador, Matilde (Sp.) (1918-)	Nana del sueno (Carmen Conde) (from Canciones de nana y desvelo)	Subtle charm. Ethnic rhythmic savor amid flowing rhythm.	UME	E$_1$/F$_2$	B
Sandresky, Margaret (Am.) (1921-)	My Soul Doth Magnify the Lord (St. Luke)	Mary's announcement of conception, effectively written for organ and voice. Recit. opens. Joyous and reassuring expression. Song of stature.	BMS	E$_1$/A$_2$	B

Sandresky, Margaret	Random and Planned Textures (composer) (in coll.: Art Songs by Women: Across Time)	Chance, aleatory acc. Atmospheric. Entrances as in "chance" music. Very vocal with particular avant garde charm.	Comp.	$-C+/G+_2$	B
Sangiocomo-Respighi Elsa (It.) (1894-)	Una sol cosa e certa (no. 2 from Dai Rubaiyat) (Omar Khayyam)	Independent melody is carried by voice against continuing accompaniment figures.	RICO	$-C/F_2$	B
Sangiocomo-Respighi, Elsa	V'era una porta (no. 3 from Dai Rubaiyat) (Omar Khayyam)	"Bell-tree"-like background given to both ascending line and repeated pitches. Some unacc. phrases. Added effectiveness gained when no. 4 follows 3.	RICO	$-C/F_2$	B
Sangiocomo-Respighi, Elsa	Vieni, riempi il bicchier (no. 4 from Dai Rubaiyat) (Omar Khayyam)	Bright, brief, quick in pace. Breathes an alert pleasantness.	RICO	$D+_1/G_2$	B
Sauvrezis, Alice (Fr.) (1885-1946)	Le Monde est plus profond (Trène) (from Trois Novains)	Sprightly harmonic changes. Chromaticism dominates. Intriguing.	SE in ROCH	$-C/E_2$	B
Schafmeister, Helen (Am.) (20th cent.)	Gypsies (Stanley Kimmel) (no. 3 from Three Songs)	Bright, rhythmic alertness stimulates this diversion of the coal miner.	SMP	$-C/G_2$	B
Scheidel, Elizabeth Rhudy (Am.) (mid-20th cent.)	Herbst Tag (no. 1 from Three Songs; text from Rilke's "Book of Pictures")	Strength within subtlety expressed by independent vocal line. Utilizes numerous octave leaps.	MS in author's library	$\bar{A}/E_2$	B

Composer	Title[a]	Character of Song	Availability[b]	Range[c]	Performance Suitability[d]
Schick, Philippine (G.) (1893-1970)	In der Nacht (no. 3 from Lieder der Sehnsucht, Op. 12) (Falke)	Individual compositional language used with rhythmic constancy—substantial flowing line, in bass clef. Vocally gratifying.	MS in BAY	$\bar{B}/D+_2$	M
Schick, Philippine	Ohne Liebe (no. 1 from Vom Frieden den Liebe, Op. 29) (Hesse)	Elongated substantial phrase lines understated dynamically, utilizing 2 against 3.	GRO in BAY	$-C/A_2$	B
Schick, Philippine	An deiner Hand (no. 7 from Vom Frieden den Liebe, Op. 29) (Waggerl)	Depicts reassured feelings on soaring vocal line amid rhythmic complexities. Designed for good musician with very light voice.	GRO in BAY	$-C/C_3$	B
Schnorr, Malvina von Carolsfeld (née Garrigues) (G.) (1825-1904)	Herbstgedanken (from Neun Lieder von Ludwig & Malvina Schnorr) (composer)	In true lieder style. Direct and gracious; enjoys a flowing momentum much of which is generated by the acc.	FA in BAY	F_1/F_2	B
Schnorr, Malvina von Carolsfeld (née Garrigues)	Lied (Geibel) (from Neun Lieder von Ludwig & Malvina Schnorr)	The undulating melody in this brief and pleasant song emerges with a	FA in BAY	$-C+/E_2$	B

light-hearted and unpretentious charm.

Schonthal-Seckel, Ruth F. (G.-Am.) (1924-)	Die Ewige Liebe (from Totengesänge) (composer)	Expresses complete earnestness within powerful dramatic impact. Complicated idiom harmonically. Substantial top range needed. Deep emotion. Closes with sprechstimme.	Comp.	D_1/B_2	B
Schumann, Clara (G.) (1819-1896)	Liebeszauber (Geibel) (in coll.: Art Songs by Women: Across Time)	A sense of fulfillment is found in nature—seen through loving eyes. Graciously set, with freshness.	BH in LoC	$-C/E_2$	B
Schumann, Clara	An einem lichten Morgen (from Rollet Lieder)	Moving acc. figure adds abandon to this song of gratification. Charm.	BH in IOA & NYP	$D_1/F+_2$	M
Schumann, Clara	Er ist gekommen (Rückert) (Op. 37/2; in coll.: Art Songs by Women: Across Time)	Impetuous anticipation exemplified in music. Generates very strong momentum. Exuberant.	BH	$E_1/A-_2$	W
Schumann, Clara	Geheimes Flüstern hier und dort (from Rollet Lieder)	Langsam. Nature, as observed by the winds. Three stanzas. Surging acc. Sensitive.	BH in IOA & NYP	$D_1/E-_2$	B

Composer	Title[a]	Character of Song	Availability[b]	Range[c]	Performance Suitability[d]
Schumann, Clara	Ich hab' in deinem Auge (Rückert) (in coll.: Art Songs by Women: Across Time)	Langsam. Endless beauty perceived. Creates sense of deep and lasting devotion. Singular expressive quality in personalized idiom.	BH in IOA & NYP	$-C/D_2$	M
Schumann, Clara	Liebst du um schönheit (in coll.: Art Songs by Women: Across Time) (Rückert)	Endearing, tender, quiet charm. Varied dynamic interest. A delight.	BH in IOA	F_1/D_2	B
Sears, Marie (Am.) (fl. early 20th cent.)	Reprieved (Charles Ludder)	Brief, direct. Ascending phrases evidence particular strength. Following marked climax through the reference to death a subdued mood closes.	GS	$D+_1/G_2$	B
Sherman, Helen (Am.) (20th cent.)	The Little Turtle (Vachel Lindsay)	Sparse. Childlike. Tastefully winsome.	SMP	$-C+/F+_2$	B
Silberta, Rhea (Am.) (1900-1959)	Jeunesse (Marjorie White)	Chromatic idiom utilized in clusters indicating "closeness." Opens with recit. followed by flowing vocal line. Meaningful idiom.	in ROCH	$-C/E_2$	B

Composer	Title	Comments	Pub.	Range	Cat.
Singer, Jeanne (Am.) (1924-)	Lament (from A Cycle of Love) (composer)	Extremely poignant text with an eloquence given to grief-torn heart in this singable setting.	HB	F_1/G_2	W
Singer, Jeanne	Summons (Patricia Benton)	Excellent as vocal vehicle. Characterful melody. Rhythmic solidarity. Harmonic color and strength.	HB	$\bar{B}/G_2$	M
Smith, Eleanor (Am.) (1858-1942)	Quest (Kate Kellogg)	In Tchaikovsky-like style. Pattern of insistence in accompaniment with strong vocal line. Tentative closing statement.	WM in ROCH	$\bar{B}-/F_2$	W
Smith, Julia (Am.) (1911-)	The Love I Hold (Karl Flaster)	Effective. Intensity of rhythmic flow essential. Of unrequited love. Tasteful.	PRE	$E-_1/A-_2$	B
Stanley, Helen (Am.) (1930-)	Credo (R. Browning)	Source of music points to inner self. Captures intuitive questioning. Conceptual quality.	MS in AMC	$\bar{B}-/F_2$	B
Steiner, Gitta (Cz.-Am.) (1932-)	I Envy Seas Whereon He Rides (no. 3 from Three Songs for Med. Voice) (Emily Dickinson)	Insistent rhythmic patterns on repeated pitches create textural strength mingled with conviction. Independent vocal line	SMP	$\bar{B}/D_2$	W

Composer	Title[a]	Character of Song	Availability[b]	Range[c]	Performance Suitability[d]
		frequently involved in the imaginative harmonic structure in accompanying figure.			
Strickland, Lily (Am.) (1887-1958)	At Eve I Heard a Flute (composer)	Lightly-sketched whimsy. Requires delicate approach. Pleasant.	DIT	$-C/G_2$	W
Strozzi, Barbara (It.) (c1619-1664)	Amor dormiglione (in coll.: Italian Songs and Arias, III) (composer)	Allegro. Rousing music to be sure! Numerous approaches used emotionally and musically. Impetuous. Moderate in length.	DIT	D_1/G_2	W
Strozzi, Barbara	Lagrimé mie (composer) (in coll.: The Solo Song: 1580-1730, ed. by Carol McClintock)	Very expressive opening in mode of lamentation. Rhythmic interest. Harmony utilizes modulations which vitalize. Vocally demanding with some coloratura. Rather long; varied moods.	NOR	$D+_1/G_2$	B
Strozzi, Barbara	Non c'è piè fede (in coll.: Art Songs by Women: Across Time) (composer)	Buoyant, fresh with rhythmic diversity. Innovative for 1600s. Fairly	BON	E_1/G_2	B

Composer	Title	Description	Publisher	Range	Voice
		high tess. Musical momentum, requires vocal command. Fairly long.			
Strozzi, Barbara	Soccorrete, Luci Avare (from La Travagliata)	Pace changes with various rhythmic patterns. Quite imaginative. Fine vocal technique required.	HAN	D_1/G_2	B
Strozzi, Barbara	Spesso per entro al petto (G.A. Cicognini) (from cantata La Fasiciuletta semplice)	Spirited. Turns phrases unpredictably. Rhythmic vitality. Three stanzas with refrain.	HAN	$-C/F_2$	B
Sutherland, Margaret (Aus.) (1897-)	The Meeting of Sighs (Shaw Neilson)	Radiates sighs and dissonance with a nearly austere harmonic structure. Leaves one with unsolved questions. Plaintive.	LYR	$\overline{B}/E_2$	B
Sutherland, Margaret	They Called Her Fair (Ester Levy)	A searching quality, with delicate appreciation in flavorful musical terminology.	LYR	$-C/E_2$	B
Swain, Freda (Br.) (1902-)	Winter Fields (Coppard)	Flowing, rhythmic adjustments effortlessly carry the melody in this descriptive and sensitive text. Well written. Brief.	NEMO	$-C/E_2$	B

Composer	Title[a]	Character of Song	Availability[b]	Range[c]	Performance Suitability[d]
Szönyi, Erzsébet (Hun.) (1924–)	Filled Up With Silence (Fenyo László)	Interesting range. Holds depth of meaning. Pacing must allow for expressive leaps. Extremities in acc. used. Excellent. Low tess.	Comp.	$\overline{\text{A}}$/E$_2$	B
Szönyi, Erzsébet	Love Song of Sappho (Ady Endre)	Strong and dynamic statement. Not long. Text Hungarian. Substantial.	Comp.	$\overline{\text{B}}$/E$_2$	W
Szönyi, Erzsébet	Nyár (Summer) (Szabo Lorinc)	Atonal. Intellectual approach. Structurally very fine. Conviction in performance, prime. Hungarian and English.	Comp.	–C/A$_{-2}$	B
Szönyi, Erzsébet	Puer Natus (biblical) (in coll.: Art Songs by Women: Across Time)	Liturgical language used from contemporary point of view. Long phrases. Excellent setting. Totally gratifying. (In Latin, mezzo and organ.)	Comp.	$\overline{\text{G}}$/G$_2$	B
Szönyi, Erzsébet	Two Little Mice (Klara Lesskó)	Allegretto. Moralistic text. Delightful busy action. Fanciful charm. In Hungarian.	Comp.	–C+/E$_{-2}$	B

Szymanowska, Maria (Pol.) (1789-1832)	Switezianka Ballada (Mickiewicza)	Interesting individual quality within format of period. Holds a buoyant charm, freshness and simplicity.	POL	$-C/E_2$	B
Taĭlleferre, Germaine (Fr.) (1892-1983)	Non, la fidelité (Lataignant XVIIIe) (no. 1 from Six Chansons Françaises; in coll.: Art Songs by Women: Across Time)	A furtive, mischievous and bright little air. Fun!	HEU in ROCH	$-C/G_2$	B
Tailleferre, Germaine	On a dit mal de mon ami (XVe) (no. 5 from Six Chansons Françaises; in coll.: Art Songs by Women: Across Time)	Harmony plays a game of surprise with a basically simple vocal line. Rhythmic teasing.	HEU in ROCH	$E_1/F+_2$	B
Tailleferre, Germaine	Souvent un air de verité (Voltaire) (no. 2 from Six Chansons Françaises; in coll.: Art Songs by Women: Across Time)	By not doubling the voice this little song adds charm to the fancy it spins.	HEU in ROCH	$-C/G_2$	B
Tailleferre, Germaine	Vrai Dieu qui m'y confortera (XVe) Old French (no. 4 from Six Chansons Françaises)	Fresh charm touched with humor and unexpected harmonic coloration.	HEU in ROCH	$E_1/G+_2$	B
Talma, Louise (Am.) (1906-)	Glory Be to God for Dappled Things (G. M. Hopkins)	Fresh. Bright. Alert text. Lively, yet lyrical. A delight.	Comp.	$D+_1/G_2$	B

Composer	Title[a]	Character of Song	Availability[b]	Range[c]	Performance Suitability[d]
Talma, Louise	Leap Before You Look (Auden)	Pseudo-waltz rhythm. Varied degrees of anger. Includes runs of unexpected intervals. Harmony and melody suit the lyrics well. Quick pace.	Comp.	E_1/A_2	B
Talma, Louise	Letter to St. Peter (Elma Dean)	Slow pace. On behalf of young men who died in the war. Highly emotional text. Harmonies complex.	Comp.	$-C+/F+_2$	B
Talma, Louise	Rain Song (Jean Garrigue)	A quick 2/4 dominates. A near spinning vitality of rhythm. Childlike charm. Diction clarity is tricky. Transparent quality and weightlessness.	Comp.	$D_1/B-_2$	B
Tate, Phyllis (Br.) (1911-)	Epitaph (Sir Walter Raleigh) (in coll.: Art Songs by Women: Across Time)	Substantial, forward moving song. Excellent setting in 3/4. Powerful.	OX	$\overline{B}-/F_2$	B

364

Thommessen, Mimi (Nor.) (c1925-)	Hvor Ofte Skal Gud Takkes? (Henrik Wergeland) (from Sommerfluge)	Recit. and chant. Prayer. Solemn, with numerous repeated pitches giving the meaningful text full sway.	NRS	$G+_1/B_2$	B
Tollefsen, Augusta (Am.) (1885-1955)	To a Snowflake (Rhonda Newton)	Swift wisp of snow's brief life in sun's rays. Child's fancy. Light. Bright.	SMP	$E-_1/G-_2$	B
Tollefsen, Augusta	Winter (Shelley) ("A widow bird sate mourning.")	Tasteful dissonances. Brief, with minimal means. Emptiness. Descriptive insight.	SMP	$E_1/G-_2$	B
Tyson, Mildred Lund (Am.) (1900-)	Like Barley Bending (Teasdale)	A meaningful substantial atmosphere is created in this melodic and brief song. Vocally grateful.	GS	$-C/E_2$ or F_1/A_2	B
Ulehla, Ludmila (Am.) (1923-)	Time Is a Cunning Thief (Shotwell)	Wordy, alert, and quickly tempoed. Clever text and an exuberant setting. Fills many programming needs.	GNM	E_1/G_2	B
Van de Vate, Nancy (Am.) (1930-)	Death Is the Chilly Night (Der tod das ist die Kühle Nacht) (from Two Songs) (Heine)	Alert and receptive awareness of symbolic night. Utilizes some long leaps. Vocally and musically gratifying.	Comp.	$\bar{B}/G+_2$	B

Composer	Title[a]	Character of Song	Availability[b]	Range[c]	Performance Suitability[d]
Van de Vate, Nancy	Youthful Age (text, Greek, from 6th cent. B.C.; in coll.: Art Songs by Women: Across Time)	Warmhearted wisp of song. Buoyant, happy spirit meshes cleverly with harmonic savor. High tess.	Comp.	E_1/A_2	B
Vannah, Kate (Am.) (1855-1933)	Bid Her Dream of Me (Emily Selinger)	Particularly low range. Different, in personal idiom.	WS in LoC	$\overline{A}-/C_2$	M
Vannah, Kate	The Way I'd Go (Marie Van Vorst)	Vocally pleasant. Traditional harmonies express sadness.	WS in LoC	$\overline{G}-/D-_2$	B
Viardot-Garcia, Pauline (Fr.-Sp.) (1821-1910)	Der Gärtner (Mörike) (in coll.: Art Songs by Women: Across Time)	In duple metre, this Mörike lied takes on a brighter atmosphere than H. Wolf's setting. Establishes individual charm.	RIES in LoC	$-C/G_2$	B
Viardot-Garcia, Pauline	Die Klagende (Dilia Helena)	Suggests Russian melancholy. Strong, haunting melody seems to pour from a heavy heart. Excellent for low mezzo or baritone.	SB&M	D_1/E_2	B

Composer	Title	Annotation	Source	Range	Category
Viardot-Garcia, Pauline	In der Frühe (Mörike) (in coll.: Art Songs by Women: Across Time)	Of substantial lieder-structure; includes personal creativity. Outstanding. Somber emotional impact dominates.	SEIT in LoC	$D_1/F+_2$	B
Viardot-Garcia, Pauline	Nixe Binsefuss (Mörike) (in coll.: Art Songs by Women: Across Time)	Animated narrative of youthful fancy. Distinct changes in attitude including the range boundaries. Excellent facile diction required on all extremities.	SEIT in LoC	$\overline{B}/G_2$	B
Viardot-Garcia, Pauline	Ständchen (Goethe) (in coll.: Art Songs by Women: Across Time)	An impetuous text gives this wooing lied a surprising and high ending. Ideal for tenor.	BO in LoC	F_1/A_2	M
Walker, Caroline Holme (Am.) (1863-?)	When the Dew Is Falling (Fiona Macleod)	Unexpected and interesting musical qualities. Steady flow amid traditional harmonies. Irish in flavor. Thought-provoking final statement.	WWP in ROCH	E_1/F_2	B
Warren, Elinor Remick (Am.) (1905-)	Snow Towards Evening (Melville Cane)	Well written. Modulates with mood changes. Dynamic control including delicacy essential.	GS	$E-/A-_2$	B

Composer	Title[a]	Character of Song	Availability[b]	Range[c]	Performance Suitability[d]
Warren, Elinor Remick	Who Loves the Rair. (Frances Shaw)	A binding melody dominates this pleasant short song. Quieting; heart-warming.	GS	F_1/F_2	W
Weigl, Vally (Au.-Am.) (1889-1982)	A Christmas Carol (Chesterton)	Interesting. Melodically and harmonically distinctive. Brief. Low tess.	MER	$\overline{G}/C-_2$	B
Weissberg, Julie (Rus.) (1878-1942)	Chanson d'Autumn (Verlaine) (from Deux Chansons)	Delicate haze of the temporal in this work for solo voice. Beautiful understatement.	PTR	$D-_1/G-_2$	B
Weissberg, Julie	Le ciel est au dessus le toit (Verlaine) (from Deux Chansons; in coll.: Art Songs by Women: Across Time)	The bell idiom opens and continues through first vocal section. All seems unreal in this questioning atmosphere. Mid-tess. Impressionistic. Eloquently stated.	PTR	$-C+/A-_2$	B
Weissberg, Julie	Die Mäuslein (Marschak) (from Funf Kinderlieder; in coll.: Art Songs by Women: Across Time)	Of a mouse's visitation at night to check on the "hour." Clever, sprightly with final scamper.	MDS	D_1/E_2	B

Composer	Title	Description	Pub.	Range	Voice
Weissberg, Julie	Rautendelein I (Hauptmann)	Allegretto. Imaginative unreality caught in this musical setting. Somewhat fragmented with colorful interludes.	PTR	E_1/A_2	W
Wertheim, Rosy (Du.) (1888-1949)	Het Narrenschip (from Twee Liederen) (Roel Houwink)	With "agitato" this frivolous disjunct composition moves boldly through recit., march, and seemingly less structured passages, giving an example of a contemporary Dutch composition. Perfect pitch would be an asset.	BRK	$-C+/G_2$	B
White, Maude Valerie (Br.) (1855-1937)	Crabbed Age & Youth (Shakespeare) (in coll: 50 Modern English Songs)	Con brio. Demands authority and a reaffirmation and belief in youth. Strong, vital.	B+H	$\overline{A}/D_2$	B
White, Maude Valerie	Liebe (Heine) (from Album of German Songs)	Sunshine and shadow effect from major to minor. Interesting setting. Strength in structure.	DIT	$-C/F_2$	B
White, Maude Valerie	Ophelia (Shakespeare) (from 50 Modern English Songs)	Andante. Repeated E_2's needed. Flowing, attractive vocal line. High tess, in one section. Effective.	B+H	D_1/F_2	B

Composer	Title[a]	Character of Song	Availability[b]	Range[c]	Performance Suitability[d]
White, Maude Valerie	To Music to Becalm His Fever (Herrick)	Pure and quaintly measured. In accord with text. Delicate.	CHA	G_1/G_2	B
Williams, Grace (We.) (1906-1977)	The Loom (G.W.)	A poignant tasteful setting of a Welsh folk ballad. Wistful sadness in minor key for mezzo.	OX	$\overline{B}-/E-_2$	W
Zaimont, Judith Lang (Am.) (1945-)	Chanson d'Automne (Verlaine) (no. 2 from Chansons Nobles et Sentimentales)	Opening notes, unacc. Thoughtful, with meaningful melody emcompassing 2 octaves. Ideal for high lyric voice. Musically rewarding.	ACA	$D-_1/D-_3$	B
Zaimont, Judith Lang	Entreaty (C. Rossetti) (from cycle Greyed Sonnets)	An underlying unrest within acc. Voice carries its poignant pleading message largely by a progression of scale patterns, of structural and musical substance.	ACA	$\overline{B}/F+_2$	B
Zaimont, Judith Lang	Love's Autumn (Millay) (from cycle Greyed Sonnets)	Interesting penetration of "Millay" in the quality of this song structure.	ACA	$\overline{B}-/G_2$	B

Composer	Title	Annotation	Pub.	Range/Tessitura	Grade
Zaimont, Judith Lang	Love's Echo (Christiana Rossetti) (from cycle Ages of Love)	Quizzical phrases which require a response. Inter-dependent rhythmical form.	ACA	$\overline{A}_1/F+_2$	M
Zaimont, Judith Lang	Soliloquy (Millay) (from cycle Greyed Sonnets)	Intervalically colorful. Yearning. Inner flutter, in keeping with text. Tonal. Rhythmic direction and meaningful patterns. Plucks reminiscently at thoughts of singer and listener. Dynamically strong. Excellent.	GAL	$E-_1/A_2$	B
Zaimont, Judith Lang	Harmonie du Soir (Baudelaire) (from Chansons Nobles et Sentimentales; in coll.: Art Songs by Women: Across Time)	Cyclical ideas create memorable environment as pitch levels parallel Baudelaire's words, forming rondo motif. Significant.	ACA	$-C+/A_2$	B
Zhulanova, Gaziza Akmetovna (Rus.) (1928-)	Pesnya pachtalyona (Tazhibaeva)	Simple charm. Unusual development of opening statement, with substantial structure.	SOV-M	$-C/F_2$	B
Zieritz, Grete (G.) (1899-)	Freunde (from Japanische Lieder) (Saito)	Straussian in harmonic and rhythmic structure. An alert awareness of new wonders.	RIES	$E+_1/A_2$	B

Composer	Title[a]	Character of Song	Availability[b]	Range[c]	Performance Suitability[d]
Zieritz, Grete	Am heiligen See (from Japanische Lieder) (Ozi)	Here the voice guides the listener through impressionistic spheres and atmospheres, cleverly focused on and guided by melodic contours.	RIES	$E+_1/A+_2$	B
Zieritz, Grete	Japan (from Japanische Lieder) (Yakamochi)	Exuberant expression of delight in Japan. Occasional motifs typify Oriental customs. Closes with joyousness. High tess.	RIES	G_1/A_2	B
Zubeldia, Emiliana de (Sp.-Mx.) (1948-)	Coplas Gitanas (from 6 Songs)	Vivace and strophic. Habanera pattern followed. Mexican ethnic interest.	ESC	D_1/C_2	B
Zubeldia, Emiliana de	Ay, que no soy! (Ana Mairena)	Curious texture and color qualities embellished through rhythmic and pacing adjustments. Interpretive sensitivity an essential.	RICS	F_1/A_2	B

| Zubeldia, Emiliana de | Jota (from 6 Songs; in coll.: Art Songs by Women: Across Time) | Well propelled spirit with limited range. Can be emotionally compelling. | ESC | $-C/D-_2$ | B |
| Zubeldia, Emiliana de | Que soy blanca Rosa (Ana Mairena) | Sparse. Creates a sense of "limbo" and mystery. Demanding dotted rhythms urge movement onward. Brief. | RICS | F_1/G_2 | B | . |

Country Abbreviations Used on Selective Song List

Am.	United States	Cz.	Czechoslovakia	It.	Italy	Rm.	Rumania
Ar.	Argentina	Den.	Denmark	Ja.	Japan	Rus.	Russia
Au.	Austria	Du.	Holland	Mx.	Mexico	Sc.	Scotland
Aus.	Australia	Fr.	France	Nor.	Norway	Sp.	Spain
Be.	Belgium	G.	Germany	Pe.	Peru	UoF.	Union of S. Africa
Br.	Great Britain	Hun.	Hungary	Pol.	Poland	We.	Wales
Can.	Canada						

373

Addresses of Composers of Unpublished Songs

Martha Alter
Connecticut College
New London, CT 06320
USA

Elaine Barkin
University of California
Music Department
405 Hilgard Avenue
Los Angeles, CA 90024
USA

Harriett Bolz
3097 Herrick Road
Columbus, OH 43221
USA

Edith Borroff
N.Y. University at Binghamton
Binghamton, NY 13901
USA

Radie Britain
1945 North Curson Avenue
Hollywood, CA 90046
USA

Roslyn Brogue (Henning)
c/o Annisquam Press
49 Leonard Street
Gloucester, MA 01930
USA

Jean Coulthard
Scores obtainable from
Canadian Music Centre
1263 Bay Street
Toronto, Ontario M5R 2C1
Canada

Emma Lou Diemer
Department of Music
University of California
Santa Barbara, CA 93106
USA

Judith Dvorkin
19 East 80th Street
New York, NY 10021
USA

Pozzi Escot
24 Avon Hill Road
Cambridge, MA 02140
USA

Blanche Gerstman
Cape Town Symphony
Cape Town, South Africa

Elizabeth Gould
3137 Kenwood Boulevard
Toledo, OH 43606
USA

Ada Jesi
Pie. Garini 8
20133 Milano
Italy

Eunice L. Kettering
Scores may be obtained from
Fine Arts Library
University of New Mexico
Albuquerque, NM 87131
USA

Many works also on file at
University of Missouri-KC
Kansas City, MO 64110
USA

Ohioana Library Association
1109 Ohio Depts. Building
Columbus, OH 43215
USA

MacDowell Colony
Peterborough, NH 03458
USA

Clare Liddle
37 Old Abbey Road
North Berwick, East Lothian
EH 39 4BP
Scotland

Elizabeth Maconchy
Shattesbrook
Borehan, Chelmsford
Essex 1, 3-27
England

Adabelle Marcus
9374 Landings Lane
Des Plaines, IL 60016
USA

Beverly McLarry
3326 N.W. 20th
Oklahoma City, Oklahoma
USA

Marian McLaughlin
(Mrs. Thomas R. Ostrom)
102 Duncannon Road
Bel Air, MD 21014
USA

Margarita Merriman
Box 704
South Lancaster, MA 01561
USA

Diane Morgan Morley
Scores obtainable from
Canadian Music Centre
1263 Bay Street
Toronto, Ontario M5R 2C1
Canada

Dika Newlin
School of Music
North Texas State University
Denton, TX 76203
USA

Blythe Owen
Andrews University
Berrien Springs, MI 49104
USA

Barberi Paull
370 Seventh Avenue, Suite 1800
New York, NY 10001
USA

Marian Peterson
Conservatory of Music
4420 Warwick
Kansas City, MO 64111
USA

Marga Richter
3 Bayview Lane
Huntington, NY 11743
USA

Donna Robertson
Box 223
Mars Hill, NC 28754
USA

Patsy Rogers
315 Fourth Street
New Suffolk, NY 11956
USA

Margaret Sandresky
Scores obtainable from
Fine Arts Center
Salem College
Winston-Salem, NC 27108
USA

Ruth F. Schonthal-Seckel
12 Van Etten Boulevard
New Rochelle, NY 10804
USA

Ersébet Szönyi
Scores obtainable from
Hungarian Copyright Office
Budapest, Vorosmarty-tei 1
1051
Hungary

Louise Talma
410 Central Park West
New York, NY 10025
USA
   Duplicating center for scores:
   King Brand
   1595 Broadway
   New York, NY 10019
   USA

Nancy Van de Vate
OMADP American Embassy
Box 2
APO San Francisco, CA 96356
USA

Publishers, Libraries, and Music Distributors

Abbreviation	Name of Organization	Location of Original Publisher	Distributor
ACA	American Composers Alliance	170 West 74th Street, New York, NY 10023	
AI	Joseph Aibl, Buch und Musikverlag	Munich, West Germany (see Library-listed)	
AMC	American Music Center	250 West 54th Street, New York, NY 10019	
AMP	Associated Music Publishers		G. Schirmer
APS	A. P. Schmidt		Summy
AT	A-TEMP Verlag	Vienna	
BAY	Bayerische Staatsbibliothek	Munich, W. Germany	
B&B	Blackmar and Brother	Augusta, GA	
BH	Breitkopf und Härtel	Leipzig, E. Germany	AMP and A. Broude
B13	Big 3 Music Corporation	729 7th Avenue, New York, NY 10019	
BN	Bibliothèque Nationale	Paris, France	
Broude	Alexander Broude, Inc.	225 W. 57th Street, New York, NY 10019	
B&H	Boosey & Hawkes, Inc.	24 West 57th St., New York, NY 10019	
BK	Book Center, Ltd.	Charlotte, NC	
BMS	Belwin-Mills Publishing Corporation	25 Deshon, Melville, New York 11746	
BO	Bote und Bock	Berlin	AMP
BON	Bongiovanni	Casa Musicale Francesco Bongiovanni	BMS
BOS	Boston Music Company	Boston, MA	Frank
BOT	Brodt Music Company	1409 E. Independence Blvd., Charlotte, NC 28201	
BRK	Broekmans en van Pappel	Amsterdam	Peters
CBD	Centre Belge de Documentation Musicale		Novello/Galaxy
CBP	Colburn Press	P.O. Box 75, Sherman, CT 06784	
CF	Carl Fischer, Inc.	56-62 Cooper Square, New York, NY 10003	
CHA	Chappell and Company, Inc.	810 Seventh Avenue, New York, NY 10019	
CHO	Choudens Fils Éditeurs	Paris	CHO/Peters
CHR	J. W. Chester Ltd	London	A.Broude/Magnamusic

CK	Copy-Kate Inc.	Silver Spring, MD	
CMC	Canadian Music Centre	Toronto, Canada	
CUC	Editioni Curci	Galleria del Corso 4, 20122 Milan, Italy	Big 3 Music Corp.
CUR	J. Curwen & Sons Ltd.	London	G. Schirmer
DAL	Geo. Dalrieu et Cie	London	Galaxy
DIT	Oliver Ditson	Nice, France	Presser
DMV	Drei Masken Verlag	Munich	
DON	Donemus Foundation		Peters
DP-H	Detroit Public Library—Hackley Collection	Detroit, Michigan	
DUR	Durand & Cie	Paris	Presser
EFM	Evans Microfilm (in Library of Congress)	Washington, DC	
EH	Elkan-Vogel		Presser
ELK	Elkin and Co., Ltd.	London	Novello
EMM	Ediciones Mexicanas De Musica		Peer
EMU	Editions Musicus	P.O. Box 1341, Stamford, CT 06904	
EN	Enoch & Cie	27 Boulevard des Italiens, Paris 2, France	AMP/Baron, M. Peer
ESC	Editions Max Eschig & Cie	Paris	AMP
EV	Elkan & Vogel	Bryn Mawr, PA	Presser
FA	Falter und Sohn	Munich, Leipzig (19th cent.—See Library)	
FL	Harold Flammer, Inc.	New York	Shawnee
FLP	Free Library of Philadelphia	Philadelphia, PA	
FOX	Sam Fox	New York	Pepper
FRA	Frank Distributing Corporation	116 Boylston Street, Boston, MA 02116	
FS	O. Flaschner Music	New York	
GAL	Galaxy Music Corporation	131 West 86th Street, New York, NY 10024	
GAM	Gambled-Hinged Music Company	Wittenberg University, Box 1101, Springfield, OH 45501	
GNM	General Music Publishing Company	Hastings-on-Hudson, NY	Chantry Music Press
GRA	H. W. Gray Publishing Company	New York	Frank
GRO	Verlag Ph. Grosch	Leipzig-Mannheim (See Library)	Belwin

Publishers, Libraries, and Music Distributors (continued)

Abbreviation	Name of Organization	Location of Original Publisher	Distributor
GRU	Leon Grus Cie, Editeurs	Paris	(Lemoine) Presser
GS	G. Schirmer, Inc.	866 Third Avenue, New York, NY 10022	
GW	George Willig, Jr.	Baltimore, MD (Early 19th century)	
HA	Handy Brothers Music Company	New York	
HAM	Hamelle & Cie	Paris	Presser
HAN	Wilhelm Hansen Edition		Broude, A/ Magnamusic
HARF	Frederick Harris Music Co., Ltd.	P.O. Box 670, Oakville, Ontario, Canada	
HB	Harold Branch Publishers, Inc.	42 Cornell Drive, Plainview, LI, NY 11803	
HEU	Chez Heugel & Cie	Paris	Presser
HMN	Editions Henn	8 rue de Hesse, Geneva, Switzerland	
IMM	Institute of Medieval Music Ltd.	Brooklyn, NY	
IOA	University of Iowa Music Library	Iowa City, IA	
JAM	Editions Musicales d'Art, Maxim Jamin	Paris	(Lemoine) Presser
JCB	Joseph Carr	Baltimore, MD (See Library)	
KUM	University of Kansas Library	Lawrence, KS	
LAG	Editorial Lagos	Buenos Aires, Argentina	
LAN	Hessische Landesbibliothek, Nassau	Wiesbaden, W. Germany	
LEM	Henri Lemoine & Cie Editeurs	Paris	Presser
LENG	Alfred Lengnick & Company, Ltd.		Harris
LL	Leslie Music Supply		Brodt
LoC	Library of Congress	Washington DC	
LYA	Lyra Music Company	New York	
LYR	Editions de L'Oiseau-Lyre, Les Ramparts	Monaco	
MBI	Magnamusic-Baton, Inc.	10370 Page Industrial Blvd, St. Louis, Mo 63132	
MDS	MacDonald-Steiner	New York	Brodt
MEN	Au Menestrel	Paris	(Heugel)-Presser

MER	Mercury Music Corporation	New York	Presser
MKB	Makeba Music Corporation	Kansas City, MO	Fox
MKC	University of Missouri (K.C.) Music Library		
MY-K	Muzyka	Kiev	Schirmer, G.
MY-L	Muzyka	Leningrad	Schirmer, G.
NEMO	NEMO: High Woods, Chinnor, Oxon	Ox 9 4BP	
NOR	W. W. Norton & Company, Inc.	500 Fifth Avenue, New York, NY 10003	
NOV	Novello & Company, Ltd.	145 Palisade Street, Dobbs Ferry, NY 10522	Belwin (rentals)
NRS	Norsk Musikforlag	Oslo	AMP & Magnamusic
NV	New Valley Music Press of Smith College	Sage Hall 3, Northampton, MA 01060	
NYP	New York Public Library	New York, NY	
OL	Olivan Press	49 Selvage Lane, London, NW 7, England	
ÖN	Österreichische Nationalbibliothek, Musiksammlung	Vienna, Austria	
ONG	Ongaku No Tome Sha	Tokyo	Presser
OX	Oxford University Press	200 Madison Avenue, New York, NY 10016	
PAT	Paterson & Sons Publications Ltd.	London	Fischer, C.
PE	Peer International Corporation	1740 Broadway, New York, NY 10019	
PEP	J. W. Pepper & Son, Inc.	P.O. Box 850, Valley Forge, PA 19482	
PLA	John Playford, Publisher	London (Fl. 1648) (See Library)	
POL	Polskie Wydawnictwo Muzyczne Editions	Krakow	Marks
PP	Personal Press (published by composer)	(See Library)	
PRA	Hudebni Matice Umelecke Besecy	Prague	
PRE	Theodore Presser Company	Presser Place, Bryn Mawr, PA 19010	
PTR	C. F. Peters Corporation	373 Park Avenue, S., New York, NY 10016	
RCFR	Ricordi (Société Anonyme des Editions)		Belwin
REM	Remick Music Corporation		
RIC	Ricordi	London	Belwin
RICO	Ricordi & Company	Milan	Belwin
RICS	Ricordi Americanas S. A.		Belwin

Publishers, Libraries, and Music Distributors (continued)

Abbreviation	Name of Organization	Location of Original Publisher	Distributor
RIES	Ries & Erler	Berlin	Peters
RINY	Ricordi-USA	New York	Belwin
ROC	Rochester Music Photo Copy Inc.	Solcus Point, New York (or see Comp.'s adddress)	
ROCH	Sibley Library of Eastman School of Music	Rochester, NY	
SA	Francis Salabert Editions	c/o 575 Madison Avenue, New York, NY 10022	
SB+M	Schliesinger's den Buch & Musikhandlung	Berlin, Vienna	
SCHA	F. A. Schaffer Publishers	Munich (See Library)	
SE	Ed. Maurice Senart	(See Library)	Salabert, U.S.A.
SEIT	Robert Steitz: Leipzig & Weimar	(See Library)	
SHP	Shawnee Press	Delaware Water Gap, PA 18327	
SIE	C.F.W. Siegel Musikalienhandlung	Leipzig (See Library)	Peters
SL	L. Schubert Music Publishing Corporation		Warner
SLK	Spencer Library, University of Kansas	Lawrence, Kansas	
SMP	See Saw Music Corporation	1966 Broadway, New York, NY 10023	
SOU	Southern Music Publishing Company, Inc.		Peer
SOV-K	Sovietski Compozitor	Kiev	
SOV-M	Sovietski Compozitor	Moscow	
ST	B. Schott & Company, Ltd.		Belwin
SUM	Summy-Birchard Company		
TROU	Eugene Troupenas et Cie	Paris (fl-1828) (See Library)	
UIN	Indiana University Music Library	Bloomington, IN	
UK	Ukrainian State Music Publications (Muzitchna Ukraina)	Kiev	
UME	Union Musicale Franco-Española	Madrid	
UMG	University of Michigan Music Library	Ann Arbor, MI	AMP

Abbrev.	Publisher	Address	Agent
UN	Universal Editions	Vienna, from Joseph Boonin, Inc. P.O. Box 2124, S. Hackensack, NJ 07606	Boonin
UNM	University of New Mexico Music Library	Albuquerque, NM	
UNS	(International Library of Music) University Society Inc.		
USC	University of Southern California Music Library	New York (See Library) Los Angeles, CA	
VOL	G. T. Vollweiller	London (1777)	
WATL	Waterloo Music Company, Ltd.	3 Regina Street, North, Waterloo, Ontario N 2 J 227 Canada	AMP & Brodt
WE	Wellesley College Publishers	Wellesley, MA (Agent: Integrity Music, New York, NY)	
WH	White Harvest Music Corporation	Box 87, Stewartsville, MO 64490	Boosey
WIN	Winthrop-Rogers	London	
WM	Willis Music Company	7380 Industrial Highway, Florence, KY 41042	
WS	White-Smith & Company	Boston (See Library)	
WWP	Wa Wan Society of America Music Press	Newton Center, MA (See Library)	

Index

About the Editors and Contributors

JANE GOTTLIEB is currently head librarian at the Mannes College of Music in New York City. Her previous affiliations include two years at the New York Public Library at Lincoln Center and five years as the principal librarian at the American Music Center. She received a Bachelor of Arts in music from the State University of New York at Binghamton and a Masters in Library Service from Columbia University.

CATHERINE OVERHAUSER is music director and conductor of the Hopkins Symphony Orchestra, the Baltimore School for the Arts Orchestra, and the York Youth Symphony. She received her conducting training at the Indiana University School of Music, the Peabody Conservatory, and at the European conservatories of Vienna, Munich, Rome, and Siena. Her conducting teachers include Frederik Prausnitz, Murry Sidlin, Hermann Michael, Sergiu Celibidache, and Franco Ferrara. She has been the recipient of numerous awards in conducting, including the Sid Guber Memorial Award given by the American Women in Radio and Television and was appointed assistant conductor to the Aspen Music Festival.

JUDITH LANG ZAIMONT is a prize-winning composer and a faculty member at the Peabody Conservatory of Music. Among her awards are a Guggenheim Fellowship in music composition, a commissioning grant from the National Endowment for the Arts, and Woodrow Wilson and Debussy Fellowships in composition. Many of her works are recorded and published and have been performed in Europe and Australia as well as in the United States. She is the coeditor of *Contemporary Concert Music by Women* (Greenwood Press, 1981).

* * *

CLARA LYLE BOONE is a native of Kentucky and a descendant of Samuel Boone, eldest brother of Daniel Boone. As a composer, she uses the pseudonym, Lyle de Bohun, the original spelling of her name from the old family seat in Normandy. She studied with Walter Piston at Harvard and with Darius Milhaud. In addition to her songs, and choral and chamber music, she has written *Annunciation of Spring* and *Motive and Chorale* for symphony orchestra. She founded Arsis Press in 1974 for the publication of music by women composers.

PATRICIA ADKINS CHITI is a mezzo-soprano who received her professional vocal training at the Guildhall School of Music and Drama under Reinhold Gerhardt and at master classes in London, Stuttgart, and Rome. She made her operatic debut in Italy in 1969 and since then has sung in major European opera houses and with symphony orchestras in Western and Eastern Europe and Latin America, South Africa, and the Orient. She has recorded for most of the European radio stations and records commercially for EDIPAN and EMI. Although born in England, Patricia Chiti now resides in Italy where, apart from her concert and opera performances, she is also well known for her musicological research. As a result of her research on women composers of the past, she was nominated artistic director of the Donne in Musica Festival, which takes place annually in Rome. She has also written a book presenting over five hundred women composers with the title *Donne in Musica*.

BEVERLY GRIGSBY is a professor of theory, composition, and music history at California State University, Northridge, where she has taught since 1963. In the early 1960s she helped to develop the school's Electronic Music Studio and in 1976 founded its Computer Music Studio; in 1980 she cofounded the State of California Consortium for Computer Assisted Instruction in Music. Grigsby's recent awards include an NEA grant for her opera, *Moses,* and her electronic compositions include a score for the feature film *Ayamonn The Terrible* (1964), *Preludes on Poems of T. S. Eliot* (1968), *A Little Background Music* (1976), and *Morning At Seven* (1981-1982). She produces electronic music concerts and is presently organizing the International Center for the Study of Women's Music at CSUN.

MARNIE HALL is the executive producer of Leonarda Productions, Inc. She received her musical training as a violinist at the University of Kansas (B. Mus., 1966) and the Manhattan School of Music (M. Mus., 1968). She performed as a member of the Kansas City Philharmonic and as a freelance violinist in New York City. In 1975 she founded Gemini Hall Records, and in 1977, Leonarda Productions.

BARBARA JEPSON is a New York City-based freelancer specializing in classical music topics and the former associate editor of the *Feminist Art Journal.* She writes frequently for *Town & Country*, and has also contributed to the *New York Times* Arts and Leisure section, *Keynote, Music Journal,* and *Heresies #10: Women in Music.*

DORIS LANG KOSLOFF, music director of the Connecticut Opera, was educated at Queens College of the City University of New York and at the Boston University School of Fine and Applied Arts. She has held positions as first coach and pianist for Wolf Trap Farm Park for the Performing Arts, principal coach for the Washington Opera Society, and coach and instructor at the Hartt College of Music at the

University of Hartford. In 1973 she was appointed assistant conductor and chorus mistress of the Connecticut Opera Association; in 1981 she was appointed music administrator, and in 1982 she was appointed music director.

DAVID W. MAVES was recently appointed composer-in-residence at the College of Charleston (S. C.), where he had been chairman of the Fine Arts Department for the past five years. He has degrees from the University of Oregon and the University of Michigan (Doctor of Musical Arts, 1973).

JILL McMANUS, a jazz pianist and composer who lives in New York, has also written music stories and reviews for *Time* magazine and the *New York Post*. In 1975-1977, she led the Jazz Sisters, and in 1980, the All-Star Band at the Kansas City Women's Jazz Festival. She has worked with the Pepper Adams Quartet, recorded with Bassist Richard Davis (*As One,* MR 5093), and her tune "Short Rainbow" is recorded on *Modal Soul* (Timeless SJP17).

CAROL NEULS-BATES, a musicologist, holds a Ph.D. from Yale University and has taught on the faculties of the University of Connecticut, Yale University, and Hunter and Brooklyn Colleges of the City University of New York. She is the author of numerous articles and books, including, with Adrienne Fried Block, *Women in American Music: A Bibliography of Music and Literature* (Greenwood Press, 1979), which was funded by the National Endowment for the Humanities and the Ford Foundation. She has also edited *Women in Music: An Anthology of Source Readings from the Middle Ages to the Present.* Currently she is an account executive with the John O'Donnell Company, a management consultant firm in New York City.

VALERIE O'BRIEN studied music and English at Oberlin College and journalism at Columbia University. Her articles on music have appeared in a number of publications, including *Symphony* and *Musical America* magazines.

JUDITH ROSEN, a graduate of the University of California at Los Angeles, has since 1971 researched and lectured on the subject of women composers. She has participated in numerous radio broadcasts and coordinated music festivals featuring women's works. Her articles have appeared in a number of publications including *High Fidelity* and *Heresies,* a feminist journal.

GREGORY SANDOW is a composer whose operas have been widely performed and a critic for New York's *Village Voice,* where he has specialized in coverage of experimental music, and the *Saturday Review.* He is presently writing a book about the musical structure of opera.

MIRIAM STEWART-GREEN, soprano, was born in 1915 in Spokane, Washington, of Norwegian-Welsh heritage. She is a graduate of the Cleveland Institute of Music and is a former member of the New York City Opera. She has appeared internationally as a recitalist and symphonic soloist with conductors including Leopold Stokowski, Arthur Rodzinski, and Rafael Kubelik. She is presently professor of voice at the University of Kansas and is a pioneer in research on women composers.

SUSAN TEICHER received her B. Mus. and M. Mus. degrees from The Juilliard School, where she was a piano student of Rosina Lhevinne and Martin Canin. She was presented in debut and two subsequent solo recitals at Carnegie Recital Hall by Artists International. She is currently completing her dissertation on "The Solo Works for Piano of Louise Talma" for her Doctor of Musical Arts at the Peabody Conservatory, where she studied piano with Leon Fleisher.

ELIZABETH WOOD is an Australian-born musicologist and writer who lives in New York City. Her dissertation was the first repertory study and history of opera composed in Australia. Her research in America centers on women in music; she has published scholarly articles on women composers and women in the avant garde of music and performance. She is currently preparing a book on women in opera and completing a novel.